Chasin' That Devil Music

Searching for the Blues

BY GAYLE DEAN WARDLOW

Edited with an introduction by Edward Komara

Backbeat
Books
San Francisco

Published by Backbeat Books

600 Harrison Street, San Francisco, CA 94107

Publishers of *Keyboard, Bass Player,* and *Guitar Player* magazines

CMP
United Business Media

Distributed to the book trade in the U.S. and Canada by Publishers Group West, 1700 Fourth Street, Berkeley, CA 94710

Distributed to the music trade by Hal Leonard Publishing, P.O. Box 13819, Milwaukee, WI 53213

Design and Typesetting: Claudia Smelser Design
Cover Design: Richard Leeds Graphic Design
Production Editor: Jan Hughes

Cover: Elmore James, Michael Ochs Archives

Library of Congress Cataloging in Publication Data:

Wardlow, Gayle.
Chasin' that devil music : searching for the blues / Gayle Dean Wardlow ; edited with an introduction by Edward Kamora.
    p. cm.
discography: p.
Includes bibliographical references (p.   ) and index.
ISBN 0-87930-552-5
1. Blues (Music)—History and criticism. 2. Blues musicians—United States—Mississippi—Biography. I. Kamora, Edward, M., 1966- . II. Title.
ML3521.W37 1998
781.643'09—dc21   98-30583
                                             CIP
                                             MN

Printed in the United States of America
06 07 08 09 10   5 4 3

◄○►◄○►◄○►◄○►◄○►◄○►◄○►◄○►◄○►◄○►

This book is dedicated to my late mother Ina Lee Wardlow (1903–1997), who talked to my many blues callers, and who encouraged my record collecting; and to Bernie Klatzko, who introduced me to the performances of Charlie Patton and the greatness of the Delta blues. Thanks also to Charlotte Moore, Ken Knight, Wendell Cook, Steve Calt, Dr. Jimmy Williams, and Dr. Bill Foster, for helping me make difficult decisions at my many crossroads.

Special thanks to Maxey Tarpley of Edisto Island, South Carolina, for the use of his record advertisements. He found the photo of Charlie Patton in the 1960s that has been used numerous times without credit to him.

Thanks also to cartoonist Tony Mostrom for use of his King Solomon Hill drawing.

Special hugs to Charlotte Moore of Dallas, Texas, who encouraged me to follow my writing dreams after many failures.

More thanks to Jim DeCola who rescued the Hayes McMullan album and repaired many guitars as we listened to the blues.

A salute also to Jimmy Phillips and Pat House of Monitor *magazine, Peavey Electronics, Meridian, Mississippi*

For more information about the Blues, visit the Delta Blues Museum in Clarksdale, Mississippi, which will have expanded facilities in mid-1999.

◄○►◄○►◄○►

Table of Contents

Foreword

Since the 1990 release of all Robert Johnson recordings, there has been intense worldwide interest in blues music. But years ago, before the rediscovery of John Hurt, Son House, Skip James, and Bukka White during the folk boom of the 1960s, the interest was limited to a select few New York City blues collectors. These men began contacting me in 1962 when I was fortunate to be living in Mississippi, the state where most of the great bluesmen had played and lived. Thus, I could search for biographical information behind the names found on old 78 rpm ("Victrola") records from the 1920–1942 time period who were thought to have been Mississippian.

Through my journalism work since 1960, I learned how to obtain and use documented evidence such as public records, city directories, and birth/death certificates required by state law. I have always been a record collector and will continue to be in future years, but I am glad I had the opportunity to develop an outstanding collection of Mississippi blues while researching and writing about the lives of then-obscure bluesmen. Although I am known as a "blues researcher" and "investigator," I hope to be eventually regarded as a "blues writer."

I have included a CD with more than 20 selections of great Delta blues performances along with the gospel singing of Rev. D.C. Rice and Blind Roosevelt Graves and Aaron. The CD also includes "Done Sold My Soul to the Devil," a 1938 Western swing release by Dave Edwards and his Alabamians. It seemed appropriate to end the collection with this song as it illustrates just how prevalent the belief by both Black and white church members that blues music was considered the "Devil's music." Also included are interviews with H.C. Speir, Ishmon Bracey, Joe Callicott, and Rev. Booker Miller, many of whom had intense conflicts between their blues lifestyles and their religious backgrounds.

Finally, to the modern connoisseur of acoustic and/or amplified blues, this collection of reprinted articles and new pieces written especially for this book will provide a ready reference on some of the blues greats.

As Son House said ("Preaching the Blues," 1930):

> I met the blues this morning, walking like a man
> I met the blues this morning, walking like a man
> I said "Good morning blues, give me your right hand."

Let's take a hand-in-hand walk with the men who made this great music.

—*Gayle Dean Wardlow,*
June 1998, Long Beach, Mississippi

Editor's Introduction

◄O►◄O►◄O►◄O►◄O►◄O►◄O►◄O►◄O►◄O►◄O►◄O►

Bluesfinders have become as legendary as the bluesmen they brought to wide public notice. Perhaps their renown is due to the fact that the neighborhoods they canvassed have long been paved over, the men and women they spoke with have died, and the recorded performances they recovered have lately become available on CD. Samuel Charters' *The Country Blues* (1959) and Paul Oliver's *Blues Fell This Morning* (1960), published before the great blues rediscovery years of 1963 and 1964, have accorded their authors awesome stature as pioneers in the eyes of the blues fans. The people who produced the blues magazines and LP reissues in the wake of Charters' and Oliver's successes are in truth no less extraordinary, even if they are known only by their bylines on articles and LP sleeve notes. Among the first writers and producers to supply the increasing demand for acoustic "folk" blues in the late 1950s and early 1960s were Pete Whelan, Bernard Klatzko, Mack McCormick, John Fahey, Kenneth Goldstein, and Bob Koester. By 1962, Whelan and Klatzko encouraged a Mississippi newspaper reporter, Gayle Dean Wardlow, to find information on some long-forgotten Delta bluesmen active 30 years past. The fruits of his searches, collected in this volume, first appeared as notes to Whelan's Origin Jazz Library LPs and then as magazine articles. However, the searches themselves became legendary among his friends and competitors alike.

Gayle Dean Wardlow was born in 1940 in Freer, Texas, but he spent his early childhood in Bienville Parish, Louisiana. When he was seven, his family moved to Meridian, Mississippi, a railroad center. In 1954, he began seeking Roy Acuff records, piecing together a near-complete collection of the Opry star's 78s by the time he graduated from high school four years later. What few blues records he acquired during the 1950s were used to trade for country and hillbilly discs.

Wardlow first paid serious attention to blues music while working full-time in Meridian, listening to the blues 78s he had not yet traded. In 1959 Samuel Charters published his seminal book *The Country Blues*, which inspired a generation of blues-seekers. After reading it, Wardlow recognized that little was known about Mississippi blues, however great Charters' and others' fascinations were for it. Thus began his search for Mississippi blues musicians and the records they made. However, the records were long out of print; the only way for him to find them was by canvassing door-to-door, asking the residents if they had any "old Victrola records" to sell.

Through a job he took with the Orkin exterminating company in 1962, he located the Jackson neighborhoods that were best to canvass. A year later, a weekend sports-writing beat for the *Jackson Daily News* enabled him to go to Mississippi Delta towns, where he would arrive early to ask for records and information.

Wardlow soon found people who had known Charlie Patton, Tommy Johnson, and their pre–World War II ("prewar") blues contemporaries. In July 1963, he located one of Patton's ex-wives, Minnie Franklin, in Bovina near Vicksburg. With the tips she gave, he returned to the Mississippi Delta the following August with Bernard Klatzko, a New York collector who was preparing the booklet accompanying Origin Jazz Library's second reissue of Patton. Together they found additional people who knew Patton in Holly Ridge, Dockery's Plantation (west of Ruleville and Drew), and Lula.

Even before his first blues article in 1966, Wardlow was welcomed in print as an investigator worthy of attention. Wardlow's midnight phone message ("I found another Patton record!") opened Klatzko's account of their fact-finding trip the previous summer, "The Immortal Charlie Patton" (reprinted in this book). That July, Simon Napier and Mike Leadbitter ran the following notice in their magazine *Blues Unlimited* (no. 13: 3): "Tom [Hoskins] thinks that the newly-found Ishmon Bracey may be recorded too; singing, like [Robert] Wilkins, gospel songs. A minor detail about Bracey's discovery is that according to Tom, he was found by a student from Jackson, Mississippi, named Dean Wardlow, not Charters as reported."

Ishmon Bracey had recorded for Victor in 1928 and Paramount in 1930, and was a close associate of Tommy Johnson. However, in later years he turned to religion and played only sacred music. Wardlow found Bracey in 1963, and from him he learned of H. [Henry] C. Speir, the former talent scout who recommended the major pre-1942 Mississippi blues musicians (including Bracey, Tommy Johnson, Charlie Patton, Skip James, and Robert Johnson, among others) to the record labels Victor, Paramount, Vocalion, and OKeh. Speir became the subject of Wardlow's first blues feature article, "Legends of the Lost," published serially in 1966 by *Blues Unlimited*, then one of the two magazines devoted solely to the blues (the other was Bob Groom's *Blues World*).

During the mid-1960s, Wardlow supplied tape copies of rare records to Bernard Klatzko and Pete Whelan for their Origin Jazz Library (OJL) reissues of prewar country blues. For an OJL supplement and a few booklets accompanying some of the OJL albums, he provided notes on, among others Tommy Johnson, Garfield Akers, Rev. D.C. Rice, Bukka White, and Charlie Patton—a difficult task, as there were no blues biographical dictionaries and little published research at that time. After Whelan left OJL in 1966, Wardlow's work with him continued with the founding of *78 Quarterly* in 1967.

About this time, Wardlow searched for death certificates on blues musicians through the the Bureau of Vital Statistics at the Mississippi State Department of Health. In 1965 he located such documents for Tommy

Johnson, Willie Brown, and Charlie Patton, the latter becoming the basis for the article "Patton's Murder—Whitewash? or Hogwash?" (1967). The most notable certificate Wardlow found, however, was that for Robert Johnson, which clearly stated the musician's age and where he had died. Until Johnson's certificate was recovered, so little was known about him that Wardlow was initially unsure about which county to specify to Vital Statistics, as he admitted afterwards in "Searching for the Robert Johnson Death Certificate" (1992).

In these early pieces, there is the excitement of the search and the immediacy of a fresh discovery. These articles are remarkable for their frequent descriptions of newly rediscovered musicians and recently recovered documents. To some extent, Waldrow's early success in finding Ishmon Bracey, Johnny Temple, H.C. Speir, and many prewar blues records led some people, including his close associates, to resent him for his apparent refusal to share what they perceived to be a vast Mississippi blues treasure.

The truth was that Wardlow had extraordinarily good luck finding people and records in Mississippi. For the most part, many prewar musicians still living had headed north during the Great Migration of the 1930s and '40s. There were few records to be found in Mississippi, where blacks could not afford them during the 1930s. As it later turned out, the rarest discs of prewar Mississippi blues were found in North Carolina and Virginia, where the black laborers in the tobacco fields and apple orchards had money to buy records, even during the worst years of the Great Depression.

After two years as assistant state editor at the *Meridian Star* newspaper, Wardlow served as public information director at Livingston (Alabama) University (1968–73). During this time, he came to know musician Willie Moore and his wife Elizabeth, who formerly ran a "juke joint" (roadhouse). (Willie Moore should not be confused with Will Moore, who brought up John Lee Hooker—or with William "Bill" Moore, who recorded for Paramount in 1928.) The Moores personally knew every recorded prewar Delta musician and a number of unrecorded ones.

Other valuable informants were Hayes McMullan and Rev. Booker Miller, both musical associates of Charlie Patton. Wardlow found McMullan in Sumner and came to value his blues musical sensibility that had not changed since the 1930s. Booker Miller continued playing blues for a few years after Patton's death, into the time of Robert Johnson's recording sessions. Although Miller had turned to the church in 1937 and later became a minister, to the end of his life he was willing to talk about his bluesman days.

Wardlow interviewed these contacts several times at length, checking names, facts, and repertoires. Although his collaboration with *Blues Unlimited* editor Mike Leadbitter on Elmore James ("Canton, Mis'sippi Breakdown," 1972) is the only major publication from these years, his taped interviews with McMullan, Miller, and the Moores would serve as touchstones for his subsequent writings. Upon their deaths, the information and memories they had became irretrievable.

In 1974, Wardlow completed a B.A. in journalism at the University of Alabama at Tuscaloosa, then earned his M.A. in communications (journalism) two years later. He published little during these years, due partly to his formal studies, and also to his work with Stephen Calt on a book about Charlie Patton and other prewar Mississippi blues musicians. Despite controversy within some blues circles before publication, the book eventually appeared in a revised version in 1988 as *King of the Delta Blues: The Life and Music of Charlie Patton.*

After brief stints at the University of North Alabama at Florence, Georgia State University, and East Tennessee State, Wardlow taught journalism and public relations at North Carolina Agricultural and Technical State University through 1990. In 1987, *Blues Unlimited* published its final issue. For the periodical's last three numbers, Wardlow brought forth his profiles on Joe Sheppard (aka Blind Joe Reynolds, 1984), Willie Brown (1986), and King Solomon Hill (1987), each the result of 20 years of research.

In his work from 1966 through 1987, Wardlow reported the facts gleaned from his sources, supporting his narratives with quotes. From the *Blues Unlimited* and *78 Quarterly* articles emerged a depiction of prewar Mississippi blues musicians as people worth seeking out, or worth remembering by those who knew them. The greatest bluesmen—especially Charlie Patton, Son House, Skip James, and Robert Johnson—performed for dancing audiences in jukes or for passersby tipping pennies on city sidewalks, but rarely did they let their audiences become part of their creative processes. Listeners were expected to laugh at some blues lyrics, but not to offer additional ones and thus shift the center of attention from the musician. Money was the object of many professionals who, not being trusted with bank accounts due to their skin color (see Bracey's story in "Got Four, Five Puppies, One Shaggy Little Hound," page 45, about not being able to cash a Paramount advance check), often spent their earnings on alcohol or gambling before there was a chance of having it lost or stolen. To ensure popularity and tips, a bluesman had to have a distinctive vocal and/or instrumental style, a steady beat, and a sense of where the next job was.

In contrast, there developed in the late 1960s an alternate depiction of bluesmen as creative folk artists. As viewed by folklorists and anthropologists, bluesmen were parts of music-making communities and were expected to share openly with their audiences the creative process of the blues, especially the selection of blues lyrics. Seldom did such researchers assign special merit and ability to one musician or another, with the result that professional bluesmen were often discussed in the same context as backyard pickers. In addition, mythical tales about the bluesmen were recorded and promoted as folklore study material. However, these myths were borrowed by some writers to describe historical people or events in the absence of factual accounts. Such a depiction was in sharp contrast to Wardlow's, and public clashes between the advocates of the two views occurred.

The most famous of those disputes was the King Solomon Hill controversy, with Wardlow, Stephen Calt, and *Blues Unlimited* on one side, and

David Evans and *Blues World* on the other. Oddly, what sparked it was Pete Whelan's *78 Quarterly*, whose first issue (1967) ran Wardlow's "King Solomon Hill" as its lead article. He based his statement that the man who recorded as King Solomon Hill in 1932 was a Louisiana musician, Joe Holmes, on the testimony of Holmes' estranged wife and several Sibley, Louisiana, residents. In a *Blues World* review titled "The King Solomon Hill Fiasco" (no. 21 [October 1968]: 17–20), Evans took Wardlow sternly to task for not decisively explaining the name King Solomon Hill, believing it was "clear" from his own research "that a singer known as King Solomon Hill (and by no other name) lived and performed in the area of McComb and Magnolia [Mississippi]."

Evans' criticism stung Wardlow and rankled him for 20 years. Yet before the review was published, Wardlow had learned during a follow-up trip to Louisiana that King Solomon Hill was the name of a community, in which there was a King Solomon Hill Baptist Church. Although he had learned this information verbally from a local informant, he felt he needed an irrefutable document recording King Solomon Hill as a Louisiana place name in order to answer Evans' identification of the name as that of a Mississippi musician, and to counteract the reliance on oral tradition favored by folklorists. Stephen Calt's defense of Wardlow in *Blues Unlimited* ("King Solomon Hill Revisited," 1970) did not end the dispute with Evans, nor could it ever have so long as both sides' arguments were based on oral testimony.

In 1986, a source of documentation for the King Solomon Hill community occurred to Wardlow: the U.S. Postal Service, which would have had to recognize and deliver any and all mail addressed to a resident living in King Solomon Hill, Louisiana, in Joe Holmes' time. It was a brilliant solution realized by the location of E.B. Walls, a retired rural post carrier who personally handled the mail route for Minden, King Solomon Hill (later known as Yellow Pine), and Sibley. His letter verifying King Solomon Hill as a Louisiana place name eliminated the possibility of its being a proper name of someone living in Mississippi. This postal solution remains among Wardlow's greatest successes and his most clever contribution to the "tool kit" of the blues researcher. As much as the King Solomon Hill controversy aggravated him, it helped Wardlow become a much stronger blues investigator.

In 1988, Pete Whelan revived *78 Quarterly* after a 20-year publishing hiatus. For him, Wardlow wrote profiles of William Harris (1988) and Henry "Son" Sims (1996), and a new biography of H.C. Speir (1994). He also cowrote, with Stephen Calt, a biography of Robert Johnson (1989) and a five-part history of Paramount Records (1988–92).

Since 1990, Wardlow has continued collecting records and acted as a consultant on the classic Delta blues. In 1991, he aided Iambic Productions in its documentary about Robert Johnson, working with musicians David "Honey Boy" Edwards and John Hammond (that documentary, "The Search for Robert Johnson," was aired on the BBC Channel 4 and is now available on Sony Home Video). In 1993, he earned an M.L.S. in library science from the University of Southern Mississippi. He has also served as an active consultant to researchers and funded projects.

The recent blues renaissance has brought with it a wealth of record reissues, lyric and melodic transcriptions, and new books about the blues and their presence in American music and culture. Among the libraries collecting jazz and blues materials for research purposes are the Blues Archive (University of Mississippi), the Chicago Blues Archive (Chicago Public Library), the Institute of Jazz Studies (Rutgers University), the Center for Black Music Research Archive (Columbia College, Chicago), the Center for Popular Music (Middle Tennessee State University), the Hogan Jazz Archive (Tulane University), and the Chicago Jazz Archive (University of Chicago). As welcome and creative as the existing literature has been, the increase in blues resources available to the public calls for new, thoroughly documented books drawing on different sources, including published research and accessible fieldwork.

Many colleges and universities now offer jazz and blues courses, whether as music, folklore, or cultural studies. Musicological history and theory techniques may not be applied to the blues as often as the ethno-musicology and cultural (i.e., American studies) approaches, yet a trend of increasing historical and analytical rigor in blues teaching and writing may emerge from the increasing availability of books and compact disc reissues. For those who have been studying the blues according to set folklore methods and perceived folk traditions, a scholarly challenge looms.

Anne and Norm Cohen's 1977 article "Folk and Hillbilly Music: Further Thoughts on Their Relation" makes a distinction between assembly music (defined as that performed for money at a public occasion or a commercial recording session) and domestic music (defined as that performed for one's own enjoyment or within a small private interactive group, or as part of a daily work routine). Applied to the blues, this distinction may enable helpful uses of commercial recordings in folklore studies. While a blues tradition is often said to be "transmitted" from one person to another, the "transmission" of blues traditions from an assembly setting to a domestic one, and vice versa, may also be noted. Such a transmission among settings may be studied with the kinds of music performed today: as long as the formal structure and melodic scales of the blues continue to evolve from the long-standing 12-measure form with flatted "blue notes," researchers may want to see who is developing these changes, and where they are being developed. If individual transmissions between assembly and domestic settings can be arranged in chronological order, this treatment of the blues may inform historical accounts.

Such a task, at least in the area of prewar blues, requires a thorough grasp of both the recordings and the secondary descriptions of them in the blues literature. Fortunately, reissue programs such as those of Yazoo and Document have brought many rare recordings into wide availability, and the current blues revival has resulted in the reprinting of many older books on blues music and culture. A sourcebook like this will encourage a new consideration of the blues, and provide techniques of inquiry for the blues and other kinds of music now and in the future.

The articles in this collection of Gayle Dean Wardlow's blues writings are like dispatches from the front, capturing the excitement of the search for lost blues artists at a time when every memory of these musicians was in danger of fading into oblivion. The book is intended to be a volume in which readers may easily enjoy individual articles without having to search for rare back issues of *Blues Unlimited* and other magazines. It may also inspire researchers who wish to use the investigative techniques in their own projects. The initial plan was to include every article Wardlow wrote for *Blues Unlimited, Storyville,* and *Living Blues,* as well as a few of his *78 Quarterly* and *Victrola and 78 Journal* pieces. At an early stage, though, some work had to be omitted.

Since Pete Whelan has kept all issues of *78 Quarterly* in print, it was decided to select only what was needed for the book. When *78 Quarterly* first appeared in 1967, it was the most sumptuously prepared periodical on blues and jazz 78 rpm records of its time, with feature articles about records and recorded artists, illustrated with rare photographs and record labels. With each subsequent issue, Whelan has carefully maintained the subject emphasis on blues and jazz records while exercising his editorial independence. There are few if any serial publications quite like this. Tim Gracyk's *Victrola and 78 Journal* is a recent newcomer, but it has ably covered the areas of classical, dance, and personality 78s. Those who wish to sample some issues should write to Pete Whelan, *78 Quarterly,* 626 Canfield Lane, Key West, FL 33040; Tim Gracyk, *Victrola and 78 Journal,* 1509 River Oak Way, Roseville, CA 95747.

A few other articles were dropped. "Son House Comments and Additions" (1967a) addressed individual points in Alan Wilson's study of Son House (as reprinted in *Blues Unlimited Collector's Classic* no. 14, 1966), and thus lacked a continuity of its own. "Bitchin' Boogie," Wardlow and Calt's open letter (1981) regarding their book manuscript *Charlie Patton and the Mississippi Blues,* and David Evans' reply as an expert advance reader of the work (*Blues Unlimited* no. 141 [Autumn/Winter 1981]: 12–13) extended the dispute over research procedure begun in the King Solomon Hill controversy; since no new research techniques or issues were discussed, this exchange was omitted. The biographical profile of Robert Johnson for Stefan Grossman and Woody Mann's *The Roots of Robert Johnson* (Pacific: Mel Bay, 1993) was not included, as the book is in print.

Pieces coauthored or authored by several other blues writers found a natural place in this book. In 1963, Bernard Klatzko joined Wardlow in Mississippi on a memorable journey through the old haunts of Charlie Patton, afterwards telling the tale in the booklet for *The Immortal Charlie Patton* (OJL-7), reprinted here under the same title. Pat Howse and Jimmy Phillips interviewed Wardlow himself for "Godfather of Delta Blues: H.C. Speir." Stephen Calt joined Wardlow (either in his own name, or as the pseudonymous Jacques Roche) to write "Patton's Murder" and "He's a Devil of a Joe."

The remaining articles were arranged in the present order. The book opens with Wardlow's 1967 King Solomon Hill article and closes with his return to King Solomon Hill 20 years later. In between, his growth as an investigator and writer may be traced. *Initial Inquiries and Encounters* contains the seeds of his research. Several articles present a collection of brief biographical entries—and one lengthy interview with Ishmon Bracey offers his recollections of many other blues artists. These tantalizing glimpses became the basis of Wardlow's later investigations.

Tips, Leads, and Documents offers case examples of the tools of Wardlow's blues research, including oral interviews, telephone directories, and death certificates. *Witnesses* treats the informants he sought when the primary subjects he pursued had died or were unavailable. *H.C. Speir* reprints "Legends of the Lost," the first article ever on the legendary talent scout (the corrected 1968 version is reprinted here), and "Godfather of Delta Blues," a vivid transcription of Wardlow reminiscing about Speir. *Retrospectives,* the culminating section of the book, combines elements of all the preceding four.

Wardlow has added three new articles especially for the book. "Bukka White: From Aberdeen to Parchman" introduces the use of court documents to blues research. "Blind Roosevelt Graves" was a piece that he had long wished to write, and it was prepared with its context in this book in mind. "Stop, Look, and Listen at the Cross Road" is a commentary asking the blues fan to entertain another interpretation of the crossroads legend.

The absence of information on some well-known blues musicians—such as Son House, Skip James, Muddy Waters, Howlin' Wolf, and Memphis Minnie—may be noticed. It is hoped that the information on performers, recordings, and documents given here will guide prospective biographers and analysts pursuing the lives of those and other blues people to the best uses of their sources.

The original articles have been edited for clarity, song title corrections, and outdated references, as well as to eliminate the redundant information inherent in a compilation such as this. A few pieces, notably "Patton's Murder" and "Canton Mis'sippi Breakdown" have been significantly revised by Wardlow and this editor to fit Wardlow's style of expression. When these articles were first printed, their pioneering authors and publishers didn't have the luxury of a copy editor like Kristi Hein, who helped produce the present texts. In a few of the early articles, the words "negro," "colored," and other now-outdated terms were used by Wardlow's informants and co-authors. Rather than removing those words, it was decided best to leave them be, as traces of the times when the research was conducted and the articles written. In no way should the retention of such terms be taken as racist or derogatory.

In addition to the new articles, Wardlow has prepared new introductions for the reprinted pieces that explain the reasons and inspirations behind their writing. For those that needed extensive updates, especially "Canton, Mis'sippi Breakdown," we have provided postscripts to make some corrections and to cite research tapes and supplementary articles.

Secondary literature is referred to by author and year of publication, with full citations given in the reference list; the list's section on Wardlow is the most complete bibliography on him to date. The fourth edition of Dixon and Godrich's *Blues and Gospel Records 1890–1943* is cited in all articles; readers should not be surprised to see a reference to this 1997 discography in an article written in 1996 or before. Specific field tapes are not cited in the body of the given article, since Wardlow would check a certain point with an informant in several interviews. Those who wish to examine the tapes may, with Wardlow's permission, do so among the 42 reels deposited at the University of Mississippi Blues Archive, or with the duplicate set of them at the Middle Tennessee State University (MTSU) Center of Popular Music. My list of the tapes cited in the articles, including the location numbers by which the tapes may be requested at the Blues Archive and MTSU, appears in the back of the book. I have also provided a list of the 78 rpm issues of the performances mentioned, and a compact disc reissue section.

I hope you will derive much pleasure from this book and its CD, whether by your stereo at home or at a table in your local library. Perhaps they will lead you to a disc or a book that you have not heard or read yet, or to relisten or reread with a fresh insight. With familiarity, the records and books will become your newfound sources to the music and ideas of the blues.

—Edward Komara,
Director, Music Library/Blues Archive,
University of Mississippi

Prologue

King Solomon Hill

As early as 1959 Sam Charters, in his book Country Blues *(p. 200), had identified King Solomon Hill as Big Joe Williams. By the mid-1960s, that suggestion seemed erroneous.*

In 1966 Stephen Calt informed me in a letter that he heard the words "goin' Minden" in King Solomon Hill's record "The Gone Dead Train." Because I had spent the first seven years of my life about 30 miles below Minden, I recognized that it was in Louisiana. When in 1967 my mother and I visited relatives in that state, I went to Minden and began asking people on the streets in the black section if they heard of a King Solomon Hill who had made records in 1932. One of them said, after listening to the King Solomon Hill cuts from the Sam Collins LP (Origin Jazz Library OJL-10), "That sho' 'nuff sounds like that Joe Holmes. You go down there to Sibley. That where he comes from."

Sibley turned out to be the hometown of Joe Holmes, and from there the article takes up. For a final word, see the epilogue, "One Last Walk up King Solomon Hill," page 208. —GDW

[Originally published in *78 Quarterly* no. 1 (1967): 5–9.]

Northern Louisiana is a barren country with few inhabitants, an abundance of red clay soil, and miles and miles of commercial timber covering the valleys, which lie between sparsely populated sawmill towns that subsist on the pulpwood industries.

Sibley, Louisiana, some 30 miles from Shreveport, and five miles below Minden, is a town of some 500 residents. Two railroads cross just outside the city limits—the Louisiana and Arkansas, and the Illinois Central.

An old man in his late seventies sat on the porch of an old, unpainted brown shack, which was reeling from the erosions of time and from lack of upkeep.

With an air of expectancy, I asked, "Ever hear of a young blues singer named King Solomon Hill? He used to live around this area and he sang a song about the 'Gone Dead Train,' and about 'Tell Me Baby, What Fault You Find in Me?'"

The old man searched his memory with a senile expression; but with a friendly smile, replied, "Don't remember no Solomon Hill, but I had a cousin named Joe Holmes who used to sing all them songs you mentioned."

Thirty minutes later I began my conversation with Holmes' wife, a gentle woman who for 31 years had lived with one of the most incredible mysteries in the history of the country blues. A three-day search in five different towns began to pay off.

Joe Holmes, alias King Solomon Hill (the name was probably given to him by a Paramount's recording director), was a native of south Mississippi. He was born near McComb in 1897.

Following Charlie, a brother ten years older, Holmes came to northern Louisiana in 1915, where, three years later, he married Roberta Allums. Their only child, Essie (who now lives in Chicago), was born in the winter of 1918.

Holmes soon grew restless in Louisiana and in 1920 returned to McComb with his wife and child. In Burgarland, the colored section of north McComb, he met its most famous blues singer, "Salty Dog Sam" (Collins). On one of the few occasions Roberta Holmes went out with her husband, she saw him accompany Sam at a juke joint. She can still recognize the likeness of Salty Dog Sam that appeared with an ad for one of his Black Patti recordings.

The family remained together in McComb for 12 months. Then Roberta and Essie went back to their home in Sibley. Joe stayed an extra six months, just playing music and doing as little work as possible.

In later years, Holmes was known for a song that began, "Going to Shreveport, tell the chief police." This may have been his version of Collins' "Jailhouse Blues" on Gennett 6167.

While traveling by train to Texas in 1928, the legendary Blind Lemon Jefferson made a brief stop at Minden. Shortly thereafter, Holmes and a close friend who lived near Minden, George Young, left with Jefferson on

Roberta Allums, who was once married to Joe Holmes, is pictured here with (unidentified) neighbor holding a 1932 King Soloman Hill record. Wardlow collection.

an Illinois Central passenger train for Wichita Falls, a favorite hangout of Lemon's in Texas.

Lemon Jefferson, named such because of his fatness as a child, always carried a pearl-handled .45 pistol for protection. A blind man with money, as Lemon had, would have been an easy target for robbery or assault.

Two months after their Minden meeting, Holmes and Jefferson parted company. After making the rounds of various Texas towns and road stops, Holmes and his friend George returned to Sibley to play in the barrel-houses and jukes of northern Louisiana.

An aftermath of Lemon's trip through Minden may have been the 1928 Paramount session that marked the debut of Willard (Ramblin') Thomas, a blues singer who probably hailed from west Texas or Arizona. It seems possible that Paramount contacted Thomas on Jefferson's recommendation.

Joe Holmes often traveled to Shreveport to play with Thomas, who later moved just north of that town, and who was to travel through many parts of Texas and Louisiana. Roberta remembers that "Joe had rather play with Thomas than with any other singer." Next to George Young, Thomas was Holmes' best friend.

When Thomas came to Sibley, he and Holmes went down in the clay hill valley area mentioned on "Whoopee Blues": "I got to go to the valley, there ain't a house for 25 miles around." They played in the small sawmill settlement of Roytown, performing at a jukehouse that was closed by the law in the late 1930s after two people were killed there in a single night.

Blind Lemon Jefferson was a companion of King Solomon Hill's briefly in the late 1920s. They played together in both Texas and Louisiana. Courtesy Maxey Tarpley.

In early 1932, a scout for Paramount Records found Holmes singing in uptown Minden and asked him if he wanted to record. Joe went home and asked Roberta what she thought about the opportunity.

She told him, "Go where you wanna go." Holmes did exactly that, although Roberta remembers that he was not too excited about the forthcoming trip to Wisconsin.

The scout in question, Henry Stephany of Milwaukee (who had replaced Art Laibley in the fall of 1931), accompanied Holmes to Birmingham, where the two were joined by Ben Curry. Curry, an old friend of Holmes', was originally from nearby Arcadia, Louisiana, where Holmes sometimes appeared in the 1930s.

These two singers, along with the

Alabama bluesman Marshall Owens and the Famous Blues Jay Singers of Birmingham, then traveled to Paramount's Grafton Studios.

The quartet opened the recording session with two sides, followed by Curry's five. On his five sides, Curry used his banjo-mandolin, the instrument he played with the greatest proficiency.

Owens, then a man in his late fifties or early sixties, recorded four sides, two of which have not been located to date by a record collector. His "Texas Blues," backed with "Try Me One More Time" (released on Paramount 13117), is a classic example of an early style of blues similar to a southern Alabama blues style. Although Owens' music has many qualities in common with Texas blues, his singing style is highly reminiscent of Ed Bell's.

Holmes was the last to record: six songs, all of which Roberta said he had been performing before his trip to Grafton. One, "Gone Dead Train," was one of the best train blues of the 1930s. Using, for some undetermined reason, the pseudonym "King Solomon Hill," he told of his experiences hoboing and hustling on the Southern railroad (which runs from New Orleans to New York via Birmingham) and on the Illinois Central (which runs through Sibley). On "Gone Dead Train," Hill also alluded to the town of Fryeburg, which consists of but a store and a post office, ten miles south of Sibley.

The flip side of that record, released on Paramount 13129, was a version of the old Memphis Minnie and Joe McCoy duet, "What Fault You Find in Me?"

His lyrics for his other two recorded numbers, "Down on My Bended Knee" and "Whoopee Blues" (Paramount 13116), express the macho attitude, a stance not unlike that taken by Robert Johnson and Isaiah Nettles.

The two songs that completed that session have never been located by a collector. One of them, "My Buddy Blind Papa Lemon," was written as a tribute to Jefferson, with whom Holmes played on at least three occasions during Jefferson's stopovers in Minden. Jefferson had died in December 1929 under mysterious circumstances.

The other missing song, "Times Has Done Got Out of Hand," was a typical "hard times" Depression piece.

On all of his extant pieces, Holmes used a cow bone for slide, in the manner that Sam Collins played with a knife.

Holmes brought copies of all three records back to Sibley with him, but all have been destroyed. He returned with Ben Curry, and both men, along with the unrecorded George Young, made a trip to Texas to publicize their recent recordings. Few copies of any single Holmes effort were sold; however, few people around Sibley even knew that Holmes had made records, because they were released under the assumed name.

Holmes continued to travel in the 1930s to nearby Shreveport and Monroe, as well as on to eastern Texas. He also spent time in small towns like Choudrant, Ringold, and Jonesboro. Roberta remembers that "He went up in Arkansas to play and people would come from Eris and Calhoun and other towns to get him to play after they heard tell about him."

A sawmill worker at Heflin, a small town south of Sibley, saw Holmes get off a train from Longview one night after he had been playing out in Texas.

"Funniest sight I ever see'd: that guy didn't stay in town 30 minutes before he got in an argument with this other guy in this joint. That other guy just pulled out his pistol and shot at him three times. He didn't stop running until he was clear out of town. Just left his baggage and guitar layin' down there on the floor." His belongings were eventually retrieved by another friend.

By the late 1940s, Holmes was drinking more and more but was still playing music. He never attended church; his wife recounts that "Joe just kept right on, just like he was going straight to the devil."

Paramount Records

2741—Born to Die Blues
Low Down Dirty Shame Blues
Moanin' Bernice Edwards

2739—Eagle Eyed Mama
Dynamite Blues
Blind Lemon Jefferson

2738—Crow Jane Woman
Marble Stone Blues.....Ida Cox

2737—Search Warrant Blues
Sweet Papa Low Down
Blind Blake

2736—Don't Break Down on Me
Baby Please Loan Me Your
Heart..Papa Charlie Jackson

2735—Tough Luck Blues
Screech Owl Blues...Ma Rainey

2734—He Just Hung His Head and
Died
Lord I Don't Care Where They
Bury My Body
Norfolk Jubilee Quartette

2731—Cincinnati Underworld Woman
Tear It Down (Bed Slats and
All)...........Bob Coleman

2729—Crawlin' Spider Blues
Ezell's Precious Five
Will Ezell (All by Himself)

2728—Competition Bed Blues
Sad News Blues
Blind Lemon Jefferson

2727—Sobbing Tears Blues
Separated Blues........Ida Cox

2726—I've Got the Key to the
Kingdom
Your Enemy Cannot Harm You
Blind Willie Davis

2724—Going South Blues
Rowdy Man Blues
Elzadie Robinson

12723—Panther Squall Blues
No Dough Blues
Blind Blake

12722—Poor Boy Blues
Ramblin' Man
Ramblin' Thomas

12721—Jungle Man Blues
Corn Liquor Blues
Papa Charlie Jackson

12718—Ma and Pa Poorhouse Blues
Big Feeling Blues
Ma Rainey and Papa Charlie
Jackson

12715—You're Going to Need that Pure
Religion
Wonder Where Is the Gamblin'
Man.
Norfolk Jubilee Quartette

12714—Selling That Stuff
Beedle Um Bum
The Hokum Boys

12710—Back Door Slam Blues
Cold Hearted Mama Blues
Blind Blake

12689—Wicked Daddy
It's Too Late Now
Elzadie Robinson

12688—Old Mill Blues
Mixed Up Rag
Will Ezell

12673—Doggin' Me Mama Blues
Hot Potatoes
Blind Blake

12662—Evil Woman Blues
Keep a Knockin' and You Can't
Get In
"Boodle It" Wiggins

This 1929 ad shows recordings by Lemon Jefferson and Ramblin' Thomas, both of whom had played together in the late '20s in Louisiana and Texas. Courtesy Maxey Tarpley.

In 1949, Holmes took sick. Roberta said, "He never went to no doctor. Take sick; laid around about three days—then he died. Been drinking before he died and he started bleeding inside. Had a hemorrhage."

Like many other great blues singers (such as Charlie Patton, Willie Brown, and Skip James), Holmes was very short. He stood only five feet and three inches. He weighed about 130 pounds, and was brown-skinned in complexion. He smoked constantly.

Roberta remembers two other facts, one pertaining to his musical development, the other to the tragedy that led to his death.

She said, "He learned himself how to play, before he ever came to Sibley." The other: "He drank all the time. He was drinking when we married."

[For much more detail from Roberta Allums and others—and the tale of the controversy launched by this article—see the epilogue, "One Last Walk up King Solomon Hill," page 208.]

I

Initial Inquiries and Encounters

Knocking on Doors for 78s:
Buying Race Records
in the South

Publisher Tim Gracyk of Victrola and 78 Journal asked me to describe how I began searching for black blues and jazz records from 1960 through the 1980s. This resulting article recaps how I searched for them, including the tip I shared with other canvassers to look for the elderly woman with flowerpots and a well-kept yard (this sort of scene was drawn by Robert Crumb in his 1975 piece "That's Life"). This reminiscence also gives a sample of what blacks purchased in the 1920s and '30s and explains why. —GDW

[Originally published in *Victrola and 78 Journal* no. 9 (Summer 1996): 9–14.]

A lthough I enjoyed blues and jazz records, I did not begin as a collector of race discs. As a teenager in 1954, I collected Roy Acuff records. After going to jukebox companies to find Acuff titles, I started buying Bob Wills 78s of the 1930s and other western swing artists. I still remember finding Mr. Freddie Okeh's "Milk Cow Blues" (OKeh 8422) in the collection of an in-law. It was one of those rare race records bought by whites. "Race records" were called as such to indicate discs made by black musicians for black buyers.

Will Roy Hearne, a Los Angeles jazz dealer, told me I could "get a whole box full" of Acuff discs if I could find some rare jazz items. One afternoon in March of 1961, I had an idea. Did any of the "colored" people near me have old records still? I say "colored" here since that is language typical at the time.

I walked three blocks down the hill to the "colored" section of town and picked out a row of houses. I went to the first one, knocked on the door, and said, "Anyone home? Can you hear me?"

An elderly woman opened the door.

I said, "I buy old records—you know, them old blues records. Do you have any?"

She replied, "Lord, no, child! We threw 'em

Freddie, who was the first Delta-sounding bluesman to record (in 1926), recorded for three companies from 1926 to 1935. Wardlow collection.

away years ago. But we used to have one of those old windup machines."

I kept knocking. After about ten houses on two streets, I spotted an old, decrepit shack with flowerpots on the porch. I knocked and said, "Anyone home?" An old woman, about 80, came to the door, we talked, and she went back inside while I waited anxiously on the porch. I never asked to come into houses. I assumed that old people felt safer if strangers stayed on the porches, especially whites. I only entered if invited. Sometimes people would invite me in by saying, "You can come look at 'em. I can't bend down that low to get 'em out of the Victrola."

This woman brought two discs out to the porch. "I found a couple," she said, modestly. "They ain't no good to me."

I looked and was surprised. One of the two discs was a red label 16,000 series Champion, the only time I found a Champion in Mississippi. In E (excellent) condition, this was #16058 by Alberta Jones, issued as Bessie Sanders and the Memphis Red Peppers. The other was a Bertha "Chippie" Hill OKeh disc, "Mess, Katie, Mess" (8437), with Louis Armstrong on cornet and Richard Jones on piano.

I concluded that here was a new and easy way to find records. I enjoyed that day what turned out to be beginner's luck. I soon learned that one could canvass all day and find nothing.

All that spring I knocked on doors, spending from one to three hours each day looking. I refined my sales approach to these words: "I buy old Victrola records—you know, them old blues records by Bessie Smith, Blind Lemon, Leroy Carr. All them old blues singers." I had learned that old people used the term "Victrola records," though sometimes they called them "Grafonola records." They remembered Bessie and Blind Lemon better than other artists.

I usually paid a quarter for each record—sometimes less, sometimes 50 cents. Normally I mentioned my price range as I made my initial inquiry. If I saw something especially desirable, I offered a dollar to be sure to get it. Selling records at the door to a white man must have struck some as unusual. Occasionally they asked if I was planning to reissue them—"You gonna make them over again?" My standard reply: "I play guitar and piano. I want to learn these old blues myself. It's illegal to put them out again."

A disappointing number were in G (good) to V (very good) condition. I came across many Blind Lemon Jefferson and Leroy Carr discs that had been played until the surface was gray. Paramounts were often cracked all the way to the label. Columbias and OKehs struck me as more durable than other discs.

I learned from experience that women had the records. Men moved around more, and they did not take records when they moved.

This pseudonym was used by Paramount on its cheap Broadway label for Blind Roosevelt Graves and brother Aaron. Wardlow collection.

I had the best luck with older women who had flowerpots on the porch, so I learned to look for flowerpots and taught other collectors to look for the same. The pots indicated that someone had lived at one location for a long time. Records were often in these homes, but they were thrown away when people moved.

Within a year I had found some choice items, including a Hattie Burleson disc from 1928 (Brunswick 7042), Robert Johnson's "Last Fair Deal Going Down" (Vocalion 03445), and Johnson's "Me and the Devil Blues" (Vocalion 04108). I bought this last one within a mile of my own home. But the prize was Mattie Delaney doing "Tallahatchie River Blues" (Vocalion 1480), a song that refers to a river flood in the Delta. My copy of this disc was the first one known to collectors. I learned this from New York collectors eager for me to trade it away.

I also discovered that women who were active churchgoers only had sacred music, never blues or jazz records. I did buy gospel records that featured singing. I recall a prize item in the home of a religious woman. I had to go back twice to get this disc. It was the fabulous Rev. D.C. Rice doing "I'm Pressing On" (Vocalion 1289). Five years later I located Rice himself in Montgomery, Alabama, interviewed him, and published his story in *Storyville*. [See "Rev. D.C. Rice—Gospel Singer," page 152.]

Usually when I found religious records, they featured Rev. F.W. McGee or Rev. J.M. Gates. Gates was the top seller of religious records. I always left these behind.

Occasionally I found discs of nonblues artists, such as Bert Williams, which were never as worn as later blues records. The white singer whose discs could be found most often in these homes was Jimmie Rodgers. His blue yodels were especially popular. I never found, say, a Caruso disc unless people hauled out 78s given to them by white employers.

Only twice did people admit that they had old discs and then refuse to show them, which aroused my curiosity, so I never forgot those houses. I stopped three different times at one house in the Delta. The other was in Natchez on the Mississippi River. I wonder what happened to those discs.

When I found houses with blues records—about one house in every ten—I generally found Bessie or Clara Smith, a Blind Lemon or Leroy Carr. Certain discs showed up often—Leroy Carr's "How Long, How Long," Blind Lemon's "Black Snake Moan," his "Electric Chair Blues/So That My Grave Is Kept Clean," Jim Jackson doing

Sam Collin's record features his slide guitar playing, while Skippy Whippy's exemplifies a small juke band performance. Wardlow collection.

"Jim Jackson's Kansas City Blues." Bessie Smith's "Down Hearted Blues" was a huge seller, and I recall Paramount scout Harry Charles of Birmingham saying in the mid-'60s, "That's the best blues record ever made."

I deduced that the old people then in their sixties or seventies had bought records mainly in the 1920s. I learned that their phonographs had been bought around 1923 or slightly later, perhaps up to 1927. The blues and jazz records would start from around 1921 and end by 1926 or 1927. People in a slightly younger age group had bought their machines and records from about 1926 to 1930.

Other discs were from the late 1930s, starting from about 1937 and ending around 1942. Not surprisingly, records from the depths of the Depression—around 1931 to 1934—did not pop up.

By 1962 I was working in Jackson for the Orkin Pest Company, and I knocked on doors at dinnertime as my interest in country blues grew.

Blind Lemon's discs were common around Jackson. He cornered the market in that area, as far as the Paramount label goes! However, I learned that small towns were the best places for finding records, not bigger places like Jackson. In every small town at least one old person still had a Victrola. An exciting find was a Black Patti 8025, "The Jail House Blues" by Sam Collins. "I brought it back from Chicago," the man said as I gave him a dollar for the prize.

One day I stopped in the little town of Edwards—close to Charlie Patton's birthplace—and found two Patton discs ("Pony Blues," 12792, and "High Water Everywhere," 12909), which was exciting. At first Charlie was hard for me to listen to because of his rough style—both playing and singing—but New York collectors had asked if I had Pattons to sell, so I knew to look for these.

I canvassed for more than ten years and occasionally into the mid-1980s. But most of the records were gone by that time, ending up in junk stores, flea markets, or trash bins. By the mid-1980s the few records that turned up were not worth the effort in finding them.

The first ad by a major record comapany to promote records made by a black singer in a white trade publication. Photo courtesy Tim Gracyk.

I noted interesting patterns. In Alabama in 1967, I met an old lady who had two Sam Collins Gennetts and ten Herwins, the best of which was 92001 by Alberta Jones with the Ellington Twins (Duke played piano on this 1926 disc). Later I learned that the Starr Piano Company had stores in Birmingham and Montgomery. Salesmen visited drug and furniture stores to convince store owners to carry Gennett discs. Herwins could be ordered from St. Louis. I found a dozen different race Gennetts in west Alabama in a three-year period.

One collector from Georgia who had begun canvassing in the late 1950s found both Black Birds of Paradise discs, Gennett 6210 and 6211, in one home in Montgomery in 1967. The music had been recorded in Birmingham in 1927, but Montgomery was the band's hometown, so it made sense that the rare discs were in that city.

My best find was not from canvassing but from visiting a junk store in 1970. The store owner had acquired the discs by going door to door. Here I found nine discs on Broadway, a label related to Paramount. Broadways originally sold for 35 cents. All were broken except for a George "Bullet" Williams (5085). I found a Ma Rainey Jug band record on Paramount 12804, a Paramount disc with Freezone on one side and Raymond Barrow on the other (12803), Vocalions by Garfield Akers (including "Dough Roller Blues," Vocalion 1481), and another copy of Matie Delaney's Vocalion 1480.

Sometimes while knocking on doors, I tried to get information about artists. Asking about singers from Mississippi helped me locate Ishmon Bracey himself, who was then a preacher. This was in 1963. I located Johnny Temple in 1965.

The 1930–32 Paramounts were never sold in Mississippi as they were in other states since the distributor, the St. Louis Music Company, had closed its Memphis distribution center in May 1930. I acquired my Paramounts from the 1930–32 period by swapping. I once calculated that I had traded with 49 different collectors since the early 1960s.

The most exciting find of all was Son House's "Dry Spell Blues" on Paramount 12990, the only known copy at the time. I found it in 1963 in Rayville, Louisiana. The disc's owners would not sell it to me at an affordable price. New York collector Bernard Klatzko sent $25, asking that I buy the record for him (that was a lot of money then!).

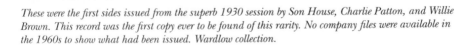

These were the first sides issued from the superb 1930 session by Son House, Charlie Patton, and Willie Brown. This record was the first copy ever to be found of this rarity. No company files were available in the 1960s to show what had been issued. Wardlow collection.

Later I got the disc back from him in a trade. It is my only Son House disc. I am also happy to own 18 Patton records, six by Skip James (not one was found in Mississippi), a Willie Brown Paramount, and two 1930 Paramounts of Louise Johnson. I have listened carefully to my records and have shared what I have learned over the years with others interested in country blues.

I bought my Willie Brown disc ("Future Blues," Paramount 13090) in the Louisiana Delta on a Saturday afternoon. I suspect a previous owner had dropped it at some point since it had been broken in half and taped back together with adhesive tape. Jim Cooprider repaired it for me. It was the first Willie Brown Paramount disc found. It had been kept in an old cheese box under a bed. The woman who sold it to me owned other records that she had—for some reason—put on a chicken coop with a tin roof, and these were badly warped. Her copy of Paramount 13006 featuring Eurreal "Little Brother" Montgomery was too badly warped to be worth anything.

Through the years I taught other collectors to canvass, most notably Nick Perls, who came south in 1964 with Steve Calt. We went to Arkansas to canvass and used my car, which had Mississippi license plates. Using Perls' car, with its New York plates, would have brought trouble that sum-

1930 OKeh ad. Courtesy Maxey Tarpley.

mer in Mississippi due to civil rights workers being in the state to register voters. It was a tense summer, with three civil rights workers murdered 40 miles from my hometown. But we had no trouble in Arkansas knocking on doors.

Records were bought in patterns. In a home near Jackson a lady had nine Supertones in the rare 2200 series. These were taken from Vocalion masters, and the big sellers among these reissues were discs of Jim Jackson, Tampa Red teamed with Georgia Tom, and Leroy Carr. When the lady told me she had some Tommy Johnsons, I was thrilled at the chance of buying some incredibly rare blues 78s, but the records turned out to be Leroy Carr discs. She had confused the names, since Carr was issued under the name Blues Johnson on Supertone. These Supertones reportedly came out in the fall of 1931.

Only once did I encounter a threat of violence. In 1967 in Pensacola, Florida, a man who had been drinking threatened me with a butcher knife when I asked to see his mother's records. I left quietly and quickly. I did not buy any records there!

In one Mississippi town a local cop stopped me as I was buying records from an elderly woman. He asked what I was doing. These were tense days during the struggle for civil rights. When the woman told the officer that I was "just buying old records," he seemed satisfied that I wasn't trying to cheat her and he left.

The early '60s were golden for canvassing. Two men in Georgia—Jeff Tarrer of Macon and Max Tarpley of Augusta—started "door knocking" about the same time or perhaps just before I did. The idea of knocking on doors for blues 78s has been satirized by artist Robert Crumb.

Even today, when I pass a row of old houses, I wonder whether there could be old records still in the homes. By this time, the precious few that remain have been handed down to grandchildren. I am sorry to say it is dangerous to be in some black neighborhoods now. That was not a concern a few decades ago.

1930 ad for new Paramount releases, featuring Charlie Patton [Paramount always misspelled Charlie as Charley], who had become their top seller after Blind Lemon died. Courtesy Maxey Tarpley.

Record Grades

By Edward Komara

Unlike compact discs, 78 rpm discs have survived in varying conditions. Dealers and collectors have devised an informal code to signify the degree of wear and tear when describing their records in catalogs and lists. Since the basis of condition grading does vary, the following is offered as a thumbnail guide for the noncollecting reader.

Mint (M) or Near Mint (NM): Unplayed (for Near Mint, played once for grading), surface very glossy and reflective with some static charge, label like new, plays cleanly. Very few blues records fit this grade; records in this condition usually come from unsold store stock.

Excellent (E): Played a few times with a sharp needle; surface glossy, but no static charge; label undamaged; one or two pops per three-minute side. Those 78s in this condition were usually kept by collectors from the time of the album's initial commercial release.

Very Good (V): Kept in good care, but played more than 50 times; surface black, but not glossy; label has some minor wear or fade; surface pops occur with the frequency of a small campfire. Records in this shape usually were from purchasers who regularly changed needles.

Good (G): Not kept in sleeve, and played often; surface has gray bands of wear; label faded or discolored; sustained groove wear resulting in high surface noise; more often than not, the disc was played with a blunt needle several times. Most records acquired by canvassers were in this condition.

Poor (P): As one dealer says, "Possibly unplayable." In other words, played and worn beyond hearing, usually with a blunt needle weighted down with coins or rocks; light gray surface, may have slight but playable cracks; label unreadable, or completely obliterated; sounds like frying bacon or popcorn. Many, many blues records were found in this condition, but few were saved by collectors and canvassers unless they were unique or extremely rare, like the sole surviving copy of Son House's "Preaching the Blues" (Paramount 13013).

The Immortal Charlie Patton

By Bernard Klatzko with Gayle Dean Wardlow

In 1963 I was working in Jackson, Mississippi. At that time I had found three Charlie Patton records. The aggressive record collector Bernie Klatzko of Glen Cove, New York, had the foremost collection of Patton's records at that time; he got my name from a Birmingham collector/dealer who informed him that I had three Patton records. He began writing to me and became the impetus behind my searching for biographical details on Patton. At that time, Bernie knew that Charlie Patton was deceased: the talented John Fahey had been to Clarksdale in 1958 and learned that Patton was dead, but not where he was buried or other biographical details. (See "Patton's Murder—Whitewash? Or Hogwash?," page 94.) Ironically, I had met Fahey in 1960 in Washington, and he had played me some Patton records; I didn't like them at first, because I was still into Roy Acuff and the dobro sound of Brother Oswald. In July 1963 I had found one of Charlie's many common-law wives, Minnie Franklin, near Vicksburg. The next month, Bernie came south to meet me and research the life of Patton. After the trip, he wrote the notes to The Immortal Charlie Patton *(OJL-7). The cover to this LP featured the only photo of Patton then found, recovered by Georgia collector Maxey Tarpley from a Paramount ad in a Victrola full of records in Augusta.* —GDW

[Originally published as a booklet to *The Immortal Charlie Patton 1887–1934, no. 2*, Origin Jazz Library OJL-7, 1964.]

It was early in December, 1963, well past midnight, when I was awakened by the shrill ring of the phone. I picked up the receiver with uncertainty. "I found another Patton record!" The exclamation was delivered rapid-fire by a familiar voice with a white southern accent. It was Gayle Dean Wardlow, and he was calling from Jackson, Mississippi, where he worked and went to school.

Gayle poured out as much information as he could in the allotted three minutes, including a summary of his latest diggings into the lives of almost-forgotten blues singers. Then he hung up, leaving me quite restless. I couldn't fall asleep after that. My mind drifted back and fastened on the images and events of a few days in August of the same year when Gayle and I were "pardners."

I remember it was August 4, a hot Mississippi Sunday, and we were riding in a Corvair I had rented in Jackson. We were driving north on US 49.

We had passed Yazoo City and the Yazoo River, the southeastern gateway to the Delta region. We swept up past Louise, Midnight, and Silver City to Belzoni. It was near the cotton fields outside Belzoni where I first caught the whiff of the poisons that fill the air. Tons of DDT are laid over the fields of the Delta by daredevil ex-fighter pilots. Flying low, right under the telephone wires, then dipping to no more than six feet above the ground, they level and deposit a thick spray on the plants. The war against the boll weevil is waged daily; insects are poisoned, but so is the air man breathes. The heavy smell of the insecticide stayed in my nostrils all through my tour of the Delta. Sometimes I can even smell it now.

Belzoni (locally, "Belzona") is a neat, clean town with recently built, modern shops and well-kept homes with trim lawns. The "Quarters"—Mississippi-ese for Negro quarters—consisted of several rows of unpainted shacks. In "High Sheriff," Charlie Patton sings, "When the trial's in Belzona/Ain't no use a feelin' proud." . . . There must have been clues to Patton's past in the courthouse there, but it was Sunday and everything was shut down tight.

Belzoni happened to be in the path of our immediate destination, Leland. We were following a lead that Dean had obtained a few months back from an old Negro named Jim Edwards. He had told Gayle that Patton had lived outside Leland, near Longswitch, and had died on Dockery's plantation, also outside Leland. This was a really good tip, and it was what prompted me to head for the Delta with high hopes of finally getting the real facts of Charlie Patton's life. Then, in

The only photograph of Charlie Patton was found in Augusta, Georgia, by collector Maxey Tarpley in the mid-'60s. Courtesy Maxey Tarpley.

July, just before my planned departure, Gayle miraculously found one of Patton's many wives, Minnie Franklin, in Bovina, not far from Vicksburg. Minnie was helpful only in fixing the year of Patton's birth—1887. The rest of the story, we felt, lay in the heart of the Delta.

After leaving Belzoni, we drove eagerly on up route 49W to Indianola, where we took refuge from the sun in a new, spanking-clean diner. Yankee that I am, I wanted to try what the menu exotically described as "catfish hush puppies," but Gayle advised me these would likely be frozen and to wait till I could get fresh ones.

We looked at our road map. Leland lay 15 miles farther east, with only Greenville, the capital of the Delta, separating Leland from the Mississippi

River. Longswitch was located on a backcountry road, off the main run between Indianola and Leland. There was a town of Dockery, but located near Cleveland, not near Leland. Could a town also be a plantation, we wondered?

We started out of Indianola a little anxiously. We had come all this way, relying on the fading memory of an old man. On the way we asked people about the location of Dockery's plantation. No one had heard of it. I was now convinced that we would find Dockery's outside Cleveland and that Gayle may have misunderstood Jim Edwards on that score.

We finally pulled off the main road onto a dirt track, which brought us to Holly Ridge, just a whoop and a holler, as they say down there, from Longswitch. A group of Negro men and women were lounging about the general store, enjoying their day of rest. Dean engaged one of the women in conversation while I waited in the car a little impatiently, anxious to get on to Longswitch.

Suddenly I heard Gayle ask the woman, extra loud, so I could hear it, "You're really Bertha Lee's cousin?" My heart jumped! My knees felt weak! I couldn't believe it. We had struck so suddenly and accurately.

I joined Gayle and the woman. She was short and dark, with a shock of grey hair that seemed incongruous around an unwrinkled face. She must have been well up in her sixties.

Patton was noted for his use of different guitar tunings and his ability to use "knocking" on his guitar sides and "stomping his feet" to keep rhythm. Wardlow collection.

"This here's Evaline Gaynes," said Gayle.

"Did you know Charlie Patton?" I asked, impatient to get to the root of the matter.

"Sure did." She pointed with a head motion at a decent-looking, white, wooden frame house. "Charlie died in Tom Robinson's house, over there."

"What was the cause of his death?" I asked skeptically, expecting to hear one more fantastic story of Patton's end.

"Charlie died a natural death."

Evaline went on to say that Bertha Lee was only 17 years old when she came out of Lula and married Charlie [Note: Further research indicates Bertha was about 30 at this time], and that they both played guitar and sang in Holly Ridge. She remembered Bertha singing a song that went "The bees buzzed around me"—a reference to Bertha's "Yellow Bee."

Patton's last Vocalin, which sold better than other releases because of its "dirty" lyrics, was issued after his 1934 death from heart failure. Wardlow collection.

We left Evaline and stepped into the general store, where we bought ice-cold Dr. Peppers and talked to the owners . . . Both men were white with watery blue eyes, and in their sixties. They remembered Patton very well. He had arrived in Holly Ridge with Bertha Lee in 1933. He was then in his forties and she was "young and wild." They sang and played together, sometimes in the back of the store itself. John Allen, one of the owners who was doing most of the talking, even played fiddle with them on occasion. He said that Patton drank heavily and he and Bertha Lee did their share of fighting with each other . . . In January 1934, Patton went to New York to record and took Bertha with him. Patton died in April of that same year and was buried in Longswitch. The two men rattled off these facts without hesitation, as if all of those events took place only yesterday. A Negro standing behind us, taking all the talk in, volunteered, "Someone put poison in Patton's whiskey!" We didn't pursue the matter.

We quit the general store and moved on to our next destination, Longswitch. It didn't take long to pass through Holly Ridge. The entire community consisted of a dozen or so shacks that lined the dirt road. The tenants serviced Tom Robinson's cotton fields. A quarter of a mile up the road, after passing two shacks and a deserted general store, we came to another group of dwellings. Confidently, we asked whether we were in Longswitch and were told we had passed it. Yes, that abandoned general

A typical store in the early 1900s in Clarksdale, one of the three biggest towns in the Delta. Wardlow collection

store was Longswitch! We went on back to Holly Ridge. I stopped at a Negro dwelling where several people were seated on a screened porch. The quizzical frowns on their faces turned to smiles when I asked about Charlie Patton.

"Oh, I sure did love that Charlie Patton. He was the best singer I ever heard," exclaimed an extremely fat woman with all the sincerity she could muster.

"He used to do a lot of tricks with the guitar when he played," recalled another woman, laughing.

"Did anyone else play guitar around here?"

"My brothers, Robert, Eugene, and Sam Riley all played the guitar," replied the same woman who had found Patton's guitar showmanship amusing.

"Where is Patton buried?"

Riley escorted me outside, pointed toward an empty field, and said, "Out there in the Longswitch cemetery."

"Does he have a marker on his grave?" If so, I wanted to photograph it. Riley said there was no marker.

"Now why do you want to know if they's a marker on his grave?" screamed an angry voice from the porch. It was the fat woman, again, and as I looked up she pierced me with a venomous stare. I dropped the subject quickly and continued to talk about Patton. The only songs they remembered were "Hitch Up My Pony/Saddle Up My Grey Mare" ("Pony Blues"), and "What You Want with a Rooster/He Won't Crow 'Fore Day?" ("Banty Rooster Blues"). This was strange, because Patton was at the end of his career when he settled in Holly Ridge and had a very large repertoire of songs. Why would they only remember these, his oldest recorded songs?

We went to the general store once more to make further inquiries and were told by several Negroes that the man who knew the most about Charlie was Charlie Watson, who ran the "crapper"—the dice game. We started for the "craphouse," which was out in the fields hidden from view by some high grass. As we approached the grass barrier, some men appeared from it with that happy drunk look. It then struck me for the first time that most of the men were shuttling between the general store and the "craphouse," getting their kicks with a roll of the dice and bathtub gin—Mississippi is a dry state.

"Don't go back there—you may get your head shot off," Gayle warned me. I never did get to see Charlie Watson. I still regret it.

The next lead to follow was to Dockery's, outside Cleveland. This would have to wait for tomorrow, as the day was drawing to a close. There were still a few hours of daylight, so we decided to canvass the country houses around Leland for "old Victrola records."

We stopped at a group of houses on a dirt road on the edge of a cotton field. At one of the shacks, we drew a young man of about 19 into a discussion of modern blues singers like B.B. King and Jimmy Reed, while an older man in his late sixties stared suspiciously at us. Although I directed questions to him about the older blues singers, he remained silent and gazed more intently than before. Finally, upon deciding that our probing was an honest effort to secure nothing more than information, he spoke up.

"I knew Charlie Patton. I ran a juke joint back in 1933 and '34 in Holly Ridge. He and Bertha Lee played there all the time. He got drunk often and would scrap with Bertha."

"Do you have any of his records?"

"I had a few, but I don't think I have any of 'em left. After so long we'd use 'em as baking plates and garden stones. I remember having 'Pony Blues' and others." He grinned, and the collector in me died one of a thousand deaths. "I live in town," he went on, "and may have some records stashed away somewhere." I got his name and address—Lonnie Hardges, 330 Blackdog St., N. Leland—and we left.

On Monday morning we started for Cleveland. It was 20 miles north of Leland on U.S. 61. After reaching Cleveland, we swung east on paved State Highway 8. We entered Sunflower County after driving three miles and in another three miles from the county line we stopped at the general store— all there was of the town of Dockery. Out beyond the general store and to its right, there was this big blue sign over an entranceway to a large plantation. Its white lettering read: WILL DOCKERY AND SON JOS. DOCKERY.

We drove in, passed some farm machinery and a cotton gin, and came upon a vast, beautifully tended cotton field. However, we turned our attention to a row of Negro houses that stood opposite the field. At the first house a middle-aged woman answered our knock at the screen door.

"Did you ever hear of Charlie Patton?" I started off.

"Charlie Patton? He's dead."

"Did you know him?"

"No. I only moved here about ten years ago. Why don't you ask some of the people who have lived here a long time? You can find them on the other end," she said, pointing to the other group of houses that lay to the left of the entrance road; we had turned right on entering. In looking over the dwellings on the plantation, they were in much better condition than the Negro houses I had seen before, and the few that I later entered were very neat.

The next few inquiries proved very fruitful. At the first house, a young woman directed us to her father-in-law, Johnny Wilder, who ran the gasoline pump in front of the general store and who had known Patton well. In the next house dwelt Patton's cousin, who directed us to the machine shop where Patton's nephew Tom Cannon worked. Sure, he remembered his uncle, but didn't know too much about him. "Why don't you ask my mother, Viola Cannon? That's Charlie's sister. She can tell you all about him. She lives in Cleveland."

We went back to the general store and bought Johnny Wilder and ourselves bottles of coke and sat on a bench in the shade—it was another blistering hot day. Johnny Wilder was brown and lean, of medium height and grey-headed. He was most amiable, but I detected an air of uneasiness about him when we started to ply him with questions.

"Charlie Patton was living here when I came here back in 1917. He traveled all around but always came back to Dockery's. Then a few years later, he left for good. Mr. Jed fired him."

What songs did he sing? Were there any other blues singers on the plantation?

"He sang, 'Hitch Up My Pony/Saddle Up My Grey Mare' and 'What You Want with a Rooster?' . . . As for other singers, there was Son House on Dockery's at the same time. He came from Drew, and Nathan Bank, also from Drew, played with them. There was Willie Brown, too. They all played for picnics and juke joints."

"Patton sang about Tom Rushen. Did you ever hear of him?" I asked.

"Tom Rushen is Iry Rushen's brother," said Johnny. "Iry Rushen was Will Dockery's bookkeeper. He just died recently."

With that, we left for Cleveland to find Viola Cannon. After several inquiries, we were directed to the "new" houses.

We arrived at a street of one-story frame homes, comparatively new and painted, but no larger than the unpainted variety. A man we enlisted for further help pointed to Viola's house and added that if we wanted to know more about Patton we should ask Millie Toy. She had been married to Patton and now lived in Boyle.

Viola came to the door. She was about five foot five, very lean, unsmiling, and proud, and seemed a little disturbed by the intrusion. She had yellow-brown skin, and a long lean face with strong regular features.

"Charlie was a great blues singer," she said. "He taught them all: Howlin'

Sharecroppers chopping "weeds" in a cotton field. All labor was done by hand, with mules, until the tractor was introduced—just before World War II. Wardlow collection.

Wolf, Willie Brown, Son House. He made up all the songs himself. He followed a guitar player around Dockery's as a boy. I forgot the guitar player's name. But Charlie didn't learn any singing from him. Charlie made up his own singing."

"Where was Charlie born?" Gayle asked.

"He was born on a farm outside Edwards in 1887. He had two brothers, William and Will C., and two sisters, Katie and myself. All are dead. I'm the last. We moved from Edwards to Dockery's when Charlie was still a young boy. He didn't start to play guitar until we were on Dockery's. My father was a very big man and my mother was short and real good-looking with long, straight hair. Charlie himself wasn't too big and he was thin."

"Was Charlie religious?" I asked.

Viola chuckled and said, "No, he wasn't religious."

"Then how did he learn all those religious songs and why did he sing them?" I felt a little embarrassed asking that question.

"My father was the elder of a church on the plantation. Charlie knew all those religious songs from boyhood and sang them later 'cause they're good songs, I guess."

"Did you ever hear of Minnie Franklin?" asked Gayle.

"Well, Charlie's first wife was named Gertrude. He met Minnie Franklin in Merigold in 1921 right after he left Dockery's. Then, he followed her on down to Vicksburg after his best gun and money." Viola recalled this incident with fits of laughter.

"Where did Charlie do most of his playing?" I interjected.

"Charlie played all over. He traveled with medicine shows and played with Blind Lemon," she replied.

"Did Charlie drink much?"

"No. He hardly drank at all," she stated flatly.

I wanted to take a snapshot of her, but she wouldn't let me. I believe this was because of her untidy appearance.

We jumped over to Boyle very quickly—it was only two miles south of Cleveland—and found Minnie Toy without much effort. She was at home with her daughter. They were very friendly, but Minnie couldn't remember much. She had married Patton way back in 1908. Her interest faded quickly and she finally withdrew her attention in favor of a mail-order catalog, while we carried on our interview with her daughter. We didn't learn anything the others hadn't told us except for some disappointing news: Willie Brown had died about 15 years earlier in Shelby. [GDW: Brown died in 1952; see "Can't Tell My Future: The Mystery of Willie Brown" page 181.]

Our next destination was Merigold. Evaline Gaynes had said that Bertha Lee was living there. It was a good place to go to continue our search into Patton's past. So far we had accounted for Patton's general movement from 1887—his birth—until 1921, when he left Dockery's, and the last years of his life, 1933 and 34. If we could find Bertha Lee, we could learn a great deal about Patton the man.

We arrived in Merigold, which lies about ten miles north of Cleveland,

and ducked off the main highway onto the dirt road leading to the cotton fields surrounding Merigold. Our first inquiries were discouraging: No one had heard of Bertha Lee. Next, we pulled up to a house to make further inquiries, and I noticed the mailbox read: Mr. Halloway. The words to Patton's "Tom Rushen Blues" flashed in my mind:

> *It was late one night*
> *Halloway was gone to bed.*
> *It was late one night*
> *Halloway was gone to bed.*
> *Mr. Day brought whiskey*
> *that went to Halloway's head.*

Could this really be *the* Halloway? That would be fantastic!

The men out in the cotton field saw us standing at the house, and started in. We started out to meet them. We met in the middle of the field. A tall, dark, heavy, but rather young-looking man greeted us.

"Where can we find Mr. Halloway?" I asked.

"I'm Mr. Halloway."

"Did you know that Charlie Patton sang about a Mr. Halloway in one of his songs?" I asked hopefully.

"Sure, but he was singing about my father. My father's dead. He used to make whiskey in those days," Halloway answered with a big grin.

"Who was Tom Rushen?" I pursued.

"Tom Rushen was the sheriff of Merigold. Mr. Day was the sheriff before him." Halloway explained. Mr. Day's losing his position would explain another verse in "Tom Rushen":

> *Got up this morning*
> *Tom Day was standing 'round,*
> *Got up this morning*
> *Tom Day was standing 'round,*
> *If he loses his office, sir*
> *He's running from town to town*

Mr. Halloway had never heard of Bertha Lee, but directed us to the other side of Merigold, where more Negro homes were strung along a dirt road that serviced cotton and corn fields stretching for miles around. We went from house to house making inquiries, but although everyone had heard of and/or knew Patton, no one had ever heard of Bertha Lee. Even the information concerning Patton was unsatisfactory, as no one knew him well enough or cared enough to try and remember that far back. But they all said, "If you want to know about Charlie Patton, ask Sam Manifield. He lives in the last house at the end of Six Mile Lake."

We followed the dirt road that ran between the lake and the cornfields to the last house. It was a crude house, but a little larger than the others I'd seen. There were several hound dogs bounding about and a few shady trees near the bank of a muddy stream. Sam Manifield's wife came out on the porch and told us we'd have to wait until Sam came off the cornfields at six o'clock. It was almost six at that moment, and we could see a tractor driven by a white man, coming toward the house. Sam, who was hanging onto the side of the tractor, alighted and came toward us suspiciously.

He was long, lean, hard, and must have been well up in his sixties, although he had the body and movements of a youth. He first interrogated us fiercely, in third-degree fashion. Suddenly, satisfied that we were only seeking information about Patton, his face broke into a big grin and he hurled himself, like a gymnast, onto the front hood of our car, and with great relish abandoned himself to his vivid memories of Charlie Patton. It was obvious from his great enthusiasm that he loved the music, more so than anyone else we had spoken to previously.

"Charlie used to play for folks right out here in front of my house. He was the only blues singer up in this section of the country. It sure was something having Charlie here."

"Did you ever hear of Minnie Franklin?" Gayle asked. "He met her and married her up here in Merigold."

"No. [I] Never did. He was living with a woman named Sudy all the time he was here. They lived near Pimbles Ferry on the other side of the Sunflower River."

"In what year did Patton come to Merigold and how long did he stay?"

Sam leaped from the car hood and pitched his back against the trunk of a tree, rubbing it very hard against the bark, trying to relieve some violent itching. "Let's see now, Charlie got here in 1924 and left in 1930. I'll never forget Charlie Patton; we sure had some good times."

Sam recalled songs like "Pony Blues," "Banty Rooster Blues," "Tom Rushen Blues," and "Mississippi Boweavil Blues." These were all recorded at Patton's first session in 1929. Mention of some of the titles that Patton recorded in his second session failed to strike a responsive chord in Sam.

We really didn't have much

1929 ad for Charlie Patton's first record in the Chicago Defender, *with first name still misspelled* Blues Archive.

time to dig deeper into Patton's life in Merigold, because it was getting late and we were keeping Sam from his evening meal. In the fading daylight we wouldn't even have time to interview Sudy, who was still living in the neighborhood. We reluctantly left Sam Manifield waving at us in the dusk, smiling with a loving and joyful smile, and absolutely thrilled that two strangers, white boys no less, were so damned interested in Charlie Patton.

For me it was like a tonic talking to Sam, who had let himself go. For the most part, our interviews before this one had proceeded painfully, with each word measured cautiously. We were always battling to win confidence of the people we talked to, never succeeding completely.

That evening we drove straight to Clarksdale where we stayed overnight. Early Tuesday morning, we left for Farrell. Farrell lies just a few miles west of Clarksdale, near the levees of the Mississippi River. There's a general store just off the main road. Another road divides the cotton fields and the inevitable Negro houses whose occupants care for them. The houses were recessed about 150 yards off the paved road with a dirt road leading to the main group, as well as to the home of a primitive country fiddler and singer who recorded four obscure sides under his own name and accompanied Patton on many others during Patton's second session. (Pete Whelan had first suggested that Henry Sims might be from Farrell.)

We approached the first house in the row of houses. A large dark woman in her late middle years came to the porch. After our usual opening with a general discussion of old-time blues singers, I asked, "Does Henry Sims live around here?"

"Henry Sims lives down in the last house."

"Does he play fiddle and sing?"

"Huh? Oh, you mean *Son* Sims. He died about three years ago." [GDW: Sims died in 1958 in Memphis.]

"How old was he when he died?"

"He was about 67 years old. You know, Son Sims was in the army in World War I."

"Did you ever hear of Charlie Patton?"

"Sure, I seen Patton and Sims playing together around here. Charlie died some time ago. Son didn't want to play anymore after that. He took it real bad."

The woman stepped down from the porch, and we walked toward a large tree where some other women had gathered to chat and relax, protected from the oppressive sun. When the women learned we were interested in blues singers, the puzzled frowns changed to smiles.

"Son Sims lived on Mr. Boyd's plantation," volunteered one of the women, pointing in the direction of the cotton fields that lay on the other side of the paved road.

"Big Joe Williams and Muddy Waters were from around here, too," volunteered another.

"What did Sims look like?" I asked.

"He was a big, heavy, dark man."

"Do you remember who played with Sims beside Patton?" Gayle asked.

"There was Son House, Willie Brown, Big Joe Williams, and Lewis Ford. Ford was older than the others."

"How much older? I've never heard of him. He never made any records."

"Let's see, Ford's about 80 now and living over in Jonestown."

There wasn't much more to be learned here and we were anxious to follow up one more lead on Bertha Lee and to check out Lewis Ford. We spent the next few hours canvassing for records around Friars Point, which is located just a few miles from there, but has a much larger community.

In the early afternoon, we started for Lula, Mississippi, which is situated on the north end of Moon Lake and about 20 miles north of Friars Point. Lula is just a few miles from the bridge that crosses the Mississippi River at Helena, Arkansas. Evaline Gaynes had told us that Bertha was living in Merigold, which turned out to be pure fiction. In view of this, we approached Lula with some misgivings.

After a few searching inquiries in the "quarters" our prospects brightened: Yes, there was a Bertha Lee Pate who lived in Lula some time ago. Yes, if you want to know about Bertha Lee, ask Fanny Baker.

Fanny Baker was a small, sturdy woman in her late middle years, very good-looking. She was quite amused that I was inquiring about Bertha Lee. "Bertha Lee was a fine-looking woman and could sing better than anyone I've heard. She ran off with Charlie Patton. Why, Bertha Lee visited Lula only two years ago. She's living in Chicago," she said, enjoying the whole business.

"Do you know where in Chicago?"

"No, but I know her sister's address."

"Do me a favor, Fanny, please write Bertha Lee's sister and tell her to write to me in New York. Here, I'll give you my name and address. It's very important. I must see Bertha Lee and speak to her."

Fanny was very agreeable. She took all the information. We left Lula with great hopes of finding Bertha Lee.

The day was drawing to a close. We still had another two hours of daylight to pursue the Lewis Ford lead. Jonestown is only about eight miles south of Lula, but there is no direct route there. In fact, the gravel road we traveled runs in a semicircle and passes lonely towns like Rich, Birdie, and Rosecreast and also traverses some of the most desolate country I had ever seen. Somehow this unpopulated, bleak countryside reminded me of the searing and seething primitive harmonica playing of George "Bullet" Williams on his "Touch Me Light Mama" and "Escaped Convict." There is a certain desperation and bite to his music that seemed to match the starkness of the landscape.

The mean mood set on the backcountry road prevailed in town. It was virtually impossible to obtain any information from anybody. If Lewis Ford was there, we couldn't find him.

This was the end of the line. Gayle had to return to work in Jackson on

Wednesday, and I decided to drive back with him, although there was one more lead to follow. We had come a long way in so short a time. Lula is only about 40 miles from Memphis, and the last stop, had we followed this last lead, would have taken us to Lake Cormorant, only 15 miles from Memphis. We were told that years ago, Son House and Willie Brown had gone up together to Lake "Carmen" (as Johnny Wilder called it) to live. Another part of the story lies there for the taking. [Wardlow treats this in "Can't Tell My Future: The Mystery of Willie Brown" page 181.]

It had been a most interesting trip. Now, drawing from my firsthand experience and with the aid of other evidence, I will attempt to make a sensible whole out of the fragments of information.

Patton was born in 1887 on a farm outside Edwards, Mississippi. Both Minnie Franklin, a wife, and his sister, Viola Cannon, testify to this. Viola, except for her frizzy hair, resembled Patton minutely. When I first saw Patton's likeness it was no surprise. He was the image of Viola. The photo of Patton that appears on the cover [of *The Immortal Charlie Patton 1887–1934, no. 2*, OJL-7] was not an acquisition made in the Delta, although Lord knows we pestered everyone we met for possible snapshots. The picture was obtained four months later from Maxey Tarpley of Georgia, who fortunately had an old record catalog supplement that contained this clean, well-preserved portrait of the great Delta bluesman.

Patton must have been of medium height—between five feet five and five feet eight. Everyone we asked indicated he was fairly short, and Viola in particular indicated he was about as tall as herself, about five feet five. The importance of his height and lean build is summoned only to dispel the inaccurate images created by hearing his overpowering, rough-hewn voice. His voice projects his overwhelming personality and talent, not his physical build.

Patton lived on Dockery's plantation in the heart of the Delta probably

Dockery's plantation, where Charlie Patton lived as he developed his "Delta Blues." Wardlow collection.

before 1900; "as a young boy," Viola remembers. Dockery's still appears to be a prosperous plantation and must have been so years ago, in Patton's time. It has better housing facilities for its Negro workers than others I saw, and must have been a preferred location for a Negro to raise a family.

Patton's country music education began early. His father led a congregation where there was probably sanctified singing, and Patton listened attentively. At an early age Charlie was fascinated by the guitar. He invented his own songs to sing along with the guitar, rather than picking up the material of others—something that characterizes the Mississippi style of blues. Minnie Franklin said that Patton was singing "Pony Blues" when she met him in 1921. This was his first record. As he was then 30-odd years old, it's safe to assume he had been singing blues for at least a decade before.

As to what type of song Patton sang in this time, we can only make some shrewd guesses. One of his songs, "Mississippi Boweavil Blues," is a virtuoso rendition of an elaborated field holler, leading us to suspect Patton adapted this sort of material (which he would have heard all around him as an adolescent) to his own uses at an early age—just after he mastered the guitar. This instrument can be a very powerful weapon. Used sensitively by a talent like Patton's, it opened up new avenues of creation and would have made whatever Patton sang something different from what had been sung before. He was probably molding the songs to blend and complement the guitar. We know that most Negroes sang in church, and many were able to pick a guitar and sing the old ballads like "Frankie and Albert," but it took special talent to become a true bluesman. The creative blues singer needed the poet's outlook—the ability to state the truths of his time and place lyrically.

It may at first seem fantastic that three of the very best bluesmen—Patton, Son House, and Willie Brown—should have been on the same plantation at the same time. However, once we accept Viola's statement that Patton taught them all, it no longer seems so remarkable. Patton's influence on Brown is easy to substantiate. In fact, on some records Brown emulates Patton in great detail. On his "Future Blues" (Para 13090), Willie uses Patton's "Moon Going Down" theme—a theme Patton himself uses on several different records. Brown has a big voice and delivers in the unrelenting manner of the master. Brown was Patton's closest disciple.

Son House, with his dark brooding singing and strange chording, started a following of his own. Robert Johnson and Muddy Waters owe a

Plantation owner Will Dockery; nearly 400 families lived on his plantation in the '20s. Wardlow collection.

great deal to House for some of their own fine work. House's close association with Patton was never obviously apparent on records because of his complete originality, but there was always something about the overall impression that House left—his big, strong voice and impassioned playing—that would place him closer to Patton's approach than to that of any other first-line bluesman. In this regard, the clincher for me is a song House recorded for the Library of Congress and recently released by Folkways through the efforts of Sam Charters. On "My Black Woman" (aka "Walking Blues," LC matrix 6607-B-3[a]), House uses the "Moon Going Down" guitar accompaniment. This wouldn't be so unusual in itself, as other guitarists influenced by Patton used it (including Kid Bailey on "Mississippi Bottom Blues" [Bruns 7114]), but it does strengthen the case that House, the younger of the two men, was influenced by Patton.

[Editor's (Pete Whelan) Note: Regarding melodies, there is the alternate possibility that "Moon Going Down" and others of Patton's themes were not invented by Patton at all, but were plantation folk airs on which all the singers drew independently. Anyone wishing to make this case, however, would bear the burden of proof.]

Patton was very successful with women and had his share wherever he went. He married young. He was only 21 when he took his second wife, Millie Toy. He traveled quite a bit. J.D. Short recalled to Sam Charters that he had worked with Patton near Hollandale, Mississippi (about 15 miles south of Leland), but Dockery's remained his permanent home until he left for good in 1921. He married Minnie Franklin that year, and from then until 1924 there is a gap in his history. He may have spent some time in Vicksburg after following Minnie there. Some lines in his "High Water Everywhere" suggest a familiarity with the town. At any rate, he returned to Merigold in 1924 and stayed for five years, in the company of a woman named Sudy.

Although Sam Manifield, the man who so freely shared his memories, believed that Patton left Merigold in 1930, 1929 seems more likely, as his first records were cut in that year and a few months later he recorded with Sims, a Clarksdale native. It seems likely he would have lived in Clarksdale for a while before recording with Sims. Clarksdale was also a much more likely spot for a recording company scout to hunt talent than the isolated Merigold.

Patton was a very popular figure around Clarksdale. Bukka White recalls on his recent LP (Takoma B1001 [White 1963]) that he couldn't fit into a room where Patton's latest record was being played. White also remarks that it was his ambition to grow up to be a great man like Patton. It's not clear where Patton lived in Clarksdale or how he made a living. Wade Walton, a Clarksdale bluesman who has recorded for Prestige, claims Patton had so many women friends he had to hire someone to fight them off with a stick when he walked through town.

At any rate, Patton wandered afield from Clarksdale in this period, and in Lula met Bertha Lee, a vivacious blues singer. They settled together in

Holly Ridge in 1933 and sang in a juke joint. Patton was drinking heavily at this time, and some of his drinking bouts ended in serious fights.

Toward the end of 1933 Patton and Bertha went to New York to make what were to be his last records. On these last numbers Patton plays in a different style. There is a new sound, the lighter sound of the 1930s. Patton's voice has lost some of its cutting edge—perhaps due to his drinking. But even though not at his best, Patton was still a breathtaking performer. Of the 14 sides Bertha Lee made at this time, only four were issued. The masters for the rest appear to be lost. Bertha's singing on the two sides I have heard is soulful, introspective, slow-paced, and somehow majestic.

Shortly after Charlie and Bertha returned to Holly Ridge, Patton died, under somewhat mysterious circumstances, at the age of 47. [For a detailed treatment, see "Patton's Murder—Whitewash? Or Hogwash?," page 94.] One of the originators of the Mississippi blues style, this great singer was buried without a marker on his grave, without a sign to attest to his greatness. But no matter, we have the music. Thank God we have the music.

[GDW: The information from Johnny Wilder concerning Son House's living on Dockery's Plantation is incorrect. House did visit Dockery's with Willie Brown, but the two bluesmen primarily lived at Lake Cormorant in the Tunica County area. Son House did not learn his guitar style from Patton. He was influenced by Willie Wilson, whom he saw playing bottleneck near Clarksdale.

Another daughter, Rosetta Patton Brown, has been found in the Delta, near Clarksdale. She is in her eighties and has many of her father's features.]

Country Blues and Gospel Pioneers

In 1963, Bernie Klatzko and Pete Whelan sent a list of bluesmen they believed were from Mississippi, and with it I began asking questions and playing copies of records in different locations throughout the state. This led to the tracking of the foremost biographical blank of the time, Nehemiah "Skip" James. I spent more than a year searching for him, but it seemed he had left no memorable trace from Jackson to Memphis. When I asked Johnny Temple in Jackson in 1964, he said, "You mean Skippy? He's from Bentonia. He used to come here and play with me." I let slip this information to Ishmon Bracey, who in turn sold it to John Fahey, Bill Barth, and Henry Vestine; these three then rediscovered James in Tunica County Hospital (see Newsweek, *July 13, 1964) before I could follow Temple's tip.*

After another year of knocking on doors and talking to people, I authored the first biographical notes on several Mississippi bluesmen, including Tommy Johnson, Sam Collins, Kid Bailey, Charlie McCoy, and Rosie Mae Moore. Additional information was supplied by Whelan and seven other researchers. —GDW

[Notes to Origin Jazz Library 2, 5, and 8 originally published as *OJL Supplement no. 1* (1965), and those to OJL 12 and 13 in the booklet to the two-LP set *In The Spirit* (1966). Author's 1997 corrections added in brackets.]

A KERS, Garfield—Born around the turn of the century in Hernando, Mississippi. Appears to have traveled little. The guitar player who accompanied him on his records, Joe Callicott, is reported still alive in the Hernando area, but Akers himself is presumed to have died about 1962. He is said to be survived by a son who plays guitar in a later style.

[See "Garfield Akers and Joe Callicott," page 118, for more information. There has been no verification about a son (that erroneous detail was provided to Whelan by Memphis researchers). GDW]

BAILEY, Kid—Probably born in the Delta, where he lived and may be still living [as of 1965]. Bailey played a number of times in Jackson and in nearby Rankin County across the Pearl River with Tommy Johnson. He was also remembered by Ishmon Bracey, Walter Vinscon of the Mississippi Sheiks, and other Delta residents in Indianola, Leland, and Morehead. A rumor has it that Bailey was killed in St. Louis while playing in a club. No information has been found to support this.

[Additional details were included by Stephen Calt and me in our book

King of the Delta Blues Singers: The Life and Music of Charlie Patton. Bailey definitely played and lived near Leland in the late 1920s. I have been unable to confirm a place or year of death. Ishmon Bracey saw him play in Rankin County (see "Got Four, Five Puppies, One Shaggy Little Hound," page 45). GDW]

BECK, Elder Charles—Played on Elder Curry's 1930 Jackson recordings. Considered by Elder Curry to be the best sanctified piano player in Mississippi. Was a member of Curry's church and then left for Memphis and later Chicago. As of 1966 he was serving as a missionary in Africa. He also recorded after World War II.

"BIG BILL"—See BROONZY.

BROONZY, Bill—One of the best-known blues players. Born in Scott, Mississippi, June 26, 1893. Moved to rural Arkansas as a child, where he played homemade violin. Worked his own farm as a young man. After service in World War I, moved to Chicago, where he learned guitar and, in the late 1920s, began his long recording career. Died 1959. [See Broonzy's autobiography, *Big Bill Blues,* 1955. GDW]

BROWN, Willie—Born 1899, probably Shelby, Mississippi. Sang and recorded with Charlie Patton. Both Brown and Patton worked on Will Dockery's plantation at Dockery, Mississippi, some 12 miles east of Cleveland. Later, Brown, who definitely learned a style similar to Patton's, traveled and worked with—and became the closest friend of—Son House, when the two worked at Lake Cormorant. Brown, who had only four commercially released sides, died in Memphis in the early 1950s. One of his most distinguishing characteristics was his use of bass strings slides, later developed by many in the Delta. This sound is prevalent on "M & O Blues," which was recorded at the same 1930 session attended by Charlie Patton, Son House, and the Delta Big Four, along with Louise Johnson, an 18-year-old female singer from the Mississippi Delta.

[See "Can't Tell My Future: The Mystery of Willie Brown," page 181. Brown died December 30, 1952, in Tunica County and was buried in Prichard. His death certificate confirms his birth date as August 6, 1900. Louise Johnson was in her early twenties when she recorded. She lived on the King Anderson plantation near Clarksdale and later moved to Memphis. The Delta Big Four recorded in late April 1930, at least one month earlier than the Patton-House-Brown session. GDW]

BRYANT, Elder Richard—A member of the Church of God in Christ in Mississippi. Recorded with both Bessie Johnson of Columbia, Mississippi, and Melinda Taylor of Forest, Mississippi. Bryant, who led various churches in the Delta, is reported to have had churches in both Hollandale and Moorehead, Mississippi, in the late 1920s.

COLEMAN, Jaybird—Born Gainsville, Alabama, 1896, and died Birmingham, 1950. A proficient harmonica player who both played and sang on records. Coleman played primarily in Birmingham and its environs, and once recorded behind J.D. Norwood (of Norwood and Duckett), a Jackson bluesman. This side was not released. Information indicates Coleman was a charter member of the Birmingham Jug Band (see OJL-4, *The Great Jug Bands*) and is well remembered around Birmingham and Bessemer for his music and comic showmanship.

[There is no information to support the theory that Coleman was actually a member of the Birmingham Jug Band. Some experts believe that Frank Palmer on Paramount is actually Coleman using a pseudonym, as his recordings apparently show many similarities to Coleman's Gennett religious sides. GDW]

Salty Dog Sam (Collins) was from Louisiana, but he was the first country bluesman to record "Yellow Dog Blues." The Yazoo and Mississippi Valley Railroad was given that name by Delta residents. Wardlow collection.

COLLINS, Sam—Although Collins was raised in McComb, Mississippi, no hard information on him turned up there. He is reported to have left home to record, returned briefly a couple of years later, and then went north. A report that he died of carbon monoxide poisoning in Chicago, in the 1950s, cannot be confirmed. So far as could be determined, as of 1965 he had no living relatives in the McComb area. His style of guitar playing—using a knife instead of the bottleneck—is typical of south Mississippi playing that has a slight Texas influence.

[Known to many informants only as Salty Dog Sam. Played with Joe Holmes in the McComb area. Remembered by Ishmon Bracey (see "Got Four, Five Puppies, One Shaggy Little Hound," page

"Yellow Dog" passenger train crew, waiting for instructions at Clarksdale in 1909. Wardlow collection.

45). Chris Smith (1990) has determined from census data that Collins was actually born in Louisiana in August 1887. Sam made the first blues recording of "Midnight Special" (1927); in another record, "Hesitation Blues" (1927), he sings of the Louisville and Nashville (the "L. and N.") Railroad that ran from New Orleans through Kentucky to Cincinnati. GDW]

CURRY, Elder—A preacher and elder in the Church of God in Christ since 1915, Curry had active churches in both Morton and Jackson, Mississippi, in 1966. His recordings were made in December 1930 at the King Edward Hotel in Jackson. Jo Ann Williams was the lead singer of a group of seven, Curry was the guitar player, and Elder Charles Beck was the piano player.

DUCKETT, Slim, and NORWOOD, "One Leg Sam"—Both Slim Duckett and "One Leg Sam" Norwood were Jackson, Mississippi, area bluesmen who recorded four gospel songs for OKeh records in Jackson in the King Edward Hotel in December 1930. Norwood, who was known as "One Leg Sam," played extensively with Tommy Johnson. Duckett, who was a stepfather to Johnny Temple, a Chicago bluesman of the 1930s, played in Jackson with Rube Lacy and others. [A photo of Norwood was published in Wardlow 1982, 8. At the 1930s session, it was the producer H.C. Speir who requested the gospel material.]

FOREHAND, Blind Mamie—Played in Memphis on streets with husband who sang blues before becoming a minister. May have come from south Mississippi originally. Probably died in Memphis in late 1930s or early '40s. [Husband and wife gospel teams often played on the same streets that bluesmen did.]

HARRIS, William—Born in the Mississippi Delta, Harris joined a medicine show organized in a south Mississippi river town and toured the Delta in the late 1920s. Harris was possibly the first bluesman to record the dynamic, driving guitar sound of the deep Delta rhythm. Harris was recorded at two sessions, but nothing further is known about him, although a musician with the same name (a common one) is reported alive in a midwestern city.

[Remembered by Delta bluesman Hayes McMullan from suppers near Glendora and Swan Lake in Tallahatchie County. Also remembered by others in Birmingham, Alabama, and Grenada, Mississippi. Wardlow's full profile was published in *78 Quarterly* (1988). GDW]

HOUSE, Eddie James "Son," Jr.—Born Mar. 21, 1902, at Lyon, Mississippi, near Clarksdale. Did not begin to play the guitar until age 26, when he was taught by an older colored musician. House met Charlie Patton in Lula, Mississippi, in 1929, where he played with him, and in 1930 went to Wisconsin along with Patton, Willie Brown, and Louise Johnson, for one of the more notable recording sessions in the brief history of race records. After returning home, House continued to work as a field hand and tractor dri-

The late Nick Perls, founder and producer of Yazoo blues reissues, photographed Son House in a 1965 visit. House was demonstrating how Charlie Patton would play on one knee for "jukers." Photo by Nick Perls.

ver. Around 1930, he moved to Lake Cormorant, where he worked on the plantation of a Mr. Cox until 1940, when he moved to New York State. He was back home in the Delta on a visit in 1942, when Alan Lomax recorded him for the Library of Congress. In 1964, House was discovered living in Rochester, New York. In 1965, he remained an extraordinary bluesman and had made many successful public appearances.

[Klatzko (1964a, 9) reported that House left Mississippi around 1940 and was visiting the Delta when he recorded for Alan Lomax and the Library of Congress in 1941 and 1942; House later (1965, 44) said he left in 1943. Died on October 19, 1988. GDW]

HULL, "Papa Harvey"—Thought to be from Mobile, Alabama. Used the recording pseudonym Long Cleve Reed. No further information available at this time.

[Hull sang of Jackson and McComb on "Don't You Leave Me Here" and "Two Little Tommie Blues," indicating a style of playing from south Mississippi and Alabama. GDW]

HURT, "Mississippi" John—Born in Teoc, Mississippi, 1892, moved to Avalon at age two. Learned to play guitar by imitating local songsters and from own relatives. Played for dances and parties in Avalon and nearby Delta towns for many years before he recorded in 1928. Hurt represents a style older than the blues, and never associated with the bluesmen of his time. After his rediscovery in 1963 by Tom Hoskins, he had an extremely successful second career, becoming one of the best known and most popular folk artists in the country. [Mississippi John Hurt died on November 2, 1966. GDW]

JAMES, Nehemiah "Skip," "Skippy"—Born Bentonia, Mississippi, June 9, 1902, the only surviving child of Rev. and Mrs. Eddie James on the White-head Plantation, a mile and a half from town. James played piano and organ in the local Baptist church and fished and roamed the bottoms of the Big Black River, a short distance from his house, where Cypress Grove is also located. James learned to play the guitar by imitating Rich Griffith and Henry Stuckey, who played "music like John Hurt." (One of them just strummed, the other finger-picked.) From them James learned songs like "Drunken Spree." Finishing high school, he went to work in a sawmill in Arkansas, where he improved his keyboard technique by listening to Will Crabtree. He went to Memphis, where he observed Clarence Williams, then to Vicksburg, where he met Little Brother Montgomery, from whom he got the inspiration for "Special Rider Blues." James seems to have developed his three-finger picking style on his own. He played the blues in the apparently widespread "cross-note" or open E-minor tuning.

In 1931, he auditioned for Paramount in Jackson, Mississippi—James says he played just two verses of "Devil Got My Woman" before he was accepted. In spring 1931, he went to Grafton, Wisconsin, for three days, to record. He remembers recording 26 sides, most of which he had composed before the session, although "22-20" was composed on the spot, when he was asked to cover the "44 Blues." Returning to the South, he played briefly in Memphis, and then in Jackson with Johnny Temple. In 1931 he went to Texas with his father, a missionary Baptist, and formed a gospel quartet in Dallas. The group toured Oklahoma, Kansas, Texas, and Arkansas for about a year before disbanding. In the 1930s, he accompanied his father to Alabama, where he attended a Birmingham seminary and became an ordained Baptist minister. The following year, he switched to his mother's faith and became a Methodist minister. He remained in Birmingham until about 1950, working in an iron strip mine. Around 1951 he went back to Mississippi and became a sharecropper. Shortly thereafter, he moved to Tunica, Mississippi, where he worked as a field hand, until his rediscovery in June, 1964, by John Fahey and Bill Barth. [For more about Skip James, see "Got Four, Five Puppies, One Shaggy Little Hound, " page 45.]

"Cypress Grove" was the B-side of "Devil Got My Woman." James was from Bentonia, a small town on Highway 49, north of Jackson. Wardlow Collection.

JOHNSON, Bessie—A member and lay preacher for the Church of God in Christ in Columbia, Mississippi. As of 1966, reported to be in a northern city still active in church work. Considered one of the greatest of all female sanctified singers.

JOHNSON, "Blind Willie"—Born about 1900 near Temple, Texas, he was blinded at the age of seven.

Johnson was known to have sung secular songs but only recorded religious music, and on this basis stands as the greatest itinerant singer of sacred music to come out of East Texas and the South. He died in Beaumont, Texas, in 1949.

JOHNSON, Buster—Probably born in Mississippi. Whereabouts unknown in 1965. Although Johnson recorded with the James Cole String Band on one occasion, he is not remembered in the central Mississippi area where the band reportedly played in the early 1930s, making it reasonable to assume that he did not form a regular part of the unit.

[Ishmon Bracey identified the James Cole String Band as being from the Arkansas Delta after hearing the "Undertaker Blues." No information to support Bracey's identification has been found. The group may have been from Kentucky or Virginia, since their recordings were done at Richmond, Indiana, and show a pronounced white string band association. GDW]

1928 Chicago Defender *advertisement for Rube Lacy's only released recording before 1942.* Blues Archive.

JOHNSON, Tommy—Born Crystal Springs, Mississippi, died there in 1956. Johnson moved to Jackson in 1926, and can be said to be one of the charter members of the central Mississippi style. For two years, he played for house parties and at juke joints, and, then, in February of 1928, recorded in Memphis with Charlie McCoy backing him on four of his six sides. In the summer of that year, Johnson recorded four more sides, again with the aid of McCoy (McCoy is said to have learned his style from his two close friends, Johnson and Bracey). In the spring of 1930, Johnson, Bracey, and the New Orleans Nehi Boys traveled to Wisconsin for further recordings. Johnson had been scheduled to make many sides but, due to intoxication, could cut only six. On some of these, he is apparently backed by Bracey, and on others, by the Nehi Boys.

Although these records were placed on sale, few have survived. Johnson continued to play in the Jackson area after this, while also traveling to distant Delta towns. His death is reported to have come from acute alcoholism.

[See "Ledell Johnson Remembers His Brother, Tommy," page 106, and "Mysteries in Mississippi," page 110, which compares the songs of Johnson and Charlie Patton. As of 1998, all six Paramount sides have been found and released.]

JORDAN, Charlie—Age and place of birth unknown. Believed to have played around the Delta and in Memphis, and to have been in St. Louis around 1925; from there he may or may not have gone permanently to Chicago. According to reports, he ran a rehearsal club with Big Joe Williams in Chicago. He lived in St. Louis during the 1930s. As a talent scout for Decca, he talked Peetie Wheatstraw into switching from Vocalion. Reportedly, Jordan limped as a result of being shot at during the 1920s for running moonshine. He was shot to death in St. Louis in 1951.

[A death certificate obtained by Stephen Calt gives November 15, 1954, as Jordan's date of death and pneumonia as the cause. This contradicts the oral testimony that Jordan was shot to death in 1951, demonstrating that public documents are always more reliable than oral traditions. GDW]

KARNES, Alfred—White country singer associated with area around Covington, Kentucky. Recorded in Bristol at the same session at which the great country singer Jimmy Rodgers recorded his first songs. Victor advertised for artists in that area to try out, which means Karnes probably just came into Bristol to record.

LACY, Rube—Born Rankin County, Mississippi, about 1895. Lacy sang both in Rankin, which lies across the river from Jackson, and in Hinds County. His style is typical central Mississippi, with a suggestion of something older. Some reports said as of 1965 he was still alive in a far western state.

[Lacy was found in California around 1967 by researcher David Evans. Died November 14, 1969 (Harris 1979). See the article "Got Four, Five Puppies, One Shaggy Little Hound," page 45 for Ishmon Bracey's comments about Lacy. GDW]

Rube Lacey was one of the premier guitarists in the Jackson area before moving to the Delta. He recorded for Paramount in 1928, and later became a minister. Photo Marina Bokelman.

MASON, Moses—No information, save the possibility that he was the same person as a minister in Mobile, Alabama, whose description he fits.

[Mason was actually from Lake Providence, where H.C. Speir remembered finding him as a black preacher for the Paramount recordings. Died late 1950s in Lake Providence. GDW]

MOORE, William—Lived, owned a barbershop, and died at age 61 in Tappahannac, Virginia. Survived by several sons, at least one of whom still played blues as of 1965.

[Moore, along with Blind Arthur Blake, was a leading ragtime guitarist of the 1920s. GDW]

NORWOOD—[See DUCKETT and NORWOOD.]

REED, LONG CLEVE —Recording pseudonym for HULL, "Papa Harvey."

RICE, Rev. D.C.—[See "Reverend D.C. Rice—Gospel Singer," page 152.]

SIMS, Henry "Son"—Appears to have lived his entire life in and around Farrell, Mississippi, where he died about 1960. He was a friend of Charlie Patton, who was instrumental in getting Sims recorded in 1929. Sims apparently stayed on the same plantation his whole life, playing only for pleasure and for the enjoyment of his neighbors. His rough fiddle playing is typical of a Delta string band musician and contrasts with the more sophisticated playing of Mississippi black and white fiddlers.

[See my 1996 *78 Quarterly* article for details about Sims' life. Died December 23, 1958, and was buried at the Bell Grove Baptist Church outside of Clarksdale, Mississippi. GDW]

This song was given "A" billing by Paramount, but the B-side, "Ham Hound Crave," was the side that sold the record to Delta residents. Wardlow collection.

TAYLOR, Melinda—A member of the Church of God in Christ in Forest, Mississippi. In 1929, recorded for Victor both with Elders McIntorsh and Edwards, and with Bessie Johnson as the Memphis Sanctified Singers in Memphis. Reported to have died in Forest in the 1940s.

THOMAS, Henry "Ragtime Texas"—The subject of much speculation. Apparently an older man at the time of his recording. No concrete information concerning him has come our way.

[See Mack McCormick's 1974 booklet accompanying the LP *Henry Thomas*, Herwin 209. GDW]

WHITE, Booker Washington "Bukka"—Bukka was born in Houston, Mississippi, in 1909. Between the ages of 10 and 15, he moved to the Delta, where he lived with his uncle. He learned to play on his uncle's piano and, in his teens, learned to play the guitar from an old field hand at West Point. In 1930, at age 20, he recorded 14 sides for Victor in Memphis. In 1934, he began living in West Point, where he played for a local barrel-house, sometimes accompanied by his relative, harmonica player George "Bullet" Williams. In 1937 White recorded two sides for Vocalion in Chicago, shortly after which he shot a

man in Mississippi and was sent to Parchman Penitentiary; he was released three years later. While "on the farm," he recorded two sides for the Library of Congress. Following his release, he returned to Chicago and recorded several sides for OKeh, composing the songs on the spot. During World War II he traveled to Baltimore, Cleveland, St. Louis, and Detroit, returning to settle in Memphis in 1943, where he worked in a tank factory until rediscovered by John Fahey in 1963. In 1966 White was living in Memphis, Tennessee.

[White died February 26, 1977. For details on his 1937 conviction, see "Bukka White: From Aberdeen to Parchman," page 101. GDW]

WILKINS, Robert Timothy— Born January 16, 1896, in Hernando, Mississippi. Learned guitar from his stepfather and other country guitarists. Played in Memphis with Frank Stokes, Gus Cannon, Jim Jackson, and Memphis Minnie. Rediscovered by Dick and Louise Spottswood in early 1964.

Fiddler Henry "Son" Sims recorded with Patton at his second Paramount recordings. Sims and Patton knew each other some 20 years before. Wardlow collection.

[Wilkins died May 26, 1987, in Memphis. He recorded for Victor (1928), Brunswick (1929–30), and Vocalion (1935, in Jackson). Soon thereafter, he abruptly left the blues to become a member of a sanctified denomination. GDW]

WILLIAMS, George "Bullet"—Born somewhere in Alabama, perhaps Selma, about 1910. Played on the streets of both Jackson and Meridian. In the 1930s he sometimes accompanied Bukka White. According to Bukka, they would play together until George passed out. Once he was revived, they would continue. Reportedly drank rubbing alcohol and shoe polish, and is presumed to have gone to an early grave, or insane, or both. There are reports he died in Alabama in the early 1940s. There is no information as to the identity of the singer on Williams' Paramount record "Touch Me Light Mama."

[No additional information has been discovered as to Williams' age at death or where he died. See Bracey's comments in "Got Four, Five Puppies, One Little Shaggy Hound," page 45, as well as Cal Stephens' "Booker White on Bullet Williams" in *78 Quarterly* no. 6 (1991): 83–85. GDW]

Got Four, Five Puppies, One Little Shaggy Hound

Although I rediscovered Rev. Bracey in 1963 in Jackson, and published some basic biographical information received from him in the Origin Jazz Library notes, I did not write a comprehensive story about him until this article.

In 1982 Stephen Calt and I decided to omit the chapter on Bracey in what was intended to be a sourcebook of all Mississippi bluesmen who had recorded before World War II (which, upon submission to the University Press of Mississippi in 1977, had received two readers' rejections). I then sent that chapter to Blues Unlimited *for publication.*

Bracey's memories give us a remarkable window on blues history; he met and played with more bluesmen during his career than any other musician I have interviewed. —GDW

[Originally published in *Blues Unlimited* no. 142 (1982): 4–11.]

Ishmon Bracey (1900–1970), considered to be one of the premier Mississippi bluesmen, was a rare combination of braggart, entertainer, musician, showman, and, eventually, an ordained minister, who held deeply ingrained religious views from his childhood.

Bracey grew up at Byram, a small town some ten miles south of Jackson, Mississippi. Bracey's first name is Ishmon, *not* Ishman, his wife Annie said. She said he was named after an Old Testament character.

Before his 1951 return to the Baptist church in which he was raised, he recorded twice for Victor in Memphis and once for Paramount in Wisconsin, and made one unreleased session in Jackson in the early 1930s for an unidentified freelancing director.

Once a friend and closest musical colleague of Tommy Johnson, Bracey parted ways with him in a dispute over both money and Johnson's self-destructive drinking. Bracey prided himself on his reconversion to the church—away from the wicked life of blues—and often said, "Thank the Lord I have changed."

Bracey's records were moderate sellers, but he did record twice in Memphis for Victor and once for Paramount in Wisconsin. Wardlow Collection.

Rediscovered in 1963 by this author, Bracey steadfastly refused to even play blues, except for one brief interlude when his wife was not able to listen. A short tape of his singing of religious songs was forwarded to a small Virginia company in the 1960s, but no positive response resulted. Bracey died in Jackson on February 12, 1970.

In Bracey's own words, here is his story as collected over six years, including almost two hours of tape-recorded interviews in which he listened to reissues of his recordings and those of other Mississippi artists. My interpolated comments clarify and augment his recollections.

◄o►◄o►◄o► Early Musical Background ◄o►◄o►◄o►

"First guitar I play, I was nine. A fella by the name of Mr. Harps at Byram bought me one . . . I worked for him and I had this little old piece of guitar,

Ishmon Bracey was a premier Jackson bluesman in the late '20s and '30s. Bracey played the "Devil's music" for many years before becoming an ordained minister in the '50s. Wardlow Collection.

didn't have no back on it, and he asked me did I want him to buy me a guitar. And he bought me a little old Stella and I started to playing around on it. I stayed up all night till I learned it. Lee Jones [Bracey's brother-in-law] showed me how to chord. Lee Jones started me out, sure enough. Louis Cooper [from Baton Rouge], he learned me more than any of them. 'Cause my cousin now, Willie Hursh taught me the first piece I ever learned . . . 'Railroad Blues.'"

◄o►◄o►◄o► Records ◄o►◄o►◄o►

"Mr. Speir got me on records [in 1928]. Me, Tommy, and Rosie [Mae Moore]. I got Tommy and we went to Memphis and we stayed three days, practicing and makin' records. On the way the bus [Greyhound] wrecked near Memphis and we ran off the road and we went into the ditch. I didn't get hurt and Tommy's okay but Rosie got skint up. I got a lawyer and got me some money and some for them. But they never thanked me. Tommy didn't appreciate what I did.

The Marsh studio in Chicago was used by Paramount in the 1920s to record its talent, but the quality of their recordings was extremely poor. Courtesy Steve Calt.

"One guy got on the bus just outside of Memphis—about two stops—and he went up the same time we did to record."

Bracey identified this man as Charlie Kyle, from Kyle's recordings and the Dixon and Godrich listing. Bracey said the town was below Hernando and was either Batesville or Senatobia. However, Bracey is confusing his two Memphis sessions—the first on February 4, 1928, had Charlie McCoy on second guitar, while at the second, on August 31 and September 1, 1928, Kyle recorded six songs.

"He had his guitar on his back. We stayed in the same hotel on Beale Street. We practiced at night before we recorded the next day at the big hall there in Memphis.

"Victory [Victor] people told me I sold 6,000 copies of 'Saturday Blues,' and I was the first colored entertainer out of Mississippi they recorded. It was in *Billboard*."

Billboard was not published in the 1920s. The trade journal for the recording industry was *Talking Machine World*. This article has not been found. Bracey may have a Speir conversation confused with the article, although he was emphatic his name was mentioned in the magazine. He also said Victor said it was "going to start putting out records solely for the colored people" (the 38500 series). Actually, Tommy Johnson recorded before Bracey at the February 1928 session and his sides were released before Bracey's.

"They said they wanted me to come back to make more records and we went back a second time that summer.

"Mr. Speir got me to go to Wisconsin [in 1930]. He got me on the Paramount Records, me and Tommy. He sent for me and told me to get ready to go up there with Tommy and to get up some new songs I hadn't made before; I sent for Tommy. He was in Crystal Springs on down there where he stayed. Tommy kept getting mixed up 'bout where we was going. He thought it was Nebraska. Tommy got sick [drinking] and couldn't record and me and 44 Charlie [Taylor] and Kid Ernest [New Orleans Nehi Boys] made a lot of records. I made six, five or six songs with my guitar. 'Woman Woman,' I had that in G minor. Mr. Layman [Art Laibley] told me that was a good idea. People don't want the same tune; see that'll make it sold more quicker and faster."

The Paramount recording director until mid-1931 was Art C. Laibley, originally a native of Louisiana, who was a salesman first and a recording director by default. Mayo Williams functioned as Paramount's first recording director in Chicago, with Laibley later joining him. When Williams left Paramount, Laibley was responsible for all recordings, including the establishment of the L series at Grafton. H.C. Speir, who went to Grafton to help Laibley set up the studio and make several acoustical suggestions, said Paramount didn't have enough treble in its recordings and conversely Victor had too much. Speir said he believed the L series stood for *Lab* and not Laibley.

"First song I played up there was 'Doodleville Blues.' 'Ain't no more whisky, Mr. Byrd done found my still. And listen here now buddy, I hid it down in Doodleville.' Everywhere I played it, white and colored would fall for that."

No copy of this Paramount recording by Bracey has ever been found. Bracey is correct in his statement that he made 18 sides for Paramount. Johnson made six, and 44 Charlie Taylor, five. Subtracting L225 from L254, the last master by Taylor, the difference is 29. Another song by the same title was recorded by David Evans on a field trip in Mississippi. Its verse structure features lyrics different from Bracey's. Evans also gives historical information in his *Big Road Blues* (1982) on the naming of Doodleville. The "Byrd" in the song was a Jackson policeman known for his bad treatment of blacks.

"I made the 'Trouble in Mind Blues.' That was a guitar solo. By myself, I made six. Rest with the Nehi Boys. Then I made the 'Farish Street Stomp' [and 'Mobile Stomp' on Pm 12980, credited to the New Orleans Nehi Boys]. That was a solo."

Bracey seems to mean that a "solo" is an instrumental, not necessarily a guitar solo, unless his memory is faulty.

"Didn't no womens at all stayin' at that boarding house in Milwaukee. We took the electric train to get there. We stayed there about two weeks. Took us 'bout ten days to record. Mr. Layman [Laibley] met us at the station and took us to his office. He showed us our contracts and how much we would make. I never got no royalties like he said.

"It's a mystery thing. I heard a lot of my records up in the Delta, like this little, old comedy song me and 44 Charlie put out. ['Where My Shoes At?' Pm 12949.] Now, I heard it up in the Delta. I haven't heard it down here."

No copies of either Bracey's or Tommy Johnson's Paramounts have ever been found in the Jackson area or even in Mississippi, to the best of my knowledge [as of 1982]. Of Johnson's two extant Paramounts, one was found in Indiana in a collection purchased by a New York collector and another was found in Milledgeville, Georgia.

According to Earl Montgomery, a former Memphis salesman for St. Louis Music Co. (which was the Mississippi distributor for Paramount), the company folded in mid-1930 as a wholesaler. H.C. Speir also reported he had a difficult time getting Paramounts after St. Louis Music folded. He said he had to write directly to Grafton and often they had already shipped their initial pressings to other areas. He had an especially hard time getting Skip James' recordings. From my personal experience as a collector and based upon Max Vreede's book (*Paramount 12000–13000 Series,* 1971), the 12950 to 13000 Paramounts are the rarest. Finally, according to Alfred Schultz of Grafton, the pressing foreman for Paramount, the company was pressing only three days a week when it folded in 1932. Schultz said a typical first pressing was 1,200 copies before the Depression, exactly the number of records a pressing stamper could produce before wearing out. Speir said it cost a company around 27 cents to make a record that would sell for 45 cents wholesale and 75 cents retail.

◄◦►◄◦►◄◦► Post-Paramount Days ◄◦►◄◦►◄◦►

"I found this man at the King Edward [Hotel]. I heard he was in town makin' records. I made three . . . made five dollars a side. I made 'Oh, Lordie Mama,' 'Come On In Ain't Nobody Home But Me,' one other I forgot."

Bracey dated the session as about 1932, when Herbert Hoover was President. However, "Oh, Lordie Mama" is a Buddy Moss song, not recorded until 1934, unless Bracey had a different song with the same title.

"Poor Boy Henderson [a blues singer from nearby Utica who had played with Tommy Johnson on several occasions in that area], he messed his whole deal up. [The recording director] was a German and when he asked [Tommy] what the title [of Henderson's record] was, he told him 'Germans in Hell' and [the director] ran him outta there.

"He's from New York. Called him Kessinger, Kissinger, something like that, Mr. Speir said he thought he knowed who he was. He said he heard he was in town."

The author once asked Speir why he did not record either Bracey or Johnson at the 1935 Jackson ARC session. He responded that "Both Tommy and Ishmon had already recorded their best songs and we were looking for new talent." However, Speir and Art Satherly, the ARC recording director, scouted Memphis, where they found Robert (Tim) Wilkins (who had previously recorded in 1929 and 1930) and Minnie Wallace (who had recorded previously with the Memphis Jug Band).

"Two white guys also recorded from Rankin County. They could play their guitar . . . I mean they could play them things. One of them went into a sink and he thought it was a bathroom and he shit there. He didn't know no better.

"Luceen [Slim] Duckett, he was there too. I don't know if they put his records out but he was in there."

Duckett and One Leg Sam recorded for OKeh's 1930 sessions at the King Edward in Jackson, and four of their sides were released. Duckett was Johnny Temple's stepfather and lived on Ann Banks Street in Jackson, where Temple later lived.

"After I made them records for the Victory company, a man came to see me from Birmingham. He wanted to carry me there to make records but he didn't offer much money. My contract wasn't up with the Victory until a year, so I didn't go."

A typical recording contract was one year's duration. Bracey said he signed one twice with Victor for 1928 and 1929. Notice that Speir did not attempt to place either Bracey or Johnson with Paramount until after August 1929, when their contracts would have expired.

TOMMY JOHNSON—"First time I met him, he came from Jackson down there [Crystal Springs] to a supper. I was playin' at the supper and he came in there with a bunch of 'em from Jackson and he was over me [better] then. Oh yes, people he was playing for ordered [asked] him to come back that next Saturday night and he couldn't get back. And then he started to comin' by Byram and then I started to playin' with him and then me and him got to playin'! After I left and went to Jackson, he's up there playing in Jackson and we kept playin' together.

"I got so I would run Tommy along [be better]. When he first came here [Jackson] he was the best, but Charlie McCoy and myself, [later] both would run Tommy along. See, he could play good until he died. But he wouldn't play 'til he got fulla that stuff and he wasn't able to play then. That was his weakness. Drink 'til he got drunk and couldn't play. One Fourth of July, he played a picnic. Got so drunk they had to carry him home before the picnic was over.

"Men, white, colored . . . we get on with them [get a music job]. White folks would give hayrides, dances. Then they'd get through. They'd have a dance at some kinda place, like a barn or something and we played. Me and Tommy would play just two guitars. We'd be *make some money*.

"I'd tell 'em just like you was the manager of us playin'. I'd tell you, 'Don't carry him nothing 'til us get through.' And he [the manager] would just give him a little and he beg, and you make out like you couldn't get it an' all that, 'cause he wouldn't play nothin' if he got high.

"Tommy kept getting mixed up about Wisconsin. I'd tell him, I'd say, 'Tommy that's Wisconsin, Grafton, Wisconsin. That's where we going.' Then he'd call it Nebraski [*sic*] again.

"Tommy got sick off Old Charter. Mr. Layman [Laibley] had this gallon barrel and Tommy, he went wild. He hadn't seen real whiskey. He was used to drinkin' that old canned heat. Had this paper cups you'd drink out of so you couldn't get the consumption [tuberculosis]. Mr. Layman got so mad at Tommy he nearly run him off. Tommy got so bad I had to play behind him on one or two songs ['Lonesome Home Blues,' Pm 13000, and more likely 'Alcohol and Jake Blues,' Pm 12950]."

Bracey said he was not certain if Paramount issued the sides he played on. He said Johnson was having difficulty getting through a take successfully without ruining it or hitting bad notes. Therefore, he took over the playing so Johnson could concentrate on his singing. No Johnson Pm reissues were available during the time Bracey was interviewed for his comments.

"[Tommy] kept ruining every record he tried to make and Mr. Layman started screaming at him and told him he was gonna send him home if he ruined any more."

Art Laibley denied in phone conversations that he ever supplied his artists with any type of liquor before or during a session. Speir said he didn't remember any liquor at Grafton but said that "talent recorded better" with "a tonic" or a drink to relax them. Bracey was emphatic on several occasions that both he and Johnson had access to bonded whiskey at their Grafton session and Johnson had a drinking problem during the session.

"Tommy was supposed to make more songs than I was. But he stayed high most of the time. Mr. Layman told me to record what I could. They put us up in this big boarding house in Milwaukee. Didn't allow no womens there. We took the electric train out to Grafton. We stayed there [Wisconsin] about ten days, then Mr. Layman asked us if we wanted to see the plant in New York. He paid us to go, but Tommy went back home. Me and 44 Charlie and Kid Ernest went."

What purpose Laibley saw in sending these artists to New York is unknown. Perhaps Laibley, who had been getting exclusive artists from Speir in Mississippi, wanted to show his generosity. Bracey said he wanted to impress them with the Paramount operation. To the author's knowledge, the New York operation would have been small compared to the facilities at Port Washington.

Bracey said he and Tommy had a "fallin' out" in the mid-1930s and didn't see each other or speak for about a year, over "Tommy's drinkin' and money." He said Johnson wanted more than 50/50 since he was more well-known than Bracey. He told Johnson that drinking was hurting the money they were making. They fought verbally about it and then split from each other.

"I was working one day down there on South Street spraying houses [in 1956]. He [Tommy] told me to pray for him, and he want to stop [drinking] but look like he couldn't. I told him he had to make up his mind and pray too. 'Thank the Lord' I told him, and he swear that he would. And he wants to be a preachin' like I was, he say. And so he left me an' it got on me so strong, I had to cry when he left. He's cryin' and I's cryin'. My wife was cryin'. And it just hurt me so bad to see him that way . . . And the next news I heard he was dead [November 1, 1956.] That hurt me worse."

KID BAILEY—"Over there in Rankin County in a juke . . . call it Gold. Tommy Johnson and Bailey were there together. He got that swing from Tommy ['Rowdy Blues,' Br. 7114] but he put different words in there himself. Cause Tommy's—the originator of makin' that kind of 'Maggie Campbell' and 'Canned Heat.' I heard him say he [Bailey] got that swing from him [Tommy]. I saw him another time in a juke at Tutwiler."

Kid Bailey has been a personal enigma. Over a five-year period, this writer was able to trace him to a plantation near Leland where he lived in the late 1920s and later to Leland and Skene, where he is remembered as appearing with Charlie Patton. Ishmon Bracey said he once saw him in Tutwiler, besides in Rankin County near Jackson, and Walter Vincson said he saw him in both Canton and Moorhead in the same time period. A black policeman from Indianola (who claims the honor of being the first black cop in Mississippi) said he saw him after World War II in Indianola, and a black funeral-home director from the same town said he saw Bailey in Moorhead in the early 1950s.

ROSIE MAE MOORE—"Rosie was Charlie McCoy's old lady. He played behind her [in local jukes] and she sang in this carnival . . . little show that went round from town to town. She's from Hazelhurst [on Highway 51, some 45 miles south of Jackson]. Rosie put out the 'Mad Dog Blues' and 'Electrocuted Blues' [Brunswick 7049, credited to Mary Butler]. She went to New Orleans, put that out, she said. That was her best song 'bout the mad dog."

(SALTY DOG) SAM COLLINS—"He used to play there on Railroad Street in McComb. I saw him there two or three times. He was there on the street takin' up collection. Called himself Salty Dog Sam. I seed him when I stopped there going to New Orleans to see my baby sister."

A McComb cab driver told me in the late 1950s that he knew Salty Dog Sam in the '20s and '30s and he had left McComb to go to either Louisiana or Texas. He declared that he saw Sam back in McComb in the mid-1950s sitting up town, obviously back in town to visit. But he didn't know where he had come from. A Clarke County blues singer, Gress Barnett, who never played professionally but more for small parties in his community, saw Salty Dog Sam also in McComb. Barnett learned at least one song, "Out West Blues," from Salty Dog Sam, whom he also identified from recordings as the same man as Sam Collins. Barnett also knew another musician, Sonny Scott, who left the Quitman, Mississippi area in the 1920s and went to Birmingham. Barnett, as Scott, played some of his material in C major. Scott died near Quitman in Clarke County in the 1950s, Barnett said.

Bracey said Salty Dog Sam had a song about "'nineteen puppies, one little shaggy hound,' but mine was the four, five puppies." Hayes McMullan, a resident of Tallahatchie County who appeared on the Mississippi ETV production "Good Morning Blues" (1978), remembers meeting Bracey in 1922 on Joe King's plantation near Webb, Mississippi. Bracey was picking cotton on Dyess' Plantation. McMullan said he was playing for "dances."

"He picked up the guitar after I put it down and he started playin'," said McMullan. "I was over him [better] at that time but man, I tell you, when he put out that record about the shaggy hound he was fiddling [playing] sure enough. He was over me then." McMullan learned a number of different styles in Tallahatchie County and played on occasions with the musician he identified as "Little Willie" Brown at Glendora, Charlie Patton's associate. Hayes identified Bracey by his photo on the Origin Jazz Library album (*Country Blues Encores*, OJL-8). Bracey said on more than one occasion he used to go up in the Delta, "'round Sumner and Webb." Bracey said he had been singing "Shaggy Hound" for about three years before he recorded it.

BULLET WILLIAMS—"He played the harmonica through his nose. Always tried to get me or somebody to go make some more records with him. He was a big, ugly blackskin man."

Johnny Temple reported the same account of Williams, saying he was often trying to get Temple to play with him so they could go and make another record. Temple did not know the singer on Bullet's Paramounts. Bengt Olsson has reported that Williams was originally from west Alabama, near Millport, close to Columbus, Mississippi, in the northeast portion of the state, not far from Aberdeen, the home of Bukka White.

KID ERNEST AND NEW ORLEANS NEHI BOYS—"I met Kid Ernest [Michall] in New Orleans. I went down there to visit my baby sister and I got in with him and I told him about us [in Jackson] and so he came back up here and went to playin' around.

"We called him and 44 Charlie [Taylor] Nehi Boys 'cause they both was little guys, not too tall. Me and Kid Ernest stayed together after we recorded and 44 Charlie went back to playin' on his own.

"One time we was up in the Delta [about 1930] and snow was up to my knees and up to his waist, 'cause he's a little guy. We played up there and in central Mississippi 'round Forest and Morton.

"And he could take the clarinet and start playing it and takes that horn off and takes the mouthpiece and pop that reed like it was a kettledrum. He could play with a band. If a musicianer with a trombone or saxophone, he could get in there with that clarinet and pick 'em up, pick their part up.

"One night at Belzona, it was wintertime, we rode the back end of a truck into town and we heard this music coming from this store. We stopped and went in, me and Kid Ernest and it was Walter and Lonnie [Mississippi Sheiks]. Kid Ernest got his clarinet and we started playin'. Man, he got down on that clarinet and made it sound so good. Peoples come over to us and left them standing. They never heard a man play clarinet like Kid Ernest did. He had that laugh in his playin' and wherever he went, people fell for it and wanted to hear it.

"I heard say he was still living in New Orleans two years ago [1967]."

Kid Ernest Michall recorded for Gennett in 1927. Bracey said Kid Ernest told him he had recorded once already but he didn't know if he was "just telling me that." Paramount spells his name Ernst on the label, 12980. No trace of Kid Ernest exists in New Orleans, although a jazz historian there said he had heard that he had recorded. The latest edition of Dixon and Godrich gives his name as Kid Ernest Moliere (1997, 677).

RUBE LACY—"No sir, I never got a record from Rubey. No! He didn't put out nothing's but the 'Cornbread Blues, Ham and Gravey.' He hadn't put out but one record [Pm 12629—'Ham Hound *Crave*' was incorrectly titled by Paramount].

"Me and Rubey worked together one time down at the lumber camp near Morton. They hired us for about a week to play music for the loggers. But I never got no record from Rubey."

Bracey denies that, as stated in the notes to Yazoo album 1007 "Jackson Blues," he learned his style from Rube Lacy. He said he learned his style from Louis Cooper and Lee Jones, but it was similar to Rube Lacy's approach. He did admit he played with Lacy at the sawmill job mentioned in this text. Often, Bracey said he could play Johnson's songs "as well as Tommy could" and "I could play what Rubey Lacy played."

BIG BOY CRUDUP—"If you a new face, you'll draw a crowd. 'Cause old Big Boy Crudup came from Bolton [a small town some 18 miles west of Jackson] up here and all the people was all around him and I says, 'That guy can't beat me.' 'Oh, man, you can't play like this man,' one said to me. He had a loud voice you know. And so hey, I fooled around in there and got my guitar tuned [cross natural] like I want and he [Crudup] wouldn't play anymore."

Several artists played or lived near Bolton, the most outstanding being members of the Chatmon family. Walter Vincson also came from the area, as did the McCoy brothers, who Bracey and Johnny Temple both said grew up near Raymond, a town near Bolton.

ROBERT JOHNSON—"Dead Shrimp" is being played.

"There's two guitars there, ain't there on that record? 'Cause you see you can't carry that bass and treble all at the same time. Charlie McCoy played that style all the time [walking bass] and Bo Carter. Bo played that style all the time too."

Bracey didn't specify when McCoy and Carter played the style. It could have been before or after Johnson recorded his walking boogie in 1936. Johnny Temple recorded a similar guitar pattern in 1935, a year before Johnson recorded, that he learned from an R.L. (Freeman), apparently one of Johnson's many pseudonyms.

CHARLIE McCOY—"I was the one who got Charlie McCoy on records. I took him to Memphis with me for the Victory [Victor] people. He was only about seventeen [years old]. He wanted to go to Wisconsin with me; begged me to go, but I wouldn't let him. I took 44 Charlie and Kid Ernest and Tommy.

"Charlie McCoy could play with a bottleneck. Most people didn't play 'round here like that. He was better on the mandolin than the guitar. He plays a guitar and mandolin alike."

The Notes to Yazoo album 1007 state that the McCoys grew up in Jackson. The McCoys grew up on a farm near Raymond, Mississippi, and then moved to Jackson in the 1920s—Joe first, then Charlie—say both Johnny Temple and Bracey.

CHARLIE TAYLOR—"44 Charlie was from 'round McComb, down there in Louisiana, them jukes in them little sawmill towns. His best song was about a railroad ['C.P. Railroad,' Pm 13121]. One night he hung up with Little Brother [Montgomery] in a juke in Rankin County [just across the Pearl River

Johnny Temple learned the "Boogie" from Johnson when he used the name R.L. Freeman during stopovers in Jackson. Wardlow Collection.

from Jackson] and Little Brother come off first. I thought 44 Charlie was better and shoulda won."

BLIND BLAKE—"I met Blind Blakes [*sic*] in Chicago. I couldn't second him. He was too fast for me. Blind Blakes, Tampa Red, Lonnie Johnson, and Scrappie Blackwell . . . all of them guitar players was buckin' one another. Blind Blakes was too fast. I used to hear a record; I don't care what kind of record I hear; I'd run over it two three times, I'd play it."

LOUIS ARMSTRONG—"Louis Armstrong offered me a job [in Chicago]. One of his guitar players had died across the water [in Europe]. His second guitar, one that play the hot guitar. I wouldn't try to play it, but he was gonna rehearse me 'til I got qualified to play with him. 'Cause I kept time that I carried. You know, time is the root of music. He came 'round here and played at the hall down there at Jackson and I's the onliest one he let in. You know it was two and a half [dollars] at the door. I played a little; I played a couple of numbers. He told them band members how good I was for time and some pieces I was familiar with, some of those pieces he played. At the time I was good at second guitar, complementing."

BLIND LEMON JEFFERSON—"Blind Lemon used to come to Greenwood every fall and let me follow him around. He didn't trust them other people. He carried a pearl-handled .45 and he could shoot the head off a chicken. And he couldn't see nar a lick. Just did it from the sound he heard. He broke time but he was good, I'm telling you. He'd be down there in the fall when people's pickin' cotton. Everybody wanted to see Lemon. I could second him but lot of guitar pickers couldn't stay with him."

H.C. SPEIR—"Mr. Speir found me up there on Mill Street on a Saturday morning. I was playing on the street and this man in a suit come up and stopped and started listenin' to me. I thought he was the law. He asked me to sing another song and I changed ['Left Alone Blues'] but he said then go back to the first one ['Shaggy Hound']. He liked that one best. He took me down to his store and I made a record for him to try out and get on [records]. He say I passed and he was gonna let me know when I was accepted. I sung the 'Shaggy Hound' ['Saturday Blues'] for him and he said that would go over."

Bracey's original title for "Saturday Blues" was "Shaggy Hound." Nowhere in the song is the word Saturday mentioned. Bracey said Speir thought the title "Saturday Blues" would help it sell better.

"He told me to go and get some other musicianers and keep practicing and I got Rosie and Tommy. He told me it was okay to use Charlie McCoy as a complementing [second guitar]. When I got my money from Wisconsin, a white man up here at McRae's Department Store wouldn't let me buy a new suit. Wouldn't cash my check for me. He said that [$900] was too much for a colored man to have. I called Mr. Speir and he came around and signed it and I put it in the bank. The bank fell [1930] and I 'bout lost it all. Only got back $600 from what I put in."

Not only did Speir send blues talent to Paramount, he also made two trips himself. On one of them he carried the Delta Big Four from Tunica County in his new 1930 automobile. His wife complained that "the smell didn't disappear for a month." At that session, Speir said Laibley told him he wanted Patton for another session, and Speir told Laibley where to find him. Subsequently, Laibley found Patton, who suggested Son House, Willie Brown, and Louise Johnson to him. Speir emphatically said that he did not carry the Delta Big Four to Grafton at the same time as Patton and House. He said that trip occurred a couple of weeks later. Dixon and Godrich (1997) report the entire session of more than 100 masters being recorded the last of May 1930. Speir said he went up in late April or early May and it was during this visit that "Old Man Moeser offered to sell me the company." Unfortunately, Speir was unable to raise the $25,000 needed to purchase the company assets and move it to Mississippi.

[For a full treatment of H.C. Speir, see "Legends of the Lost," page 126, and "Godfather of Delta Blues," page 131.]

ONE LEG SAM (NORWOOD)—"Tommy was scared of him. He used to bully Tommy 'round and he was scared of him. No sir—*I* wasn't scared of him and he knew it. He was a hard man to be 'round. He lost his leg when the train [Panama Limited] hit his gravel truck. Tommy ran around with him. He stayed with Luceen [Slim] Duckett up there on Ann Banks [at number 905]. Tommy wouldn't fight nobody, but One Leg Sam would, and Tommy stayed with him to protect him [Johnson from being hurt]."

Notes to Yazoo album 1007 "Jackson Blues" are erroneous. They listed "Peg Leg Sam" as Norwood's name. Temple said he was always called "One Leg Sam."

ROBERT WILKINS—"I saw him in Memphis, just outside of town in a juke playin'. Didn't drink nothing but a little wine. I never saw a man drink so little."

SKIPPY JAMES—"He played with Johnny Temple. Me and 44 Charlie and Kid Ernest was playin' one night up there 'round Pocahontas [a small town near Bentonia, James' home] and he and 44 Charlie got in a contest. 44 Charlie won. We told him we had made some records and he wanted to know how we made them. He used to come to Jackson and stay up there on Ann Banks Street with Johnny Temple."

Temple lived at 905 Ann Banks Street until his death in 1968, from urinary tract carcinoma. In this fabled house he hosted such blues figures as Tommy Johnson, Norwood, the McCoy brothers, Skip James, and Elmore James, who roomed with Temple just before James' death in 1963. Temple said he had been "knowing Elmore James since the 1930s."

BLUE COAT (TOM) NELSON—"He played over there for picnics in Vicksburg. He had a little string band. He always wore a blue coat [army style]. That's how he got his name. Washboard Walter was over there too playing on the street. He played the rub board [and recorded duets for Paramount with John Byrd]."

Speir recalled finding a washboard player in Vicksburg and recording him, but he didn't remember a name.

JOHN BYRD—"He told me he was from Red Lick [near Pattison] and he stayed in Natchez a lot. He used to come in here with Tommy on weekends [about 1930]."

A 1966 trip to Red Lick in rural Jefferson County produced no leads that could either refute or substantiate Bracey's statement. The community no longer exists, except for a rural store. Temple said John Byrd came to Jackson with Tommy Johnson on at least one occasion, and Byrd told him he was living at Georgetown, a small town south of Jackson, where he was playing for workers at a sawmill. A trip to Georgetown did produce witnesses who remembered Byrd, but they said he had moved to Bogue Chitto, another sawmill town on the way to Brookhaven on Highway 51 south. Temple said Byrd did play 12-string guitar, the only person he ever saw in Mississippi who played one.

GEECHIE WILEY—"She lived 'round there on John Hart Street for a while. Charlie McCoy got her for his old lady. She could play on the guitar as good as on that record ['Eagles on a Half,' Pm 13074]. She said she was from Natchez; close by Natchez was her home. She didn't stay here long, couple of months and she done left."

Bracey said he was not confusing Wiley with Rosie Mae Moore. He said McCoy lived with both of them at different times. He said Wiley played guitar and accompanied herself when she sang. [Her "Last Kind Words Blues" was prominently used by Terry Zwigoff in his documentary film on Robert Crumb.]

MISSISSIPPI JOHN HURT—"In this juke in Greenwood, I walked in and heard this little guy playin'. I took out my guitar and started playin' when he finished and I had the crowd and he wouldn't play no more. He come up to me later and says, 'How you tuned?' and I shows him. We got to be friends after that but he didn't ever get over me [play better]."

JUKE HOUSE DAYS—[Bracey illustrated the dangers of playing in the jukes.]

"She gave me a dollar every time she'd come there to play the 'Vicksburg Blues,' like Little Brother Montgomery; so see that was when that bonus came out, and some of them gettin' $400. He had done got a $400 bonus, and he had done cashed his check and he was 'round there and she had the biggest of the money, see! And she was a nice lookin' little woman too.

And so she came over where I was and she asked me to play the 'Vicksburg.'

"She said, 'Here's a dollar, play it again.' And I played it and she came back over there and say, 'Here's another dollar, play that again.' I played it and so she came over there the third time. After she left he came over

A typical, small Delta town with "jukes" in the 1950s. Wardlow Collection

there. 'Say you, see that woman over there in that corner?' I say, 'Sho'! I see her.' I'se tryin' to be lively and friendly, and so he say, 'That's my wife.' I say, 'Yeah! I said that the first time I seen her, I say you have a nice-lookin' wife.' He say, 'Well listen, don't you let her come over here all up in your face no more.' I said, 'Okay.' I say, 'She just asked me to play a piece and tippin' me, wasn't nothin' to it, that's the first time I see her.' He said, 'I done told you.'

"So time he left, she came back. She said, 'Here's a dollar, play the "Vicksburg Blues" for me again.' I take'n the dollar; that's the fourth time. I said, 'Isn't that your husband?' She said,: 'Yeah, how you know?' I said, 'He came over and told me; say you was his wife and for you not to come up in my face no more.' I said, 'Now, I play this "Vicksburg Blues" till day, long as you give me [money].' I said, 'Now I'd ruther for you not to come. You want me to play a piece now, you send me somethin.' She said, 'Okay, ain't nothing; he know it's the first time I seed you too.' I said, 'Yes mam.'

"Fourth time she left here, he come back with a crab-apple switch . . . draw it back at me, he said, 'You so and so you, all right, and I tell you to keep my wife out your face.' He breakin' up to me. I had that Washburn guitar, juked him back offa me and hit him and bust the guitar on his head; see knocked him down under me. And that time he got up and was comin' on at me. Then I hit him with a Coca-Cola bottle case.

"The guy I was playin' for was tough, Marshall Serge, so he came in there and got his gun, and made him beg my pardon and everything, so he got kinda quiet down and so he went on out 'bout a half hour, 45 minutes, somethin' like that, and brought in a little old whiskey bottle. He said, 'Aw, let's drink it off and be merry!' I said, 'You drink; I don't want no whiskey; I been drinking.' I said, 'I'm playin' for a man that sells whiskey; you know I got plenty, as much as I want.' He said, 'Oh you have got the devil in you, eh?' He broke at me that time and Marshall ran in there with his gun. And ran him home.

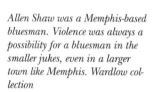

Allen Shaw was a Memphis-based bluesman. Violence was always a possibility for a bluesman in the smaller jukes, even in a larger town like Memphis. Wardlow collection

"An' I looked down there; could put my fist through [the hole in the guitar]. If he'd been there then I'da kill him. So another boy there name Robert Bearman, and I got his guitar, and I finished the party out with it."

[EK: Bracey's claim to have been offered a job by Louis Armstrong must be discounted. Armstrong's first trip abroad was in 1932, by which time both his musicianship and his showmanship were extremely polished. Hardly ever did his band feature two guitarists—one exception is documented on his December 1927 OKeh recording, "Savoy Blues," with Johnny St. Cyr and Lonnie Johnson.]

◄◦►◄◦►◄◦►◄◦►◄◦►◄◦►◄◦►◄◦►◄◦►◄◦►◄◦►◄◦►◄◦►

Memphis City Directory Blues

While working as a reporter for a Meridian newspaper, I learned to locate people's addresses in city directories. Today researchers use these routinely, but my Blues Unlimited *article (68: 16–17, reprinted here in condensed form)—documenting a 1969 search in Memphis—described the first pioneering use of the directories to locate old musicians.*

Be prepared to spend time and swallow disappointment. In my few hours in Memphis, I found only half the musicians I sought. Still, given more time in a city where the blues have flourished, you may unearth new information on some little-known artists. See the following sidebars for intriguing Jackson city listings of Ishmon Bracey and Tommy Johnson.—GDW

City directories from the years 1925 to the early '60s generally fail to list many well-known black blues singers and sanctified singing-preachers of the area. For example, although a photo of Elder Lonnie McIntorsh ran in the *Memphis Press-Scimitar* (May 12, 1966), he was not a resident of Memphis, as confirmed by his absence in the directories I checked. The 1934 church listings include 16 sanctified ministers of the Church of God in Christ, but not McIntorsh. He never lived in Memphis, but was a resident of Caruthersville, Missouri.

Members of Jack Kelly's South Memphis Jug Band appear in some directories. As early as 1925 and as late as 1937, Higgs (Daniel M.) is listed as a physician living at 218 Cambridge Avenue. A Will Batts shows up in one 1934 listing: William Batts, porter for the W.P. Moore Dry Goods Co., 713 Simmons Avenue. However, their leader Jack Kelly had no listings.

The mysterious Allen Shaw (in 1965, Furry Lewis recalled Shaw as living on the North Side) appears in 1930 and 1934 as a laborer, living at 248 Webster Avenue. But is this *the* Shaw? Unlike census records, city directories don't identify race, so it helps to know whether an address is in the white or black section for the time period.

Gus Cannon appears in the 1930 directory as a laborer, married to Olyda, at 1331 Hyde Park Blvd. There are *four* Robert Wilkins listed in 1934, along with a Willie Borum at 751 N. Montgomery with wife Sophronie. After a solitary 1925 listing as a laborer, Frank Stokes, he reappears in the 1937 directory as a blacksmith at 461 Wicks Avenue. But are any of these *The Man* who made the Victor and Paramount recordings?

Gus Cannon, a jug band leader and a major competitor of the Memphis Jug Band, who was listed at various times in the city directory. Wardlow collection.

◄◦►◄◦►◄◦►

Searching for Bracey and Johnson: Jackson City Directories 1927 to 1956

These city directory listings include the occupation, wife's name in parentheses, and residence.

Listings for Ishmon Bracey
1927/28 Employee Panhandle Oil
  725 W. Earl
1930 Ishmael [*sic*] musician
  730 W. Earl
1935 Musician
  730 W. Earl
1937 Laborer
  905 W. Lynch
1939 No listing
1940 No listing
1943 913 Lynch St.
1945 No listing
1947 Painter
  917 Dalton
1950 (Annie M.)
  916 Dalton
1956 No listing

Listings for Tommy Johnson
1927/28 Thomas (Maggie) landscape gardener
  1390 St. Ann
1930 Musician (Rosa)
  703 S. Jefferson
1935 Thomas (Maggie) laborer
  1209 N. Grayson
1937 Thomas (Maggie) laborer, Blue Ribbon Creamery
  732 W. Monument
1939 Blue Ribbon Creamery
  1029 N. Bradley
1940 Same address
1942 (Maggie)
  840 Monroe
1943 Laborer (Maggie)
  930 Monroe
1945 Same listing as above
1948 Same listing
1950 Laborer
  834 Monroe

NOTE: It is assumed that the above Johnson is Tommy for all listings, based on information given by Bracey and the Rev. Ledell Johnson that Tommy was married to both a Rosa and a Maggie Bedwell. There is no foolproof way to guarantee these listings are correct. In some directories Bracey was listed and Johnson not, and vice versa. In some years no directories were published. Obviously, both Johnson and Bracey moved many times.

◄o►◄o►◄o►

A Quick Ramble

with Ramblin' Thomas, Jesse Thomas, Will Ezell, Bessie Tucker, and Elzadie Robinson, and the Texas talent scouts, R.T. Ashford and the Kendall Brothers

In 1972, at the request of Blues Unlimited *coeditor Mike Leadbitter, I interviewed Jesse Thomas, who had recorded in 1929 and after World War II. This assignment led to the first publication of information on Louisiana-Texas musician Willard "Ramblin'" Thomas, Jesse's older brother. It also contained details on Will Ezell, who reportedly brought Blind Lemon Jefferson's body home to be buried in Texas. In addition, there were some comments on Elzadie Robinson, Bessie Tucker, and, not least, talent scout Harry Charles of Birmingham, and the Texas talent scouts R.T. Ashford and the Kendall brothers (misspelled as "Kendle" in the original article). The latter three were primarily responsible for most prewar recordings of Texas bluesmen.*
—GDW

[Originally published in *Blues Unlimited* no. 148 (Winter 1981): 14–15.]

Shreveport bluesman Jesse Thomas recorded and released at least two postwar recordings on his Club label, but the evasive Thomas, who has lived in Shreveport's black section since moving back from the West Coast in the 1960s, is one of a few Louisiana-Texas bluesmen who recorded before 1930, and in the 1946–60 postwar era.

Thomas, a mild-mannered, shrewd businessman who operated a small club in Shreveport in the early 1970s, was the younger brother of Willard "Ramblin'" Thomas, known for his Paramount and Victor recordings of 1928–32.

Jesse also did a session in 1929 for Ralph Peer and Victor in Dallas, playing guitar behind Bessie Tucker, and was in the studio in Dallas in 1932 when his older brother Ramblin' recorded for Victor.

Born around 1910 (no exact birth date has been found) in Loganport, Louisiana, a small community on the Louisiana-Texas state line, Jesse auditioned for Paramount in 1929 in Chicago after being sent there by Dallas talent scout R.T. Ashford.

[Ashford, a record store retailer on Dallas's West Central Avenue, was Paramount's talent scout for Texas, according to Art C. Laibley, the PM sales and recording director who died in Chicago in the mid-1970s. Laibley told this researcher that Ashford, H.C. Speir (Mississippi), and Harry

Charles (Birmingham) were the three main scouts Paramount used in securing talent in the South. Originally from Louisiana, Laibley worked for Paramount from the mid-1920s until 1931, when he left to join an insurance company in Chicago. In Max Vreede's Paramount book (1971), Ashford is also listed as a PM dealer in a published ad in the *Chicago Defender* in March 1923.]

Paramount Records

Blind Blake   Ramblin' Thomas

HITS

Yes, sir—your latest Blues hits are out on Paramount by the great exclusive artists. Look at this blues extravaganza—everything and anything you want. Also remember that on Paramount you hear those sublime spirituals everybody loves, sung by master artists. Every number a good record. Let us play them for you.

Vocal Numbers

12771—**Oil Well Blues**—Vocal—Guitar Acc.............Blind Lemon Jefferson
        Saturday Night Spender Blues—Vocal—Guitar Acc..Blind Lemon Jefferson
12769—**Ghost Woman Blues**—Vocal—Guitar Acc.................George Carter
        Weeping Willow Woman—Vocal—Guitar Acc.............George Carter
12768—**Cheatin' Daddy**—Vocal—Piano Acc........Will Ezell—Elzadie Robinson
        This Is Your Last Night with Me—Vocal—Piano Acc.
                                          Will Ezell—Elzadie Robinson
12767—**New Style of Loving**—Vocal—Guitar Acc.................Blind Blake
        Ramblin' Mama Blues—Vocal—Guitar Acc.................Blind Blake
12765—**Hot Papa Blues No. 2**—Vocal—Banjo Acc.........Papa Charlie Jackson
        We Can't Buy It No More—Vocal—Banjo Acc....Papa Charlie Jackson
12758—**Wasn't That Doggin' Me**—Vocal—Guitar Duet Acc....Beale Street Sheiks
        Rockin' on the Hill Blues—Vocal—Guitar Duet Acc...Beale Street Sheiks
12773—**Bucket of Blood**—Piano Solo.............................Will Ezell
        Playing the Dozen—Piano Solo............................Will Ezell

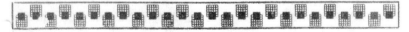

Willard "Ramblin'" Thomas was a major selling bluesman for Paramount in 1928 and 1929. Courtesy Maxey Tarpley

Jesse recalled, "I went into Ashford's Record Shop with some other people and he listened and told me where I could go. They told him I was Ramblin' Thomas' little brother. I went up there [Chicago] in 1928 or '29 and auditioned but they told me I didn't have enough original material. They didn't use me."

[Both Laibley and Mayo Williams conducted auditions for Paramount in Chicago in the 1920s. Paramount had an office in Chicago where Williams worked with talent and songwriters. Laibley commuted back and forth between Grafton and Chicago for recording sessions. According to Harry Charles, Williams was constantly "pushing songs."]

Within a year, Jesse had another opportunity when Victor came to Dallas to record blues and hillbilly artists. Strangely, he was living in Oklahoma City, more than 200 miles away, when he was offered the opportunity to audition for the session by a pianist he knew only as "49."

"I was in Dallas to record, but they sent for me from Oklahoma City . . . through this piano player I knew . . . called him '49.' I didn't know his real name." [According to Dixon and Godrich (1997), this was probably K.D. Johnson.]

"I played on Bessie Tucker's records . . . 'Katy Blues' and some others like that. He ['49'] played piano and I played the guitar and this other guy played the bass horn, maybe a drum. There was two more on there."

[Dixon and Godrich list four sides made by Bessie Tucker on August 10, 1929, with a guitarist credited as either Bo Jones or Carl Davis. "Katy Blues" is one of the four sides recorded with an unknown bass, piano, and guitar accompanist. Brian Rust's Victor Master Book (Rust 1969b) has consecutive masters (55324 to 55331) for sides by Thomas and Tucker.]

Jesse also recalls that America's Blue Yodeler, Jimmie Rodgers, recorded at the session and was having a drinking problem that attracted the attention of Victor field recording director Ralph Peer.

"He was drinkin' pretty heavy; that's what Mr. Ralph Peer said. He was singing some blues that day."

[Both Ishmon Bracey and Tommy Johnson played for Jimmie Rodgers in Jackson, Mississippi on at least one occasion. Rodgers, who was appearing at the King Edward Hotel, heard them performing on the street in front of the hotel and invited them to the roof, where he allowed them to perform for his audience. Bracey said, "He was struck by that 'yodel' of Tommy's and asked us if we had recorded. We told him we had made records for the Victory [*sic*] people in Memphis." On another occasion, Bracey and One Leg Sam (Norwood) were invited by Rodgers to perform on the roof at the King Edward.]

Despite other reports of an unknown artist being limited to four or six sides (H.C. Speir, who was involved in many sessions with different companies, is one very credible witness), Jesse claimed Peer had no limit on the number of sides an artist could record. However, Thomas only recorded four masters.

"He didn't seem to have any limit on how many songs you could do. He let you record as many as you wanted to as long as he had enough time.

"It was either twenty-five dollars a side or twenty-five dollars a record they paid," Jesse recalls. "We needed the cash, so we took the money." [Speir always tried to get his talent fifty dollars a side. Both Bracey and Johnson were paid this sum, according to Bracey, for their Victor sessions with Peer.]

Jesse's recordings were poor sellers; one, "Blue Goose Blues," which provided the name for a New York specialty label, was probably released in late 1929. The other, 23381, was not issued until 1932 or 1933.

[Dixon and Godrich show four masters by Jesse Thomas, recorded in Dallas, August 10, 1929, with two sides issued on Victor 38555 and two on 23381. New York collector Don Kent has a copy of the latter that he acquired from a Virginia hillbilly collector.]

The Dallas–Fort Worth area remained Jesse's home grounds in the 1930s and he never returned to Oklahoma City. In 1932 he was playing with a small band in Fort Worth, when his brother Ramblin' was recorded by Victor.

"That was through the Kendall Brothers in Fort Worth. They had this record store and they sponsored this radio show that you could play on. Ramblin' used to play for them. I happened to go along with him that day to the session."

[The Kendall Brothers Furniture Store and one of the brothers are mentioned in Charles Townsend's biography of Bob Wills, *San Antonio Rose*, published by the University of Illinois Press (1976).]

Jesse remembers Jimmie Rodgers again at this session and says Rodgers listened to Ramblin's song about a groundhog, reworked it, and recorded the song with a slightly different approach.

"He called it something like a 'rootin' hog' . . . he changed it around."

[Rust's Victor Master Book (1969b) shows Rodgers recording "A Blue Yodel (Ground Hog Rootin' in My Back Yard)" on February 6, 1932, the last of six songs he recorded at the Dallas session. Thomas recorded three days later, February 9, and did four songs, two of them being versions of this song: "Ground Hog Blues" and "Ground Hog Blues No. 2." Ironically, two artists who were to become as famous as Rodgers—Bob Wills and Milton Brown—recorded masters immediately after Thomas, as the Fort Worth Doughboys.]

Jesse was not to record again until the late 1940s, when he recorded for a number of California labels including Specialty. He had previously met a specialty representative in Tucson, Arizona, in 1947, he says, but didn't try to record for that company until the early 1950s, when he auditioned personally at the company's offices.

Later, Jesse Thomas went into the record business himself, recording songs at Universal Studios in Hollywood, paying for the pressings, and releasing the records under his personally owned Club label. [The Leadbitter & Slaven discography (1969) shows four sides recorded by Thomas on the Club label. Former Shreveport postwar collector Bill Woodward—who joined the author in the 1972 interview with Jesse Thomas in Shreveport, Louisiana—reported that a West Coast collector has found a third Club by Thomas. The discography on Thomas shows he recorded for Miltone, Club, Freedom, Modern, Swing Time, Hollywood, Specialty, and Elite, a who's who of West Coast postwar labels.]

Jesse also recorded and released a recording by a woman gospel singer, paying for all releases on a "collect as you go" basis.

"I put one out, and see what it would do, then put another one out," he recalls. "They were made down in the Universal Studios in Hollywood and it was sometime around the Korean War."

Jesse returned to Shreveport in the 1960s and was still active in 1980, playing at a supper club, according to *Living Blues* editor Jim O'Neal.

WILLARD THOMAS—Jesse says his older brother Willard was discovered in Dallas for Paramount and the record company gave him the name of "Ramblin'." "He got on there in Dallas, that's what he told me," Jesse remembers. "He and Lemon [Blind Lemon Jefferson], they run together quite a bit and played together. He played quite a bit with him in Dallas."

[Jefferson may have directed Ramblin' to R.T. Ashford—a major retailer of Jefferson's records—or Thomas may have approached Ashford independently. Jefferson also played in the Shreveport area, as did Thomas. Mrs. Joe Holmes (Roberta Allums) of Sibley, Louisiana, reported to this researcher in the 1960s that her late, estranged husband, who recorded for Paramount in 1932 as King Solomon Hill, often played with Thomas in Shreveport and in some of the towns surrounding Sibley.]

Jesse says that Ramblin' was a transient between Dallas and Shreveport and spent most of his time playing in those towns. "He spent a good time in both of them [Dallas and Shreveport] . . . about the same . . . He'd mostly get hisself a room to hisself and play on the streets, in a barbershop, on a corner or even in the alley. In those days it wasn't against the law to play on the streets.

"Ramblin' always traveled a lot. We didn't play together that much. He died in Memphis sometimes in the '40s of TB. We never got word where he was buried, 'cept he died in Memphis." [A search by the Vital Statistics Department of the State Board of Health in Nashville failed to find a death certificate for Thomas.]

Jesse said, "He liked that bottleneck style best. Wasn't no one he learned from particular [guitar style]. Several people down there [Loganport] played that style with a bottle."

ELZADIE ROBINSON—"We knew her when she wasn't nothin' but a young lady there in Loganport. She sang in our church there 'fore she made records.

"We just stopped hearing from her after a while. She never moved back from Chicago but she would come through and 'holler' at the people. She

Spirituals — Sermons

12772—**Cool My Scorching Tongue**—Preaching with Singing
Rev. C. H. Welsh and Congregation
Abraham Offers His Son Isaac—Preaching with Singing
Rev. C. H. Welsh and Congregation

12749—**I'm Going Through**........................Norfolk Jubilee Quartette
Sinner, You Can't Hide......................Norfolk Jubilee Quartette

12744—**Religion Is Something Within You**—Vocal—Two Guitars
Blind Joe Taggart
Mother's Love—Vocal—Two Guitars.................Blind Joe Taggart

12630—**His Eye Is on the Sparrow**—Vocal.............Norfolk Jubilee Quartette
I Wouldn't Mind Dying If Dying Was All.....Norfolk Jubilee Quartette

---

Have You Heard These Releases?

12770—**South African Blues**
Piggly Wiggly Blues
Windy Rhythm Kings

12764—**Rock My Soul**
Whoopee Stomp
Broadway Rastus

12766—**Hard Hustling Blues**
High Powered Mama Blues
Moanin' Bernice

12761—**Old Country Rock**
Raggin' the Blues
William Moore

12760—**Blame It on the Blues**
Sleep Talking Blues..Ma Rainey

12757—**The Devil in the Church**
Jesus Healed the Blind
Rev. C. H. Welsh

12756—**That Black Snake Moan No. 2**
Tin Cup Blues
Blind Lemon Jefferson

12754—**Notoriety Woman Blues**
Walkin' Across the Country
Blind Blake

12753—**Barrel House Woman**
Heifer Dust..........Will Ezell

12752—**Good Time Blues**
New Way of Living Blues
Ramblin' Thomas

12751—**Dentist Chair Blues Part I**
Dentist Chair Blues Part II
Hattie McDaniels and Papa
Charlie Jackson

12750—**Rising River Blues**
Hot Jelly Roll Blues
George Carter

12746—**I Had to Give Up Gym**
Pat-a-Foot Blues
Hokum Boys

12745—**Unsatisfied Blues**
Need My Lovin', Need My Daddy
Elzadie Robinson

12743—**Newport Blues**
George St. Stomp
Cincinnati Jug Band

Elzadie Robinson

Elzadie Robinson, who often recorded with Will Ezell, an East Texas pianist, hailed from the Shreveport, Louisiana area. Courtesy Maxey Tarpley

always went to Chicago to record and then finally moved up there."

[Dixon and Godrich show Elzadie Robinson's first recording session for Paramount as 1926 and Ezell's first solo session in 1927. It is logical that Ezell teamed up behind Miss Robinson in Loganport, as both were in the area. No information is available as to how the two were found by Paramount.]

WILL EZELL—"He played around Loganport at this big mill there at Hasland [*sic*] Texas, just across the water, about a mile from Loganport. I think he drifted in there playin'. In those days there weren't no jukeboxes or many bands. He was the piano player there in the big dance hall at the mill."

[Of all the Paramount artists Art Laibley knew, he remembered Will Ezell most vividly. Laibley had seen Ezell at a dance hall in his hometown of Fullerton, Louisiana, when Ezell played for white dances around World War I, years before Laibley left the South to begin working for the Wisconsin Chair and Manufacturing Company, which owned Paramount.

Birmingham talent scout Harry Charles considered Ezell to be one of the two best pianists he had ever heard (the other was Cow Cow Davenport, who Charles discovered in Birmingham and brought to Paramount). Charles, who also brought Lucille Bogan to Chicago, reported to this researcher that Ezell and Bogan "got something going" and "Ezell used to come to Birmingham to see her to work on songs." In fact, when Bogan came into Charles' Birmingham office around June 1927 to see about getting on records, she was involved in a divorce proceeding with her husband, a railroad man, because of her affair with Ezell. Bogan had met Ezell in Chicago when she was recording for Paramount in March 1927 with her first accompanist (according to Godrich), Alex Chaney; Charles confirmed that he brought Chaney, a Birmingham pianist, to play behind Bogan.

Charles worked in Birmingham, Atlanta, and Charlotte, North Carolina, in the years 1924–31, freelancing talent to Paramount, Gennett, Vocalion, Columbia, and QRS before opening a successful piano business in downtown Birmingham. Another Birmingham pianist Charles recorded was Sid Harris, who wrote "Mountain Jack Blues"—recorded by Harris on piano rolls, and by Ma Rainey for Paramount. Charles was *not* responsible for recording either Walter Roland or Jabo Williams, but he did find Ed Bell in Alabama, and the man he nicknamed "Barefoot Bill" in Atlanta, Georgia, "where he just walked into my office."

Charles suffered a stroke in 1977, and is now deceased.]

[EK: Jesse Thomas died on August 14, 1995, at the age of 84.]

Six Who Made Recorded History (1926–35)

These capsule biographies cover several blues figures whose biographical details were previously unknown. Freddie Spruell's widow gave me historical data on her husband, the most interesting of which pinpointed "Mr. Freddie" as being from Lake Providence, Louisiana, just across the Mississippi River from Issaquena County. The first information I found on Isaiah Nettles came from H.C. Speir, who said he found him in the little railroad stop of Rockport for the 1935 Jackson session for Vocalion, and thought his guitar style was different from those in Jackson or in the Delta. Gress Barnett, an elderly bluesman in Quitman, Mississippi, spoke about the Sonny Scott who recorded with Walter Roland; Scott, who was from below the Shubuta community, was known under two nicknames. The note on Geeshie Wiley came from Ishmon Bracey, who on his "Suitcase Full of Blues" borrowed Wiley's rough-edged style of guitar. The details on John Byrd came from Johnny Temple and Bracey; Bracey said that Byrd told him he came from the Red Lick community (near Natchez), which name was apparently adopted by the Red Lick record distributor of England for its mail-order operation. —GDW

[Originally published in *78 Quarterly* no. 5 (1990): 93–96.]

JOHN BYRD— Byrd appeared in a variety of recording roles: as accompanist for Mae Glover for Gennett in 1929, as a sermonizer at the same session, as a recording partner of Washboard Walter for Paramount the following year, and as a self-accompanied blues singer at the same session. Although Delta bluesman Booker Miller likened Byrd's "Billy Goat Blues" to Delta guitar playing, Byrd was apparently from South Mississippi. Ishmon Bracey thought he hailed from Red Lick or Patterson, two towns in the vicinity of Natchez ("Washboard Walter" was from Vicksburg, according to Bracey). The Jackson bluesman Johnny Temple twice saw Byrd perform locally with Tommy Johnson. "He's about my size," Temple said of him. "[A] kinda dark fella . . . he looked like he and Tommy were just about the same age." (Johnson was born around 1896.) Temple recalled that Byrd played his 12-string guitar with an unusual flatpick: ". . . He had a great big old pick like a toothpick, you know . . . He could play it, though." Byrd is also said to have visited Georgetown, Mississippi, with Tommy Johnson and to have worked there in a sawmill for about a year. Another artist he performed with was Blind Roosevelt Graves: "I think they played together at Morton, Mississippi," Graves' one-time associate, Chester House, recalled.

ISAIAH NETTLES— Nettles' forceful brand of dance music was one of the few bright spots in a dismal blues recording era. Unfortunately, only two of the four sides he recorded for ARC were issued. His discoverer, H.C. Speir, located him at the train station in Rockport, a small settlement 20 miles southeast of Crystal Springs that consists of two stores. Although local residents could not recall him when queried three decades later, it is probable that Nettles hailed from another town in the vicinity. A 1960s employee at Belhaven College, Jackson, saw him perform both in Jackson and other towns in the vicinity of Rockport. This informant recalled that Nettles would enhance his musical appeal by tap dancing in his bare feet as he played. (He also performed the strange stunt of spearing bottle tops with his toes, and walking with the tops between them.)

Nettles appeared on an October, 1935, session held on the second floor of a building located near Speir's Farish Street Music store, and supervised by Speir, Art Satherly, and W.R. Calaway. (Both Robert Wilkins and Will Shade, who performed at the same session, had a vague memory of Nettles' presence there.) The recording name "Mississippi Moaner" was apparently given to Nettles by Satherley, for Speir did not recall it.

According to the college employee, Nettles served in World War II and spent two or three years afterwards in Mount Olive and Taylorsville, two large towns in southeastern Mississippi. Then he left the area, remarking that he was headed "up north."

SONNY SCOTT— A native of Alabama, Scott never achieved the popularity of his one-time associate Walter Roland, with whom he shared his first and last recording session in 1933. A singer named Gress Barnett knew Scott from the early 1930s, when he lived at Quitman, Mississippi. Scott, he said, was actually surnamed "Scarborough," and was known as both "Sonny" Scarborough and "Babe" Scarborough. For a time, Scott acted as Barnett's musical coach: "He tried to get me on piano chords on the guitar," Barnett said. "He could make a piano and a guitar say its prayers; he'd get on me a heap of times, he say, 'You just stay around here, you oughta go about, you could be *learnt*—but you won't go nowhere.'" According to Barnett, he died shortly before World War II in Shubuta, where he had once lived and where his sister lived. "He had a so-called son, and the last time I see'd his son, he said his daddy had passed," Barnett said.

FREDDIE SPRUELL—One of the first self-accompanied Delta bluesmen to record, if not *the* first, Spruell lived in Chicago when he made his debut for OKeh Records in 1926. Although his musicianship had a decidedly Southern slant, it

Freddie Spruell, who moved to Chicago as a boy from Lake Providence, Louisiana, was the first bluesman to record in the Delta style. Wardlow collection.

was apparently developed in the North. "Freddie was only a boy when he moved to Chicago with his parents," his widow recalled in 1981. Formerly, he had lived in Lake Providence, Louisiana, the one-time residence of Blind Joe Reynolds. "When I met him in the late '20s, he was already makin' records," she said. Apparently seeking to enlarge his reputation, he told her that he was the composer of "Mr. Freddie Blues," which was originally recorded by Priscilla Stewart in the summer of 1924 and credited to her piano-playing accompanist, who later recorded as Freddie Shayne.

Spruell's secular musical career ended by the end of World War II: "The last thing he played for I knew about, was his mother's birthday . . . She asked him to stop playin' (blues), and he did it after that. She wanted him to go back into the church, and he did. That's why he quit playing the blues and started preaching." She added, "He was preaching by 1945. He was a Baptist . . . but he didn't preach that much and didn't play in church." Spruell, she said, died in Chicago in 1956 after a lengthy hospital stay. Yet, no local death certificate for Spruell appears to exist, possibly due to the many spelling variants of his name.

GEESHIE WILEY and ELVIE THOMAS—The four tunes that Wiley recorded solo and with Elvie Thomas for Paramount in 1930 and 1931 establish her as one of the greatest female blues artists. According to Ishmon Bracey, she hailed from the vicinity of Natchez. In the 1920s she spent three months in Jackson as a resident of John Hart Street; while there, she played in a medicine show. "She could play a guitar, but she had a guitar player with her," Bracey said. "She'd play a guitar, and a ukulele, too." While in Jackson, she took up with Charlie McCoy.

A woman matching the description of Elvie Thomas was remembered as living near Palmer's Crossing, a small community outside of Hattiesburg. No other information is available.

Gress Barnett of Quitman knew both Sonny Scott, who recorded in 1934, and Salty Dog Sam (Collins) from the McComb area of South Mississippi. Wardlow collection.

◄◦►◄◦►◄◦►◄◦►◄◦►◄◦►◄◦►◄◦►◄◦►◄◦►◄◦►◄◦►

The Story of Charley Booker . . . Greenville Smokin'

While listening to various postwar Mississippi records, I was intrigued by the prewar sound of Charley Booker, who recorded the lyric "Greenville smokin', Leland burnin' down" in his record "No Easy Riding Blues," with Houston Boines on harmonica (see accompanying CD). Since Booker sang about Greenville and Leland, I took copies of his records to both towns, and discovered that both he and Boines were from the Leland area. As a result of leads gathered there I found Booker living in South Bend, Indiana. He would die there in 1989. Houston Boines remains a biographical mystery, having left the Leland area years ago.

Blues Unlimited editors Mike Leadbitter and Simon Napier were keen to run a story on Booker and Boines, since they considered their records to represent the pinnacle of jukehouse blues in Mississippi at a time when Howlin' Wolf and Muddy Waters were recording their Chicago club blues. —GDW

[Originally published in *Blues Unlimited* no. 99 (February/March 1973): 12.]

Reared in the same Delta area that brought fame and attention to Charlie Patton, Charley Booker was born in 1925 on a plantation between the tiny Mississippi communities of Moorhead and Sunflower. His 1952 recordings dramatically proclaim and reflect, partially, the older Delta style that he heard as a youngster around the town of Drew—a prime stomping ground for bluesmen in the late '20s and early '30s.

Booker now [1973] lives in a South Bend, Indiana, rooming house. When interviewed by telephone, he said that his uncle, a major influence, played around Drew with Charlie Patton: "I was copyin' 'No Ridin' Blues' on the guitar from my uncle," he added, and, if one listens closely to it, the Patton "Green River Blues" note pattern is most noticeable. In fact, as a child, Booker once saw Patton performing near Indianola.

Boyd Gilmore, a friend of Booker's uncle, was another boyhood influence and companion. Booker said, "I used to stay in his

Charley Booker played with Houston Boines in the Delta in the early 1950s. Their sound is more "rural" and "rougher" than the Chicago sound of the early 1950s. Wardlow Collection.

house when I was a kid." He thought that Gilmore had lived in both St. Louis, Missouri, and Hughes, Arkansas, and would be in his early sixties.

When World War II broke out, Booker, by then a competent singer and guitarist, was living in Leland. In 1947 he arrived in Greenville to start a short-lived career as a professional entertainer.

Burl Carson, a Greenville resident, met Booker in 1947 and remembered: "Charley played with a slide. He could play in the style of Elmore James. He also played regular guitar. He was an old country-type boy . . . cotton-patch singer."

Booker became a much-liked singer and would usually play at a local jukehouse owned by Bay Jennings, in the company of Cleanhead Love, a drummer. When not at Jennings' Booker could be found at Henry T's Pool Room on Nelson Street or at dance halls in Hollandale and Arcola.

In Greenville Booker met or "ran with" Little Milton, Rice Miller, Willie Love, Ike Turner, Elmore James, and many others, and by 1951 had his own radio show (possibly on station WDVM). In January 1952, Ike Turner approached him about recording and on the 23rd he went into a makeshift studio in the Casa Blanca Club (or was it the Castle Farm?) to cut some sides for Joe Bihari, with Cleanhead Love and Houston Boines— whom he'd first met in Belzoni—in attendance.

Booker recalled that "'No Ridin' Blues' sold real well," but alleges that he never received all the royalties due to him. The disc was a smash hit around Greenville and Leland, earning him a reputation as a prophet, for he sang of "Greenville smokin', Leland's burnin' down . . ."

A month after the song was issued, Leland did indeed nearly burn down. A terrific fire in the downtown area wiped out a block (according to reports) and the blaze could be seen eight miles away! Apparently, airplanes from the Greenville Air Force Base had to be called in to help fight a fire that at one stage was out of control and endangering the whole of Leland.

After Booker's move to South Bend in early 1953 with his wife and children, his music had become a sideline, but following our conversation Steve Lavere interviewed him in depth and arranged a recording contract. Charley Booker was due for a comeback after 20 years of obscurity.

[EK: Early in his search, Wardlow was told that Booker had died and Boines was in Florida (and reported this in his notes to the editors, *Blues Unlimited* 73 [1970]: 3). However, he followed other tips that led to Booker, very much alive and well in 1971.

Charley Booker died on September 20, 1989. His career after Wardlow's article is recounted by Steve LaVere in his obituary in *Living Blues* no. 89 (1989, 38–39).]

This record shows the influence of Charlie Patton on the postwar sound in the Delta, and Charley Booker's "licks" on this 1951 recording. Wardlow collection.

◄◦►◄◦►◄◦►

II

Tips, Leads, and Documents

The Black Birds of Paradise

Pete Whelan supplied the background detail that the Black Birds of Paradise had recorded in Birmingham for Gennett Records in 1927, and he speculated that the band had come from Birmingham, Montgomery, or Mobile, Alabama. I then went to Montgomery to canvass, and after a few inquiries I was able to locate Thomas Bell, one of the original members. He led me to Tom Ivery, another member who had two 1927 photos of the band. Together, they gave me enough information to write the lead story of the second issue of 78 Quarterly. *Afterward,* 78 Quarterly *mysteriously lapsed into obscurity for 20 years until magazine editor Pete Whelan published the third issue in 1988. —GDW*

[Originally published in *78 Quarterly* no. 2 (1968): 7–12.]

What happened to Alabama's legendary jazz band? Who were they? Gayle Wardlow uncovers surviving members of one of the greatest jazz bands to come out of the Deep South . . .

MONTGOMERY, ALABAMA: The old colored woman said, "Go and see James Bell, if you want to know about old bands. He was one of the original members of that band you're talking about."

Thirty minutes later, I was knocking on the door of Bell's home. Bell came to the door and invited me in. He was medium-sized, brown-skinned, and he looked like a fashionable bartender at a country club.

I hoped that I had found my source of information. I got straight to the point.

"Were you familiar with the Black Birds of Paradise, a band that played here in Montgomery in the 1920s and made records for the Gennett Record Company?"

"Familiar? Of course," said Bell. "I was one of the original members of the band. But those were old days, way on back there."

After more questions, answers, statements, Bell got on the phone and called another original member of the band, Tom Ivery, who lived about four blocks away. He asked Ivery if we could come over and talk to him about the band.

So, armed with an Origin Jazz Library reissue of the Black Birds of Paradise recordings (*By Ways of Jazz*—OJL-9), we started for Ivery's house.

Ivery, tall and slender, with an air of leadership and a flair for creative conversation, was more like the stereotype of a university professor than that of a former musician.

Both Ivery and Bell seemed somewhat aloof for the first few minutes of our conversation. Perhaps they wondered about this author's interest in a dance band 40 years in the past.

However, after listening to various cuts of the band on the Origin reissue, Ivery launched full force into the answers I sought.

The Black Birds of Paradise became a band in 1925, when a group of local colored musicians from Montgomery, coupled with graduates and ex-students from Tuskegee Institute (located in nearby Tuskegee, Alabama), came to Montgomery to seek work.

Originally, there were eight members in the band. They were Willie "Buddy" Howard, trombone and vocalist; Samuel Borders, drums; James Bell, clarinet, alto, and soprano saxophone; Philmore "Shorty" Hall, trumpet; Tom Ivery, banjo; Melvin Small, piano; Walter Boyd, tenor saxophone; and Ivory Johnson, tuba.

Borders, Small, Hall, and Bell had all attended Tuskegee and had played in the school band at that college.

The first name of the new band was "the Black Birds." "This was such a common name," said Ivery, "that we decided to change it to the Black Birds of Paradise."

Bell added, "I don't remember who came across that name, or who suggested it, but we all liked it. So we took it."

In 1927, Willie Howard, called "Buddy," secured a recording contract with the struggling young Gennett Record Company of Richmond, Indiana.

The contract was made possible by a Mr. Swett, the manager of a local music store where the group bought and serviced its instruments. Swett contacted Gennett executives in Birmingham, and the company sent one of its talent scouts to negotiate a contract with Howard.

All eight members of the band were required to sign the contract, which prohibited the band from recording with other interested companies for a certain length of time.

One morning in July 1927, the group left for Birmingham and spent an entire day recording at the company's studios at 1820 Third Avenue South.

"We were all tickled to death," Ivery said of the trip. "We didn't even think anything about the amount of money involved, just that we were having a chance to record."

Bell remembers "that company was to have paid us royalties, but we never did get any. They said we had to sell so many records in such a period of time, and we could record again."

Rust's *Jazz Records 1897–1931* (1962) shows six sides were recorded at the first session, probably on July 9, 1927.

"Muddy Water," an old song rearranged by the band, was the first song recorded at the session.

"Bugahoma Blues," the second song of the session, was named after a rough colored neighborhood in Montgomery, near where the band often played (when it played at Washington Park, a local Negro recreational area).

"Tishomingo Blues" was a version of an old blues that the band rearranged and improvised to suit its membership.

"Sugar" was taken from sheet music that the band had bought at one of the local music stores.

"Shim-Me-Sha-Wabble," another instrumental, was taken from a dance by the same name that was popular in the 1920s.

"Razor Edge," another instrumental and the last number in the session, was released on the Gennett-produced affiliate label, Black Patti.

Within three weeks, the band was back in Birmingham, recording three more masters for the Gennett Company. Strangely enough, Ivery can't remember the trip. However, an employee of the local music store owned by Swett does remember the band making two or three trips to Birmingham, since he helped to arrange travel expenses.

Rust shows three titles for the second session of August 10, 1927. Two of the masters, "When Jenny Does That Low Down Dance" and "Indiana Mud" (taken from sheet music), were never released.

The third title, "Stompin' Fool," another wild instrumental, was released on Black Patti 8053 with "Razor Edge" on the reverse side.

Neither Ivery nor Bell can recall having seen the Black Patti issue. This particular record has never been located by a collector and is considered to be one of the unfound masterpieces of jazz.

Evidently, the unreleased titles were not issued, possibly because the band's other titles sold poorly, or because they didn't match the musical quality that Gennett wanted for its race issues.

When the band returned from the recording trips, it went to a photography shop on Dexter Avenue in downtown Montgomery and had two publicity shots made: one, a still with the band's members posed around their instruments; the other, an action shot similar to those made by Chicago photographers of jazz bands in that city.

Ivery, the publicity-minded member of the band, erected a little sign that said EXCLUSIVE GENNETT RECORDING ARTISTS and set it on the floor to be included in one of the photographs.

Apparently, the recordings did little to enforce the Black Birds' reputation in the central Alabama area. The band already had that part of the state completely in its grip.

Bugahoma was a local community in the Montgomery area, where the band sometimes played. Wardlow collection.

Its only competitors in the Montgomery area were the Original Alabama Dominoes (a white dance band), and a colored band that Ivery vaguely remembers by the name of the Triangle Harmony Boys. This band also recorded for Gennett.

The Black Birds consistently outdrew both bands, and each week, for a number of years, the band appeared on Saturday nights at the white country club near Harragut Springs, a small resort area on the outskirts of town.

Most of the Black Birds' music was based on sheet music that the band had purchased in local music stores. The other songs were made up by the various members of the band.

"We had a bushel of music," Ivery said. "We mainly tried to introduce something new that the people had not heard."

This is the method by which such songs as "Bugahoma" were written. Bell played clarinet on "Bugahoma" and "Tishomingo," and alto sax on "Sugar."

Ivery and Bell both agreed that Howard was the best trombonist they ever encountered. "Buddy was an extraordinary trombonist. He played as good with his feet as his hands. He played the slide with his feet to show off. He was just a naturally born musician."

Although members of the Black Birds had listened to early jazz recordings by other bands before they began recording as a unit, both Ivery and Bell felt that this had little effect on their styles.

Notice their closeness to the Frank Bunch sound (also on Gennett)—a Birmingham band, some of whose members were also originally from Tuskegee Institute.

This sound is almost identical in arrangements and ideas. Thus, one may deduce that the Negro musicians of Alabama were developing their own individual style and sound, just as were the New Orleans musicians who had been developing jazz in that area for a number of years.

Both Ivery and Bell recalled hearing older musicians in their area while they were still youngsters. The styles and approaches played by these older

This jazz band, with two records issued on the Gennett label, had its own regional sound, not influenced by typical jazz records recorded in the North. Wardlow collection.

musicians were similar to those used by the Black Birds in their 1927 recordings.

This Alabama jazz style may have evolved from street bands or college and school bands that had been a part of the Negro school education in Alabama's larger towns.

One summer, the Fess Wately band of Birmingham, with the Bunch brothers as members, paid a visit to Washington Park in Montgomery. The two bands engaged in a marathon "jam and battle" session that lasted for hours.

Ivery remembers that it was a close contest but, in all truthfulness, audience applause made the Wately band a slight favorite.

"But we both got paid the same amount, and that was what counted," Ivery said, amused.

In 1930, the band arranged a tour of the middle west, beginning in Texas. This tour caused the first breakup in band membership.

Ivery did not want to make the trip, since he had a steady job as a postal clerk. Others, who had full-time jobs, also did not wish to make the trip. Actually, Howard was the only member of the band who made his living by music alone.

The band, under Howard's leadership, finally broke up in Omaha, Nebraska, in 1931, when Bell and others who did make the trip returned to Montgomery.

Howard stayed in Omaha and played with other bands in that area. He subsequently formed a band of his own.

(It is interesting to speculate whether Howard might have become a member of the Frank Perkins band, a local Negro jazz band in that city. This group appeared on Gennett's subsidiary label, Champion, and was recorded in Richmond, Indiana in 1931. Perhaps, if he was with the band at that time, Howard was the connecting link in securing a recording contract with Gennett.)

By the deepening days of the Depression, the Black Birds of Paradise had disbanded. The members who stayed in Montgomery became part of a new band—the Black Diamonds—under the leadership of Bell.

This band is considered by some in the Montgomery area to have been a better unit than the outfit that spawned it. Unfortunately, it never had a chance to record.

As of 1968, three members of the original Black Birds of Paradise were deceased: Johnson, Small, and Boyd.

Howard was still living in Omaha, and Hall was active in music in North Carolina. Borders had last been heard from in a small town in California.

Bell had only recently retired from the music business and was still actively employed as a top-notch brick mason. He resided at 1209 Roanoke Avenue in a fashionable Negro neighborhood.

Ivery had retired from the U.S. Postal Service and lived close to Bell at 1200 Thurman Avenue.

Ivery summed it all up in these words, "We were a pretty good little juke band, even if I have to say so myself."

Down at the Depot: The Story of John Lee

In 1971, after listening to John Lee's "Alabama Boogie" and his stunner "Blind Blues" recorded for Federal in 1951, I decided to look for him in the Selma-Montgomery area. An indication that Lee knew contemporary acoustic blues was that "Alabama Boogie" was based on Lightnin' Hopkins' "New York Boogie." By playing tapes of his Federal records around Montgomery, I located John Lee in a matter of days. BU editor Mike Leadbitter and others had speculated that John Lee must have had a last name, since John Lee Hooker had one. Surprisingly, he was listed in the phone books as "John A. Lee." Later, he recorded an LP in Montgomery for Rounder (for which I wrote the notes), after I had failed to record him on my own due to his $500 recording fee. Lee was a fantastic knife (not bottleneck) guitar player, a style he learned in 1930 from his uncle.—GDW

[Originally published in *Blues Unlimited* no. 113 (May–June 1975): 12–13.]

"John Lee must be another name. That can't be his full name!" Mike Leadbitter wrote me in 1967. And now that John Lee has been rediscovered, played a concert in Boston, and recorded an album for Rounder Records, the big secret can be let out.

Indeed, this sensitive Alabama bluesman *has* another name—it's simply *Arthur* and it fits nicely between the John and Lee. John Arthur Lee is his complete name and that's it! However, I hasten to add that the 190-pound artist with tints of grey in his hair calls himself John Lee, and he abbreviates the middle name to an "A." He is just plain John A. Lee in the Montgomery phone book, in which he's been listed for more than 25 years. Ironically, the 1951 listing 4-8582 has been altered only by an additional prefix of 264. (This is another story—how much time was spent searching for an artist who was presumed dead or in the northern cities while he was listed in the Montgomery, Alabama, phone directory all the time?)

In retrospect, it's easy to determine the conjecture and speculation for a more complete name than John Lee on the 1951 Federal recordings. The early 1950s belong to another John Lee—Hooker. Therefore, it stands to reason that the John Lee on Federal must have another name, and that the Federals were issued as such for any value the company might accrue from their association with the Hooker name. Composer credits to a mythical-sounding Charles Wersing added to this thinking.

But in the blues we have often found the logical to be the illogical.

When a pattern seems standardized, there arises a finding to counter our theories and assumptions. Well, then, who is John Lee? Where is he from? What's his background, and with whom and where did he play his music?

Born May 24, 1915, at Mt. Willing in Lowdnes County, Alabama, Lee spent his first seven years on the Judge Wood plantation, six miles from nearby Fort Deposit. In 1922, his father moved to better work conditions on a plantation in Conecuh County near Evergreen, Alabama. "We lived out six miles from Evergreen on Mr. Milton Moore's place," Lee recalls. "That is where I really first began to learn about music."

In 1930 the Lee family moved out to Old Spotty, a community where "Evergreen was in slavery times." Lee stayed there until the late 1930s. He visited Youngstown, Ohio, in 1937; worked in Cantonment, Florida, for a year or so in 1938–39; and moved to Montgomery in September 1945.

"When I came to town I came in grand fashion," he says. "I come in on a wagon with a mule. The wagon broke down and I left it standing right there in the middle of the street, downtown. And I ain't left here since!"

Musical ability was abundant in the Lee family—it seems everyone was musically inclined. All of Lee's six brothers, a sister, his parents, an aunt, and an uncle (who also played piano) played the guitar. Father Climon [*sic*] and mother Vallie used a natural or standard tuning when John was still living at Mt. Willing, and an Aunt Cora played in Spanish tuning. "Sometimes I'd just rake my hands across the strings of her guitar," he recalls. "It sounded so good and the way she played made it sound better."

Lee's father played only occasionally; the main influence on Lee's distinctive Alabama style was Uncle Ellie [*sic*] Lee, the best slide guitarist in Evergreen and the county, according to Lee.

Uncle Ellie was to teach Lee to play on both natural and cross natural (open E) tunings. He showed

John A. Lee pictures are hard to come by; there were only 200 of this promotional shot made. Wardlow collection.

Lee the basic structure of "Blind's Blues" and "Depot Blues," both postwar legendary slide performances.

"I got a lot of 'Blind's Blues' from Uncle Ellie," Lee admits. "I'll sing some of his verses now that I learned from him. He was the first man I ever seen play with a pocket knife. I learned how to use a knife from Uncle Ellie and another old man. Coley Smart, from Evergreen, showed me how to hold a bottleneck. But I always like the knife better. It would break and I could hold it better."

Lee holds the knife between his fourth and baby fingers on his left hand and uses one blade approximately five inches long. The dull side of the large blade is used as the slide.

"Down at the Depot" ("Depot Blues") was heavily influenced by Uncle Ellie, but Lee adamantly declares he wrote the lyrics. "That first verse is about me and a fellow who were hoboing out of Brewton. I had the money to buy a ticket, he didn't. He asked the porter—we called him the conductor—if he could ride the train. That man told him the train wasn't his, and he couldn't let him ride. So he got under the train and rode the blinds!"

A third influence on Lee's style was Brewton–East Brewton, Alabama, bluesman Levi Kelly, "who taught me how to choke them strings on a googie to make it sound better. That's what I'm doing on 'Women Blues' (one of the songs recorded for Rounder)," he says. "First songs I ever learned were 'Crow Jane' and 'How Long, How Long,' I learned them both in natural. Uncle Ellie told me that if I learned in natural first, I could play in any chord and play any song I wanted."

John A. Lee, who played in open tunings with a knife, not a bottleneck, recorded four songs in 1951 for Federal at a Montgomery radio station. Blues Archive.

Lee prefers this tuning and the key of C for the majority of his repertoire, which includes songs influenced by Blind Blake, Blind Lemon Jefferson, Leroy Carr, Bessie Smith, and Furry Lewis. Some of these influences are subtle, others are from records, and some are from cross-pollination with other singers who were singing the verses from records.

Lee was also playing a segment of "Blind's Blues" about this same time (1930) and was adapting other songs from records, making up his own verses. This is shown in his adaptation of songs such as "Sloppy Drunk," which has a personal anecdote of a local moonshiner who was almost apprehended by the county sheriff. The man ran into church with the whiskey as services were being conducted, Lee laughingly recalls, and the man received a strong tongue-lashing from the minister who had to hide him from the law!

From these years, Lee sings songs like "Up North Blues," based on the 1937 Youngstown trip, "Women Blues," about a coal-black woman he had one time, "Circle Round the Sun," about an incident in the cotton fields when he was talking "pretty things" to a girl, and a hilarious "Somebody's Been Foolin' You," which represents another side of the man not evident from his Federal recordings. This song is about an old girlfriend, Lottie Stallworth. "She wudn't pretty nor special," Lee says. "But that's the only kind of woman we had way back there in the country then."

"Baby Blues," recorded at the 1951 session, is an original composition, both lyrically and musically. Lee claims, "I was working down in Florida, Cantonment, and I had this woman, she was one of twins. There was two of them looked just alike and I could tell the difference because of this little mole, but no one else couldn't. That is why that verse goes, 'Got two little women, can't tell them apart . . .'" One verse in the song that says, "I love goin' back to Florida where I can have my fun . . ." was *not* lifted from the Tenderfoot Edwards 1929 recording of "Florida Bound." It was based on Lee's experience of working on the paper-mill construction job he had in Cantonment, which is just across the state line and only about 30 miles from Evergreen.

Did Lee ever know Ed Bell? "Nope, I never seen nor heard of the man. I played up around Greenville, but I never met him." What, then, about the mysterious Barefoot Bill, who is often identified as Ed Bell? From his recordings and the Columbia promotional drawing, Lee identifies the man as *Jimmie Lee*. This Jimmie Lee was no relation, and John Lee says he met him in Montgomery at two house parties after World War II.

"Old Pellham, a friend, he introduced me to this fellow. He said something about him making records. I never paid no attention to it though. He had the funniest way of playing, he'd lay the guitar down across his lap and then chord it. He was on his way to Atlanta both times I heard him play, Pellham said he lived over there. He was coming out of somewhere south of here and just passing through." John Lee is convinced Jimmie Lee is the same man, based on the aural evidence presented. A close listening to "Squabblin' Blues" seems to affirm this statement. In the fifth verse, Barefoot Bill says (to the author's ears), "Give it to Amy Lee, Amy don't want it . . ." It seems reasonable to deduce that Jimmie Lee's wife would be Amy Lee and the artist is thus identifying his last name in the song.

Another artist John Lee remembers from a Birmingham gig was 1932 Paramount artist, Jabbo Williams. He says he played a club with Williams and that people also called him "Dink." This was after World War II.

Lee spent most of the 1930s playing fish fries, jukes, and house parties before settling in Montgomery. He says he took the town fast. "There wasn't no musician in here that could run me. They'd see me coming and turn the other way. I had this town sewed up!" According to Lee, there were not as many guitarists in Montgomery as would have been in a town of comparable size in Mississippi.

And that Federal session? Ralph Bass, travelling from Los Angeles, visited the city in 1951 and advertised for talent over radio station WMGY. Bass auditioned Lee and recorded him on the basis of his original material.

He heard Lee play "Blind's Blues" in a practice session in the studio and quickly added it to the titles to be taped. Bass thought it would be the session hit. Instead, "Alabama Boogie," written for the session, was the best seller.

Lee says, "Now Lightning Hopkins had cut a song 'New York Boogie' about his own state" (Lee thought this was Hopkins' residence) "and I decided that I could put one out about my home state. That is how come I wrote 'Alabama Boogie,'" he brags. A local dee-jay, Chuck Elliot, who used the personality name of Charles Wernsing, was involved in the session. Wernsing's name appeared on the records as composer and this led to the conjecture that Wernsing was Lee's last name.

Regardless of the role played by Wernsing, Lee was bitter over the session, claiming that he was never properly paid and never received royalties promised. He says he still has his contract, and split the $100 dollars paid for the session with Wernsing. Wernsing has been unavailable for his side of the story.

By 1960 Lee had discontinued his musical activity and was dormant until he was rediscovered by this writer.

[EK: There had been some interest in John Lee before Wardlow published this article in 1975. As early as February 1965, *Blues Unlimited* (no. 19: 11) printed an extract of a letter from Bernard Pearlman of the King and Federal labels, stating emphatically that John Lee was not the same person as John Lee Hooker. Nevertheless, speculation about who John Lee was continued at such a pitch that in February 1966 *BU* editor Mike Leadbitter (no. 30: 13) reminded readers to take Pearlman's statement into account. Wardlow's 1971 rediscovery of Lee led to a 1973 Rounder recording session, an appearance at the 1974 National Folk Festival at Wolf Trap (Vienna, Virginia), and a *Living Blues* profile by Frank Scott (1974).]

Searching for the Robert Johnson Death Certificate

(1965–1968)

In the late 1950s I began reading articles on jazz and blues, including Paul Oliver's book Blues Fell This Morning *(1960). Another book, Orrin Keepnews and Bill Grauer's* A Pictorial History of Jazz *(1955), contained a death certificate for Bix Beiderbecke. In 1965 as a newspaper reporter, I discovered that birth and death records were kept by the state of Mississippi. Armed with four dollars (one dollar per document), I sought out the Bureau of Vital Statistics in Jackson and filed for death certificates on Charlie Patton, Willie Brown, Tommy Johnson, and Robert Johnson. Within a week I received the Patton, Brown, and Tommy Johnson certificates, but not the one for Robert Johnson based on the information I supplied. The Patton and Brown documents were published, and the details from the Tommy Johnson one were provided to a California researcher, David Evans. I then spent three years requesting a Robert Johnson death certificate from the states of Texas, Arkansas, and Tennessee. The correct location of Greenwood, Mississippi, as the site of Johnson's death was given by David "Honey Boy" Edwards to Pete Welding (in an interview conducted on July 29, 1967, but not published in* Blues Unlimited *until June 1968), and with that detail I found the certificate on January 11, 1968. —GDW*

[Originally published in *Blues Revue Quarterly* no. 6 (Fall 1992): 26]

By 1965, a number of legendary country blues singers had been redis-covered, including Son House (1965, 42), who told of memories of having Robert Johnson listen to House and Willie Brown's playing at house parties around Tunica County and the Robinsonville and Lake Cormorant areas. House told interviewers that he had heard Johnson was murdered, but he didn't know where.

All that was known of Johnson had come from Don Law (Driggs 1962), ARC's Dallas recording director, who had recorded Johnson in San Antonio in 1936 and 1937. He said Johnson was barely out of his teens and appeared to be only 18 or 19 years old when he had recorded.

No one knew where Johnson died. Was it in Mississippi, Arkansas, or Texas?

That same summer of 1965, I located Willie Moore and his wife Elizabeth Glynn Moore living at Tutwiler. Both had known Johnson in the Robin-

STATE OF MISSISSIPPI

MISSISSIPPI STATE DEPARTMENT OF HEALTH
VITAL RECORDS

BUREAU OF VITAL STATISTICS — **STANDARD CERTIFICATE OF DEATH** — State File No. 13704

MISSISSIPPI STATE BOARD OF HEALTH

1. PLACE OF DEATH

County _Leflore_ .... Registered No. ....

Voting Precinct .... or Village ....

or City _Greenwood (outside)_ (No. .... St., ... Ward)

(If death occurred in a hospital or institution, give its NAME instead of street and number)

Length of residence in city or town where death occurred? yrs. mos. ds. How long in U. S. if of foreign birth? yrs. mos. ds.

2. FULL NAME _Robert L. Johnson_ (Write or Print Name Plainly)

(a) Residence: No. _Greenwood Miss._ St., ... Ward.
(Usual place of abode) (If nonresident give city or town and State)

PERSONAL AND STATISTICAL PARTICULARS	MEDICAL CERTIFICATE OF DEATH
3. SEX _M_ 4. COLOR OR RACE _B_ 5. Single, Married, Widowed, or Divorced (write the word) _single_	21. DATE OF DEATH (month, day and year) _8-16-38_
5a. If married, widowed, or divorced HUSBAND of (or) WIFE of	22. I HEREBY CERTIFY, That I attended deceased from ...., 19...... to ...., 19...... I last saw h...... alive on ...., 19...... Death is said to have occurred on the date stated above, at .... m.
6. DATE OF BIRTH (month, day, and year) 7. AGE Years _26_ Months Days If LESS than 1 day, ... hrs. or ...... min.	The principal cause of death and related causes of importance in order of onset were as follows: Date of onset
8. Trade, profession, or particular kind of work done, as spinner, sawyer, bookkeeper, etc...... _Musician_ 9. Industry or business in which work was done, as silk mill, saw mill, bank, etc......	Contributory causes of importance not related to principal cause: _2-2 B_
10. Date deceased last worked at this occupation (month and year) _July 1938_ 11. Total time (years) spent in this occupation _10_	_no Doctor_ Name of operation (if any was done) .... Date of ....
12. BIRTHPLACE (city or town) (State or country) _Hazlehurst Miss_	What test confirmed diagnosis? .... Was there an autopsy? ....
13. NAME _Noah Johnson_	
14. BIRTHPLACE (city or town) (State or country) _D.K._	23. If death was due to external causes (violence) fill in also the following: Accident, suicide, or homicide? .... 19......
15. MAIDEN NAME _Julia Major_	Date of injury .... 19......
16. BIRTHPLACE (city or town) (State or country) _Miss_	Where did injury occur? .... (Specify city or town, county, and State) Specify whether injury occurred in industry, in home, or in public place
17. INFORMANT (and Address) _Jim Moore_	Manner of injury .... Nature of injury ....
18. BURIAL, CREMATION, OR REMOVAL Place _Zion Church_ Date _8-17_, 19_38_	24. Was disease or injury in any way related to occupation of deceased? .... If so, specify ....
19. UNDERTAKER (and Address) _Family_	(Signed) .... M. D.
20. FILED _8-18-38_, 19...... _Cornelia J. Jordan_ Registrar.	(Address) ....

THIS IS TO CERTIFY THAT THE ABOVE IS A TRUE AND CORRECT COPY OF THE CERTIFICATE ON FILE IN THIS OFFICE

F. E. Thompson Jr. MD
F. E. Thompson, Jr., M.D., M.P.H.
STATE HEALTH OFFICER

JUL -9 96

Nita Cox Gunter
Nita Cox Gunter
STATE REGISTRAR

WARNING: A REPRODUCTION OF THIS DOCUMENT RENDERS IT VOID AND INVALID. DO NOT ACCEPT UNLESS EMBOSSED SEAL OF THE MISSISSIPPI STATE BOARD OF HEALTH IS PRESENT. IT IS ILLEGAL TO ALTER OR COUNTERFEIT THIS DOCUMENT.

THE FACE OF THIS DOCUMENT HAS A COLORED BACKGROUND ON WHITE PAPER. THIS IS WATERMARKED PAPER. DO NOT ACCEPT WITHOUT FIRST HOLDING TO LIGHT TO VERIFY WATERMARK

Text on left margin: FORM V. S. No. 1 — N. B.—WRITE PLAINLY, WITH UNFADING INK.—THIS IS A PERMANENT RECORD. AGE should be stated EXACTLY. PHYSICIANS should be careful to state CAUSE OF DEATH in plain terms, so that it may be properly classified. Exact statement of OCCUPATION is very important. See instructions on back of certificate. MARGIN RESERVED FOR BINDING. Every item of information should be carefully supplied.

This document—the first published information on Johnson's life from public records—was found in 1968 after "Honey Boy" Edwards said Johnson was killed near Greenwood. A larger 1996 copy is used here for better legibility. Wardlow collection.

sonville area, and on one occasion Willie was even jailed with Johnson (who called himself Robert Sax) for singing disrespectfully about the high sheriff of Robinsonville, a Mr. Woolfork. They stayed in jail only a few hours.

When I interviewed Willie further, he told me he had been in Missouri when Johnson's death occurred. He said he heard that Johnson was shot to death near Eudora, Mississippi, on the way to Hernando from Robinsonville. Like other rumors of Johnson's death, Willie heard Johnson reportedly was murdered over a woman.

That same summer, using a device I had learned as a journalist, I went to the Bureau of Vital Statistics—part of the State Department of Public Health—and filled out the forms for death certificates on Charlie Patton, Willie Brown, Tommy Johnson, and Robert Johnson.

The bureau found the certificates on Patton (1934), Tommy Johnson (1956), and Brown (1952). But they did not turn up a certificate on Robert Johnson, after checking the files for 1937 to 1940. At that time it was assumed Johnson must have died in 1938, because of the publication about a scheduled appearance at Carnegie Hall in December 1938 that John Hammond had put together (Hammond 1938, 27).

So, it was back to the basics. Maybe Johnson died in Arkansas, as Elizabeth later told me. She was living out of Mississippi when Johnson was reportedly killed. When she came back to Mississippi in 1939, she heard that Johnson was shot to death in Helena, Arkansas, where he was playing at a club called the Hole in the Wall, a juke in the downtown black section of Helena.

This blues standard was popularized by the Rolling Stones in the 1960s. Blues Archives.

So I wrote to the Bureau of Vital Statistics in Little Rock and requested a search be made for a death certificate. Back came a negative reply. No death certificate existed for a Robert Johnson in the State of Arkansas in those years specified. Perplexed, I decided to send a request to the State Health Department in Austin, Texas. Perhaps Johnson was killed in that state. The Health Department replied with a certificate for a Robert Earl Johnson who died in 1938. The only problem was that this Johnson was white, and obviously not the right man.

The record exemplifies "damping" by Johnson, or holding the palm against the strings to get more bass rhythm. Blues Archives.

That left one other possibility: Tennessee. So in 1967, I tried the state of Tennessee and they came up negative also. Logically, it seemed that if Johnson was murdered, then perhaps it was never reported to the authorities—not an unbelievable situation for a black man in the 1930s in the Deep South.

Late in 1967 Pete Welding, a blues columnist with *Down Beat*, interviewed David "Honey Boy" Edwards of Greenwood about his past associations with Mississippi bluesmen. Edwards told Welding that Johnson was killed near Greenwood, and that he was living in Greenwood when Johnson died in 1938 or thereabouts (see Welding 1968, 10–11).

One more time I decided to try the Bureau of Vital Statistics in Jackson to see if they could find a certificate. I didn't have much hope, as they had already checked from 1937 to 1940 two years earlier. Strangely, a letter came back with a death certificate on a Robert L. Johnson who died August 16, 1938, in LeFlore County near Greenwood. In the earlier search they had looked only in Montgomery and Tunica counties. When they searched in LeFlore County, of which Greenwood is the county seat, they found the document and dated it January 11, 1968.

As *Blues Revue Quarterly* (1992) readers now know, the certificate con-

Both Willie Moore (Moses Alexander) and his wife Elizabeth Glynn Moore knew Robert personally. Elizabeth knew Johnson's mother and Willie was once arrested (and jailed for a few hours) with Robert. Wardlow collection.

firmed that Johnson was at least 26 years old and had been born in Hazelhurst, Mississippi—previously unknown information. The certificate also listed his mother's and father's names. There was no doubt it was the right Johnson because of the occupational listing of musician.

The death certificate was first published in 1971 in *Blues Unlimited* of England (Calt 1971).

In retrospect, the document easily could have been found in 1965 if authorities had looked under LeFlore County as well as Tunica and Montgomery counties.

[For more on Johnson, in addition to the following article, "Robert Johnson: New Details on the Death of a Bluesman," see "Stop, Look, and Listen at the Cross Road," page 196, for a detailed exploration of the legend that Robert Johnson sold his soul to the devil.]

Robert Johnson: New Details on the Death of a Bluesman

Johnson's Death Certificate and Its Previously Unseen Flip Side

[Originally published in *Guitar Player* 30, no. 11 (November 1996): 29–32]

Robert Johnson's death in 1938 has spawned more questions and controversies than any other event in blues history. A recently discovered document sheds new light on what may have happened.

After a three-year search through four states, I found a copy of Robert Johnson's death certificate in '68, and it was first published in '71. In the space for the cause of death, the certificate simply stated "no doctor." Through the years, rumors circulated that Johnson had been poisoned at a house party and died a few days later in Greenwood, Mississippi. His friends "Honey Boy" Edwards and Johnny Shines recalled that near the end, "Robert was crawling along the ground on all fours, barking and snapping like a mad beast."

A recent search of the Vital Statistics section of the Mississippi State Department of Health turned up previously unknown information on the back of the original Robert Johnson death certificate. The document contains this investigative report by LeFlore County Registrar Cornelia J. Jordan:

I talked with the white man on whose place this negro died and I also talked with a negro woman on the place. The plantation owner said this negro man, seemingly about 26 years old, came from Tunica two or three weeks before he died to play a banjo at a negro dance given there on the plantation. He staid [*sic*] in the house with some of the negroes saying he wanted to pick cotton. The white man did not have a doctor for this negro as he had not worked for him. He was buried in a homemade coffin furnished by the county. The plantation owner said it was his opinion that the negro died of syphilis.

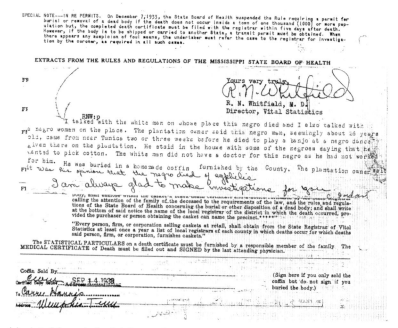

Inquiries into Johnson's death led to an investigation which ultimately determined his death was not a murder. Wardlow collection.

The document also reveals that on September 14, 1938, a copy of the death certificate was made for a woman who may have been Johnson's relative, Carrie Harris of Memphis, Tennessee.

Dr. Walter Holladay, who headed a state charity hospital for more than 20 years, offers the opinion that if Johnson had congenital syphilis—meaning he was born with it—an aneurysm of vital blood vessels could have caused his death at age 26. Johnson's medical problem could have been compounded if he were drinking moonshine, which he was known to do. The descriptions of Edwards and Shines suggest another possibility to Holladay: "A combination of poison, drinking moonshine, and liver damage could have caused pneumonia." Penicillin, the first cure for syphilis and an effective treatment for pneumonia, was not available to the public until after World War II.

"As to what finally killed him," says Holladay, "it's still just speculation. Without an autopsy it would be impossible to know for certain."

[EK: The publishing history of the Robert Johnson death certificate has been a curious one. Although Wardlow found it in 1968, he retained it among his research papers for a book he was cowriting with Stephen Calt. Evidently the *Blues Unlimited* editors soon learned of this document, for it appended "Quo vadis Robert Johnson?" to a caption for the Joe Hill Louis death certificate it published in February/March 1971. Nine months later, the obverse of the Johnson certificate that Wardlow recovered in 1968 was published, with a commentary by Stephen Calt ("Robert Johnson Recapitu-

VOCALION RECORDS 11

BERTHA "CHIPPIE" HILL
(Vocal Blues with Inst. Acc.)
04379 Georgia Man
04379 Trouble in Mind

HUNTER & JENKINS
(Vocal Blues with Inst. Acc.)
02613 Lollypop
02613 Meat Cuttin' Blues

ROBERT JOHNSON
(Vocal Blues with Guitar Acc.)
04002 Honeymoon Blues
03416 Kind Hearted Woman Blues
04108 Little Queen of Spades
04630 Love in Vain Blues
03665 Malted Milk
04108 Me and the Devil Blues
03665 Milkcow's Calf Blues
04630 Preachin' Blues
04002 Stop Breakin' Down Blues
03601 Sweet Home Chicago
03416 Terraplane Blues
03601 Walkin' Blues

BLIND WILLIE JOHNSON
(Sacred Singing)
03095 Dark Was the Night—Cold
        Was the Ground
03021 If I Had My Way I'd Tear the
        Building Down
03095 It's Nobody's Fault But Mine
03021 Mother's Children Have a
        Hard Time

**L. JOHNSON and
CLARENCE WILLIAMS**
(Vocal Blues with Inst. Acc.)
03013 Wipe It Off

03953 My Baby's Getting Buggish
04570 Night Life Blues
04162 Palace Blues
04392 Pocket-Book Blues
05071 Private Talk Blues
04080 Reckless Life Blues
04520 Reefer Hound Blues
04693 Roll Me Mama
04857 Sad, Lonely and Crying Blues*
04520 War Broke Out in Hell
04950 Who You Lovin'
04330 Who You're Hunchin'
03756 You Got Good Business

FRANKIE JONES
(Vocal Blues with Inst. Acc.)
04206 Bring Your Mud and Let's
        Dab
04266 Gamblin' Man
04266 Jockey Blues
04206 My Lincoln

SONNY JONES
05056 Dough Roller
05056 Love Me With a Feeling

LILLIE MAE KIRKMAN
(Vocal Blues with Inst. Acc.)
04951 Hop Head Blues
04951 It's A Hard Way to Travel
04991 What Evil Have I Done?
04991 When You Leave Me Honey

LITTLE SON JOE
(Vocal Blues with Inst. Acc.)
04776 A. B. C. Blues
04776 Bone Yard Blues
04707 Diggin' My Potatoes
05004 Key To The World
04978 My Black Buffalo
04707 Tuff Luck Blues

04356 I Hate to See the Sun go Down
04506 I'd Rather See Him Dead
03285 If You See My Rooster
03258 I'm a Gamblin' Woman
03474 It's Hard to be Mistreated
04250 I've Been Treated Wrong
03046 Joe Louis Strut
04295 Keep on Eating
04356 Keep on Walking
04858 Keep Your Big Mouth Closed
04506 Long as I Can See You Smile
04797 Low Down Man Blues
03474 Man You Won't Give Me No
        Money
03285 My Strange Man
03966 New Caught Me Wrong Again
03697 No Need You Doggin' Me
05004 Poor And Wandering Woman
        Blues
03966 Walking and Crying Blues
04898 Worried Baby Blues
03697 You Can't Rule Me

**MITCHELL'S CHRISTIAN
SINGERS**
(Spiritual Singing)
04783 Ain't Gonna Lay My Receiver
        Down
04844 Are You Living Humble
03235 Blessed Are the Poor in Spirit
04472 Brother Come On In
03016 Come on Ezekiel Let's Go
        'Round the Wall
03016 Count Out the Angels
04844 Drinkin' of the Holy Wine
03099 Got My Ticket
03279 Hide Me, Oh Lord
04394 How About You
03180 I Don't Care Where You Bury
        My Body
04418 I Got a Letter from Jesus
03409 I Got to Go to Judgment
04913 I Have A Home In Yonder
        City

1939 Vocalion catalog page with listings for Robert Johnson. Blues Archives.

lated," 1971). Oddly, the detail from the reverse about the coffin provided by LeFlore County later showed up in print, in Alan Greenberg's published screenplay *Love in Vain* (1983, 248), and in Steve LaVere's booklet to *Robert Johnson: The Complete Recordings* (1990, 18). Only with Wardlow's 1996 publication of the document were both sides presented.

At first, the certificate was thought to have been illegally filed, casting doubts on its contents. In his 1971 analysis of the obverse alone, Stephen Calt thought the document was "illegal," since a 1925 Mississippi state law required a notification of a "local health officer" to investigate any death unattended by medical aid. With the reverse now available, it confirms that LeFlore County Registrar Cornelia Jordan conducted the investigation for the state director of Vital Statistics, R.N. Whitfield. Regardless of the extent to which Jordan's 1938 inquiry gave the certificate legal status, it has not dispelled the doubts of some readers about its credibility, such as that expressed by *Blues Access* (Winter 1997, 108): "On the other hand, as a friend of ours notes, we wonder how many blacks in [19]30s Mississippi were pronounced dead of syphilis . . . with bullet holes in the backs of their heads?"

Such a casual dismissal as that of *Blues Access* should not be made until individual details are fully verified. Chief among the unanswered questions is Jim Moore, the listed informant. If his identity and plantation affiliation can be found, then the specific "Zion Church" (a common name for black churches) can be pinpointed, and thus the vicinity of Greenwood where Johnson died and was buried can be better established. However, if doubts about the certificate's credibility remain after all the notes have been accounted for, then the document may be taken at less than its face value.]

Patton's Murder— Whitewash? Or Hogwash?

Gayle Dean Wardlow and Jacques Roche [Stephen Calt]

In the first issue of 78 Quarterly, the diplomatic Pete Whelan paired Stephen Calt and me for an article on Charlie Patton on the death certificate I obtained in 1965. This was the first such certificate to be published in the blues literature. To meet the publisher's request, this article has been shortened. —GDW

[Originally published in *78 Quarterly* no. 1 (1967): 10–17.]

One of the more peculiar aspects of blues research is the frequency of encounters with conflicting and even preposterous death stories concerning a well-known blues singer. For reasons to be explained later, such an aura of mystery tends to surround the deaths or disappearances of certain singers that the features of their actual lives become eclipsed in the minds of both the public at large and singers' own contemporaries.

In some cases, particularly that of Bessie Smith—who died, according to her last manager, not dramatically on the doorstep of a segregated hospital, but in a car collision (Oliver 1961, 70–71, but see also Albertson 1972, 215–226)—the myth is bound up in cultural lore. In the lesser known example of Charlie Patton, the intrigue mushrooms the more one approaches direct sources of biographical information.

Blues research can bare hysterical rumors in the context of their broad cultural function. The Patton researcher confronts a credibility gap from the outset, in which rumors of both violent and natural death are *equally* suspect. This is due to the fact that legends of Patton's violent death did not spread far beyond the confines of rural black society. Whatever function such stories did serve must be limited to that culture that was shaped by the cotton economy of the flat Mississippi Delta.

As of 1967, no one has come forth from the Delta with a Bill Broonzy–like claim of "telling it the way it was" in regards to Patton. As Skip James—who in Mississippi 30 years ago frequently encountered rumors concerning the violent deaths of both Patton and himself—put it: "A lot of people may say a lot of things about Charlie's death, and a lot of 'em weren't with him when he died, either; that much you can bet on."

This death certificate was first found in 1965 in Mississippi's Vital Records department. Public records like these are more reliable than oral reports. Wardlow collection.

In May 1963, sharecropper Jim Edwards of Cleveland (a small town some 30 miles south of Clarksdale, Mississippi) stated that Patton died from heart trouble in 1934 in the town of Longswitch, near Leland.

Two months later, one of Patton's many wives, Minnie Franklin Washington, remarked that although she had heard that Patton died in 1934 of natural causes following a prolonged illness, she strongly suspected that he drank himself to death.

Both Edwards and Mrs. Washington were correct in one statement: Patton did die in 1934.

In July 1963, Bernard Klatzko and Gayle Dean Wardlow were told in tiny Holly Ridge that Patton died there and not in Longswitch, which, though a mere mile away, no longer even existed. It was then "established" that Patton died in a house across from Tom Robinson's store (the only one in Holly Ridge) immediately after returning from a recording trip to New York—probably in late February or March of 1934. A grave site, which they were not allowed to inspect, added credence to these statements. An elderly black woman who guarded Charlie's grave was not interested in how he died. [EK: See Klatzko's "The Immortal Charlie Patton, " page 18, for an account of this incident.]

After the trip, Mr. Wardlow was told independently that Patton died from a slit throat, having bled to death in the aftermath of the butcher-knife attack inflicted by a woman with whom he was then living.

The story of a cutting, which did actually take place (in Cleveland around 1930, shortly after Patton's arrival there from Will Dockery's plantation nearby), was widely repeated throughout the Delta, and over the years eventually was carried to Chicago. There, in a small club, even Howlin' Wolf recounted the story to Mr. Klatzko in the presence of other former Patton acquaintances.

This story was, in effect, repeated by Booker Washington White on an album recorded for Takoma (White 1963) wherein White, in a breezy manner, implied that Patton had been knifed and killed by a "sandfoot" (or "no-good," barrelhousing woman).

Since Patton bore an ugly, wicked scar across the side of his throat, it is easy to guess where this rumor originated. Yet, actual members of Patton's family, while confirming a knifing episode, squashed the rumor of death by that means.

The process of zeroing in on Patton's few intimates has otherwise served only to bring old legends to light. Hayes McMullan, an acquaintance of Patton and Willie Brown, heard that Patton was struck and instantly killed by a lightning bolt. This rumor may be taken as a fulfillment of the prophecies of zealous churchgoers who believed that God would literally strike down those who followed the devil in singing "his" blues.

Regarding the clergy, Patton used "Elder Greene Blues" as a vehicle for attributing to them—with some justice—all of the vices that made the blues singer unacceptable to them. Yet, through his own penchant for preaching without credentials, Patton called flagrant attention to himself as an imitator of the Elder Greene ilk and thus made the "lightning bolt" rumor plausible.

The explanatory telegram Son House (who often performed with Patton) received from Patton's averred widow stated that Patton died from the mumps (House 1965).

However, the recently recovered death certificate reveals that he died of a heart attack. From this document the true facts can be reconstructed—assuming the reliability of the on-the-scene witnesses.

According to his attending physician, whose handwriting is difficult to transcribe, Patton died of a mitral valve disorder. Both Klatzko and Wardlow were told as much, along with the (now substantiated) fact that Patton had visited a doctor as late as the week before his death.

A number of interesting biographical points are suggested by the jumbled notations, which will now be examined in full.

Patton died in Sunflower County on April 28, 1934, and not February as reported. At the time of his death, he was living at 350 Heathman Street in the black sector of Indianola, a town some ten miles from Holly Ridge. This structure, in which Patton undoubtedly died, no longer stands.

Surprisingly, Patton's age was given as 44, indicating a birth date of 1890 or 1889 (from May onwards). Previously, it was thought that Patton had been born in 1887 because his sister, Viola Cannon of Cleveland, and a former wife, Minnie Franklin Washington, had concurred on that year.

The new date probably came from Patton himself. Since the name of the informant, Willie Calvin, was entered in the handwriting of the registrar (one Dollie Trotter) on the day after Patton's death, the witness in question would seem to have collaborated on early-acquired information. Although an informant for a death certificate is usually a relative, spouse, or close friend, the name "Willie Calvin" had never been encountered in the course of extensive research on Patton. Since the informant no longer lives in the vicinity of Indianola, and left no relatives or forwarding address behind, the possibility still remains that the birth date for Patton could be erroneous.

However, for Patton to speak of his birth to Willie Calvin would mark a departure from his general rule of not discussing his personal life. Son House could never get Patton to reveal his birth date, which by House's own guess would lag some ten years behind the Mississippi certificate date.

Other facts, such as the listing of his birthplace (Hinds County) and that of his parents' names (Bill and Amy), agree with the previously collected data. The centrally located county of Hinds, with its seat at Jackson, was Patton's home until around 1900. Thus, an original master of the Delta blues probably did not move there until the Delta blues style had already begun.

The certificate shows that the registrar completed the listing of Patton's address (which was probably furnished by Willie Calvin) and respelled his name as "Charlie." This revision is favored today by his *Origin Jazz Library* reissuers, who have dropped the "Charley" used on his Paramount recordings, while maintaining both the ARC-Vocalion and Gennett ledger versions. Patton himself, who could neither read nor write, spelled his first name orally as "Charlie."

The undertaker's name is listed as the Central Burial Association, which was a local black funeral home. The mere fact that Patton received a formal burial tends to suggest that he had met a nonviolent death.

Other debatable aspects of Patton's death arise from the certificate's more important entries. Two are the cause of death and the duration of Patton's last illness. Although the doctor wrote that he treated Patton from April 17–20, he gave an oddly precise figure—92 days—to represent the duration of the fatal illness. This figure seems to have been written over an earlier notation of 13 days.

Any explanation of the discrepancy between the two dates must be purely conjectural. One possibility is that the entry of 13 days, which goes back to the day before Patton originally visited the doctor, was given by Charlie himself and referred to his awareness of acute symptoms. The 92-day figure, which would closely correspond to the date on which Patton's final recording session was completed, might have been written in after someone (possibly Willie Calvin) suggested that Patton had been feeling sick "since he came back from New York."

Another misleading impression comes from the alleged cause of death, for mitral valve trouble is only a secondary cause of general heart failure and would normally be listed as such on a death certificate. In itself a *sequela* (a diseased condition resulting from a previous disease), a mitral valve disorder does not lend itself to a "duration of illness" entry at all.

This ad was featured in late 1929 in the Chicago Defender, *the premier black paper before World War II that ran weekly ads for race records. Blues Archive.*

Although a mitral valve disorder would have been obvious to a doctor of Patton's generation, its actual role in the death could not be stated without an autopsy. Considering the other factors in Patton's medical history, his doctor should have ruled on its potential for causing Patton's death. (The severity of a mitral case cannot be determined via stethoscope.)

Unless congenital, Patton's mitral valve defect could have been caused either by rheumatic fever before puberty, or by syphilis some 20 years before the appearance of heart symptoms. In the early 1900s, the chances were "99.9 to .1," according to one medical source, that rheumatic fever would produce a mitral heart condition.

Patton's mitral valve defect could have fallen into one of two categories, which would in turn have determined the severity of his symptoms. If his was a mitral stenosis case (suffering from a contracted valve), Patton's ensuing symptoms would have been manifest over the last five years of his life. In a case of mitral insufficiency (with a loose valve), these symptoms would have appeared, in an acute form, during the last three months of Patton's life.

Although the severity of the symptoms would vary from case to case, they would have limited his performance as a musician and as a laborer, and would have progressively worsened without medical treatment. By the time Patton was treated in Indianola, the effects of his heart condition—such as shortness of breath, general anemia, stomach disorders, and the presence of blood in his phlegm—could easily have indicated that his case had reached the terminal stage.

Confronted by such an unfavorable prognosis, Patton's doctor might have seen hospitalization as useless. At the same time, he would have seen enough evidence of a rampant heart condition to have accurately certified Patton's death. The fact that Patton paid at least two visits to the doctor would indicate that he was instead being treated with a drug (digitalis) to make his enlarged heart work faster.

Patton's earlier heart symptoms would have been masked by heavy drinking and chain-smoking, to which his physical condition could have been wrongly attributed. Contrary to the belief of one ex-wife, Minnie Franklin Washington, Patton's drinking could not in itself have affected his heart condition. Despite a report that Patton ignored a doctor's advice to stop drinking, alcoholism was rightly omitted from the death certificate.

On the other hand, that Patton slept or rested little during the last week of his life could have hastened his death.

If Patton's heart condition

Blind Lemon, who was Paramount's best seller from 1926 until his death in late 1929 in Chicago, visited Mississippi on at least two occasions. Courtesy Maxey Tarpley.

had been of a stenosis character, his career as a blues singer would have been hampered by the time of his first Paramount session in June 1929. Significantly or not, Patton gasps for breath at one point on "High Water Everywhere, Part II."

According to Son House, Patton's records greatly surpassed his live performances, and that could conceivably be explained by his medical condition. During live performances, which according to House might extend for three hours or more, Patton was sometimes known to favor a "lazy" vocal style (such as can be heard on "Green River Blues") and to rely on clowning techniques as much as actual blues-playing to keep his audience.

But House saw no visible trace of heart disease during his acquaintance with Patton. Some symptoms, which must have developed unobserved by House, were noticed by others who knew Patton. These, imparted to Bernard Klatzko by Bertha Lee (who accompanied him on his last recording trip), consisted of the exhaustion that Patton felt after a night's performance and the pain experienced whenever he tried to sleep on his back. The latter symptom may be the result of poor blood circulation and is typical of heart disease. (From another view, House said that Patton never slept on his back, but would often turn and bellow in his sleep.) Neither House nor Bertha Lee knew Patton before 1929. It is thus unlikely that origins of his mitral valve disorder will ever be verified.

The existence of this death certificate clarifies some of his personal history. None of Patton's known wives bear initials that match or are even similar to "W.K." (or, possibly, "D.K."). The absence of Bertha Lee Pate's name as wife or even as informant tends to bear out the persistent report that Patton, for all his "marriages," was anything but monogamous. However, Patton did not die in Holly Ridge where she had previously lived with him.

The fact that Patton's last address was apparently given by a Willie Calvin, further suggests that Patton had been living with her when he died. None of his long-standing male companions recognize the name "Willie Calvin."

That Patton is listed as a farmer—and not as a musician—indicates the lack of social status for blues musicians in Patton's time. Such a listing, however, does not imply that music was a "personal pastime" for a professional bluesman.

In 1929, while living on Jeffrey's plantation near Lula (across the Mississippi from Helena, Arkansas), Patton told a friend in reference to his wife: "She's killing me. She's starving me." Son House laughingly recounted Patton's successful ability to live off food stolen by ever-obliging cooks. Patton's possibly recurrent belief that he was being poisoned would be explainable on quite simple grounds: an undiagnosed "mitral" stomach.

Bukka White:
From Aberdeen to Parchman

The background on Booker T. Washington "Bukka" White came from court documents in the Monroe County Circuit Court clerk's office in Aberdeen, Mississippi. The records there factually document that White was sentenced to life imprisonment in Parchman Penitentiary for murdering another man. In contrast to some recent academic trends—which maintain that oral evidence is fully trustworthy—court records are irrefutable concerning marriages, alleged crimes until proven, transfer of property, and actual court testimony. —GDW

One of the major hazards for a prewar bluesman was the ever-present danger of violence from jealous or drunken husbands and boyfriends. As Mississippi Delta musician Willie Morris told Stephen Calt of Delta males: "Shit man, them guys down there, if they see you around their woman and they caught up with you, they'd kill you. They'd go out there and get their cotton field women; you know, if one quit 'em, and they couldn't get another one, they'd kill you." (Wardlow and Calt 1989, 226).

It was not uncommon in the rural South for a county sheriff to be called to a juke house or a house party to break up a drunken disturbance, or to investigate a reported felony such as aggravated assault (intending to kill someone with a weapon) or an actual slaying.

Most bluesmen had violent encounters that led to scars or even death. Charlie Patton, according to David "Honey Boy" Edwards, received a slit throat at a Holly Ridge frolic. "One of the old guys cut him," Edwards remembered. "It was a deep cut in his vein . . . a bad cut" (Wardlow and Calt 1989, 226–227). Earlier in his career, Patton was shot in a club in Helena, reportedly at the Hole in the Wall; later Patton himself told his protégé Booker Miller that his limp had been caused by a gunshot wound (Wardlow and Calt 1989, 149).

Bukka (Washington) White, who served time at Parchman for a 1937 murder conviction, recorded a number of spirituals at his 1930 blues session.

Miller himself, who always carried a .38 pistol in his belt, once was almost killed when a drunken partygoer tried to get his guitar and play it. When Miller refused him and then turned around, the drunk swung with a "dog iron" from the fireplace, missing when Miller bent down in the nick of time. "I guess it wasn't my time to go," Miller recalled in a 1968 interview. "If I hadn't bent over, he would have killed me for sho'."

Ishmon Bracey remembered a south Jackson party at which a man objected to Bracey's friendly exchanges with the man's wife. The dispute was resolved by another's intervention, but when Bracey later turned down the man's offer of whiskey, the man attacked him. (For the whole anecdote, see "Got Four, Five Puppies, One Little Shaggy Hound," page 45.)

The mostly widely publicized blues crimes and convictions involved Booker T. Washington "Bukka" White and Eddie "Son" House Jr., both of whom were sentenced to Parchman for felony convictions (a crime that requires jail time in a state penitentiary, from one year to life or execution). By contrast, a misdemeanor conviction (or a less serious crime) placed a number of bluesmen on the county farm for terms up to a year.

In his *Story of the Blues* (1969, 121), the legendary Paul Oliver reported that Bukka White "drew a gun in a muddled fracas and killed a man. Though he recorded a couple of titles in early September [1937]—one story says he broke bond to do so—he was in Parchman Farm within the month. Conditions on Parchman at this time were vile and Bukka was lucky that his playing saved him from too much heavy labor. When his release was secured after two years by Lester Melrose, he could think of hardly anything else but trains, drink, prison and death, the subjects of all his blues."

In a 1981 interview essay on the life of Bukka White, folklorist researchers F. Jack Hurley and David Evans reported that Oliver's research was incorrect. They wrote (p. 172): "For example, as recently as 1969 the noted English blues writer, Paul Oliver, in *The Story of the Blues*, wrote that Bukka killed a man 'in a muddled fracas' and was sentenced to a long prison term. Oliver also states that his release was obtained after two years by his music agent, Lester Melrose. None of this fits the facts as Bukka related them. Bukka did not kill a man. He shot a man, as he said, 'where I wanted to shoot him.'

In Mississippi in those days such a scrape between two blacks was common enough to elicit little reaction from the courts. Bukka was, in fact, sentenced to two years. He served his time and was duly released. It is true that he was under contract to Lester Melrose of Vocalion Recording Company, and Melrose does seem to have secured one favor for him—Bukka was allowed to make a short trip to Chicago to do one recording session before his prison term began."

The Confiners, a four-piece group of Parchman inmates, made this record for a small Hattiesburg company in 1961. The band made public appearances. Wardlow collection.

Hurley and Evans then implied the "story" that Oliver received and published about White breaking bond was a direct quote from Oliver himself: "Oliver says that he [White] jumped bail to attend the session, but if this were true it seems likely that his stay in prison would have been longer and considerably more unpleasant than it was."

Oliver's information, based upon interviews with Big Bill Broonzy and others in Chicago, is closer to the court documents than Hurley and Evans' erroneous assumptions and comments. Bukka White's Vocalion session in Chicago, which produced the major hit "Shake 'Em On Down," took place on September 3, 1937. Court documents from the Monroe County Circuit clerk's office at Aberdeen show that Washington (Bukka) White was indicted by a county grand jury during the October 1937 session of Circuit Court, and that an arrest warrant was issued for him. On November 8, White was tried by a petit (12-man) jury and convicted of murder: "We the jury find the defendant guilty as charged but fail to agree to punishment." Trial judge Thomas Johnston sentenced Bukka to serve "the term of the balance of his natural life in the state penitentiary" and to be carried immediately to Parchman by a county deputy.

Presently, a search for Parchman files has revealed no surviving information before World War II confirming the date of Bukka's release or how it occurred. Obviously, he was not released for any error by Monroe County officials, but for his commercial possibilities as a Vocalion/OKeh blues artist. Paul B. Johnson, the Mississippi state governor in 1940, had the authority to order Bukka's release. In like manner Leadbelly was pardoned from the Texas state penitentiary at Huntsville, and was released from the Louisiana state penitentiary at Angola under the "time off for good behavior" policy, as reported

Bukka White, who recorded two sessions before World War II, was one of the re-discovered bluesmen who played the blues festivals of the 1960s. Photo by Dick Waterman.

This Monroe County court document shows that Bukka White was convicted of murder in 1937 and sentenced to life in the Parchman penitentiary. Wardlow collection.

by Texas blues scholar Mack McCormick and by authors Charles Wolfe and Kip Lornell in their exhaustive biography *The Life and Legend of Leadbelly* (1992).

Today, the pardon of a convicted murderer by a Mississippi governor would create intense media reports and harsh criticism, especially if the offender had served less than three years. Bukka's OKeh/Vocalion session occurred in April 1940 in Chicago, two and a half years after his conviction.

Presently, the Monroe County Circuit clerk has been unable to locate the grand jury indictment that would have given the actual place of the slaying, the name of the victim, and the date it occurred.

Likewise, concerning Son House, no court files have been discovered in Coahoma County (Clarksdale) concerning his 1928 conviction and self-explained (House 1965 and Wilson 1966) two-year incarceration at Parchman.

III

Witnesses

Ledell Johnson Remembers His Brother, Tommy

This was the first in-depth article on Tommy Johnson's lifestyle and music. After finding his brother Mager at Crystal Springs, Mississippi, on a tip from Ishmon Bracey, I gathered basic information on Tommy and his brothers that was published in the OJL 1965 notes (see Section I, Initial Inquiries and Encounters, page 10). (For Bracey's recollections of Tommy Johnson, see "Got Four, Five Puppies, One Little Shaggy Hound," page 45). In 1967, Pete Whelan requested that I do a feature on Tommy Johnson, and so that July I sought out Ledell Johnson in south Jackson. I played him copies of Tommy's songs and those by other artists, including Willie Brown from the Paramount issue. The next month, I conducted the first-ever interview with Dick Bankston, a former Delta musician who had played with both Johnson and Patton; much of his information was published in my "Can't See My Future" article in 1986. Immediately after the Bankston interview, I revisited Ledell Johnson at his home at 1520 Barrett Street in Jackson, and he recounted Tommy Johnson's "crossroad" story in an alternate "graveyard at midnight on the darkest night of the month" version. Although Ledell knew of Tommy's musical relationship with Ishmon Bracey, he considered Tommy the more talented of the two, and he did not personally "like" Bracey. —GDW

[Originally published in *78 Quarterly* no. 1 (1967): 63–65]

Jackson, Mississippi: The tall, skinny elderly man sat on a straight chair under a magnolia tree in his front yard. He leaned back and said: "Yes, I'm Ledell Johnson . . . and Tommy Johnson was my brother."

I began asking Ledell Johnson, the brother of one of country blues' most famous singers, about Tommy Johnson's life and music.

"Tom, he was four years younger than me. I was born in 1892, so Tom must have been born in 1896." (Other sources list Johnson's birth date as 1894).

"Now, Tom, he was the seventh child out of 13. First there was Pearly, then Viola, George, Jim, Ida, Ledell (myself), and then Tom."

Tommy Johnson's father was a slave. Ledell remembers that "Daddy was born a Stratton in Atlanta, Georgia, and he was sold to a family in Copiah

County, Mississippi, where we were all born. He was sold to some Johnsons—so that's how we got our names."

The father, Idell Johnson (Stratton), married Mary Ella Wilson, who was also a native of Copiah County. Ledell's father died in 1924 in Crystal Springs.

Concerning Tommy's early childhood, Ledell remarked, "I learned Tommy how to play the guitar first. I learned myself from watching my uncle play, I learned Tommy the guitar long before he ran away from home."

When I asked Ledell when Tommy left his father's farm near Crystal Springs, he said, "Tommy just up and ran away when he was 12 years old with this older woman.

"Tom, he had been working for Mr. Lynfield Redmann down at Terry, and because he was so good a worker, Mr. Redmann gave him a horse and buggy to carry home. My brother gave the horse and buggy to our mother, and it wasn't two weeks later that Tom up and left with this older woman to go up in the Delta.

"She come and got Tommy from Terry, where she lived, and they took off and went up near Rolling Fork. She could have passed for his grandmother. She had a daughter herself as old as Tom was."

Ledell thinks that the real reason the woman stole Tommy Johnson away from home was that Tommy could play the guitar well enough to make money, and she would get the money. He remembers that the woman's name was Moore.

When I asked Ledell what year this was, he replied that it was 1914. This is confusing, for Ledell had declared that Tommy was only 12 when he left home. Yet, Ledell also said "Tommy, he nursed for me after I got married in November, 1912, and that was before he ran away." If Tommy's birth year was 1896 as Ledell calculates, in 1914 he would have turned 18.

Tommy stayed up in the Rolling Fork area and in the Delta for about two years. Then, he returned to the Johnson's farm just west of Terry, a small town closer to Crystal Springs. He then returned to the Delta for a short while, living at Boyle in Sunflower Country.

In 1916, Tommy came back to Terry again and married Maggie

This photo of Tommy Johnson, taken from a 1929 Victor Race Catalog, is the only known photograph in existence. Wardlow collection

Bedwell (Campbell) from Terry. Ledell and Tom "stole" Maggie away from her father and took her to Crystal Springs, where Tommy married Maggie in Ledell's house.

When Maggie's father came looking for her, Tom and Ledell hid her, so that she could not be located. Maggie was only 14 at that time and a very attractive young woman.

In the fall of 1916, Ledell Johnson and his wife Mary, and Tommy Johnson and his wife Maggie, all moved to the Tom Sander plantation at Drew, another small Delta cotton town in Sunflower County.

"While we were up there, Tom started playing music with Will (Willie) Brown and Dick Bankston," said Ledell. "Tommy, he played more than I did though, but I was playing a lot in those juke houses or for parties in those days."

When I asked Ledell if he ever heard of anyone named Patton, playing around Drew, he said, "That guy named Charlie Patton came in there at times and we played together. I saw Tommy and Patton play together many times. We all got together and played for jukes or for dances and parties."

Deep in thought, he continued, "I didn't see him much, but all three of them guys (Patton, Bankston, and Brown) were singing that song about 'Hitch up my pony and saddle up my grey mare, I'm gonna find my baby out in the world somewhere.'"

Ledell remembered that Brown and Patton were about the same age, although Patton was maybe a little older. "Will, he was married to Josie Brown . . ."

Just then, Ledell's wife, Mary, added, "You know both of them played the guitar. Josie, that's Will's wife, was from Crystal Springs . . ."

I asked Mary if Will and Josie had any children. She said, "No, not as far as I remember."

In December of 1918 (Ledell remembers that the war in Europe had been over one month) Ledell left Drew and returned to Crystal Springs.

The best-selling 1929 record was Tommy Johnson's signature song. Wardlow collection.

Tommy Johnson stayed up in the Drew area for a longer period of time, then came back to Crystal Springs. Then he went to south Mississippi and Louisiana.

Ledell saw Tommy at various times in the next few years in different places. Sometimes the two brothers, along with a younger brother, Mager, played uptown in Crystal Springs in the mid-'20s in front of Thaxton's drug store.

Johnson, like other blues singers of that period, had countless women. Ledell remembers that Tommy had so many wives that Ledell could hardly count or keep up with them.

"Tommy he never kept no woman very long.

He had one for a while and then just up and left her when he had a notion. He stayed on the move all the time, moving from one town to another."

When I asked him more about Maggie Campbell, made famous in Tommy's 1928 Victor record, Ledell laughed lightly and said, "Yes, I remember Maggie. Her and Tommy fought all the time. They would make up and then start right back fighting and arguing again.

"One night up there in the Delta where they were living, Tom and Maggie got in a bad fight with snow all over the ground, knee deep. She started hitting Tommy with pots and pans, and finally bit him on the ear. Tommy, he got up a runnin' and ran right out the front door in his underwear into the snow with her right behind him chasing him. Both of them were barefooted. A few minutes later, I looked over there and they were walking arm in arm back to the cabin, already made up."

It took Ledell quite a few minutes to remember the names of all of Tommy's wives.

"He had this woman in Arkansas—I don't remember her name—for a while. Then there was a creole woman named D'Ella, and then Ella Hill; a woman named Emma, who I think was from Tylertown; and there was another woman who lost her mind, Sophronie."

I asked, "What about Rosie?" She was one of Johnson's wives that both Ishmon Bracey and Johnny Temple remembered.

"I remember that name, but I don't remember what happened to her."

Ledell's reminiscence took a new direction. "You know, Tom once asked me to go with him to Omaha, Nebraska, to make some records with him, but I never did back him up on his records. I let him make them by himself." (Ledell Johnson often referred to Grafton, Wisconsin, as Omaha.)

"Tommy, he said that he stopped making records because he sold all his rights, but he stayed drunk so bad and so much, it was hard for him to make any records. That boy would drink anything—bay rum, canned heat, shoe polish, moonshine, Solo—anything that had alcohol in it."

Tommy Johnson always spent a lot of time talking before he got around to playing songs. Ledell recalls one harrowing incident when Tommy's guitar was "busted up" for just that reason.

"Tommy, he was sitting down at this store, and this white man came along and asked him to play some piece for him. Tom, he just sat there for a few minutes and kept saying yes; but he never would start the song. After a while the man told Tom to give him the guitar and he would play it himself.

"Well, Tom handed him the guitar and told him to go ahead—'I wanna hear you.'

"Well, he made that white man mad, and he just took the guitar and hit Tom right on the head with it and kept trying to hit him with it until Tom got up and ran away from him. Busted that guitar all to pieces.

"So there we were, with no guitar, and we were supposed to play a party down there in south Jackson. We had to go borrow a guitar from someone to play the party that night."

Tommy Johnson had little "respect" for musical instruments. Ledell recalls, ". . . wasn't nothin' for him to break or tear up a $50 or $60 guitar when he got mad at a woman."

When I asked Ledell if he knew how Tommy died, he told me that "Tom was next door at my daughter's house, Ella Lee Hampton, playing for a party. Been drinking all night and when he finished this last song and the party broke up, my daughter went into the kitchen.

"She heard someone out on the couch, groaning and dying.

"Tom, he was already embalmed before he died. He drank so much of that Solo [a paint remover with a high alcohol content] that it ate his insides up. One pint of that stuff makes a gallon of whiskey. That's what killed him, drinking that kind of stuff."

I asked Ledell if the last song Tommy sang that night at the party might have been "Big Road Blues."

He said, "I don't know what it was, but he sure took that last trip down the Big Road by himself that night." (His death certificate states the year as 1956.)

This year [1967], Ledell Johnson turned 75. How would I describe him? As a gentleman who lives a Christian life, is still active, preaches when the opportunity arises, and has a keen memory.

Ledell Johnson sits in the shade under the trees and reminisces about events that took place a half-century ago, or more—now fragile memories that may be wiped clean by a capricious flow of time that drifts down the unending Big Road of Life.

Mysteries in Mississippi

Blues Unlimited *was the first blues magazine in the world, starting in 1963. After getting some sample copies, I sent this article to its editors Mike Leadbitter and Simon Napier. Here I point out the similarity between the melodies of Patton's "Pony Blues" and Johnson's "Bye Bye Blues." This is the first connection between Patton's and Johnson's respective performance styles. See also "The Immortal Charlie Patton," page 18, and "Ledell Johnson Remembers His Brother, Tommy," page 106.—* GDW

[Originally published in *Blues Unlimited* no. 30 (February 1966): 10.]

Mississippi blues hold many mysteries, but one of the more baffling is the origin of the melody of a song titled "Pony Blues" recorded by Charlie Patton in June 1929 on Paramount 12792 and by central Mississippi bluesman Tommy Johnson for Victor 20439 in February 1928, under the title of "Bye

Bye Blues." The great importance in the linkage of these two songs is that the same melody used by Patton for his version of "Pony Blues" is one of the two main melodies he employs for almost all of his recordings. The other melody (which, oddly enough, is called by many "Moon Going Down" after its best usage on Paramount 13014) is also used by Johnson on another 1928 Victor recording.

The main question is, Who influenced whom? Did Patton teach Johnson the melody he used on "Pony Blues," or did Johnson teach Patton? The question becomes more involved when considering statements made by many who knew both singers and were in musical contact with them. Both Ishmon Bracey and Walter Vincson (one of the Mississippi Sheiks of OKeh and Paramount recordings) were playing with Johnson at jukes and parties in the Crystal Springs, Mississippi, area as early as 1921. At that time, both Vincson and Bracey said Johnson was singing the song "Bye Bye Blues" to the same melody that was used by Patton on his 1929 recording.

Bracey further complicates the matter by saying that he and Johnson went into the Delta each fall to play in the small cotton towns and jukes, and that Johnson first sang the song. Bracey said, "Tommy taught Patton that song. He gave it to Patton over in Greenwood or either Moorhead, while they were playing together in a juke. It was about 1923."

Bracey has admitted that he was not with Johnson when this occurred, but that Johnson told him about it, after it had happened. Both Johnson and Bracey traveled into the Delta beginning in the years right after the close of World War I, when cotton laborers migrated to the Delta to bring in the big fall crops.

Now the complication really deepens, for Patton was born in rural Hinds County, Mississippi, in either 1887 or 1890, and this section of the state is firmly associated with the central Mississippi style of blues! Johnson was born at Crystal Springs, Mississippi, in 1894, which is a little more than 30 miles from Edwards, Patton's birthplace, so their ages do not place them in different blues generations.

Mattie Franklin, a wife of Patton's for a short time in 1924, said he was singing his version of "Pony Blues" and the song "Banty Rooster Blues" by that same year, and that Patton told her he had been singing them for a couple of years. So, whether Johnson taught Patton or vice versa will surely continue to be a controversy among blues analysts for years to come.

The importance of the melody is simply this: If Johnson influenced Patton, then Johnson's rating as a bluesman must advance and Patton's diminish. Patton is generally considered the greatest of the Mississippi bluesmen, while Johnson's authority has not been fully established. Most of Patton's greatness is based on the central theme of "Pony Blues" and "Moon Going Down"; but is this theme his? If it is, and Patton taught Johnson this melody, then Patton's greatness must be considered intact, as an originator of a style that directly influenced Willie Brown, Kid Bailey, and Son House.

◄o►◄o►◄o►

Luther and Percy: The Huff Brothers

In April 1968 at Mike Leadbitter's request, I sought out the Huff brothers, who had recorded their prewar sound during two 1951 Trumpet Records sessions. I easily found Percy Huff, who was a Jackson cabdriver and cafe operator. He gave information that linked their recording style to prewar Jackson musicians Charlie McCoy (the greatest influence on Luther Huff), Tommy Johnson, Ishmon Bracey, and Slim Duckett (Percy Huff's favorite guitarist). —GDW

[Originally published in *Blues Unlimited* no. 56 (September 1968): 4.]

Jackson, Mississippi—in 1950. Luther Huff set up a recording session with Trumpet Records—the Diamond Record Company—with its headquarters located on Farish St. Huff showed up at the studio late in the afternoon on a chilly, windy, wintry day with his younger brother Percy, who played the lead guitar on the four sides released under the name of Luther Huff. Luther, who has been an obscure figure, but who has received considerable praise from blues critics, played the mandolin (or the "banjo-mandolin," as Percy called it).

Percy claims that they made two sessions for Mrs. McMurry, both set up by Luther, but that he wasn't paid for either session. "She paid him; I never got nothing out of it," Percy said. "She just paid him—we made them together but she just paid him." Within a month after the sessions, Luther had left for Detroit, Michigan, hoping to get work and capitalize on his recent releases.

For the first session, cut in the '50s, the brothers recorded "Dirty Disposition" and "1951 Blues." Luther recalls being partially sick and having a hard time playing, "I was sick that night and she [had] taken me in her car to get some black coffee; and I got okay and went on back down there and played. I was having a chill before I got the coffee."

The Huff brother's sound on this record is reminiscent of a 1920s style played by both Slim Duckett and Charlie McCoy. Blues Archive.

While Mike Rowe (1966) states that the song "1951 Blues" represents an early Delta style of blues, it is actually reminiscent of a 1920s style practiced by Slim Duckett of Jackson, Mississippi, who was an obvious influence on Percy's guitar playing. Although both brothers had moved into the lower Delta in 1938 or 1939 (according to Percy) and undoubtedly absorbed segments of the local styles around Belzoni, where they sharecropped, the real influence of the two Huff Brothers can be traced not only to Duckett, but to Tommy Johnson, Charlie McCoy, and Ishmon Bracey as well.

Both brothers were born in Hinds County—Percy on November 7, 1912, Luther on December 5, 1910. Each listened to Johnson, Duckett, Bracey, and McCoy at local parties and on the streets of Jackson in the 1920s. Duckett, Percy's favorite guitarist, was almost an unknown in the Jackson sphere, but he played extensively for 25 years, often with his close friend Tommy Johnson.

Johnny Temple, a former recording artist now living in Jackson, is very familiar with the influence and musical background of Slim Duckett (who was, in fact, his step-father). Temple claims Duckett died in Jackson in the early '40s. Before then, Percy watched him play guitar at the parties they attended, often switching instruments with him. "We would just go where they were, and if they were there, we'd just play their instruments," Percy said. Duckett was well known for one song in particular, probably called "Black Spider Blues," which Percy sang at the time.

Similarities between Percy's guitar work on the Trumpets and Johnson-Bracey's on the Victor sessions, with McCoy's second guitar work, is easily recognized. Percy said that Luther "followed behind Charlie McCoy. He played guitar some, but he mostly played the mandolin unless a string broke on it or something like that."

[EK: Seven years after this article first appeared, Bob Eagle published

Percy played lead guitar on his brother's 1950s Trumpet session. He holds a copy of one of the two records he made with his brother. Blues Archive.

"Luther Huff" (1975), presenting Luther's account of the Trumpet session. He had left Mississippi for Detroit, Michigan, in 1947 and found work as a sander. During a return visit to Jackson in 1950, he realized too late that he didn't have enough money to return to Detroit. Through Sonny Boy Williamson and Elmore James, Luther learned of Lillian McMurry's Trumpet Records label, and he approached her as a prospective artist. McMurry worked with him and his brother Percy through three days of sessions, on January 10 and 16, and February 21, 1951, and formally signed Luther alone as a Trumpet artist on January 23, (the contract is now in the McMurry/Trumpet collection at the University of Mississippi Blues Archive). Although by signing the contract Luther agreed to pay the side musicians he brought with him, he evidently kept all of the money received from Trumpet and returned to Detroit after the sessions. Percy Huff's complaint to Wardlow that he received nothing for the session should pertain not to McMurry but to his own brother.]

The Huff Brothers, noted for their prewar guitar and mandolin sound, recorded four songs for Trumpet in 1950. Blues Archive.

This contract verifies Luther Huff's session with the Diamond Record company in 1951. Blues Archive.

Highway 80 Blues

A Mike Leadbitter request led to the 1969 rediscovery of Tommy Lee "Legs" Thompson, of Rankin County, Mississippi. In the early 1950s, Tommy Lee had recorded "Highway 80 Blues," a guitar solo for the short-lived Delta label. Thompson also recorded some sides for Ace, but none was released. This article also provided the first explanation as to the origins of the "Catfish Blues" B-side to Elmore James' "Dust My Broom" on Trumpet. —GDW

[Originally published in *Blues Unlimited* no. 66 (October 1969): 12–13.]

I was born down here in 1915. I would say I was somewhere about 15 when I started to playing. Made me a guitar. Taken me a cigar box and a guitar neck and I played several parties with it. I worked places. I could play behind most anybody when I was working and recording. I saw Charlie Patton back there in the '30s. Someone would say Charlie Patton was at the juke house and we would go round and see him. Tommy Johnson, whooo! Did I know him! I used to play everything he played. I seen him in Jackson, I'd follow with him."

[Listening to Tommy Johnson's "Cool Drink of Water Blues," 1928—"That's Ishmon Bracey with him? It isn't!" It was Charlie McCoy on second guitar.]

"You got Tommy Johnson's 'Weeping Willow'? He put that out. It was on RCA; I bought the record. [Note: The label was Victor, which was bought by RCA in 1929.] Mr. Speir was involved in him. Tommy, when he was recording, nobody in Jackson could beat him on blues. I met him on the street mostly. I sure wish you got to hear 'Canned Heat' by him! Before he died, he couldn't sing at all! He would go and run the red light and they'd put him in jail, and put him on the street. I seen him lotsa times, working on the streets in the city, Jackson. He'd work his fine out.

"I made records before I met Elmore James—he had made 'Dust My Broom'—he sure did! I met him in Jackson. He wanted for me to play second guitar for him. I never did play on records with him. Well, he usually, it was another fellow he had with him—came from Chicago with him. Fact about it, Elmore stayed here. I was talkin' with him about two weeks before he died. They say he died in Chicago. He had a brother up there in Canton; I forget his name. 'Dust My Broom' was recorded down here at her place [Lillian McMurry's Trumpet Records], that's what he told me. Robert Johnson? He used Bob's records. Robert Johnson, he was a pretty rough fellow; I never did hear what did happen to him. He was real nice—

you know 'Terraplane'? I played bass behind Elmore. We played at a big club up there in Belzona and then we played up there in Louise. Played around the Delta a lot too.

"Sonny Boy? [Aleck Miller, aka Sonny Boy Williamson II, who recorded for Trumpet and Chess.] He played by himself."

[Here Wardlow plays the mysterious "Catfish Blues," released on Trumpet Records by Elmo' James.]

"That's Sonny Boy and Bobo! Call him Bobo. He was from Jackson. He was a Thomas—Bobo Thomas. He played guitar. He should have been around 30 years old when he made that record. He talked about it the way it was. He went out there to record that record by himself [i.e., under his own name], but she [Mrs. McMurry] wouldn't let him. So she, the Elmore James record ["Dust My Broom"] was on the other side and then Sonny Boy Williamson blowed the harmonica for them. I saw Bobo about a month ago. He came by where I was working. We was workin' at the 'Playhouse' on Farish Street [in Jackson].

"Charlie Booker? I never did hear of him. Willie Love didn't talk 'bout him." [Thompson worked with Love's Three Aces for a while.] "I never did know Willie Nix. Did you know Memphis Slim? I seed Boyd Gilmore a time or two and listened to him play. He came by the studio when we was working for Ace [in Jackson]. He wanted to record and he [a Mr. Vincent, of Ace Records] took some tapes on him, but he never would process them.

"Just like Junior Parker, he [Vincent] said like that first song Junior recorded, that 'Feelin' Good,' we went to his house, and he say no, I don't want that, and he [Jr.] took his group to record it! And he [Jr.] say, man, you don't know what you're doing and he [Vincent] say, no, I couldn't sell it—and so that man up there in Memphis, he cut it for them and it came out red hot." [laughter]

[Here Wardlow plays Thompson's own "Highway 80 Blues," made for Delta Records.]

"That record was made somewhere about 1951. I made it in Jackson. Mr. Ammons had his own studio out on Raymond Road, about where the TV station is. John Thorn was on piano. He was from Jackson. Myself and another boy was on guitars. I forget his name . . . he helped me out on that one. I played it in 'E', E natural; Highway 80, that's the highway that runs through Brandon and Jackson. I wrote it in about a day, and cut it in two, three days after. I never did know how many copies it sold—that's why I never would record for him any more. Six cents a copy was what I suppose to get out of that one. I never did get any advance. The title of the other side is 'Packin' Up.' Well, I wrote that myself. I sure did hear that on the juke boxes!

"I cut one for Mr. Vincent at Ace. Well, I got about better 'n 200 dollars out of that . . . I met Frankie Lee Sims, Big Boy Crudup too. Frankie was from out there in Texas. He came into Jackson, you know, to record. We did some recording in the studio there [Jackson]—the radio station. I believe it was WLBT at that time. It was on a Sunday if I'm not mistaken and we did, we cut a record for Ace. 'Sleeping in the Ground'—I wrote that and 'My Love Is Here to Stay.' I'm quite sure you heard THAT record! I had the record and somebody stole it. I just played guitar on it. Myself and Sammy Myers and King Mose. Sammy blows harp—he's here in Jackson! King Mose played drums. We had Walter on piano. He worked for the University Hospital last I heard. Walter Berry. Now we, uh, I myself and Sammy and, er, we was the music. King Mose just played drums. We was the Royal Rockers. I can find Sammy at any time!"

[EK: There was more to the Bobo Thomas story than Thompson learned. According to Lillian McMurry (O'Neal 1986, 20, and letter to Komara, October 22, 1997), after the 1951 "Catfish Blues" session she paid Thomas outright for recording and lent him a guitar and amplifier with which he could develop a B-side. She heard nothing more from him for almost a year, not even when she released "Catfish Blues" as the B-side to Elmore James' "Dust My Broom" (see the postscript to "Canton, Mis'sippi Breakdown," page 159, for more on that Trumpet release). Finally, in 1952, she heard that he was arrested on a charge involving the guitar, and that he had been waiting eight months for the hearing. With the assistance of McMurry and a lawyer, Thomas pleaded not guilty and "got off" the charge. This court episode wound up costing Trumpet $250.

On Tommy Johnson's "Cool Drink of Water Blues," Charlie McCoy accompanies on second guitar, not Ishmon Bracey as Thompson had thought.

There was no such "Weeping Willow" title or related lyrics by Tommy Johnson released on Victor (later RCA Victor) or, for that matter, on Paramount. A well-known blues record of the 1920s was Bessie Smith's "Weeping Willow Blues," recorded on September 26, 1924, and released on Columbia 14042-D; its flip side was "Bye Bye Blues," a title that is the same as Johnson's treatment of "Pony Blues" for Victor (see the "Mysteries in Mississippi," page 110). It is likely that Thompson had Johnson's "Bye Bye Blues" in mind, but had confused its title with that of Columbia 14042-D.

"Catfish Blues" is the B-side to Elmore James' "Dust My Broom." Blues Archive.

No information on Thompson since 1969 is available. Jim Pratt's article "Tommy Lee's D.J. Jamboree" (1994) is about Tommy Lee Griffin.]

Garfield Akers and Mississippi Joe Callicott:
From the Hernando Cotton Fields

This article is the foremost in-depth report on Garfield Akers and his music. On a trip to Memphis in December 1967, I searched for Joe Callicott, who reportedly was still living in Nesbit, Mississippi, near Hernando. Bill Barth, who was living at Memphis, visited him before I did, and was learning guitar from the older master. During my visit with Callicott, I played Garfield Akers' four songs and Joe's two while he listened with glee. He recalled the influential musicians who had taught both Garfield and himself. Disposed much like John Hurt, the affable Callicott happily recalled working and recording with Garfield. The interview was not published until this Living Blues *article in 1981. —GDW*

[Originally published in *Living Blues* no. 50 (Spring 1981): 26–27.]

Mississippi Joe Callicott died in early 1969 in his home town of Nesbit, Mississippi. Born in 1901, Callicott was influenced by Frank Stokes, one of the many noted blues guitarists based in the Hernando area during the 1920s. Both Callicott and Garfield Akers worked with Stokes, and the Akers-Callicott guitar duets have been compared to those of Stokes and Dan Sane. In *Sweet as the Showers of Rain*, Samuel Charters writes, "People still remember him [Stokes] working for the Doctor Watts Medicine Show with Akers—both of them with their faces blacked up, except for the usual painted white mouth."

Callicott made only one prewar record (reissued on Yazoo L-1009 and OJL-11), but after field researcher George Mitchell found him still living in Nesbit in 1967, Joe recorded a few albums and appeared at the 1968 Memphis Country Blues Festival. His 1968 *Blue Horizon* LP (7-63227 [U.K.]/BM 4606 [U.S.]) contains a version of Garfield Akers' "Dough Roller Blues." The field recordings for Mitchell included an LP on the Revival label (1002) and half an LP on Arhoolie (1042).

In the fall of 1929, Brunswick/Vocalion Records made its initial field trip to Memphis to record talent for its Vocalion 1000 and Brunswick 7000 Race Series. The session at the Peabody Hotel was highlighted by the first recorded appearances of Garfield Akers, Mattie Delaney, and Kid Bailey, concomitantly with veterans Memphis Minnie and Tampa Red.

The recording of "Cottonfield Blues Parts 1 and 2" (Vocalion 1442), by Hernando's Garfield Akers, accompanied by his friend Joe Callicott on second (complementing) guitar, represented a classic Mississippi blues approach.

"Garfield had been playing that song for about two or three years before," Callicott explained in a December 30, 1967, interview. "That rhythm came from around in here. He didn't have too many songs. That was his main song and he practiced on it all the time." [A similar rhythm was used by Joe McCoy on his Decca recording of "Look Who's Coming Down the Road," recorded in 1935 but released around 1940, and by Robert Wilkins on "Get Away Blues."]

This 1929 release, one of the classic prewar records, features Garfield and Joe Callicott on acoustic guitar, which provide the amazing rhythm behind Garfield's moanin'. Wardlow Collection.

Callicott remembered that he and Garfield were carried to Memphis by Hernando native Jim Jackson, already a race recording star with his massive hit "Jim Jackson's Kansas City Blues," and the three stayed two nights in Memphis at a hotel on Beale Street.

[Jim Jackson was discovered by talent scout H.C. Speir in Memphis on Beale Street while Speir was in town for a recording session. Speir sold Jackson's services to another local Memphis scout, who in turn carried him to Vocalion, which was the company Speir was already working with. Speir

Blues music is inexorably linked to the plantation experience. Here, a fieldhand plows for spring planting. Before the tractor came to the Delta, all fields were ploughed with mules and cotton was chopped by hand. Wardlow collection.

had doubted that Vocalion would have taken Jackson. Speir had seen Jim Jackson on the streets of Jackson, Mississippi, for a number of years and he described him as a "cocaine head."]

Callicott said, "Jim Jackson come and got us. We tried out and Mr. (J. Mayo) Williams, he liked that hummin' in there." Callicott said that Williams was particularly "struck" by Akers' singing, especially the high-pitched wailing or humming, and their rhythm.

Akers' vocal style confused some early collectors and researchers as a trademark of Texas singers. "Garfield got that hum from Ed Newsome around here two or three years before he recorded," Callicott said. "He just took it up and made it better. If it sounded good, we put it in."

After their audition, Joe Callicott and Garfield Akers had the same problems as many blues artists in preparing for the three-minute record: "We started one and messed it up and did another, and then we got it down pat." Callicott remembered that before the session, the two got enough liquor to "wash your mouth out right good." Afterwards, he said, "they give you a little."

Between takes the two waited about 15 minutes, watching the same type of start and stop lights that other companies used to tell talent when the allotted three minutes of wax was recorded. Akers recorded three different takes of both sides, probably to insure on "Part 2" that more than one master was available if the better take was ruined by accident or by weather. H.C. Speir has confirmed that "hot weather" would ruin a wax master and that companies would pack a master in sawdust and ice to prevent spoilage immediately after a recording take. He also said that companies stayed out of the South during the hottest summer months—which explains the higher number of fall and spring sessions in the Godrich/Dixon discography *Blues & Gospel Records 1902–1943* (1997).

Joe Callicott remembers seeing "two little guys" recording this song. Bailey was a rambling bluesman who had played with both Patton and Willie Brown. Wardlow collection.

Although Akers only recorded two sides at the 1929 session, Callicott recalled, "Garfield had two or three more songs, but Mr. Williams didn't want them." One of the rejected songs was a version of "Bo Weevil." At least three other musicians from the Hernando, Mississippi, area also auditioned, according to Callicott: "Dusie, a girl who sang, well, she didn't pass. Major Strong, a guitar player, and Louisa, they didn't pass either."

Callicott remembered peeking through a glass window and seeing "two little guys" making a record. After hearing the Kid Bailey Brunswick record, he surmised, "That's the same guy who was here then . . . It was two of them together. He was little: Who was he? I remember seein' them same guys, was right here." Callicott didn't ask questions nor did he converse with the two. He only listened as they recorded.

Memphis Minnie was also in the studio, preparing herself for recording one of her major hits, "Bumble Bee."

"When she got up [from practicing] she was more than feelin' good [drinking]. She was ready. She and Tampa Red had the first steel boxes we ever saw."

"Steel boxes" were National tri-cone guitars. In a taped 1968 interview, Johnny Temple claimed that these were first brought to Jackson by Memphis Minnie and Joe McCoy in either late 1929 or early 1930, when the pair came from Chicago to play a club date.

Callicott continued playing after the first session, and researcher George Mitchell reports that Callicott did some traveling before he considered himself "good enough" to record on his own. He recorded two sides for Brunswick in February 1930 at a second Memphis session, where Akers also recorded again.

Callicott claimed that Akers backed him on "his recordings and I backed him on mine," but the aural evidence on Callicott's lone Brunswick record, "Fare Thee Well Blues"/ "Traveling Mama Blues" (7166), fails to substantiate this claim. (Akers probably played with him during practice sessions but not on the actual recordings.) However, it is possible that Callicott is playing such a "tight" second guitar that he could be playing on Akers' two 1930 sides, "Dough Roller Blues" and "Jumpin' and Shoutin' Blues" (Vocalion 1481).

H.C. Speir has reported that a second guitarist was usually paid $5.00 a song. Speir encouraged a singer to use "a complementor" if it enhanced his song, as in the case of Ishmon Bracey, Tommy Johnson, and Charlie Patton. However, some companies refused to pay the accompanying artist, their policy being that a country blues artist should be able to record alone with only his own instrument.

Callicott considered Akers to be a better artist than himself and he had planned only to back up Akers' playing, as he had been doing for almost a decade in the Hernando area. Callicott enjoyed his role as Akers' "complementor" and did not feel competition or jealousy existed between them.

"I kept him chorded up good, trackin' him . . . You hear them basses [on 'Cottonfield Blues']? Well, that's me. Hear them little strings? Well, that's him . . . And when that guy would get to playin', I'm tellin' you the truth—we'd sit face to face. And we changed up [i.e., swapped guitar leads] . . . and you wouldn't know it."

Callicott did not know who developed the "stompin' bass" that both men featured on "Cottonfield," but he believed that Akers was the originator of the rhythm—"that comes from around here." (Robert Wilkins reported to Stephen Calt that two Hernando area brothers named Byrd played the same rhythm as in "Cottonfield" in the 1915–20 period.) Callicott never asked Akers in their years of playing who developed the "Hernando style." To Callicott, that information was not important. What mattered was that he and his friend played together, partied together, and enjoyed their local popularity.

Callicott did not buy a copy of his recording when it was stocked by a furniture store record retailer in Hernando. "I went down to hear it after I heared it come out. I never did get one. I knew it was me singing, I didn't need one." He believed that Akers never bought copies of his records, either.

Akers was born near the turn of the century near Brights, Mississippi (another Hernando resident reported that Akers was "from around Batesville"), and reportedly died in Memphis in the late 1950s or early 1960s. A search by the Tennessee Bureau of Vital Statistics failed to locate a death certificate for Akers between 1955–64. Most reports have located his death in Memphis around 1960, although Nate Armstrong says it may have been in the early to mid-'50s (see part two of this article by Jim O'Neal [see Editor's note]).

Akers was already playing guitar before he moved to the Hernando area as a teenager around World War I. Locally, Akers was nicknamed "Newd" (pronounced "nude"); another local resident recalled that he also had a nickname pronounced "Par-Tee."

According to Callicott, Garfield Akers married his only known wife, Missie, in the mid-1920s, and the couple never had any children. This contradicts a 1965 report that Akers was "said to be survived by a son who plays guitar in a later style." (This report was based on information given researchers looking for Son House in 1964 and was incorporated by Origin Jazz Library producer Pete Whelan into *OJL Supplement No. 1*, the liner note pamphlet to OJL albums 2, 5, and 8 written by this author. Akers' recordings were reissued on these three LPs.)

Akers and Callicott met in the 1920s and their musical relationship continued into the 1940s, when they stopped playing together for "suppers and frolics."

"We just run up into one another around here, playin' at these frolics; he liked the way I played and I liked the way he played; so we just hung up together. Stayed together."

Callicott described Akers as a "buck dancin' guy" and said that at the Vocalion session, a photographer went downstairs with them and took their photo outside of the Peabody on the sidewalk. In the photo, Callicott said, "Akers, he was dancin' and I was playin' the guitar."

Both Akers and Callicott played the bluesman's standard guitar, the cheap Stella. "Right on Beale Street there, I bought my Stella . . . paid $11 for it. It was hangin' in a window. I played it till it wore out."

The Akers family lived on Chambers' Place most of Akers' early life. Akers worked as a typical Southern sharecropper who made yearly crops. He and Callicott played for parties on weekends, but at the time neither was the typical "blues traveler" like Ishmon Bracey, who traveled from New Orleans to Memphis in the fall, or Tommy Johnson, who ranged from Tylertown and Franklinton, Louisiana, northward to Inverness and Tutwiler, Mississippi, during his record-producing years.

Although the Delta is less than 30 miles away, neither Garfield nor Joe ventured into that unfriendly territory to play parties and dances. This hometown approach was for two reasons: to ensure security against hostile attack by unfriendly persons, and to make money from the guaranteed popularity they had in the Hernando region.

When they played away from home, Callicott said that he might even claim that he was from a different state rather than say he was from Hernando.

"Me and my nephew went down the road here to play for people at Oak Hill near Zion Hill [both communities below Hernando]. Never been there before and we didn't know them folks. This guy come up to us and he asked me where I was from.

"'I'm from St. Louis,' I told him.

"He asked my nephew where he was from.

"'I'm from Alabama' [the nephew told the man].

"Man, I'm tellin' you. They'll kill you in a moment. When them old women get to shakin' them bottoms, their old mans get to gettin' jealous. They'll sure kill you now."

Callicott and Akers' motto was "People get over you [trying to start fights], let them go on." This advice failed for Aaron Holcomb, the man who taught Joe guitar: "They got in a fight; this guy who was playin' with

New Vocalion Race Records

Tampa Red

Christmas Man Blues   Vocal with Piano   1224
and Guitar   Chippie Hill and Tampa Red
Weary Money Blues   Chippie Hill

Begin a New Life on Christmas Day–Part 1   1217
Begin a New Life on Christmas Day–Part 2
    Rev. A. W. Nix and Congregation

The Wrong Way to Celebrate Christmas   1221
This Time Another Year You May Be Gone
(The Guitar Evangelist)   Rev. E. W. Clayborn

There Was No Room at the Hotel - -   1222
Seeking for MeLucy Smith Jubilee Singers

Grievin' Me Blues - - - - - - -   1216
    Vocal with Piano, Guitar by Tampa Red
    Georgia Tom
It's Tight Like That Vocal with Piano, Guitar
    Tampa Red and Georgia Tom

Michigan River Blues - - - - -   1223
You Can't Come In
Vocal with Piano Accompaniment   Bert M. Mays

Shake Your Shimmy - - - - -   1218
    The Midnight Rounders
Crying My Blues Away
With Vocal Chorus A. Wynn's Gut Bucket Five

De's Bones Gwine Rise Again - - -   1219
My Lord Delivered Daniel
    Southern Plantation Singing

Down by the Levee - - - - -   1220
    Vocal Chorus Wynn's Creole Jazz Band
Parkway Stomp
Skee Da Vocal A. Wynn's Gut Bucket Five

Hard Hearted Mama Blues - - - -   1187
Niagara Falls Blues
    Voice with Harmonica and Guitar   Kid Cole

Joe Callicott, who met Tampa Red, Georgia Tom, and Memphis Minnie at their February 1930 session in Memphis, said, "She [Minnie] and Tampa Red had the first steel boxes we ever saw," referring to their National tri-cone guitars. Courtesy Maxey Tarpley.

him. They took him and cut him up so bad he'd been better dead, and they shot him [Aaron Holcomb] and left him piled up on the floor."

[EK: George Mitchell is widely credited for rediscovering Joe Callicott in 1967 and helping him make several recordings, the most widely available of which are on *Mississippi Delta Blues Vol. 2* (Arhoolie 1042).

Callicott and Akers were taken by Jim Jackson to two Vocalion/-Brunswick sessions in Memphis, one in the fall of 1929 and the other in the winter of 1930; Callicott's memory combined the two occasions. Nevertheless, the artists he mentioned to Wardlow were confirmed by the session data provided by Dixon and Godrich (1997). A partial recording order and the respective matrix numbers for the 1929 session are: Garfield Akers (M201–202), Jim Jackson with Tampa Red and Thomas A. Dorsey (M203–206), Joe Callicott (M207), Kid Bailey (M209–211), then Jim Jackson again (M214–215). Those for the 1930 session were: Tommy Griffin (MEM767–770), Bozo Nickerson (MEM771), Kansas Joe McCoy and Memphis Minnie (MEM772 and 773, the latter matrix for what would be the hit version of "Bumble Bee"), Jed Davenport (MEM774–775), Garfield Akers (MEM776–777), Joe Callicott (MEM778–779), then later Mattie Delaney (MEM785–786) and Jim Jackson (MEM804–805).

"Garfield Akers . . . to Beale Street and the Juke Joints," Jim O'Neal's account of Akers' later years, was published as a companion piece to this Wardlow article (*Living Blues* no. 50, 26–28).]

Plantation owner instructs a sharecropper where to plough during the spring planting. When Saturday night came, the [laborers] went to "suppers" or "jukes" to party. Wardlow collection.

IV

H.C. Speir

Legends of the Lost
(The Story of Henry Speir)

This series of articles in Blues Unlimited *in 1966 was the first published information on the music scouting career of the legendary Jackson music store owner H.C. Speir. Speir's memory of some of the many artists he recorded has been proven erroneous, but many of those about which he had doubts have been confirmed as his discoveries. —GDW*

[Originally published in four installments in *Blues Unlimited* (1966). The corrected text from Simon Napier, ed., *Back Woods Blues* (1968) is the basis for the present version.]

No other legend stands out as indelibly across the grooves of recorded music in memoirs of Mississippi blues and sanctified music as does Henry C. Speir.

The legendary H. C. Speir as a young man in the early 1920s, when he worked at a Victrola plant in New Orleans. Wardlow collection.

Speir, a Jackson, Mississippi, music store owner for nearly a quarter of a century, searched the entire Southern area from Virginia to New Mexico for talent to send to the various recording companies. He was also an active artist and repertoire director and supervised three sessions: one in Jackson in 1930 for OKeh, which is erroneously listed in the OKeh files for Atlanta, Georgia, one in Jackson in 1935 for ARC, and one in Hattiesburg in 1936.

He helped record various artists in Houston, New Orleans, Birmingham, Chicago, Grafton (Wisconsin), and Dallas. Speir once said, "I've recorded in almost every major city in the nation over a period of 23 years. I've found so many singers I can't remember many of their names, and I've forgotten about many others."

Speir, who was reported by Skip James and Son House as having perished in a 1942 fire (which did end his music ventures), lost an address book as big as a novel in the fire, filled with names and addresses of the artists he had recorded and their home addresses. (This in itself was a disaster, for Speir does not remember many of the artists he recorded, only towns where he found singers. Because of personal beliefs, he has steadily refused to listen to my collection of blues and sanctified recordings, but he has mentioned towns where he found artists or verified towns for me after I had located these areas with my personal research.)

When I asked Speir, in one of our long interviews, who he considered the best of all the singers he located in the blues field, he replied, "Ole Charlie (Patton) was the best I ever seen. But, you know, James, Skippy James, he was real tough! Catch Skippy on the right day—mind you now—the right day and he was as good as Patton, but overall Patton was the best. His little friend Willie Brown was the best guitar player I ever heard in 23 years of talent hunting. He could really make it talk, great guitar player."

This man was a giant among talent scouts. He not only knew the artists, he knew what the record companies wanted and he gave it to them. Speir recalled, "I sent artists everywhere, and tried to work with all the companies, but I probably did send the best artists to Grafton, Wisconsin—the Paramount Record Company. We worked real close, me and Art Laibley!" He added, "I worked with Laibley and also with Ralph Peer of Victor, and P.C. Brockman of OKeh. That place in Richmond, Indiana [Gennett], got lots of my artists in my early years."

When one looks at the Paramount roster of recorded artists, it becomes obvious that Speir not only found almost all of its Southern talent, he even helped record it in Chicago and Grafton, and helped Laibley remodel the

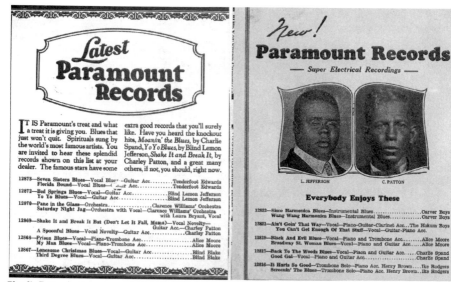

Charlie Patton's status as a blues musician was instantly elevated when he was featured next to Paramount's best-seller, Blind Lemon Jefferson, on this 1929 brochure. Courtesy Maxey Tarpley.

Grafton studios to get a better sound on the later (1929–32) Paramount recordings.

In December 1930, OKeh Records asked Speir to direct a session in Jackson to record various artists living in the area. Speir directed nearly 100 masters in the King Edward Hotel, recording such artists as the Mississippi Sheiks, Bo Carter, Charlie McCoy, Slim Duckett and Pig Norwood, Elder Curry, the Campbell College Quartet, Elder Charles Beck, and Mississippi Coleman Bracey and his wife.

As recording activities declined in the early '30s with certain companies' changing policies, Speir began a closer association with the expanding American Recording Corporation of New York City and its two field directors, W.R. Calaway and Art Satherly. In 1933, Speir made tests of Charlie Patton, his wife Bertha Lee, Son House, and Willie Brown, on recording equipment that he kept on the second floor of his business for testing purposes. These tests were forwarded to Calaway, and early in 1934 Calaway made the trip to bring Patton to New York for his last session.

In 1934, Speir began work with Decca and its subsidiary label Champion, and was responsible for Kokomo Arnold being waxed. In the fall of 1935, Speir set up a session in Jackson on the second floor of an old dance hall on Farish Street, one block above his music store, and recorded nearly 120 masters. Speir brought Robert (Tim) Wilkins from Memphis, along with Will Shade, Minnie Wallace, and Little Son Joe, and scouted the Helena, Arkansas, region for blues piano players.

Young Isaiah Nettles came to the Studios one Sunday to record four songs in the old country style—probably some of the last, with the exception of Booker White's 1940 session in Chicago.

In 1936, Speir directed a session in Hattiesburg, Mississippi, recording such artists as Blind Roosevelt Graves, Cooney Vaughn, Zeke Bingham, the Laurel Fireman's Quartet, and other sacred and secular items. This was the session that produced the now-famous Mississippi Jook Band records.

Because of ARC administrative policies, he discontinued working relations with the corporation shortly after the session, but he vaguely remembers Calaway coming through Jackson in the fall of the year on a trip into the Mississippi Delta, searching for talent to bring to Texas for a session that was to begin in a couple of weeks. From all available circumstantial evidence, Calaway evidently discovered the most controversial Mississippi blues singer of all generations, Robert Johnson, in one of the small Delta towns near Memphis that Speir and Calaway had searched for talent on previous trips. [For accurate information on Johnson's discovery, see "Stop, Look, and Listen at the Cross Road," page 196.]

Speir remembers, "That 1938 was the worst year of all for new talent; the record companies just didn't want any new talent for records." This fact is further borne out by the sale of ARC to Columbia Broadcasting System in March 1938, which included all the ARC masters.

After the 1942 fire that destroyed part of his music store, Speir discontinued his musical interests. Undoubtedly adding to this situation was the record ban of 1942, which was precipitated by American Federation of Musicians head James Patrillo, who was in dispute with the record labels.

Speir recalls the search for talent as an exciting one, for often he would drive hundreds of miles to listen to a group or individuals that he heard of in rumors from other musicians. With blues singers, he usually used an approach such as "I hear you're a good singer, how about singing some of your songs for me?"

After the singer finished, he would tell him, "You sound pretty good. You know, I make records; if you will keep practicing and get your songs together real good and come to Jackson in a couple of days, I see that you get on records." If the singer questioned whether Speir was really a recording company's talent scout, he would recite a long line of musicians he was responsible for recording, such as Charlie Patton, Tommy Johnson, and William Harris.

When the singer showed up in Jackson, Speir reimbursed him for his travel expenses and gave him a couple of extra dollars for spending money while going to a session.

When travelling to a session in Texas or an alternative site such as New Orleans or Memphis or Atlanta, Speir would either drive the artist in his car or use a rented vehicle. He also remembers that each year for many years he ran a special train or cars on a train from Fort Worth to New York, picking up talent in various cities from his own research or from scouts with whom he worked closely. Although many artists were paid little for their services, Speir's were probably the best paid of all the artists

Speir's furniture and hardware store during World War II after relocating from downtown Jackson. Wardlow collection.

recording for various scouts. His average fee was either $50 a side, or ten percent of the royalties on the sale of issued titles. [*BU* Editor's note: This is considerably more than many artists were paid per side, even ten years later.]

The race artists that stand out most in Speir's memory are Charlie Patton, Tommy Johnson, Ishmon Bracey, Skip James, William Harris, Kokomo Arnold, and "the red-headed woman" (probably Lucille Bogan)—but he vividly recalls many others once their names are brought up.

Speir also recorded many of the finer jazz groups. "I found five or six bands in New Orleans." He also tried to get Louis Armstrong to record, after he spent an evening—as the only white man present—on board a pleasure ship on the Mississippi River at New Orleans, listening to an Armstrong group. However, Armstrong told Speir that he was already recording in Chicago and had been for about a year. Speir told him he would be a great artist, and this has certainly proved correct.

In addition to the vastness of his blues, jazz, and sacred recordings, he was responsible for many hillbilly and country artists being recorded. One of the many he remembers was Uncle Dave Macon, whom he recorded in Jackson—after Macon wrote him from Tennessee about the possibilities of doing such. Later, Speir traveled a number of times with Macon into the Appalachian Mountains on talent hunts.

"That was the most dangerous place I ever went in my life. Once they knew you, the people were as friendly as could be; but until they found out you weren't a revenue agent, your life was in real danger."

Speir was the first person to locate Jim Jackson, whose rights he sold to another talent scout in Memphis, named Loren Watson. Jackson, of course, made a remarkable hit of his "Kansas City Blues," which he was singing when Speir found him in Hernando, Mississippi.

On the question of why the Mississippi blues singers seemed to stand out more than other artists in different states, he said "the Negroes in Mississippi played more music and were friendlier to each other than in other areas. There were more of them living closer together, and they swapped a lot of ideas among themselves."

At the age of 70 in 1966, Speir divided his time between his gardens and a part-time real estate business.

A true legend, though almost forgotten by the historians of modern jazz and blues, this man indeed was a visionary and a gentleman of great insight and ability.

[EK: Speir himself actually recorded two L masters (314-1-3) at Grafton and had Paramount press 100 copies of his talks—satirical attacks on Mississippi Senator Theodore Bilbo and state politics. This disc is now kept at the University of Mississippi Blues Archive.

Speir died in 1972. Readers interested in more on Speir, in addition to this piece and the "Godfather of Delta Blues" interview that follows, should look up David Evans' "An Interview with H.C. Speir" (1972) and Wardlow's complete biographical piece, "H.C. Speir (1895–1972)" (1994).]

Godfather of Delta Blues: H.C. Speir

Pat Howse and Jimmy Phillips

In 1991, Peavey Electronics' Monitor *magazine worked with me on a comprehensive article about Mississippi bluesmen and research techniques, featuring color reproductions of rare record labels. More than 200,000 copies of that issue (vol. 10, no. 3) were distributed to worldwide locations, including Australia and New Zealand, from which I received telephone calls about bluesmen. As a follow-up a few years later,* Monitor *featured this article, the most in-depth treatment to date on the "talent brokering" of H.C. Speir and his recollections of the race recording industry from 1926 through 1940. —GDW*

[Interview with Wardlow conducted by Patrick Howse and Jimmy Phillips and originally published in *Monitor* (Peavey) no. 13 (1994): 34–44.]

Blues scholar Gayle Dean Wardlow "discovered" H.C. Speir in 1964, while a student at Belhaven College in Jackson, Mississippi. At that time, Speir was selling real estate, but from 1925 to 1935, during the golden age of blues recording, he was a central figure in the rise of country blues. During this period, the Mississippi "talent broker" supplied major record companies such as Victor, Columbia, Brunswick, and OKeh and minors such as Paramount, Vocalion, and Gennett with a veritable breeder reactor of Delta and other regional bluesmen: Charlie Patton, Skip James, Tommy Johnson, Ishmon Bracey, Bo Carter, the Mississippi Sheiks, William Harris, Blind Joe Reynolds, Blind Roosevelt Graves, Washboard Walter, Geeshie Wiley, Elvie Thomas, Isaiah Nettles, and Robert Wilkins, among others. In addition, Speir was indirectly responsible for the recording careers of Son House, Willie Brown, and Robert Johnson.

Initially, Speir approached talent scouting as a means to promote his music store business, which he had established in 1925 at 225 North Farish Street, in the black business district of Jackson. In lieu of royalties, he preferred standard fees and expenses from the record companies for his discoveries and recording activities. He frequently attended sessions at his own expense, sometimes supervising the recording process. From 1929–32, Paramount was the principal beneficiary of Speir's findings, accepting his recommendations at his word, without demonstrational acetate discs. To accommodate Victor and other prospective companies, in 1926 he installed an audition recording machine upstairs in his store, which he also made available to the public at five dollars per recording. In 1944, convinced that the record business was dead, he moved to North Jackson and opened a used-furniture store.

Pat Howse interviewed Gayle Dean Wardlow in February [1994] regarding his association with Speir from 1964 until his death in 1972. What follows is an illuminating look at the blues subculture of 1920s and '30s Mississippi, juxtaposed with a white man's intuitive grasp of the significance of the music and his indefatigable efforts to preserve it.

How did you establish the connection between Speir and these bluesmen?

I found Ishmon Bracey first, who recorded for Victor and Paramount, and I was inquisitive. I said, "How did you get on records, Ishmon?" He said, "Mr. Speir got me on records." I said, "What do you mean?" He said, "He owned a music store, and he sent me to Victor and he sent me to Paramount." I

H.C. Speir was responsible for the recording careers of the major Delta bluesman. By 1929 he became an exclusive scout for Paramount, discovering artists such as Charlie Patton, Tommy Johnson, Ishmon Bracey, and Skip James among others. Wardlow collection.

said, "Is he still alive?" He said, "Yeah, last time I heard, he was living over in Rankin County somewhere, and he was advertising real estate in the paper."

So I looked in the phone book, called him up, and said, "I'm in college and I'm interested in these old singers. Can I come out and see you?"

I went out to see him, started talking to him, and then I tried to pick his brains over a period of time. He was about 65 to 70 at that time, and he was into religion and the church. He didn't want to talk that much about his old days in the record business. He said, "I was never dishonest with anybody—I didn't cheat them. But those days are gone." He really did not realize the importance of what he'd done.

You've got to remember, in the 1960s this was still "race music," and good white people just did not associate themselves with that kind of music. And so Speir did not treat blacks bad, but he also did not associate with them socially. He didn't go to places to hear them play that much. He told me, though, that on some Thursday afternoons he would drive up in the Delta and go where Charlie Patton was and listen to Charlie and Willie Brown on Thursday nights. He said he'd spend the night and come back down to Jackson or come back that same night.

Speir started working about 1926 as a "talent broker"—his own term—picking up talent and carrying it to the record companies. And he did three sessions in Mississippi for companies: 1930, Jackson for OKeh; 1935, Jackson for ARC [American Recording Corporation]; and 1936 in Hattiesburg for ARC.

Was he already in the talent-broker business, or did he start this after a couple of these bluesmen came to him?

No, I think what happened is, he was buying records from the companies and he got the idea himself. He said he'd known for years that they ought to be recording southern talent, you know, black blues—and the record companies weren't. So about 1926, he tried to interest the companies in recording black blues. And it's really about April 1927 before he really got somebody on record. He got a singer called William Harris that he found outside of Jackson, and he sent him to Birmingham to record for Gennett. That's the first blues guitar player that I know that Speir found. Now he may have found some before that—I don't know who they are. He found Tommy Johnson and Ishmon Bracey in 1927. He found Charlie Patton in 1929—and Skip James in 1931.

In December of 1927, he found Bracey on the

Speir recorded the first three records listed on this flyer at the 1930 OKeh session in Jackson. Courtesy Maxey Tarpley.

streets of Jackson, up on Farish Street, took him to his store, had him play for him. Bracey thought he was a detective because he came up in a suit and a tie, and Bracey followed him back to Speir's Music Store at 111 North Farish. His first store was at 225 North Farish, and he stayed about two or three years, then he moved to 111. And 111 is where this picture ᶜ was made, in January of 1929.

But he found Bracey about December of '27, and he took him and made a test upstairs on his recording equipment. And he made a test of Tommy Johnson—he got Tommy Johnson to come in. He made those tests and sent them to Ralph Peer at Victor. Peer is the same guy who recorded the Carter family and Jimmie Rodgers in Bristol, Tennessee, in 1927. He sent it to Victor. He said he'd never heard anything back from Ralph Peer. He said he thought they weren't interested, and suddenly he got a telegram from Ralph Peer saying, "Have these guys in Memphis on such and such date to record." So he sent them to Memphis.

None of these demos that he recorded were finished?

No. Well, not where you could tell they were done on an acetate.

But they were never issued as a finished product.

Oh no. They were totally tests, so the companies could hear how the voice sounded and the guitar sounded. And you gave them a chance to pass or reject the singer.

Speir's store on North Farish Street, 1929. At right are booths to listen to records. Speir had a custom recorder upstairs to cut acetates for a $5.00 price. Most all of the great Delta musicians came here to get on record or buy blues records themselves. Wardlow collection.

And they were doing it on acetate disc?

Yeah, doing it on metal disc. It's kind of like a metal base or an aluminum base. And you record with a diamond needle into the grooves, and it's called an acetate—that's what we call it today. But it was on metal in those days.

Do you know if any of them still exist anywhere?

I don't know of any. Mr. Speir's son had some, and he sent them to someone in Jackson and they kept them. Speir is the only person I've ever known who had a recording machine in the 1920s. He did what was called vanity recording. He would charge five dollars and he'd take somebody upstairs and let them make their own record.

Was this an electrical process or a mechanical process?

Electrical—by 1926 they had electrical machines.

So it went right from a microphone through an amplifier stylus and just etched it right into the plate.

It cut a groove into the metal. What, in effect, it was doing was cutting a record. But it was doing it in a metal-based surface. The companies cut on about 1 to $1^1/_2$ inches of beeswax, hard beeswax; they cut with their diamond needle into the beeswax. That was the master, then they made a pressing mother from the master.

That's where the expression "cutting a record" came from.

Right. You actually cut a record into beeswax in the 1920s and '30s. And they kept this wax under ice, and in the summertime, as soon as they recorded something, they'd put it into a refrigerator so it would not be affected by the intense heat in the South. They had a lot of trouble recording in the South, because the heat ruined the masters. And this is also why they made at least two takes of every song. Every song you did, you did at least two takes, three minutes long. Now the difference is, you might do 50 right now in the studio with tape, but in those days they didn't have tape. They had a wire recorder in the '30s. You could record on wire, but none of the companies ever recorded on wire, they recorded on hardened beeswax.

Victor didn't trust Speir's own judgment on Bracey and Tommy Johnson, so Ralph Peer wanted a test to pass on. Victor was called the Victor Talking Machine Company at first, then the Victor Phonograph Machine Company. Then RCA [Radio Corporation of America] bought out Victor about 1929, and it became RCA/Victor.

But Paramount would accept any artist Speir recommended. All he had to do was send them a telegram: "I'm sending so and so up, meet him in Milwaukee at such and such time." Charlie Patton, Skip James, Bracey, Johnson, all the people from Mississippi—Paramount took his word for it. They would take anyone he sent them.

Was Paramount the label that Patton, Willie Brown, and Son House recorded for when they went to Wisconsin? And was that through a Speir connection, too?

Yeah. Here's the story. First, Speir found Charlie Patton at Dockery's plantation.

So he scouted, as well? He didn't wait for them to come into the store?

No, he scouted. When Speir got in it about 1926, he began to hunt talent. He used to go looking for talent. He would go out with Art Laibley. He said he went to Birmingham, Mobile, New Orleans with Laibley. He said he found a lot of talent in Memphis and New Orleans—he said they were the best two towns for talent. He'd find people singing on the streets, he'd walk up to them and listen to them, and if he thought they were interesting enough to make a commercial record, he'd ask them to play some more of their songs to see if they had four songs. You had to have at least four songs to be able to make a record.

Bracey came in and auditioned, and Bracey told him about Tommy Johnson. So he went to hear Johnson up on the Pearl River, in a little camp where he was living. He went up there and listened to him, and he said he had one complete song—that's all he had. And he said, "You got to have four songs, Tommy, to record." So he started working on more songs.

What was that, "Big Road Blues"?

The first time, he cut "Big Road Blues," "Maggie Campbell Blues," "Cool Drink of Water Blues," and "Bye Bye Blues." But Bracey and Johnson both sold well enough. They recorded in February of '28 in Memphis, and Victor brought them back to Memphis to record in August of '28. So both of them sold.

Now Bracey told me that his record of "Saturday Blues," his first record out, he said Victor told him it sold 6,000 copies. That doesn't sound like a lot today, but you broke even when you sold 500 copies. So 6,000 made Victor some money, enough so that they'd bring Bracey back to record. Now Johnson had a big hit with "Canned Heat Blues," recorded that August. "Canned Heat Blues" came out in 1929—that was a big hit. And of course, that spawned the name of the band, Canned Heat, in the '60s; that's where they got their name.

Speir told me he went over into Mexico looking for talent to bring to San Antonio to record for the record companies. When he'd go up to St. Louis to place orders with the St. Louis Music Company, which was a major distributor, he would go out on the streets and hunt talent. He said one time he was up there, he picked up about five or six acts and sent them to the St. Louis Music Company. And he said the St. Louis Music Company arranged for them to be recorded, probably with Gennett. So he was traveling.

He told me when he went to Louisville, Kentucky, to buy carpet, he hunted talent on the streets there. Now he was also responsible for most of the string bands out of Mississippi: the Leake County Revelers from near

Carthage; Freeny's Barn Dance Orchestra from the little community of Freeny; the Newton County Hillbillies, from right in there between Newton County and Leake County where Carthage is—he recorded them for OKeh.

He recorded the great Grand Ole Opry star, Uncle Dave Macon. Uncle Dave Macon wrote him a letter from Murfreesboro [Tennessee], where he was living at that time when he was playing on the Grand Ole Opry, and said he wanted to record. Speir wrote him back, or wired him a telegram, and said, "Be in Jackson on such and such date." And that's some of the rarest of the Uncle Dave Macon recordings; he made six sides for OKeh in December 1930, in Jackson.

So he picked up string bands. As a matter of fact, when I found him in the '60s, he had orchestra and string-band records—he still had some fiddle bands. He didn't have any blues. He didn't have any Skip James, any Tommy Johnson, or any Charlie Patton.

He heard about Charlie Patton probably through Bo Carter. After receiving a letter from Patton, he went to Dockery's plantation to find Charlie and get him to audition. Then he brought him back to Jackson, put him on a train, went to Chicago, from Chicago to Richmond, Indiana. At that time the Gennett Company of Richmond, Indiana, owned by the Starr Piano Company, was making masters for Paramount, which did not yet have a studio. They were paying, I believe, $40 a side for masters in those days, and the masters were shipped to Wisconsin, then they made the records from them.

So Charlie went first to Richmond and recorded about 16 sides. Then about December of 1929, his records were selling really well, so Paramount wired Speir again to have him sent back. This time he went to Grafton, Wisconsin, where they had just opened a new studio. Paramount was actually located in Port Washington, but they recorded about three miles away in Grafton. So at Grafton, Patton made another session with a fiddler named Henry "Son" Sims from Clarksdale. He backed him up on a number of sides, and Sims recorded four sides himself. Sims was not a singer, but Paramount was willing to record anything by him, and it sold a few copies. That was December of 1929.

In April of 1930, the owner of Paramount, Otto Moeser, got Art Laibley, who was the Paramount sales manager and recording director, to wire Speir and then to call him on the phone and ask him to come to Grafton—they wanted to sell the company to him. He drove all the way to Grafton in April of 1930, he talked to Otto Moeser, and they offered him the Paramount Company lock, stock, and barrel for $25,000. That's how much it would take to move it from Wisconsin to Jackson, all the pressing equipment and all the facilities. Paramount, which

Speir discovered Skip James (from Bentonia some 35 miles north of Jackson) and sent him to Grafton, WI, to record in February 1931. Wardlow collection.

had been in the race record business since 1922, could have ended up in Mississippi, where all the great singers were.

But Speir didn't have the $25,000. He came back to Jackson and tried to raise the money through the Chamber of Commerce, and nobody would back him.

Now here's what happened: Speir would have had the money to buy it if he had known about four months earlier. He put $30,000 that he had made off his record store—five of them went into business and raised $150,000 to go over in Rankin County and drill for oil in 1929. They drilled, but they struck natural gas. And natural gas wasn't worth anything at that time. That particular natural-gas field is now the major gas field for the state of Mississippi. Mississippi Valley Gas still pumps out of that station. So he lost his money. If he'd have known he was going to be offered Paramount, he'd have had $30,000. But he said, "I'd have been a rich man if the oil had come in."

Speir's store was in the black neighborhood on Farish Street. He set it up specifically to sell to black customers in 1925, when he went into business. Ninety percent of his trade was black, ten percent was white. He stayed in the black district on Farish Street from about 1926 to about 1937. Then he moved up on West Capitol, and he stayed there until 1944. Then he moved out in north Jackson and opened a furniture store and got out of the record business.

In 1942 James Petrillo, head of the American Federation of Musicians union, called a strike against all the major record companies until they agreed to give union musicians more wages. And so the record companies just shut down for about 18 months, didn't produce any new records. All they could do was reissue what they already had in their catalogs. So when this happened, Speir got out of the record business—he thought the record business was dead.

Now what's interesting to note is, sometime after World War II, the Mc-Murrys went into the used-furniture business on Farish Street. And Speir said Lillian McMurry either called him or came by to see him and asked him about starting a record label, would it go? And he said, "Well, it could, if you got the right backing." And he told her she had plenty of good talent. And they started the Trumpet label. She had Elmore James on the label, Big Joe Williams, Sonny Boy Williamson, all Mississippi artists—Willie Love from Greenville and a lot of white hillbilly artists, also. Trumpet lasted from about 1950 to about 1955, about five years.

So would Speir be considered the one who discovered Son House and Willie Brown and those guys?

In May of 1930, Charlie Patton had moved from Dockery to Lula, Mississippi, and he ran into Son House and Willie Brown. He had played with Willie Brown many years earlier, but he met Son House.

So what happened is, Laibley wired Speir. Paramount wanted to get Patton back for a third session in May of 1930, after Speir had been up there in

April. He didn't want to go up himself and carry them, so he went to Patton and gave Patton the information. Laibley got the name and the address where Patton was, Laibley came down to see them, gave them expense money, and they drove up to Grafton. Had it not been for Speir, Laibley would never have found Patton, House, and Willie Brown. So Patton actually arranged for Willie Brown, Son House, and the piano player Louise Johnson to go with him to record the third time. But Speir was indirectly responsible.

That was Son House's first recording?

That was Son House's only recording commercially. He recorded in 1941 or '42 for the Library of Congress, but the only commercial records he made were 1930 in Grafton; he recorded at least eight documented sides.

All of them were issued?

All were issued. One record called "Clarksdale Moan" has never been found. There's one copy of "Preaching the Blues"; there are about three or four copies of "My Black Mama" and "Dry Spell Blues."

One of the Willie Brown Paramounts has never been found. They issued four sides by Willie Brown, and one of the records has never been found. They never showed up—no one's got a copy anywhere. Nobody knows how they sound. It was late 1931 or early 1932 when these Son House and Willie Brown records came out, and they didn't sell at all. Seventy-five cents was a tremendous amount of money for a poor black person in the South. They may have sold a few copies in the cities. The only place the late Paramounts show up is in, like, Virginia, where there was apple money and tobacco money. But where there was cotton money, there was no money anymore— the cotton fields provided the chief income of the black people [in the deep South].

When Paramount would call Speir and say, "Send so and so up to Wisconsin," would they pay the artist's fare up there?

Speir paid the expenses and they reimbursed him. Speir bought the train ticket and gave [the artist] some spending money, and the company reimbursed him. Now what Speir normally got, he said if they had four or six songs, "I got a hundred fifty cash." He said, "I got a hundred fifty for finding Charlie Patton." So he probably got paid $150 all three times Patton recorded, just for finding him for the company. But normally, he got $150 if the artist he picked could sing at least four songs. Now one he missed was Mississippi John Hurt—he didn't record John Hurt. John Hurt was found by a fiddle duo called Narmour and Smith who lived in Carrollton. They got John Hurt to come to Memphis with them and record for OKeh. That's the only major Mississippi artist that I know of that Speir missed.

So would you speculate that if it hadn't been for Speir, most of these artists would have never been heard of?

No doubt about it—they'd have never recorded, they'd have never been heard of. They'd just have been local names, you know, somebody who played on the streets. If Speir hadn't been there, the greatest of the Delta blues singers would probably have never recorded. I mean, Patton had been performing since 1910 in the Delta. It's 1929 before Speir hears about Patton. Now Patton had a chance to record.

There was a man in Itta Bena, Mississippi, called Frank Lembo—had a record store and sold Victrolas and furniture. He picked up two or three artists in 1927. He picked up Rube Lacy, and he picked up Washington White [Bukka White] for his first Victor session in 1930. So he got some talent. But he tried to get Patton to go and record for Columbia, and Patton wouldn't go because of Lembo's reputation—he didn't trust him. If Patton had come on down to Jackson, he could have walked into Speir's music store, and Speir would have probably sent him off a couple of years earlier. He told me Patton had the greatest talent of anybody he ever saw. He said he had six, eight, ten songs or more. He said, "I knew he'd go over well because he had so many songs, and they all belonged to him."

Tell me the Robert Johnson–H.C. Speir story.

In 1935, Speir recorded for ARC, worked with Art Satherly and Don Law and W.R. Calaway at Farish Street for a record session. In July of 1936, he met Calaway down in Hattiesburg. They recorded about 100 masters; they released something like 20 or 30, maybe 40 at the most. Calaway never paid Speir. Speir said he never was paid, although I would've thought Art Satherly would have made sure he was paid, because Satherly was the president of ARC, and he went to Columbia later on and recorded people like Roy Acuff and Bob Wills. But Speir didn't get paid by Calaway.

Robert Johnson came into his store, went upstairs, and made an audition record.

This was Robert Johnson's first recording.

Yeah. Now Speir did not remember making a demo for him. Steve LaVere says he talked to one of the relatives of Johnson, and Johnson brought a demo, or a little acetate, to play on the wind-up Victrolas. So that would have come from Speir's store. But Speir did remember him singing and throwing his voice up on "Kindhearted Woman." And I played him "Kindhearted Woman" by Johnson and he said, "Oh, I remember that guy—he threw his voice up like Bracey did."

So probably, if he made a demo there, it would have been "Kindhearted Woman."

Oh yeah. It would have been "Kindhearted Woman" or "Terraplane Blues." Now Speir sold his records, but he remembered the song, "Kindhearted Woman." He said the guy threw his voice up in falsetto.

What you've got to remember is, even though Robert Johnson's considered a great talent, Speir had heard plenty of great talent. He'd heard Charlie Patton, Skip James, and Tommy Johnson. So Robert Johnson was just an unknown blues singer trying to make a buck and get on records. But for some reason, he thought Johnson would go commercially. He took his name and address and sent it to the ARC salesman in New Orleans named Ernie Oertle. Oertle called upon Speir once a month, coming out of New Orleans, bringing sample records for him to order from ARC. ARC is five labels: Melotone, Perfect, Banner, Oriole, and Romeo. But they also owned the Vocalion label at that time. Most of Johnson's stuff came out on either Melotone or Perfect, or on Vocalion. When they did the Robert Johnson reissue, they put a Vocalion label on the front of the box.

So what Speir did is, he sent Johnson's name to Ernie Oertle—wherever Johnson could be found. I don't know if it was an address in maybe Hazelhurst or an address in Jackson, where a relative was supposed to be living. But Oertle went and found Johnson, whether it was in Robinsonville or whether it was in Jackson or Hazelhurst, and took him to San Antonio, Texas, to record.

Now ARC, in 1935, had started recording in San Antonio and Dallas to open up the jukebox market in Texas. And what they were doing, they were recording a lot of the western-swing bands like Bob Wills at that time. And this was going on the jukeboxes throughout Texas and was making them money, because a lot of the copies could be sold and played on jukeboxes. So Johnson went to San Antonio, where they were recording at that time, in November of 1936, and made his first sides. Then he came back in June of 1937 to Dallas.

So Robert Johnson probably heard about Speir through—

Oh, he heard about him through all the black musicians he played with. If he played in Jackson, he's bound to have known that Tommy Johnson and Ishmon Bracey and Bo Carter and all these guys had made records, and he'd asked them, "How'd you get on record?" Robert Johnson told Elizabeth Moore Glynn when he was a teenager that he was going to make records someday, that he was going to go to New York and make records someday. She quoted me that particular statement. (That was Willie Moore's wife. She lived on the same plantation near Robinsville near Robert's family. She was married to a man named "Hard Rock" Glynn at one time first, and then she became Moore's wife later on in her lifetime.)

She said Johnson told her he was going to make records someday and that he was going to be famous, that he was going to New York to make records—that was his goal in life. And he accomplished it. But if it hadn't been for Speir, Robert Johnson probably would have never been recorded. You see, you got to look at it—Johnson was playing his style by 1931 or '32, and most of the songs in his repertoire he'd probably known for four or five years and had his number-one pieces down. Why didn't he come to Jackson earlier and see Speir? Either he didn't feel he was good enough, or he never found out that Speir was the man to get you on records. You just have to speculate which it would be.

But all these guys did go to his store.

They auditioned at his store. If he found them on the street, he'd listen to them on the street and then bring them down to the record store. If he thought they were good enough talent to record, he'd make an acetate to listen to them himself and to send off to the company.

Now Paramount didn't require an acetate at all—they took Speir's word for anything he'd send them. Skip James brags that he came into Speir's store with another musician—Slim Duckett was his name. Slim Duckett and One Leg Sam Norwood recorded in December of '30 for OKeh. Now here was Skip James, living at Bentonia, 35 miles out of Jackson, and he didn't get on the OKeh sessions—Speir didn't find him, see. So Skip James, about February of 1931—about two months after the recording session at the King Edward Hotel—comes into Speir's store to audition.

Now James said in all these interviews that there were 20 or 25 people lined up to audition, and he was the only one that passed. The truth is, Mr. Speir told me he never set aside days for musicians to line up. He said they would come into his store to talk to him, but he didn't set aside certain days as audition days—he didn't want to have that many people coming in his store at one time. So Skip James' story was a falsehood. Speir said it didn't happen that way.

What he did is, James came in and played four or five songs. James said he played "Devil Got My Woman," and Speir passed on him [said he passed the audition]. That may be possible. He probably had him play a couple of more songs to make sure he knew at least four songs.

So then in two or three days, he bought him a train ticket to Milwaukee. They went to Chicago on the Illinois Central, then they rode the "electric train" from Chicago to Milwaukee. And Art Laibley from Paramount met James in Milwaukee, took him in the studio, and he recorded over a period of a couple of days.

Now Speir told me another interesting story. He declared that he took Skip James to Memphis to record him, and James got religion on him and wouldn't play the blues. Now this would have to be after 1931. I think it was probably the Jackson session in 1935, and he got his towns mixed up.

So was Speir saying [James] got religion on the trip?

He got religion in the studio. He started singing gospel songs and wouldn't sing any blues; he got religion and wouldn't record at all. He was very moody, Speir said. He and Bracey would have these religion spells, where they'd stop singing blues totally and go back in the church.

So there was complete separation between blues and church.

You were either serving the Lord or you were serving the devil. And if you played blues and lived that lifestyle, you served the devil and you were going to hell. Good church people didn't have anything to do with blues singers.

Why would a poor black pay 75 cents for a record?

You got to realize this. In the 1920s, there was no black radio, there was no television. The only medium they had was the wind-up Victrola and the record. So they listened to the records for relaxation, or they played them to dance by. All you could do was hear a live singer on the streets. You could come into town on a Saturday and you'd hear somebody on the streets playing for a nickel or a dime and taking up collection. And people like Bessie Smith, Ma Rainey were big, they were giants to the black people. Ninety percent of Speir's customers were black. Of that 90 percent, probably 90 percent were women. Seventy-five cents was a lot of money in the 1920s. But the sharecropper didn't buy the records. The woman who worked for the white man as a cook or a maid in his home bought the records—she had money. People bought records when they got their cotton money in the fall. Or if they got their spring planting money, they'd go buy some

Hayes McMullan (1902–1990) was a local Delta bluesman who played dances and "suppers," but made his living from sharecropping, not music. He recorded a 1968 album that is unreleased. Wardlow collection.

records. But the women bought the records, not the men; the women owned the Victrolas, not the men. And if you had a Victrola, you had a lot of prestige in your community.

A lot of the song lyrics had sexual symbolism.

Oh yeah, they were sexually explicit sometimes, or double-meaning songs.

So in a way, it was like buying pornography. I mean, a black wouldn't spend 75 cents to buy a record like "Terraplane Blues" just for the music.

But it had that great dance rhythm, too. And blacks loved big cars. If you owned a big car, that was a symbol of affluence, of success. However, I don't know of any blacks who owned a Hudson Terraplane or a Cadillac in the 1930s.

But when Johnson was singing about his car, that was a woman he was talking about.

Yeah, he was using the symbolism of the Hudson Terraplane being like a woman. I mean, that sold. But Johnson was nowhere near as explicit as Bo

Carter, who recorded "Let me squeeze your lemon" and "Your biscuits are big enough for me." And Victor kept recording him because he sold so well. He was the dirtiest man on records.

But the record companies had to know they were exploiting this sexual thing among blacks and charging them 75 cents for a record.

They probably didn't, because most of the white executives working for the record companies didn't understand the double meaning of the black language. Speir said Art Satherly understood what they were saying the best and what they meant. But he said the rest of those guys had no idea what those lines meant. He said, "I knew, because I grew up around Negroes in the hill country, and I hear them singing. So I knew what they were talking about." And the black public knew what they meant, the person buying the records knew what they meant, because they'd heard this kind of talk all their lives on the streets.

Would you speculate that because of the sexual content of the blues, there was that separation between the church and—

Well, that's one thing. But it was not so much the sexual meanings. Blues was associated with gambling and drinking. Remember, we had Prohibition in the '20s. If you played blues, you played where people drank and gambled and carried on and committed adultery—all the things that the black church and the white church stood against: gambling, fornication, adultery, violence, murder. A lot of people got killed or stabbed or cut up at a juke house. Or at a house party, somebody would get shot sometimes.

See, there weren't any commercial places to go. If you lived in a small town in the Delta, you went to a house party. Some plantation owners might have a place they could open up as a juke on weekends, but most didn't and you played house parties. That's what Hayes McMullan played, that's what Bracey played, Tommy Johnson, Patton—they played dances or "suppers" mainly. Somebody like Patton would be hired for a dance on Saturday night, and he would attract a large audience.

This song about sex (jellyroll) was a big seller for Paramount in early 1930. Wardlow collection.

Speir told me that on a good day in the springtime or summertime, he sold anywhere from 300 to 600 78s. He was open from eight o'clock in the morning till ten at night. You see, in those days, the poor blacks and poor whites all came to town on Saturdays. They came into town in old cars or even wagons in those days, in the '20s and '30s. But it wasn't in the '30s that he sold as many records as the good days in the '20s, when everything was booming. Speir said he stocked 3,000 78s, and 90 percent were race records ordered for the blacks and sold to the blacks. Sometimes the whites bought dance music, like Bennie Moten's

Kansas City Orchestra or Jelly Roll Morton. But in those days, every record company had a separate numerical series that they called "race." Paramount started about 1921 or '22, and everything in the 12,000 series was race. Columbia: 14,000 was race, 15,000 was white hillbilly. Victor had a 38,000 and a 23,000 series that was nothing but black music. Now Victor mixed a lot of their stuff in between for a long time and didn't start till 1928 making a black series. Gennett mixed theirs in. On certain records, it would say, "Race Record Blues" or "Old Timey Singing" or "Old Time Fiddle Band," things like that on the label. On Johnson's record, it says "Vocal Blues with Guitar Accompaniment." But 90 percent of the black blues songs had "blues" in the title somewhere, so you'd find blues.

Speir paid 45 cents for the record and retailed it for 75 cents. He said the major companies told him it took about 28 cents to make a record. So they made 17 cents off the record and he made 30 cents. There was no return in those days; in other words, if you bought something and didn't sell it, you didn't get your money back. Columbia and Victor were shipped out of New Orleans. Paramount and Vocalion were shipped by the St. Louis Music Company. OKehs were shipped out of Memphis. They shipped records in every week by railway express. The St. Louis Music Company wholesaled all the types of guitars, musical equipment, Victrolas.

Now Speir carried Victors and Columbias. Victor called its machine the Victrola, and Columbia called its machine the Graphonola. [Speir] said you could get a machine for under $100, and some of the big Victor Orthophonics sold for $150–$200, but the blacks couldn't afford it. If you look at the picture [1929 photograph of Speir's store], you see he's got a lot of suitcase models. You could buy a suitcase model for $9.95 up to $14.95. All these were pre-electric wind-up machines.

Now Victor came out with an electric motor in 1927, but the majority of blacks didn't have electricity. The Victrolas were shipped in from New Orleans and New York City. Victor had an assembly plant in New Orleans. As a matter of fact, Speir said he went down there when he got out of the Navy and worked about two years, and this is where he got the idea to go into the music business. And so he came back to Jackson eventually and borrowed a little money and got into the business.

Speir sold Stella guitars for $9.95. He sold Nationals. He said he had some of the big jumbo metal-bodied guitars that he sold for $32.50. I don't know how anybody had that much money to buy one. Johnny Temple told me that Memphis Minnie and Kansas Joe McCoy said they went up to Chicago to record in about 1930, and they came back driving a new Winston car with two brand-new Style 1 Tri-cone Nationals—the first metal-bodied guitars anybody had ever seen in Jackson. And those sold for $125 apiece.

Did Speir mention what kind of instruments any of these guys played?

Stellas. He said they played the old, cheap Stella guitars—across the board. Speir said Martins weren't very good guitars; he said they didn't work at all for blues.

He sold violins and what looks like banjo ukes back there hanging up. You walk in on the left, and you got the Victrolas and the portable wind-up Victrolas on the right. That's a radio standing by him. And there were four listening booths, where people took the records in and listened to the 78s. I don't know if he sold sheet music; it looks like he may have some sheet music there. If you look up there, there are advertisements for Art Gilham and Paul Whiteman. He said Columbia and Victor sent out a lot of promotional material; he said somebody like Paramount didn't send much.

People like Muddy Waters and Howlin' Wolf, who were not contemporaries of the bluesmen Speir recorded, were influenced mostly by the records.

Right. The first-line singers of the '20s weren't influenced by records, they were influenced by people they heard playing live. Robert Johnson heard a hell of a lot of good records somewhere. He copied Charlie Patton. He took some melodies from Skip James. "Hellhound on My Trail" is the same song as "Devil Got My Woman"; his "32-20 Blues" is the same melody as Skip James' "22-20 Blues." "Preaching Blues" was Son House's song. Son House recorded "Preaching Blues" in 1930. So Johnson was tremendously influenced by records.

So indirectly, what Speir did influenced postwar blues.

Sure. Speir recorded the prewar Mississippi guys, and then people like Muddy Waters and Elmore James took it up to Chicago and it became postwar blues. Robert Johnson is kind of the link between the old and new. That's why Johnson has such a reputation; that's why Johnson is the man. They took Johnson's music and went to Chicago with it, played it on electric guitar and created Chicago blues.

You see, in those days, every company had a hillbilly series, a pop series, and a race series, and they just tried to retail them in different markets. They found out about 1921 or '22 that they could sell white fiddle music down south. And it was about 1926 before anybody ever recorded guitar blues, really. In 1926, Paramount found Blind Lemon and Blind Blake, and both of them started selling really well.

So all the other companies jumped on the bandwagon and tried to find guitar blues from real southern artists; they started coming down south to places like Atlanta, Memphis, Dallas, Jackson, and Louisville, Kentucky, to set up and record once or twice a year. And Speir would take people and go to these recording sessions. He told me he went to recording sessions in New Orleans, Memphis, Chicago, Atlanta.

Now remember, he was taking not just black, he was taking white people, too. He was taking white artists like preachers or fiddle string bands; he was taking them to places to record, also. Normally, you think about him as the guy who was responsible for all the great black talent, but he found a lot of white talent, too. He loved white fiddle music. He found a Choctaw Indian fiddle band from Oklahoma that was at the Philadelphia

Choctaw Festival in the summertime and got them on Victor. Big Chief Henry was his name.

But he missed on Jimmie Rodgers. He told me that Jimmie Rodgers came in his store to audition. He said Rodgers sang a couple of songs and he said, "Jimmie, you're not ready to record right now." He said, "I didn't think much of his songs. I told him to go back to Meridian, and when he worked up four or six more good songs, bring them back and see me again and I'd listen." He said the next thing he knew, he looked up one day and Jimmie Rodgers was on RCA Victor.

How old was Jimmie Rodgers?

He was about 30 years old when he auditioned for Speir, but he didn't do a "Blue Yodel." You got to remember, Jimmie Rodgers' first record for Victor was "Sleep Baby Sleep," and it sold just enough copies that Victor brought him back in the studio and then he made "Blue Yodel." And "Blue Yodel" started selling like hotcakes, and he was set from then on as a big recording star.

So Jimmie Rodgers probably heard about Speir the same way as the other guys did. So would you say, on a small scale, Speir in Jackson was kind of like Nashville today?

He was. He told me people would write the companies saying they wanted to get on record and they were a good talent, and the companies would write them back and say either write Mr. H.C. Speir in Jackson, Mississippi, or go there. He said he actually had people from out of state come to his store to audition. And he would tell them, "Go home, work some more, and come back someday when you've got some more songs."

He said the main reason most people didn't get recorded was because they didn't have enough songs, original material. The record companies didn't want material that had been done by somebody else, they wanted original material. That's why Charlie Patton and Skip James were so big— because they had a lot of material. Skip James recorded somewhere around 16 to 20 sides for Paramount. Patton probably did 12 or 14 sides the first session, about 15 or 16 the second session, and four the last session with Son House and Willie Brown. By then, May 1930, the Depression was starting.

John Hurt's first record, "Frankie," sold so well that Tommy Rockwell, who was the director for OKeh Records, wired Hurt and went him money to come to New York. So he went to the New York studios. Speir said if they thought the talent was good enough, really worthwhile, and would make them some money, they'd bring them up to New York to record in their best studios. So John Hurt was good enough in OKeh's eyes to go to New York to record.

The only other Mississippi solo artist I know of that ever went to New York to record was Charlie Patton. Speir had made a demo of Son House, Willie Brown, and Charlie Patton and sent it to W.R. Calaway. And Calaway came down to Speir's store in 1934 to get their addresses. He went into the Delta and found Patton in jail in Belzoni—finally tracked him down to Belzoni from Holly Ridge, where he was living at that time, which is in Sunflower County. He took him back to Meridian, and they rode the train from Meridian to New York City. And Patton recorded up there for a couple of days, Patton and his wife Bertha Lee.

Getting back to Tommy Johnson, didn't you tell me he had a speech impediment?

Yeah. Speir said Johnson stuttered a lot, and he couldn't speak plain when you were talking to him. He'd have to start singing before he'd stop stuttering. And he said he kind of hissed when he talked, and that was a natural distraction. So he said he kind of felt sorry for Tommy because he was tongue-tied or something. He didn't hiss or stutter on records.

He was a chronic alcoholic.

He drank canned heat. The amazing thing is, Tommy Johnson lived from 1896 to 1956: he lived to be sixty years old, as much rot-gut whiskey and canned heat and antiseptics as he drank.

How do you consume canned heat?

You boil it down and melt it, and the alcohol comes out. Then you drink the alcohol.

Speir said that every blues singer is going to drink at least a little bit. He'd not going to make music or have an emotional feeling until he gets a little alcohol in him. He said he'd buy antiseptic or he'd buy canned heat. He said most of them drank antiseptic—they could buy that when they couldn't obtain bonded alcohol in those Prohibition days.

Ishmon Bracey told me that when he and Tommy Johnson went to record for Paramount in Grafton, Wisconsin, at the studio there was some Old Charter whiskey in a barrel. Tommy had never seen bonded whiskey before. This was 1920s, prohibition. Where would you see Old Charter in Mississippi if you were a poor black guy? Johnson drank so much he was ruining the takes. [For more, see Bracey's recollection in "Got Four, Five Puppies, One Little Shaggy Hound," page 45.]

Speir said one time, Tommy got thrown in jail and called him, and he went and put up $150 bond. He remembered it was $150, because that was a lot of money in tight times, Depression days—must have been the early '30s. And he said Tommy jumped bail and went to Crystal Springs. And Speir went looking for him, couldn't find him in Crystal Springs, went on down to Louisiana, and they told him he was living in a little town called Angie, Louisiana. And he walked up on in a garden and he said, "Tommy, you got to go back with me," and he put handcuffs on him.

He said Johnson begged him, "Don't make me go back, Mr. Speir." He said, "Well, I'll lose my hundred fifty dollars." So he took him back to Jackson.

He said later on, he saw him on a county road one time or a city work crew around town. [Johnson] was drinking a lot, so he probably got arrested for public drunkenness. [Speir] really must have felt for Johnson.

Who was Isaiah Nettles?

Isaiah Nettles made four sides in 1935 for ARC. In October of 1935, ARC came to Jackson and they did this session upstairs on Farish Street—lasted about ten days. But earlier, in December of 1930, OKeh Records came to Jackson, to the King Edward Hotel, and they recorded for about ten days, too—recorded hillbilly, blues, and gospel. And Speir was responsible for all that talent.

What about Blind Joe Reynolds?

Blind Joe Reynolds, also known as Blind Willie Reynolds, grew up in Tallulah. Speir found him at Lake Providence and sent him to Paramount. He recorded a song called "Outside Woman Blues." In about 1967, Cream recorded it. He only recorded four sides for Paramount, and only two sides, "Outside Woman" and "Nehi Mama," have ever been found. He also recorded two released sides for Victor in 1930.

Anyone else you can think of?

Speir told me there was an old woman in the Meridian train station he used to love to come by and hear. She was a train caller, and he said she'd sing out where the trains were going. He said she was fabulous. He said, "I tried to get her to go on records, but she wouldn't do it." He said, "I'd have put a harmonica or something like that behind her." He said he'd come here to Meridian just to hear her. He also recorded a guy in 1927 named Moses Mason from Lake Providence, Louisiana, who sold hot tamales and played a guitar and sang out, "Get your hot tamales . . ."

How would you appraise the Speir legacy?

Speir was the godfather of Delta blues. H.C. Speir was to '20s and '30s country blues what Sam Phillips was to '50s rock 'n' roll—a musical visionary. If it hadn't been for Speir, Mississippi's greatest natural resource might have gone untapped.

[GW: The Mississippi Sheiks also did a 1931 session in New York studios.]

V
Retrospectives

Rev. D.C. Rice—
Gospel Singer

While knocking on doors for records in 1967, I encountered an elderly black man who said he had no blues records but had "some of those good gospel records, not those 'devil's records.'" After talking about religious artists such as Revs. J.M. Gates, F.W. McGee, and D.C. Rice, he said, "I knew D.C. Rice, I used to go to his church in Chicago. He's over there somewhere in Alabama, last time I heard." That tip led to a quick check of phone books in Selma and Montgomery; Bishop D.C. Rice was listed in the Montgomery directory. I called him about his old recordings, and when he responded with a letter, I went to Montgomery for an interview. This was the first article on a major sanctified preacher who recorded in the 1920s. —GDW

[Originally published in *Storyville* no. 23 (June–July 1969): 164–167.]

Rev. D.C. Rice recorded some of the greatest gospel records of the era. Rice left Chicago in the early 1930s and returned to Montgomery, where he pastored a Holiness Church. Wardlow collection.

Montgomery, Alabama—"Within thirty days, my records were all over Chicago, and Mr. Kapp told me it would take 10,000 records to even try to fill up all the music stores in the country with a copy."

The gentleman talking—already established in the history of recorded sanctified music—recalled with serious interest his days of recording for the Vocalion Record Company as Rev. D.C. Rice and his congregation.

In 1969, almost 40 years later, Rice was still active in church work in the South. He was Bishop of the Apostolistic [*sic*] Overcoming Holy Church of God for the states of Alabama, Georgia, and Florida. Besides this honor, Rice was pastor of a local church in Montgomery—the Oak Street Holiness Church at 805 Oak Street—a member church of the denomination that Rice had belonged to since his arrival in Montgomery in 1932.

Bishop Rice, as his friends called him, was born in rural Barbour County, Alabama, around 1888. Although Rice did not divulge his exact age, a friend said that he was close to 80 at this writing.

Rice's father was a member of a local Baptist church, and Rice recalled that he was converted in his father's church, but not "really saved" until 1917, when he joined the Holiness Church in Chicago. He had left home and the South to live in Chicago in 1915 or 1916.

He soon became interested in the music that was sweeping the Holiness Churches of the Chicago area and began to attend a local church, the Church of the Living God, Pentecostal, served by a Bishop Hill.

According to Rice, this particular church had been organized by Hill to offer an alternative to the Church of God in Christ (COGIC), whose movement was spreading through the U.S. The formation of the national COGIC organization took place in Los Angeles, California, in 1906; there, Bishop Mason and Bishop Jones, a noted song leader of the era, had broken relations over which types of music arrangements were "holy" and which were "not holy" in the House of God.

Mason had developed the new "sanctified" movement in his church. From the first congregation in 1897 in the small Mississippi town of Lexington, the movement spread like wildfire across the country.

By World War I, the sanctified movement had spread among different denominations, and Rice recalled that "there were thirty to forty Holiness churches in Chicago" when he arrived from the South.

Many collectors consider Vocalion tops in its quality of artist selections and recording sound. Courtesy Maxey Tarpley.

Rice's fate was determined in 1917, when he was "really saved" at a Sunday morning service at Hill's church on Chicago's crowded East Side. "I got saved at 11:40 AM," he said. "I'll never forget the time or place. I thought I was saved before that, but I really wasn't."

Rice continued to attend Hill's church for some three years more, until Hill died. Then Rice had the opportunity to accept a small and struggling sanctified congregation of the same denomination on Chicago's West Side.

The church had only about 15 members when Rice took charge, but it grew steadily under the powerful musical leadership of the pastor, who brought ideas and concepts he had learned at Hill's church to his new membership.

At Hill's church, a variety of instruments—almost anything that could make a sound—were used by the congregation. These included bass fiddle, tambourine, cymbals, triangle, guitar, cornet, trombone, and drums.

In 1928, Rice heard the first race releases of Revs. F.W. McGee and J.M. Gates. Immediately, Rice decided that he could make recordings just as good.

After a few days of hard thinking, Rice went to downtown Chicago to talk to a representative of Vocalion Records.

Rice nervously approached the artist and repertoire director for the company, Jack Kapp, and told him that he would like a tryout to see if he was good enough to record.

Rice was scared, "plenty scared" he remembers, but he said his courage helped him. "You got to have courage."

Kapp agreed. He told Rice to bring his congregation the following Saturday for tests to determine the value of the music.

When Rice arrived in the Vocalion studios with about ten members of his congregation, Kapp told him to "preach like you are preaching to the whole world out there." Rice did just that and used songs he had written himself for the audition.

When the tests were finished, Kapp walked up to him and said, "I wouldn't give you a nickel for your music." He told Rice he was sorry, but he couldn't use him at that time.

One of Rev. Rice's greatest records was "I'm Pressing On." Rice believed, "The spirit moves through the music." Wardlow collection.

Rice left the studios heavy-hearted and full of disappointment, but on the following Wednesday, he received a phone call from Kapp telling him to be in the Vocalion studios on the following Saturday morning and be prepared to record.

Rice never understood what prompted Kapp to tell him he was of no use to Vocalion after the tests, then call him later in the week, unless Kapp was either trying to put Rice to a test, or get him to work for less money than other artists were receiving.

Rice appeared at the studios on a Saturday in April 1928 and recorded two titles, making three

VOCALION RACE RECORDS

SUPPLEMENT FOR NOVEMBER, 1931

When Can I Get It?   Vocal with Two Pianos   .   .   .   1642
That Thing's a Mess   Kansas City Kitty, Georgia Tom

Beat It Right   .   .   .   Vocal with Guitar   .   .   .   1643
Preachers Blues   Guitar by Memphis Minnie   Kansas Joe

I Want God's Bosom to Be Mine   Spiritual Vocals   .   .   1644
Join the Band   Birmingham Jubilee Singers

Tight Haired Mama Blues   Vocal with Piano and Guitar   1645
Days of the Week Blues   Charley Jordan

Straddle the Fence   Fox Trots   With Vocal Chorus   .   .   1646
Levee Low Down   Jackson and His Musical Champions

We Got That Same Kinda Power Over Here   .   .   .   1647
New Born Again   Sermons with Singing   Rev. D. C. Rice

Five Minute Blues   .   .   .   Vocal with Piano   .   .   1648
Better Bring It Right Away   Lee Green

Ain't It a Pity and a Shame   1649
Don't Hang My Clothes on No Barb Wire Line
   Vocal, Guitar (The Devil's Son-in-Law) Peetie Wheatstraw

ALL VOCALION RECORDS SEVENTY-FIVE CENTS

Rice's last record was issued in late 1931 when record sales had plummeted since 1928; few copies were sold at the 75 cent retail price. Courtesy Maxey Tarpley.

takes of each song, with the best one of each three chosen for release. (Whereas Godrich and Dixon do not give take numbers on the Rice releases, Rice insists that this practice did exist and this is how Vocalion recorded him. Perhaps by this date the company made no distinction between different takes of the same song, and thus did not list them separately.) The first two recorded sides were "A Sure Foundation" and "The Angels Rolled the Stone Away," released on Vocalion 1178.

Rice would not accept a royalty basis contract from Kapp, but insisted instead on being paid $75 a side or $150 a record.

Within a short time—according to *Blues & Gospel Records* and Rice himself—he was back in the studios, obviously because his first release was selling well. In Rice's powerful singing and sanctified arrangements, Vocalion apparently had found its answer to Victor's Rev. McGee. Rice kept, as nearly as possible, the same personnel for all his sessions for Vocalion, but Kapp also brought in union musicians to back Rice on some occasions. These were usually either a trumpet player or a bass tuba musician.

The piano player on Rice's records was Louis Hooper (not to be confused with the New York blues pianist of the same name), while a "Mr. Hunter," his first name now forgotten, played the trombone. Hunter's father played the drums and Hooper's father also played the trombone as well as the bass viola. Rice's wife played the tambourine and also sang on some titles. The cornet or trumpet player, whose identity has long been a mystery of some debate in jazz circles, was furnished by Vocalion. Rice did not remember his name; he said he never really knew him that well. (Some jazz authority may wish to speculate which musician Kapp might have used on the sessions. Punch Miller's name has been mentioned.)

Louis Hooper and his father were both members of another Holiness Church in Chicago—the Holy Nazarene Church—while both Hunters were members of Rice's denomination. Hooper actually played for many church revivals in the Chicago area; Rice mentioned that Hooper had played frequently at Rev. McGee's church on Chicago's North Side.

So, a closeness between the ideas and musical adaptations of Rice and those of McGee can be noted. (Some authorities on sanctified recordings consider the records of Rice and McGee to be the best of those recorded in the 1920s.)

Rice remembers that it usually took about an hour and a half to record a session. Rice used a radio station's studio adjacent to the Vocalion studios to broadcast his services, beginning each Sunday at 12:45 PM. Thus, many recording sessions were set for Sunday mornings; when the session was finished, Rice went on the air with his regular Sunday program.

Rice reflected on the difference between the new sanctified music and the church music of his childhood.

"The Baptist Church didn't allow us to play music in church when I was growing up," said Rice. "Anything besides the piano was considered to be the music of the devil and was frowned upon. People just sang the old songs in those days, just like a choir or in groups of three or four. Our music went just the opposite way and got away from this. We put rhythm into the church because the people wanted it."

Rice also remembers that the blues "were played down in Alabama, when I was a little boy, and they said that they had been playing them before that time."

Rice, however, saw no religious singers playing guitars on the streets, until he reached Detroit on a revival and promotion trip and ran into such a group on the city streets singing and playing for the public.

Rice had a masterful feeling for his music. "My ideas would come to me in my sleep," he said. "At times I would just wake up and the words would be in my mouth, and I would have myself another song."

Recounting how he developed his recordings, Rice said he, not Kapp, decided when a solo was needed to give a song such as "Pressing On" more impact—and greater sales. "People need to feel the rhythm of God."

Rice also had one advantage over McGee: he did almost all of his own lead singing, backed by his congregation. McGee's records often feature solos by other singers.

Once, Kapp tried to get Rice to do some sermons on subjects such as "Tight Like That," the same type of material that the Rev. Emmett Dickenson (a Baptist preacher on Chicago's East Side, according to Rice) did for Paramount, but Rice refused. "It was not my type of music or preaching," he said. He also refused Kapp's requests that he take a trip to Atlanta to record a session with some members of a congregation there.

In the summer of 1930, Rice wrote Paramount asking for the opportunity to record. Paramount responded agreeably, arranged for two test recordings, and paid travelling expenses to Grafton, Wisconsin, for Rice and other members of the party. The group stayed for two days in a boarding house the company had leased for its artists, and Rice recorded two titles, now lost from his memory. At one time he owned the test pressings, which Paramount gave him, but both have been lost. This is unfortunate, for Paramount issued very few sanctified recordings that were actually made at Grafton; as of 1969 I can only recall the Rev. T.T. Rose, issued on Pm 12966.

Toward the end of 1930, after it became impossible for his church to support him, Rice left Chicago. He moved south to Jackson, Alabama, and served as pastor of a small church in that locality for two years.

In 1932, Rice became the pastor of the Oak Street Holiness Church in Montgomery and joined its denomination. In 1941, he was made Bishop over the three-state area already mentioned, and became responsible for the growth and the administration of denomination churches within that area.

Since then, his church modernized its music somewhat, using the electric organ in preference to the piano. The big bass drums were still present, but there was no one in the church capable of playing trombone or cornet effectively. His second wife (his first was killed in an automobile accident) led the choir and did a magnificent job of lead singing.

She performs in the manner of Rosetta Tharpe. Miss Tharpe, who is one of the best-known sacred singers, was first discovered by Rice. "I got Rosetta Tharpe into music when she was just a child. I helped her then, but later she went to New York and sold out to the devil." (Perhaps Rice was judging according to his concept of Christian living and performing.)

Many of Rice's recordings were adapted from standards. "Pressing On," Rice said, came from "I'm Pressing On in the Heavenly Way," an old standard still sung in southern white Protestant churches. Other songs came from Bible verses like "No Night There" and "The Wise and Foolish Virgins." Obviously, almost all sanctified songs recorded in the 1920s by various artists were written in that time period. This likely came about from the new sanctified churches; sanctified music did not really begin to spread until shortly after 1900.

Finally, Rice said that he did record titles for Kapp that were released on the Brunswick label. He identified "Soon We'll Gather at the River" and "Where He Leads Me I Will Follow" as songs he recorded. He said Kapp wanted to get some of his music on another label besides Vocalion. This should help clear up the mystery of the Brunswick recordings released under the name of the Southern Sanctified Singers on Brunswick 7074—despite the skepticism, based on aural study, expressed by *Blues and Gospel Records.*

[EK: Rice died in March 1973 in Montgomery (Misiewicz 1991).]

Canton, Mis'sippi Breakdown

Gayle Dean Wardlow with Mike Leadbitter

After writing several articles, including the one on Tommy Lee "Legs" Thompson, at Mike Leadbitter's requests, I received yet another one from him in 1971—this time for information to be used in what would be the first in-depth Elmore James article. I had previously heard from Johnny Temple that James had an adopted brother, Robert Holston, in Canton, Mississippi. With the premier Carolinas researcher-writer Pete Lowry of New York State, I followed Temple's tip during a weekend investigation in the Canton area and interviewed Holston. The details gathered were sent to Leadbitter, who then added information about James from interviews with Sonny Boy Williamson II (Aleck Miller) and Homesick James.

One bit of information that has not been confirmed is the report of James' early marriage to Josephine Harris. The leading Elmore James researcher in Mississippi, Pat LeBlanc, has been unable to substantiate this detail.

Additionally, the account that Leadbitter gleaned from Sonny Boy Williamson II and Homesick James—that Lillian McMurry recorded James without his knowledge—is erroneous. Mrs. McMurry has stated in print that she recorded James with his full knowledge (for more, see the postscript). After reading her Living Blues *interview with Jim O'Neal (1986), listening to a tape of a 1955 telephone call between McMurry and James, and examining James' signed Trumpet contract and advance check (at the Blues Archive, University of Mississippi), I realized that the account of the Trumpet session was in error and decided to correct it myself, since Leadbitter had died in 1974. With Mrs. McMurry's Trumpet documents presented after the original article, Ed Komara and I are happy to set the record straight. —GDW*

[Originally published in *Blues Unlimited* no. 91 (May 1972): 5–10.]

Elmore James (1918–1963) has been dead for nearly a decade, but his legend continues to grow. Much has now been written about his life. So much, in fact, that a fresh attempt to piece together a biography based on articles already published becomes a hopeless task. Faced by a mass of conflicting data, we decided to ignore almost everything and return to square one for our research.

Only a deep interest in the man's life, inspired by the adulation he still receives, kept us going, for the task was far from easy. After a year of checking official records and chasing down misleading clues, while interviewing friends

This legendary recording has influenced legions of young blues players. Elmore used a bottleneck in open E tuning with a Kay flattop guitar and a pickup across the sound hole. Wardlow Collection.

and relatives in Mississippi, the facts that we now present came to light. The result is a brand-new story, of interest to all enthusiasts. We both hope that some readers will be fascinated enough to hunt out the last few pieces missing from a very complex jigsaw. Though this article is only one in a series dealing with Delta happenings, it is, for us, perhaps the most important of all.

Elmore James was born Elmore Brooks at 7 o'clock PM on January 27, 1918, the illegitimate son of Leola Brooks, a 15-year-old farmhand. His birthplace was Richland, Mississippi, a small Holmes County community near Pickens. He was raised in the Canton area, a land of low, rolling hills with towns dependent on farming or sawmill operations, nestling by the Big Black River.

James' childhood was spent on farms near Lexington, Goodman, Durant, and Pickens. Leola bore no more children, even though she soon set up home with a man named Joe Willie James, nicknamed "Frost." No one remembers why the lively and mischievous little Elmo' wanted to play music, but all his attempts were encouraged. By the age of 12 he was making sounds on broomwire strung up the shack wall; two years later he was picking on a "lil ole two, three string box made out of a ole lard can." He was living in the vicinity of Goodman at the time, calling himself Elmore or Joe Willie James, but nicknamed "Clean-head" because he liked to shave his head.

Depression years were tough for this small family; they appear to have moved around constantly seeking better work. Their teenaged son Elmore was considered a man by Mississippi standards, doing his fair share in the fields.

John Jr. Gueston, a second cousin, still lives in Goodman (in 1971) and has vivid memories of the '30s. Elmore James was singing "Smokestack Lightning" or "Dust My Broom," accompanying himself on a cheap six-string guitar, using only his "naked hand." He is remembered by Gueston as "the only guitar picker down there" in Goodman and could usually be found at "Mr. Victor Samples' place in Franklin" where he performed at Saturday night dances.

"Homesick" James Williamson, another cousin, often came into Canton to see his relatives, making his last visit in 1936. While working on the Kincaid plantation, they adopted Robert Earl Holston—an orphan—as a brother for their son. The boys were the same age and shared common interests; their friendship continued until Elmore James' death.

By 1937 Frost and Leola had moved into the Delta, settling at Belzoni on the Turner Brothers plantation. (They continued to move around fairly frequently, trying one plantation after another in the locality before splitting up to move north after World War II.) Though the stay in Belzoni never led to an easier life, it did help James in terms of music.

He was in the right spot at the right time to benefit enormously.

He was, by 1937, an 18-year-old man who no longer enjoyed working. He had also developed a taste for liquor, especially moonshine, that was to last throughout his life. He was very popular with the women, trying his hand at marriage after meeting a local girl called Josephine Harris, with short-lived results. He started rambling and bought his first real guitar—a National—for 20 dollars in Belzoni. It was a year of unrest and dissatisfaction, with the weekends becoming more important than the week.

In Belzoni, or nearby, he met two people who were to influence his music greatly. Robert (known to James as "Dusty") Johnson, and Aleck "Rice" Miller, who was passing himself off as the original "Sonny Boy Williamson." (The *original* Sonny Boy—John Lee Williamson—was "easily the most important harmonica player of the pre-war era" [*All Music Guide to the Blues* 1996].

As Miller rose to stardom on the KFFA Helena "King Biscuit Time" radio broadcast in the early '40s, his Interstate Grocery Company sponsors supported his pose as the Chicago harmonica star, putting his image on sacks of its "Sonny Boy" Corn Meal. When John Lee Williamson was murdered in 1948, Miller supplanted him as *the* Sonny Boy.)

Both Johnson and Miller were hard-drinking lechers, but were still fine musicians with a large following. Johnson was soon to die at Greenwood, but "Elmo" and Miller became firm friends. Although Kokomo Arnold's records once appealed to James, it was Johnson's bottleneck playing that inspired him to use a piece of metal pipe and the open E tuning to play "Dust My Broom."

With Robert Holston supporting him as rhythm guitarist, Holston

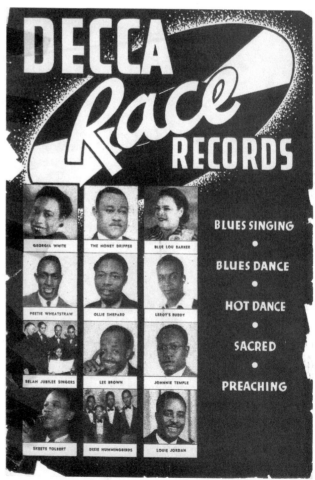

This 1940 Decca Race Records brochure depicts Johnny Temple (3rd down on right) who rented a room to Elmore James in the late '50s. Courtesy Maxey Tarpley.

remembers, "He would sing 'Dust My Broom' and 'Black Mattie's Face Shine Like the Risin' Sun.' He played mostly 'round plantations, but sometimes, late in the evenin' [would] play out of the back of a truck or go 'cross the tracks to the juke houses . . . play all night, drinking moonshine!" In Belzoni the popular juke joints were cafes owned by Jake Thomas and Percy Simpson. Here James would pick up two or three dollars, plus all he could eat and drink, for a Saturday night's work.

By 1939, he was on the Daybreak plantation playing for "suppers." Meanwhile Miller was hanging around Greenville, often coming into Belzoni to help his friend with the music. Though James preferred to work alone or with Robert Holston, he sometimes accompanied pianist Carter Gayten (brother of Paul) and guitarist Peter Brown at Lexington. But in keeping with the changing tastes, he got his own combo together to play for dancers. Precious White played sax, Tutney Moore was on trumpet, Holston continued to play rhythm or bass guitar, and "Frock" O'Dell sat in on drums. These were the men who backed up James or Miller for gigs at the Harlem Theatres in Belzoni and Hollandale, owned by Mr. Osborne, Willie James' place and the Peacock Inn in Belzoni, and a joint remembered by Holston as located "out of Goodman run by Big Boy McCray—he had little dances at his house—Elmo' would play for him." "Broom" and "Smokestack Lightning" were the big numbers, and Elmore used a cheap pickup on an acoustic guitar and an amplifier. The band usually entertained in the winter when things got quiet. "Wintertime we just balled all weekend," recalled Holston. "No work to do, cotton all picked." If very hard up, James would go to churches pretending to be a preacher and hoping to pick up the collection, after delivering a sermon. This became another lasting habit, added Holston.

It was during these slack winter months, too, that James wandered, sometimes just vanishing without a word. "He'd be gone—hoboin' mostly. He didn't stay away too long, usually 'bout two weeks," Holston said. Apparently, Miller had gotten another sponsor, Max Moore's Interstate Grocery Company, for his 15-minute radio show on KFFA, a Delta sensation. This sudden success for Miller must have unsettled James somewhat—jobs were plentiful in Arkansas, not in Belzoni. Then World War II took over, changing his life. On July 24, 1943, Elmore James found himself in the U.S. Navy.

Elmore James—number 8439732—saw active service, went to Guam with his guitar, and got an honorable discharge after war's end in 1945. He didn't see Mississippi for two years, returning to find that his family had left Belzoni. Learning that Holston was running a radio repair shop in Canton, he moved there, making it his base for the next ten years. At this time his heart was suddenly troubling him, forcing him to go to Jackson for medical treatment from time to time. But the trips to Helena continued during 1946, where he stayed with Peck Curtis and often bumped into Miller.

A year later (1947), he was back in Belzoni, rooming at Henry Flowers' boarding house and working on the Silver Creek plantation. Here he married Georgiana Crump, another local girl, while continuing his musical activities. He played mostly "around the country" (according to Holston), but his usual playing spot was Webber's Inn, a barrelhouse owned by Cornelius Horton. His reputation was still strong in the area, but even with appearances on the King Biscuit Time he wasn't getting wide recognition.

In 1947 Miller moved to Belzoni to advertise on radio a new patent medicine, Talaho (pronounced "Tally-Ho"), for the O.J. Turner Drug Store. Miller invited Elmore to appear with him whenever he wanted the airtime. Belzoni had no radio station of its own until 1957, so the new 30-minute show was recorded at Turner's store and broadcast from either WAZF in Yazoo City, or WJPJ in Greenville.

From Monday through Saturday, Miller as "Sonny Boy Williamson" sang blues; on Sunday his program was devoted to spirituals. He had developed his own sound by using Hohner Old Standby harmonicas, which he had tampered with—unscrewing the sides and slightly bending the reeds with a toothpick—to achieve a loose, resonant effect. When combined with the then-novel amplified guitar style of James, Miller's distinctive harmonica sound attracted a lot of listeners, selling Talaho as fast as it could be produced. Two years later, Hadacol offered to sponsor Sonny Boy under better conditions. So, in 1949 he moved to West Memphis and station KWEM, leaving James behind.

However, James may have appeared on the Talaho Show irregularly, but it was this "Belzoni Radio Show" that really introduced "Broom" to the Delta. There had been many gigs in both Mississippi or Arkansas during 1948, which gave James the opportunity to play with other bluesmen: Willie Love, "Big Boy" Crudup, Charlie Booker, Johnny Temple, and Boyd Gilmore.

With Miller gone, James joined Love's Three Aces at Greenville, where they appeared on WDVM as part of a show run by disc jockey Eddie Williams (now with WESY in Leland). Sponsored by local merchants, Love had a daily 30-minute show, using James, Frock O'Dell, and Little Bill, a guitarist or bassist from nearby Leland. Love and Miller were also close friends. Although based in different towns in 1949, they continued to play together whenever possible.

James wasn't too happy about traveling; he preferred to be near a hospital due to his illness. He realized that his music opportunities still lay with Miller, not Love. In 1950 he too moved to Arkansas.

In West Memphis he heard that Miller was hoping to make some records for the Diamond Record Company in Jackson. When this became reality, James went back to Canton and the radio repair shop, to be near the Jackson studio when needed. In January 1951 Miller arrived in Canton and took Elmore into Jackson for a session. With Willie Love and Joe Willie Wilkins, Miller—as Sonny Boy Williamson—recorded "Eyesight to the Blind" on Trumpet, which became a hit. Throughout the year James returned to the studio with Love and Miller for more record dates, but because of stage fright he couldn't record one of his own songs. "Broom" was cut during a rehearsal with Miller and O'Dell in August. When he understood the rehearsal had been recorded, James froze, unable to make a second side. [For the corrected account of this session, see the postscript following this article.]

"Broom" was on sale by October, with an anonymous flip side, and entered the R&B charts in early 1952. Collecting royalties, James bought himself a car. He continued to make live appearances between visits to the hospital. Both Modern and Chess were after him to record, and offers of better money were extended. James did nothing, ignoring everyone. Finally, in the summer of 1952, Joe Bihari found him at a Jackson club and persuaded him to come to Chicago to record. There James was reunited with his mother.

James had signed a contract with Trumpet, and, as was then general, it would have lasted for a year with options. He recorded for the new Meteor label, with the Johnny Jones Band around October. An announcement in *Billboard,* dated December 13, 1952, states that Lester Bihari, Memphis rep for Modern, "who will continue to headquarter in Memphis, has signed Elmo James, ex-Trumpet warbler, whose first release is 'I Believe.'" Though nothing more than a heavily amplified version of "Broom," the disc shot into the 1953 charts at high speed.

Before "I Believe" was in the charts, James had already cut some titles for Checker. "She Just Won't Do Right," an answer to "Broom," was recorded on January 17, 1953, again with the Jones band, and duly released. However, the scarcity of copies suggests that the single was quickly withdrawn from sale.

By November, James had made a whole batch of records for the Bihari Flair label. He also played guitar on Big Joe Turner's "T.V. Mama," for Atlantic. With "I Believe" still a national hit, he headed south to cash in while he could.

Back in Canton, Clarence Shinn booked him into the Club Bizarre, where he got a warm welcome from his friends and the patrons. His heart ailment forced him to go to Jackson regularly and restricted the frequency of live appearances. He would often perform at a big sawmill near Canton, with Willie Love in Greenville or in Jackson with Sonny Boy (Miller). When Flair wanted him again they had to come looking—usually sending Ike Turner on ahead. Robert Holston still remembers Turner, plus "the men from California" hunting all over town for their elusive star. "Please Find My Baby" was recorded at an auditorium outside city limits (see Saul Bihari's words in *BU* 74 [Scott and Paulsen 1970, 11], but "1839 Blues" and "Sho' Nuff I Do" were recorded in the Club Bizarre.

In 1954, James hired a manager, Otis Ealey of Atlanta, as reported by Bruce Bastin and Pete Lowry (1970, 4–5). Otis booked James for the Elks Convention in Atlanta, helped him settle in town at 384 Pine Street, and employed him to assist at the Lithonia Country Club.

James was by now married to a woman named Janice, whom he'd previously met in Jackson. After about six months the couple quarreled, causing Elmore to "dust his broom" and head for Chicago. Otis' services continued, arranging bookings for many years.

Chicago was a good spot for club work, but by late 1954 James' record sales were diminishing, possibly because of the overuse of the "Broom" theme. In an effort to improve matters, Joe Bihari took James to good professional studios in New Orleans and Hollywood between tours. These dates produced two minor hits, "Standing at the Crossroads" and a new "Dust My Broom"—but by 1956 Flair let their contract expire.

No longer a recording artist, James carried on with the club work in Chicago. A long engagement at Sylvio's was supplemented by the occasional set at the Key Largo, Club Alex, or other joints on the South and West sides. At the same time James met a young harmonica player from Jackson named Sammy Myers. Sammy took to sitting in with Elmore's Broomdusters before heading back south for good.

In 1957 Mel London signed James to his new label, Chief. Five records were released, but unfortunately no hits occurred. Becoming very thin and bronchial, James began wearing heavy glasses, looking much older than his 40 years. The next year he was back in Jackson, where he got a job as disc jockey for WRBC. Within a few months James, restless as ever, was back in the Windy City.

He now went to live with Homesick James, the two working the clubs with occasional help from J.T. Brown, "Sneaky Joe" Harris, and other friends. When work was slow, James sat in with Otis Rush, or Sonny Boy Williamson (Miller), who was touring major northern blues centers such as Gary, Detroit, or St. Louis. Then in 1959, Bobby Robinson offered him a contract with Fire Records in New York. Sessions took place late that year in Chicago, and by April 1960 even Chess was again interested in his services. By 1961 James was touring again with his own band, changing musicians with great frequency. But he ran into trouble with the American Federation of Musicians union for employing nonmembers, upon which he returned to Jackson.

During 1961 and 1962 he lived with Johnny Temple on Ann Banks St. Whenever Fire wanted him to record, he flew or drove to New York. But he was really sick and getting much weaker. He kept his performances in the Hinds County area—backed by people like Big Moose, Sammy Myers, King Mose, or Robert Robinson—where, luckily, his following was as great as it had ever been. Warned by the doctors about heavy drinking, he spent his days in lazy fashion—often visited by Homesick James and other musicians.

Chicago too had not forgotten. James was well liked both as a musician and as a person. In 1963 Big Bill Hill, the promoter and disc jockey, brought him to Chicago for a comeback, after clearing up his union troubles. With Chicago club work now possible, he took living quarters at 1503 North Wieland Street.

Just as everything was about to go smoothly, Elmore James died from organic heart disease on May 24, 1963.

Big Bill Hill took care of the funeral expenses, and after a well-attended wake in Chicago James was buried near Durant on May 29th. His mother, now known as Leola Randoll, gave his name as Elmore (Joe Willie) James to the coroner, stating that he had resided in Chicago for ten years, and was a self-employed musician and unmarried. She could not remember his date of birth, giving his age as about 44 years and birthplace as Lexington, Mississippi.

James was survived by several children, at least two common-law wives, his mother, his stepfather "Frost," and many uncles, aunts, and cousins.

[EK: Wardlow and I rewrote much of this article for its inclusion here, and perhaps we should have replaced it with an entirely new version. This is a rare example of Wardlow's being involved in a project where some oral testimony was used without checking other informants, sound recordings, and written documents. In this faulty manner was written the false description of Lillian McMurry recording Elmore James' "Dust My Broom" without his knowledge and consent.

Wardlow believes that one source of the "Dust My Broom" story may have been Aleck Miller, as he was the only participant to have gone to England and talked with the blues journalists there. From 1963 through 1965, Miller made frequent extended visits to England and Europe, spending much time spinning tales about bluesmen to *Blues Unlimited* and other British blues publications. However, Bob Groom of *Blues World* seemed wary of such stories, admitting shortly after Miller's death: "Known far and wide as a teller of tall tales and as a flamboyant personality, he impressed his wizard-like image indelibly on the Blues 'scene'" (July 1965). In addition, in a special *Blues Unlimited Collector's Classic* (no. 7 [1965], 7) Pete Welding relayed Homesick James Williamson's claim that James was recorded unaware by McMurry. Leadbitter may well have taken these yarns as facts, using them as such in "Canton, Mis'sippi Breakdown" and his biographical article on Aleck "Sonny Boy Williamson" Miller ("Bring It On Home," 1973). Whether it was Miller, Homesick James, or another informant who told the "'Broom' rehearsal" story to Leadbitter, the source is not identified in the article.

The studio tape recorder was added to the "Dust My Broom" session myth by Robert Palmer in his *Deep Blues* (1981, 214): "He [Elmore James] wouldn't [record 'Dust My Broom'], but in October [1951] he was tricked into rehearsing it in the studio with Sonny Boy and

This contract between Lillian McMurry of Trumpet Records and Elmore James refutes the often-told rumor that Elmore was recorded without his knowledge, which began with a story apparently by Homesick James or Sonny Boy Williamson in the early 1960s. Blues Archive.

Frock while McMurry surreptiously ran a tape." Since Palmer's *Deep Blues* has been the best-selling and most influential book on Delta blues, its depiction of James' Trumpet session has been cited more often than its apparent Leadbitter and Wardlow source.

This check shows that Elmore knew he would be recorded, and this $35.00 was an advance on future royalties. "Dust My Broom" became a national hit and a present-day standard. Blues Archive.

What follows is a version corrected according to the Trumpet Records files (now housed in the Lillian McMurry/Trumpet Collection, Blues Archive, University of Mississippi), Jim O'Neal's interview with Mrs. McMurry, Marc Ryan's *Trumpet Records* (1992), and various 78 rpm records. Although I have discussed this session with Mrs. McMurry, J. Woody Sistrunk (who is writing a com-

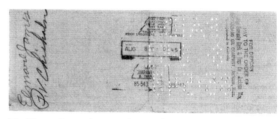

The Elmore James signature is a trademark of the James estate. Blues Archive.

plete account of it with the surviving musicians and technicians), and Gayle Wardlow, I will refer to issued records, written documents, and published statements. In her written comments to me (letter, October 22, 1997), Mrs. McMurry wrote: "Proof of the truth herein should make all repetitive, non-investigative writers ashamed and lose their credibility."

Elmore James' performance as issued on Trumpet 146 sounds well prepared. Lasting two minutes and 42 seconds, it encompasses six blues choruses, the middle four of which are sung, and the final chorus ends with the ensemble concluding together. Had the music run over the three-minute limit for 78 rpm discs or been faded out, or had the ending been ill-timed and ragged, then a suspicion of its being a rehearsal take could be raised. However, such is not the case: all musicians are well miked, and James' voice is heard clear and unmuffled. According to Marc Ryan's Trumpet discography, the session was held on August 5, 1951, with James, Sonny Boy Williamson, bassist Leonard Ware, and a drummer (possibly Frock O'Dell). It took place in Jackson at Ivan Scott's Radio Service Studio, which used one microphone and a direct-to-disc recording process instead of the then-new tape technology. Hence not tape, but only discs could be "surreptitiously" run at Scott's, and the cost and short running time of each recording blank would have made such a recording expensive and not technically feasible.

On August 4, 1951, the day before the session, Elmore James signed a one-year Trumpet contract with Lillian McMurry, received an advance of $35, and witnessed McMurry's beginning of the copyright process for "Dust My Broom."

While registering the song in 1951, McMurry thought James was the composer, not realizing at the time the words and music had been frequently used before. Robert Johnson had recorded the song as "I Believe I'll Dust My Broom" in 1936, but even that version had its precedents. Aaron and Milton Sparks recorded the same melody and similar lyrics as "I Believe I'll Make a Change" in February 1932. In 1933, Jack Kelly and his South Memphis Jug Band recorded the same melody and similar lyrics as "Believe I'll Go Back Home" for the American Recording Company, and the following year both Leroy Carr and Josh White covered the melody as "I Believe I'll Make a Change" for their respective labels. Although it seems James may not have been the original composer of "Dust My Broom," he was the first to copyright it, and he had absorbed its style enough to be able to make any other song sound like it.

Although James played at a Jesse "Tiny" Kennedy session for Trumpet on October 22, 1951, he never made another side of his own to be paired with "Dust My Broom." He left Jackson later that fall, and the following January he broke his Trumpet contract by recording for the Bihari Brothers' labels Flair and Meteor. By the summer of 1955 he recorded a cover of "Dust My Broom," which was released on Flair as "Dust My Blues." Meanwhile, Lillian McMurry released his record (with "Catfish Blues" by Bobo Thomas on the flip side—see "Highway 80 Blues," page 115, for more details) in early 1952 with considerable success. Despite his departure, she took careful note of James' activities. When he made a long-distance telephone call to her late in 1955, he was reminded of the "Dust My Broom" copyright:

Lillian McMurry: Well, you know that I leased out "Dust My Broom" to another label and re-released it [EK note: On Ace Records 508].

Elmore James: Is that right?

LM: Yeah, this fellow leased it from me and so it's out again on the market; and the Biharis . . . you recorded a number for them just like it called "Dust My Blues." "Dust My Blues," which is the exact same music and you know we had the music on that, don't you?

EJ: That's right.

LM: And yet they claim they got "Dust My Blues" see, which is exactly like "Dust My Broom" only it says "Dust My Blues."

EJ: It's the same music.

LM: It's the same music, isn't it?

EJ: That's right.

LM: That's just what I said.

EJ: It is the same music.

LM: Well, that's been copyrighted, you know, ever since 1951, Elmo. You knew . . . you remember when I copyrighted the thing?

EJ: Sure do, right there in the store when the man wrote it.

LM: Um-hum. That's what I call high-powered stealing. Just stealing.

EJ: What is Sonny Boy doing now?

(O'Neal 1986, 28)

This exchange proves that Elmore James was personally involved in the registration of "Dust My Broom," and it confirms the business steps he and McMurry took before the session. From these documents and the one record that he made, it is evident that James acted carefully and deliberately before and during the session, if irresponsibly thereafter.

Despite this effort to correct one tall tale, the other legends about Elmore James will persist. Few artifacts remain from his itinerant life. There are the records of course; most of them are in mono, but several of the later ones for Bobby Robinson are in stereo. Precious few photographs exist, although fortunately some of them are in color. If any film or video footage of him exists, none of it has been shown to the public. With so many aspects of his life left to the blues fans' imaginations, the mythical stature given to James is quickly growing to equal that of Robert Johnson.]

Johnny Temple, who was a major city blues artist in the late '30s for Decca records, often offered Elmore room and board in Jackson. Wardlow collection.

He's a Devil of a Joe

Gayle Dean Wardlow and Stephen Calt

The 1968 posthumous rediscovery of Blind Joe Reynolds, whose real name was Joe Sheppard, required three years of the most intensive tracking I ever did. In 1965, H.C. Speir said he found Blind Joe at a lumber camp a few miles above Lake Providence. So I searched Lake Providence and stumbled upon information on Moses Mason, whom Speir hadn't yet mentioned to me. Blind Joe (he was not known by his last name) was well remembered, but all informers were wary of a young white man asking about a blind blues singer who, it turned out, had served time in both Louisiana and Arkansas prisons. Blind Joe had left Lake Providence shortly after World War II with a big fat woman guide, who had beaten the hell out of him on a street corner during a dispute over tips that he suspected she had stolen.

I was to hear about two more Blind Joes in the Louisiana Delta, one of whom was solely a sacred singer. After searches of Tallulah and other Louisiana Delta towns, I tracked a Blind Joe who played the blues on the streets of Monroe, Louisiana's fourth largest city. In its black section in 1967, I sought out information about a Blind Joe who was seen playing outside a cafe there. Surprisingly, the cafe owner said Blind Joe was still alive in a little community just south of Monroe. When I found his actual house, it was closed up, and no one knew where he was. Nine months later, while on a return visit in 1968, I learned Blind Joe had died. When I had found his nephew and played him the Reynolds recordings, he said, "That's old Joe. That's my uncle, that's old Joe."

Some of the "street sources" we talked with refused to give their names, fearing how the information might be used against either them or Blind Joe Reynolds. This attitude was especially severe during the tense civil rights period of the 1960s, when a white man "from out of town" talking to black men certainly received attention in both black and white neighborhoods.

Interestingly, Joe Sheppard (his real name, not Reynolds) was the only bluesman surviving from the classic prewar period who was actively playing an electric (not acoustic) guitar in 1967; that same year, Cream with Eric Clapton included their version of Blind Joe's dynamic 1930 Paramount piece "Outside Woman Blues" on their album Disraeli Gears *(Atco SD 33-232).*

The photo of Blind Joe Reynolds on page 171, apparently taken in 1947, was obtained by Stephen Calt in 1968 when privacy laws were not restrictive. The second photo, published in BU *14 (Wardlow 1982), and again in this issue, came from his relatives, who gave it to me. —GDW*

[Originally published in *Blues Unlimited* no. 146 (Autumn/Winter 1984): 16–20.]

Perhaps the brashest and bawdiest blues singer of the prewar era was the mysterious guitarist known to posterity as Blind Joe Reynolds, composer of the minor rock hit "Outside Woman Blues." Blind Joe was that rare figure who not only lived up to the church stereotype of a sinner, but flouted social taboos with positive relish.

"Anything 'bad' was Joe," recalled Jack Brown, a gregarious black store owner in Monroe, Louisiana, who was "raised up together" with the badman. "Yes sir; anything 'bad' was Mister Joe . . ." Despite his own respectability, Brown was titillated by the unsavory qualities that often shocked Joe's other neighbors. "Oh, Joe was somethin'!" he declared not long after the singer's death. "He's a devil of a Joe."

But the devil was something of a fabulist. Using falsehood and evasion for both his own amusement and protection, he left contradictory accounts of his past. Thanks to his well-known wariness of the law, his associates had to guess his proper surname, as he changed identities often. "Blind Joe Reynolds" was but one of several aliases.

"His name was Joe Sheppard from his birth," insisted Jack Brown. "I don't care what anybody tell you."

With similar finality, another neighbor scoffed: "His real name wasn't no Sheppard." Joe's nephew from Monroe, Henry Millage, gave real credence to this doubt. "Before he put his name into a 'Sheppard,'" Millage confided, "he was 'Joe Leonard.' And after he got on the run—you know, got into a little trouble . . . then he changed his name over to Blind Joe Sheppard . . . What he was on the run for I don't know, but I do know he was on the run."

Blind Joe once told Millage's wife Bess that he could never divulge the nature of the trouble that prompted his changes of names. (The use of assumed names was not an unusual tactic for an entertainer. Robert Johnson used several, including Robert Dusty, Robert Sax, and R.L. Joe Callicott told these authors in 1968 that often, traveling no more than 20 miles from home required altering one's name for self-protection.) To judge by his self-admitted crimes—the alleged shooting of an uncle, and of one white man—it must have been formidable. He certainly wasn't ashamed of his "rap sheet," which included two penitentiary terms. A Monroe acquaintance, Jack Sewell, who knew him personally in the 1960s, said, "If he'd been in jail he'd tell it: if he'd been to the penitentiary, he'd tell it; he didn't care . . . Maybe his woman cared, but he didn't care."

It was as Joe Sheppard, the name by which he was most commonly known, that he was buried. He sometimes adopted

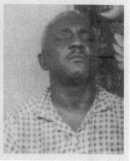

THIS IDENTIFICATION CARD IS ISSUED TO HOLDER BASED ON HIS OR HER ACCEPTANCE OF THE CONDITIONS SET FORTH ON THE INSIDE FRONT COVER OF EACH CERTIFICATE BOOK OF COUPONS.

IMPORTANT

THIS IDENTIFICATION CARD MUST BE PRESENTED TOGETHER WITH BOOK OF CERTIFICATES.

Blind Joe Reynolds (Sheppard) used this identification from a blind organization to ride trains or buses at no cost in the 1950s and '60s. Wardlow collection.

the surname of a stepfather, Eddie Madison, even after his mother had remarried. As with his rightful name, Joe's age and birthplace were often changed with the telling. "He'd jump up and tell me one age, and then he'd jump and tell me another age," recalled a Monroe friend named Arnella Strickland. She said Joe told Bess Millage that he was born in 1904 at Tallulah, Louisiana, but his death certificate gives his birthplace as Arkansas and his birth year as 1900.

Tallulah, where Joe was raised as Joe Sheppard, is a small cotton town located almost 20 miles west of Vicksburg, which is on the Mississippi River. It numbered 3,300 residents in 1930, the year the newly completed Vicksburg Bridge provided a nonferry passage between the two states. According to Brown, Joe's musical career began there during the World War I era, when he was (in Brown's words) "eighteen, nineteen, maybe twenty years of age." Two local guitarists who only "rapped" (strummed) their instruments—Louis Martin, and a man known as "Hey Willie"—numbered among his earliest tutors.

"Joe would be right with 'em," Brown recalled. "After he commence to learnin' good, then he would get one of 'em's box, and he would play his part." When he had no guitar to play, he added percussion to their efforts with his own washtub. "He wasn't too good then but he was learnin' then," Brown said of Joe's early years. A fiddler known as "Deaf John" sometimes joined the trio, but normally, "it wasn't nothin' goin' in them days but just guitars and accordions."

Although "not too many" traveling minstrels ever passed through town, by Jack Brown's report, those who did all added something to Joe's growing repertoire. "He stay there with 'em, tryin' to learn what he could, offa what they doin'. He listened and then he sing the same songs . . ." Tactfully, Joe would not offer his copies to local audiences until their originators had left town.

By the end of World War I, word of Joe's musical prowess had spread from Tallulah to a desolate nearby country area known as "Kansas-Kansas," where he frequently entertained railroad workers for tips. One of his local listeners, Jack Sewell, reminisced: "Ain't but one man I would stop and hear his music before I do Joe's. And that was the man that was teachin' him."

The anonymous teacher was an itinerant guitarist who stood "right at fifty," or more than twice Joe's age. He was a brusque taskmaster. "If Joe didn't have a tune like he wanted it," our informant recalled, "he'd stop him right quick, say now, 'Get right!'"

Although impatient with Joe's progress, the tutor accepted whichever name he was then using easily enough. He never addressed his pupil as "Sheppard," but as "Joe Madison," "Joe Reynolds," or "Willie Reynolds." (There was a tiny community named Reynolds just a few miles north of Tallulah, and Joe may have taken its name as his own to distance himself from the local law.)

Only as a musical apprentice could Joe be properly termed submissive. Marital and religious bonds held no charms for him.

"He tried to get all the women he seed and all that they had," Jack Brown recounted. "I don't know what was his object." Joe never sang spirituals in the fashion of other blues singers. "Never knowed Joe to go to church much," Brown said. "If he did, he'd be off from the church arguin' and cussin' and raising sand." Episodic shooting scrapes and what Brown termed "much devilment" punctuated his Tallulah days.

In the early 1920s his career was temporarily foreclosed by Arkansas authorities, who arrested him in Tallulah and carried him to a state penitentiary east of Pine Bluff. "He mighta been stealin'; anything," Brown remarked. "When he come back, he rest hisself up; then he come ramblin' round through the country, bein' 'bad' as usual."

Our informants said Reynolds was arrested by Arkansas authorities. More likely he was first arrested by Louisiana officials, then turned over to Arkansas authorities who came for him. Conviction of a felony such as murder, armed robbery, and assault with intent to kill required imprisonment from one year to life or execution under United States laws at that time. A misdemeanor such as petty theft, assault, or prostitution required up to "11–29" (11 months and 29 days) on a county farm where chain gangs worked. Reynolds may have been carried to Arkansas for a misdemeanor offense, thus serving less than a full year.

Management of the Arkansas State Penitentiary, located just east of Pine Bluff at Cummins, has been highly controversial through the years. In 1968, a national story concerned the finding of bones of "escaped prisoners" in a grazing pasture. One old inmate claimed there were "more bodies than you can count," alleging that authorities killed the inmates and buried them there, then told the next of kin that the inmate had escaped.

Once released from prison, Joe's freedom did nothing to curb his tempestuous spirits. Instead, it destroyed his sight. "Brudell Scott shot his eyes out with a shotgun," recalled Brown, who witnessed their shootout in Tallulah some time between 1925 and 1927.

"They's drinkin' and got drunk," Brown explained. "And got to cussin' and arguin'. One broke to get his gun, and the other 'un had his gun hid out there at the edge of the woods; he went and got *his* gun. And he's hidin' behind a tree . . . and Joe happened to peep out too quick."

Scott's birdshot ("I don't know whether they was shootin' sixes or fours") caught him full in the face, leaving it disfigured with pellet scars. "It turned his face blacker than what it was," Brown added.

The shooting caused Joe to reflect on the wisdom of remaining in Tallulah, where he would have been an easy target for any local enemies. "When they carried Joe to the hospital and Joe got healed up where he could kinda get about, Joe left there," Brown said. "He didn't stay up in there no longer after this shootin' come up."

Asked if Joe ever contemplated revenge upon Scott, Brown laughed: "No; hell, no." Perhaps from wounded pride, Joe was anxious to forget and falsify the episode. He later told Bess Millage that his blinding was accidental, that his brother had done the deed with a shotgun as he attempted to make peace with the brother and another man. He also took pains to avoid a repetition of the Scott disaster by learning to shoot a pistol at audible targets. He not only publicized this expertise, but took to displaying a .45 pistol as a conversation piece, Brown remembers.

But the years in which Joe adjusted to his handicap are obscure. Summing up his life of vagabonding, Bess Millage said, "I'd say you can't pronounce where he *ain't* stayed. He used to go all over the United States." In search of musical audiences, he traveled the same territory as other deep Southern bluesmen, such as Mississippi's Skip James. Within the span of a few months in 1926, James saw him perform at a black cabaret on Memphis's North Nichols Street, as well as on the streets of Sun, Louisiana, a small riverside town near Bogalusa. Sun was the location of the annual Strawberry Festival, which drew crowds who might well donate to a blind street singer.

A year or so later, Joe cropped up briefly in Clarksdale, Mississippi, in the company of a nearly 250-pound woman. She collected their earnings from passersby in a clay water jug through which she sputtered out a tubalike accompaniment to his songs. In 1929 he was back in Kansas-Kansas, Louisiana, diverting himself with self-proclaimed gamblers like Jack Sewell. "I was wild; he was wild," recalled Sewell, who knew Joe as "Willie Reynolds."

By then Joe had become a blues "professor" himself with at least two local proteges, whom he groomed as bottleneck guitarists. "He went home and got him some bottles himself," Sewell recalled. "And told them, say: 'Now if y'all wants me to teach you, put them bottles on your fingers.'" Joe's own bottleneck slurs greatly impressed Sewell: "Look like to me it would 'talk.' He was makin' it 'talk' . . . I ain't heard none of 'em played no better than him, and I heard a lotta musicians."

Store owner Brown agreed that Joe could at least hold his own against any rival. "They didn't 'run' Joe *no* kinda way."

Among those who tried and failed to "run" Joe was Ishmon Bracey, a well-known bluesman from Jackson, Mississippi, who, one Saturday afternoon around 1930, thought to dislodge him from a Vicksburg street by pitting his playing against Joe's. "He worked me over on that guitar," Bracey freely conceded. "He had two, three pieces there he could 'stop' anybody with." Bracey highly respected Reynolds as one of the few men ever to "run him." (This information is further discussed in *BU* 14, Wardlow 1982.) In such situations the judgment of listeners, rendered in the form of tips and acclamation, produced the day's "winner."

Before Joe did battle with Bracey, he had found a home of sorts in Lake Providence, Louisiana, the first train stop north of Tallulah on the Missouri Pacific line. Local legend states that the town was so named because pirates who once massed in nearby river coves were so pernicious that only Providence could steer the frontier boatman safely past them. When the Mississippi riverbed shifted around 1940, the town literally lost its riverside identity, the importance of which had vanished with the passing of the steamboat era.

Early in 1930, Jackson talent broker H.C. Speir ventured into a sawmill camp barrelhouse about three miles from Lake Providence and heard Joe's playing. He was sufficiently impressed to invite him to Jackson for the purpose of arranging a recording session. Shortly after Joe arrived, he was dispatched by train to Grafton, Wisconsin, where, in February 1930, he cut four sides for Paramount Records as "Blind Joe Reynolds." (Speir said he had heard of Reynolds' talents from some of his other artists who brought him news of singers he should seek out. He said it was either "Bo [Carter] or Charlie [Patton] who told me about him." Therefore, he was willing to travel to Lake Providence to find Reynolds.)

More than 35 years later, his friends and relatives in the vicinity of Monroe had little inclination to discuss his reason for adopting a recording pseudonym. When the subject was broached with one relative, the authors were told ominously: "Now we're on another conversation altogether." A second old associate declared: "I ain't sayin' nothin'." Jack Sewell snapped: "I ain't gonna talk about that . . . I told you nice as I could."

On the other hand, Jack Brown soft-pedaled the name change, shrugging: "He just put that 'Reynolds' there." Henry Millage offered a more functional explanation: "He told me that he was makin' records, but he wasn't usin' his real name 'cause he was on the run."

The subterfuge was hardly necessary, for the Depression cloaked Joe and other blues singers of the period in contemporary obscurity. To date, fewer than five copies of Paramount 12927 have been found by collectors. (The first Reynolds Paramount was found in rural Georgia in 1963 by collector Jeff Tarrer, who later sold the record to New York collector Bernie Klatzko. Gayle Dean Wardlow found a copy of Victor 23258 in 1965 in Charleston, Mississippi. The Victor 23000 series (Godrich 1964) showed 23258 as an unissued number.) When these recordings were found by collectors, they immediately established "Blind Joe Reynolds" as one of the outstanding artists of his recording era, a maestro with a seemingly original sense of timing and phrasing. His lyrics, delivered in a raucous rasp, were no less astonishing; instead of the jumbled lyrics that cluttered up some blues songs of the period, they were cohesive, caustic comments intended to provoke jaded sniggers from listeners. Their conceits were as dated as the knee-length skirt (the craze of 1925) that was the subject of "Nehi Blues":

> *Some girls wear short dresses*
> *and these married women wears 'em too*
> *That's the reason the single men*
> *Lord don't know what we want to do.*
> *Wish the proper judge'd*
> *make the women let the dresses down*
> *Told that tremblin' soul: "Doggone!*
> *What you learnin' in town?"*
> *Women tarry too long,*
> *pullin' this short dress style*

So we single men can't tell
a married woman from a child.
Let me tell you boys
what these knee-high dresses will do
Get you broke, ragged, and hungry boy
and then come down on you.
All of you young women
sure Lord oughta be 'shamed
Makin' these old men naughty
when they're walkin' on walkin' cane.
A old man ain't nothin',
but a young woman's play
She works hard all the time
tryin' to change we young men's ways.

While one cannot always decipher Joe's diction or the intended meaning of each word, there is no mistaking the leer within the lyrics. It was such stuff that had led W.C. Handy to originally decry blues as fit for "small-town rounders and their running mates" (Handy 1941, 77), before he decided to dilute the raw product with Tin Pan Alley earnestness.

For his part, Reynolds had decided to make a living by being unacceptable to respectable people. Unlike most blues singers, he worked with a pretense. In place of earnestness he substituted mock exasperation with inconstant women, or devoted ones, according to his choice of songs. The crass humor of his approach lay in the fact that he sang from the frank viewpoint of a predator who in life (as his associates knew full well) presented little but trouble for the opposite sex. It was his audacity that made him "acceptable" to those he did not offend.

He served his pretense well on "Outside Woman Blues," which had been his signature song for almost a decade when he finally recorded it. "He could clown with it," Jack Brown said. The song (whose title phrase signifies a mistress) eventually became his unwitting contribution to rock, by virtue of a best-selling album selection by Cream (who garbled its lyrics).

When you lose your money,
great God don't lose your mind
And when you lose your woman,
please don't fool with mine.
I'm gonna buy me a bulldog,
watch my old lady whilst I sleep
'Cause women these days, get so doggone crooked,
till they might make a 'fore day creep.
. . . Tell you married women,
how to keep your husbands at home
You oughta take care of the man's labor,
and let those boys alone.

> *You can't watch your wife,*
> *and your outside woman too*
> *While you're off with your woman,*
> *your wife could be at home,*
> *Beatin' you doin', buddy what you tryin' to do.*
> *Mmm . . . buddy what you tryin' to do.*

Though on the run, Joe tried his best to be available for recording. Periodically, after his first session, he would dictate letters to a female traveling companion who mailed them to his discoverer H.C. Speir. The letters were inquiries about his future recording prospects. Eight months after his initial session, his efforts were briefly rewarded by Speir (who remembered "feeling sorry" for the man he knew as Reynolds), who sent him to a makeshift Victor studio in Memphis. Another four sides resulted, two of which were never issued by Victor.

Reynolds apparently spent time in Vicksburg, and very possibly the fat woman described as his "wife" who begged for him may have been from that river town. According to Bess Millage, both Third Street and Goose Hill, named in two song titles, were in Vicksburg, the apparent setting of "Third Street Woman Blues."

> *She's a big fat mama with the meat shakin' on her bone*
> *And everytime she shake it Lord a hustlin' woman lose her home.*
> *She got somethin' that the men call a stingaree*
> *Four o'clock every mornin', you turn it loose on me.*
> *Mmm—where my Third Street woman gone?*
> *Believe to my soul she would hustle everywhere but home.*
> *If you can't be my rollin' mama you can't spend your change*
> *If you can't be my rollin' mama you can't spend my change.*

The singer ran out of time before he could deliver the final line—a blind singer would not have been able to see the red light the recording companies used to show that the allotted three minutes were completed. (It's notable that Paramount recordings of artists who were on other labels reveal a more relaxed artist. Possibly Paramount gave its talent all the time they needed to record. It should be noted, too, that Paramount had more commercial blind singers than any other company: Blake, Jefferson, Willie Davis, Percy, Taggart, Reynolds, and Graves, to name the more outstanding.)

In later years, Joe developed or feigned qualms about the propriety of performing the song for his nephew, whom he liked to warn about the perils of crime.

"I tried many times to get him to play that all the way through," Millage said of "Third Street Woman," "but he go to laughin', say: 'No, that'll learn you bad habits,' and he just cut it off."

A decade of wayfaring, with alleged interludes at the Mississippi State

Penitentiary and the town of Leland, Mississippi, followed his fruitless session. Around 1944 he returned to Lake Providence with his enormously pudgy companion and rented one of five or six run-down apartments that constituted the upstairs of Chink's Boarding House, a block from the town's main street. Its ground floor was a combination cafe and beer hall, and Joe often played for tips on its front steps.

There, a quarter that an appreciative listener tossed his way provided a twisted moment of comic relief for the small group of spectators, who watched his wife (if wife she was) lunge for the coin.

Joe took this action less graciously than did the philosopher who sang "When you lose your money, great God don't lose your mind." It drove him to a "near-frenzy," an eyewitness said. Unable to see his intended target, he beat the air with angry blows until his wife suddenly capsized him. To a combined chorus of his raging curses and appreciative howls from bystanders, she beat him unmercifully, said one of the bystanders. "Funniest damn thing I ever saw in my life," he said. (The name of the bystander, a black town constable who recounted the tale in 1965, has been lost.)

On a spring day around 1947, Joe and the same woman were seen ambling down U.S. 47, which runs south out of Lake Providence. They never returned. On June 30th he presented himself at the American Foundation for the Blind on West 16th Street in New York City. After being legally certified as blind, Joe was handed a book of travel coupons that enabled him to ride free on buses and trains in the company of a sighted guide. He left no home address and had no further contact with the agency for many years.

Although his coupons were good for any destination, he soon turned up in the small town of Bastrop, only 40 miles west of Lake Providence. In Bastrop he gave a succession of house parties and, according to Arnella Strickland, "used to have two women stayin' in the house together." This story became a local fable: "I heared everybody say that," remarked Jack Brown.

Some community-minded spirits did not hail his attempt to domesticate an "outside woman." Informants indicate that Joe left Bastrop under duress.

Monroe was better suited for his behavior. Arriving in the outlying neighborhood of Richwood in 1957, Joe quickly set about impressing his neighbors with his personable roguery. "He's still talkin' 'bad' talk, like he's a 'bad' man, you know," recalled Brown, who had himself settled there on the south side of town, operating a small grocery store where later Reynolds would sit and sing for his boyhood friend from Tallulah.

There was at least some substance to his boasts, though Bess Millage felt ashamed by his degradation: "You know, he was this kinda man: I'm sorry to tell you, but he had two wives."

Upon the death of one "wife" he formally married the other, a reclusive woman who preferred that her name not be disclosed. She had first met her future husband as he played blues on the streets of Monroe. "A little boy was leading him," she remembered. "He's 'round about ten years old."

Though she became Joe's new guide, there were times when he fended for himself, as when he leveled one of his .45s at a dog that snipped at his feet during one street concert. A single shot obliterated the animal and established the point that Blind Joe was nobody to trifle with.

In respectable company, his only social asset was his wife. "That woman would hustle for him; she'd beg for him," said Jack Brown. "Yeah, beg: tell the people, 'Would you help me for Joe? My husband blind, would you help me for Joe? . . . Gimme a quarter, gimme a dime, gimme a nickel . . .'"

As for Joe, Brown insisted stoutly that "he did not beg," as though this had been a point of honor with him. He literally sang for his supper. Often Brown would drop a quarter in the tin cup Joe attached to his guitar, or would entertain him with drinks of liquor at his grocery store on Lincoln Drive, the street where the "Reynolds" lived in "one of these old rent houses." In turn, Joe made an amusing spectacle of himself for the benefit of Brown and his drop-in customers. On the occasion of his first appearance, Brown related joyously, "The folks commence to come in; he commence to lyin'. I wish you could have been here with Joe . . ."

His debut at Brown's store was marked by a public boast relating "how he preached for money." Brown elaborated: "He go different places, you know, with his blues-singin'. And it wouldn't work out too good; he'd get hungry and broke, then he'd 'change' and tell the folks God sent him to preach. I'm tellin' you right—Joe was *somethin'!* I wish you coulda seen Joe."

Arnella Strickland, whose Washington Street home was another favorite hangout, recalled: "He told me he gonna play music out yonder and sing the blues; the next Sunday he'd go to church and get him a pulpit and *preach!* And say, he just had the people just *fallin'!* Had 'em call a collection and he'd be sittin' up there in the pulpit half-drunk, and say, 'God-damn!'"

Although Monroe's black churchgoers held regular religious services, Joe did his "sham preaching" in neighboring areas. "He couldn'ta done that at home," Jack Brown laughed, "'cause we knowed him too good."

Not everyone did, however. One incredulous guest of the Stricklands was shocked by the disclosure of his blues-singing. "He told me he don't play music," she said, prompting another visitor to muse: "I never heard him sing too much, but I know he used to call hisself preachin'."

Some time in the 1950s or early '60s, Reynolds switched from acoustic guitar to electric. Sources in Bastrop said he was playing such when he lived in that small paper-mill town in northeast Louisiana, some 35 miles above Monroe. Bess Millage said his favorite song in the '50s was "Going Down in Louisiana, Just Behind the Sun" (Muddy Waters' "Louisiana Blues").

His presence on the local welfare rolls made it impractical for him to perform on town streets, which gave credence to his self-woven myth of musical retirement. By the mid-1960s he not only had a new electric guitar ("It wasn't no cheap one, either," said Bess Millage) to supplant his outmoded acoustic one, but a chauffeur to supplant his travel coupons, which he replenished in 1965. The driver, his nephew Henry, took him to such places as Shreveport, Jackson, Greenville, and Pine Bluff, where he played on the streets, and Natchez, where he posted himself outside the gates of a lumberyard and entertained employees as they changed shifts.

Neither he nor anyone else had any idea that he had become the last active prewar blues minstrel of any historical importance. His few contemporaries were either dead, retired, or living "folk" exhibits who played occasional concerts for middle-class white audiences. None were active tradesmen working in their original musical environment, as Joe was. It is doubtful that Joe was remotely aware of the blues' new respectability or of his own status as the composer of a minor hit record recorded in England.

On a Saturday evening in 1968 he capped a visit to the Millages with a performance of "Outside Woman," set to electric guitar. On the same night he was disabled by a stroke and removed to a Monroe hospital. Two weeks later, on March 10, 1968, he died of pneumonia.

"He died actin' bad," Jack Brown said with a grin. "He died actin' bad."

Joe's remains lie in the Richwood Gardens Cemetery on the outskirts of Monroe. But his social wrongs were not buried with him. It was perhaps to protect his widow and the several bastard children he was said to have allegedly fathered that, in the first year after his death, his neighbors (with the exception of Jack Brown) were "cool to strangers" asking questions about him. Some were openly wary of being interviewed by an (as they imagined) "FBI man" posing as a music researcher. Even those neighbors who took pains to reassure Helen Sheppard that her unexpected caller had "only come to find out about records and things" were themselves vexed by such questioning. Having communicated their impression of a man who showed a colossal indifference to propriety, they decided to say nothing to besmirch him.

Can't Tell My Future:
The Mystery of Willie Brown

Willie Brown's contributions to Delta blues had been seriously underestimated, and some, if not all, of the information on him was included in the Charlie Patton biography King of the Delta Blues Singers *(1988). I decided to include additional data taken from interviews with Willie Moore and his wife, Elizabeth, who had known Willie Brown and Son House personally. This article published Brown's death certificate, which proved that he died in 1952, the same period that Son House remembered him dying.*

Because of several conflicting descriptions of the Will Brown living in Drew remembered by Ledell Johnson, Dick Bankston of Memphis, Hayes McMullan, and others, I reported here that there were two Willie Browns who played guitar in the Delta region before World War II. A third Brown, William, of the Sadie Beck plantation in the Arkansas Delta, who recorded for Alan Lomax in 1942, has been confused with the "Little" Willie Brown of Robinsonville who recorded with Charlie Patton. [EK: This latter confusion with William Brown has been made by Lomax himself (1993, 494, chap. 1, n. 2), who asserts: "I believe this [the William Brown recording with Willie '61' Blackwell] was the same William Brown who recorded later in the narrative with Son House and earlier with Charlie Patton."] —GDW

[Originally published in *Blues Unlimited* no. 147 (Spring 1986): 6–9.]

Like his longtime acquaintance and fellow legend Charlie Patton, with whom he recorded, Willie Brown was buried quietly in a small cemetery, in rural Tunica County—to be forgotten by all except a group of blues fans who, for the most part, did not become aware of his role in Mississippi blues history until more than ten years after his death. And as is true of Patton—who lies in an unmarked grave at Holly Ridge in Sunflower County—Willie Brown's legend has grown, supported chiefly by anecdotes from Son House and other artists who remembered him as one of the outstanding guitarists in blues history.

Willie Lee Brown was only 52 when he died on December 30, 1952, after a long battle with alleged alcohol problems that led to the deterioration of both liver and heart. Shortly before his death he was hospitalized in Memphis. Some people in Tunica County, around Robinsonville, claim he actually died in a Memphis hospital, though this is not confirmed by his death certificate. Willie was buried in Prichard, next to the Good

Shepherd Baptist Church, one he probably never attended, and no grave marker was evident when this writer visited the area in the late '60s.

A common-law wife—said to be a recent acquisition—named Annie Lee Brown had moved from the Prichard area, where Brown was living at his death, to Memphis (just as the obscure Louise Johnson was reported to have done in the '40s, from the King-Anderson plantation near Clarksdale). Efforts to locate Brown's widow in Memphis were unsuccessful. Therefore, Son House, rediscovered in 1964 in Rochester, New York, became the primary informant for stories about Willie Brown. An interview with House was published in 1967 in the first issue of *78 Quarterly* (Perls and Calt 1967).

Willie Brown's death cetificate shows he died at age 52. He had been musical partners with both Son House and Charlie Patton. Wardlow collection.

But Willie Brown left lasting memories and sentimental ties with a number of persons in Tunica County, especially those who lived in both Robinsonville and nearby Lake Cormorant (which locals pronounce "Carmen"). Among these sources were Willie (Moses Alexander) Moore and his wife Elizabeth (Glynn) Moore, who both knew Brown, House, Patton, and Robert Johnson independently before they became common-law spouses. They were living in Sumner, Tallahatchie County, where Hayes McMullan introduced them to this researcher.

To the Moores, Willie Brown and Son House were household names, better known than Charlie Patton, who stayed in the Tunica County area for only a short time. Robert Johnson, also known by the names Robert Sax(ton) and Robert Dusty, was only a teenager when the Moores knew him.

Willie Moore, a professional gambler who changed his first name from Alexander after an alleged slaying of another man during a gambling brawl, met Brown as early as 1916 in rural Tunica County. "I'd almost growed up with him," Moore recalls. "I was 16 when I first got acquainted with Willie Brown. He'd play anything on that guitar. I mean anything—he could play it. He always say, 'Them blues ain't nothin' but a lowdown dirty achin' chill'."

Moore accompanied Brown's playing and sometimes his singing. He says Willie never prided himself on his singing and considered himself a better guitarist than vocalist. But Willie sang blues and Moore would accompany him on the bass string. "His favorite song was 'Old Cola,'" Moore remembers. This was Brown's version of "Pony Blues." "Sometimes he'd sing and

Willie Moore of Sumner (1960s) knew and played with Willie Brown near Robinsonville in the 1920s. There are no known pictures of Brown. Wardlow collection.

sometimes I'd sing but you know I loved to hear him sing about...that old pony!"

Brown had a sizeable repertoire "but mostly he wanna play 'Old Cola.' But he'd get drunk, man, and he'd sing 'Coley' 'til he just poured it on." And when he would really get "to feeling good [high]," Elizabeth Moore says, "I say he gonna hit them bass strings. I knows he gonna be draggin' it down." She is referring to Brown's slapping the first bass string, as he did on "Future Blues" (Paramount 13090).

Moore says Willie Brown told him he was from "down there near Cleveland" and never lived in Drew (as reported by David Evans 1982, 176–178). "He used to be down there [visit] Dockery's where Charlie Patton lived, but you know he never did say he lived there. He told us he had stayed at Cleveland first and he stayed at Shelby." Other friends in Tunica County said Brown talked about a sister who lived near Cleveland, but a search proved unfruitful. However, Brown did travel to towns such as Hollandale and Glendora, and was seen in Helena and in the Leland area, but not necessarily with Charlie Patton, with whom he "often fussed and fought" over how to play music. "Willie Brown said he wasn't too fond of him [Patton] because he played too fast and then he would argue." According to Moore, Brown told him Charlie would argue "over about anything." "Sometimes they'd get to talkin' about what [key] was the 'Jelly Roll Blues' played in or what was the 'Down Home Blues' played in," Moore says. "I tell 'em, I'd say, 'You all ain't gettin' nowhere.'"

But playing with Son House was an easier task for Brown, as Moore remembers: "He wanted to play with him [House], didn't want him to preach, you know. The folks would get around Son House, you know, and he'd preach a year, somethin' like that, and then six months later he's playin' blues. But he could preach, you know! Willie Brown would go to church where Son House was pastoring but he never got in the church. Son would tell Willie Brown he done quit playin' 'em blues and Willie would say, 'Well, I sho' need you [to play music].' Willie would swear that Son done quit, and next time Willie would hear [from folks] he'd be playin' again."

By 1930, when House and Brown teamed up, Moore and Brown had been playing for some 14 years irregularly. They even went into the army together in 1918; along with a third man from the Bedford plantation they registered for the draft in nearby Hernando. Months later, all three were drafted at the same time and ended up in Camp Shelby, Mississippi, near Hattiesburg (where ARC recorded in 1936, and where in the early 1950s Cooney Vaughn was reportedly killed in a drinking daze on a railroad track where he was sleeping or had fallen down).

Decca Records reissued the Brown songs in 1935, three years after Paramount folded. Wardlow collection.

"Me and Willie Brown registered over there in Hernando and they made us Class 1." The two friends discussed the war in Europe, having heard tales about French women. "He asked me what did I think about it?" Moore remembers. "I told him, I say, 'I wanna go 'cause I ain't never been to France,' and he say, 'I'm goin' but it's a risk to run.'"

Neither Willie made the trip overseas. They did make it to Camp Shelby, where Willie Brown had a fateful meeting with the camp doctors. "Willie Brown just fell down cold," Moore recalls, laughing. "When they give him the three Cs [shots] he just fainted." Shortly after the inoculations, during the basic training program, Moore says, "Peace was declared," and both Willies went back to a life of making music, working very little, and being local celebrities.

"I'll tell you one thing," Moore says, "he says he didn't, you know, like to drink so much whiskey . . . but looka here, he'd drink it, man, just as sure as you born to die! And whenever you hear him slappin' that guitar, he been had some too. And look, he wouldn't shoot no dice, play no cards, no, sir. There's one thing I know him to do . . . two things. He'd drink that whiskey and play that guitar."

Willie Brown was a soft-spoken man and, because he didn't brag a lot, some residents of Robinsonville didn't believe he made records. Elizabeth Moore recalls, "Well, him and that Kid [Bailey] made music together sometimes. That fellow's been with Willie Brown playin' right there at Lake Carmen. I seed him in person. I don't know where he lived at. I just know they'd be over there to the juke on Saturday night. Willie Brown comes back home on Saturday and we asked him, 'Old Cat'—we called him that—'where's you been?' and he say, 'Me and Kid been out makin' some records.'" But Elizabeth didn't believe him until she heard the Kid Bailey recordings. She quickly identified "Rowdy Blues" (Brunswick 7114) as a song that Brown both played and sang. "They didn't go in the time Willie and Son House made records," she recalled. "Him [House] and Willie went another time to make some records."

Besides these associations, Brown also played with Kid Douglas, later known as Memphis Minnie, who lived in nearby Walls, just above Robinsonville on Highway 61. "When she's playin' with us she played lead all the time, he'd [Brown] played second and I'se played third. She'd do the singing." When Moore first saw Minnie, "her and a boy was playin' mandolin and a guitar together . . . All of us called her Kid Douglas. Everything Willie Brown could play [songs] she could play, and then she could play some things he couldn't play."

In the early '40s Moore—who was later to move to Missouri, where he was living when

Willie Brown's "M & O Blues" was enough of a seller in 1932 to merit reissue in 1935 on Decca's 35 cent label. Wardlow collection.

Brown died—heard from friends that there was to be a recording session at Clack's store. "Up there on the mill job at Lake Cormorant, right there this side of the depot, left hand side of the road, Son House and them made some records and they wanted me to come make some too."

But a logging commitment for a "boss man" prevented Moore being there, and by the time his obligation was completed, Alan Lomax and company had left for Memphis. The store owner obviously lined up talent for the session from the local musicians he knew. "They had a juke right there, what you call at Clack's. White fella run it, was a dago white man. Well, he had it, he opened it up for the colored folks." As late as 1967 Clack's store was standing but unoccupied. The main Illinois Central railroad from Clarksdale to Memphis ran behind the store for some 50 years, and a train can be heard passing Clack's on one of the Lomax recordings.

Willie Brown continued to play throughout the '40s, though not as often after Son House moved to Rochester. But his drinking had had its effect and he was hospitalized in 1952.

"Willie Brown went to that hospital in Memphis and when he come outta that hospital they put him in the undertaker's parlor there [Tunica]. And they didn't have 'nough money to bury him with."

The death certificate says he died at home and lists heart failure as the cause of death.

"My uncle says they buried 'im over in Prichard. You know, my uncle knowed 'im good. That's the reason I know he didn't die in Fiddlin' Joe [Martin]'s arms or nothin' of that kind," Moore says, adding he was living in Missouri when Brown died. Martin had asserted that Brown died that way, but Moore and other residents refuted the claim. "Fiddlin' Joe, he's kinda funny. He'd kinda make 'em up, you know," Moore says. "Play that box, that's all I ever know him [Brown] to do. Fishin', nothin' else. All I'd see that fella doin' is drinkin' and playin' that guitar. He sure could do that. He sure could work that whiskey out, man!"

◄◊►◄◊►◄◊► The Two Browns ◄◊►◄◊►◄◊►

Hayes McMullan and Dick Bankston were each acquainted with a Willie Brown.

In 1962, when this researcher began to question Mississippians about Charlie Patton for historical documentation, many of the sources questioned remembered seeing Patton when he was playing at suppers and parties with another guitarist they identified as Willie Brown.

Hayes McMullan saw Patton with Willie Brown and later teamed with Brown himself. Brown mostly played behind McMullan's singing, since he didn't (McMullan said) like singing as much as playing.

After this researcher took Bernard Klatzko, a noted Patton record collector, to the Delta to Dockery's plantation in 1963, Bernie speculated that both Willie Brown and Charlie Patton had lived at Dockery's. Brown especially had been visible in the Dockery's area just before and after Patton's 1929 sessions.

In 1965 this writer secured death certificates from the state Bureau of Vital Statistics for Patton, Brown, and Tommy Johnson (and three years later, for Robert Johnson). The Patton death certificate was published in *78 Quarterly* in 1967 (no. 1, 10–17). [See "Patton's Murder—Whitewash? Or Hogwash?," page 94.]

Prodded by Pete Whelan of Origin Jazz Library Records, this writer taped interviews with Rev. Ledell Johnson, brother of Tommy, and his wife Maybelle in south Jackson in 1967, using the Origin reissues to elicit comments about musicians both Ledell and Tommy had known. Both Ledell and Maybelle told anecdotes of

Nathan "Dick" Bankston, who played in the Drew-Dockery area, was active as a bluesman in the 1920s. He knew a different Willie Brown than the one who played with Charlie Patton and Son House in Tunica County. Wardlow collection.

Hayes McMullan of Sumner (1968), who played extensively in the Tallahatchie County area in the 1920s and 1930s, performed with Willie Brown, who played "second" guitar behind Hayes' singing. Wardlow collection.

years they had spent individually in the Drew area from about 1913 to 1923.

Both Johnsons described a Willie (Will) Brown—they used the names Willie and Will interchangeably—as being married to a Josie Bush from near Crystal Spring, the hometown of Tommy Johnson, as this writer originally reported in the first Origin notes on Mississippi artists.

Mrs. Hattie McMullan sits on a typical Delta sharecropper house built in the 1930s. Few of these houses had plumbing or electricity until after World War II. Hattie convinced Hayes to give up blues playing in the '30s, after marching him home from a juke brandishing a pistol. Wardlow collection.

Listening to the 1930 Willie Brown Paramounts, they said: "The music ['Future Blues'] sounds like Willie Brown but the voice don't." Asked to describe the Brown they had known in Drew, Ledell said, "He was chunky and heavyset; he had a big, round face." Maybelle added, "He was heavyset; he was 'bout big as you." (The researcher is six feet tall and weighs 230 pounds.) Maybelle also said that the Brown she knew looked "'bout 25" in the late 1910s. Ledell agreed.

Perplexed by this description—radically different from that provided by sources who said the Willie Brown they saw with Patton was "smaller than Charlie" or "no bigger than Charlie"—this researcher sought out Dick Bankston in Memphis in the summer of 1967. This was the first-ever interview on tape with recordings played for the former Drew musician.

Bankston (who was also interviewed by David Evans later that summer) could not identify the 1930 Paramounts credited to a Willie Brown as being by the Brown he had known at Drew, who introduced him to Charlie Patton around 1912. He described the Drew Willie Brown as "as tall as my son [six feet or over]" and "'bout your size." Asked about a small Willie Brown, Bankston replied, "I didn't know him." He also said the Brown he played blues with "never made no records" and had moved to Memphis, where he died somewhere around 1940. He described Brown as being in his early twenties when he met him in 1912.

Could there have been two Willie Browns who played with Charlie Patton in the Dockery area, before Willie Lee Brown teamed with Son House just before the May 1930 Paramount session?

Or was there confusion about the two men?

The death certificate obtained in 1965 said that Willie Lee Brown was born August 6, 1900, died on December 30, 1952, and was buried near Prichard. Son House had confirmed to Stephen Calt in a 1966 interview that the Brown he had played with for more than 15 years before he moved north had died around New York in either 1952 or '53.

In 1978, the Wardlow-Calt manuscript on Patton and the Delta blues was submitted to the University Press of Mississippi and ultimately rejected by its reader David Evans, who commented, "The thesis of the two Browns is extremely unlikely and borders on the absurd." No reasons were given why our descriptions of two men, based upon information from the Johnsons, Bankston, Moore, McMullan, and many others, were considered absurd.

Then, in 1982, Evans' *Big Road Blues: Tradition and Creativity in the Folk Blues* was published. It described the Willie Brown from the alleged Drew tradition as "born sometime between 1890 and 1895 either in Drew itself, in Shaw (about 20 miles to the southwest), or somewhere in Tennessee. In any case by 1911 he was living near Drew on Jim Yeager's plantation and playing guitar . . . Brown remained on Yeager's plantation until about 1929, playing his blues mostly right around Drew" (p. 176). Furthermore, Evans wrote about Josie Bush: "She was about seven or eight years older than her husband to whom she was married by 1911" (p. 176).

Earlier in the '70s, Steve LaVere, working out of Memphis and researching Robert Johnson, had found a gambler-turned-preacher named Ernest Brown living in Tunica. He had known Patton, Robert Johnson, and Willie Brown, and said that he lived on the Peerman plantation as a youth with the Willie Brown that he later met again in Robinsonville. Willie had lived on the same plantation from about 1909 to about 1915, Rev. Brown said, but he left Peerman's after he learned how to play the guitar. Willie Moore said he met Willie Brown around 1916 in Tunica County.

How could the Willie Brown (called "Bill" by his closest associates in Robinsonville and Lake Cormorant) have been married to a Josie Bush in 1911 and also living near Drew, when Rev. Brown knew the same man on Peerman's plantation at that time?

Also, Willie Moore said that the Willie Brown he knew married "a woman out there on the Dog [railroad] in 1918." Unlike Josie Bush, this woman never played guitar.

In determining that two Willie Browns did indeed play music with Charlie Patton during his career, we based our findings upon the following evidence:

- the different physical descriptions of the two men from at least nine sources;

- reactions to the 1930 recordings by Willie Brown; and

- the death certificate and Son House's statements about when the Brown he knew had died.

The following quotes from taped interviews constitute the evidence referred to in the first item of evidence cited above.

Leroy Willis (Helena 1967): "They called him 'Bill'; everyone called him 'Bill.'" Frank Howard (Triplett, 1967): "They called him 'Little Bill.' He stood 'bout five foot four, weighed about 135." Hayes McMullan (Sumner/Tutwiler, 1967–71): "I called him 'Little Willie Brown.'" Mandy Wigham (Swiftown, 1967): "They would mostly call him 'Little Willie Brown.' He was low, Willie was lower [smaller] than Charlie." Willie "Have Mercy" Young (Leland, 1967–70): "He was a little bitty old guy." Elizabeth Moore (Tutwiler/Sumner, 1967–71): "Willie Brown didn't weigh over 135 . . . that was his size."

Contrast these statements with those of Bankston and the Johnsons: Ledell Johnson (Jackson, 1967–68): "Willie Brown was chunky and heavyset. He had a big round face." Maybelle Johnson (Jackson, 1967–68): "He was heavyset, fat, big as you." Dick Bankston (Memphis, 1967): "He was as tall and heavy as you. He was as tall as my son [six feet or over]."

Blind Roosevelt Graves
(1909–1962)

In 1968, I came across information that Blind Roosevelt Graves came from Laurel, Mississippi, some 60 miles from Meridian. Upon reaching Laurel, I headed to the shoeshine stands, the black barber shops, and the cafes, asking about Blind Roosevelt Graves and playing tapes of his music. An old friend of his, Chester House, who had known Graves and his brother personally, said that Graves had died in Gulfport in 1963. In 1990, University of Mississippi Blues Archive Research Associate Walter Liniger accompanied me to the Gulfport area, where he actually found the informant who verified where Graves was buried, and with whom and where he had lived. —GDW

In the 1920s and '30s, the only way for a blind person to earn a living was to play music on a street and beg for nickels and dimes. However, in 1926 a door was opened when Paramount executives discovered that records by both Blind Lemon Jefferson and Blind Blake were excellent sellers. Before then, Paramount had never recorded a blind musician.

As the '20s roared on and country blues flourished on record, Jackson music talent broker H.C. Speir began sending talent to Paramount. The label did not require a test record as other companies such as Victor did (see "Godfather of Delta Blues," page 131).

In the fall of 1929, one of the most impressive Mississippi blues and gospel singers was dispatched to the Gennett Records studio in Richmond, Indiana, to record masters for the Paramount label. Those 15 sides by "Blind Roosevelt Graves and Brother" are excellent representatives of the finest blues and sacred music with piano and cornet.

Roosevelt Graves, son of William Graves and Maggie Booth, was born blind on December 9, 1909, in the Summerland community, some 15 miles west of Laurel on State Highway 16. His brother Aaron, who accompanied him as a street guide, was reportedly blind in one eye also, according to Ishmon Bracey, who saw the two perform on Jackson streets.

Aaron (not Uaroy, which is possibly a misinterpretation of Leroy) played a tambourine when

This recording, similar to Western swing records of the 1930s, could be considered the first rock 'n' roll recording. Wardlow collection.

needed. (See Ishmon Bracey's memory of the Graves brothers in "Got Four, Five Puppies, One Little Shaggy Hound," page 45.) He bore the dubious distinction of being credited on both Paramount and American Record Company (ARC) issues as merely "Brother."

In several 1960s interviews, Speir remembered the Paramount recordings by Graves with piano specialist Will Ezell of east Texas. Ezell was employed by Paramount as a staff pianist on many sessions. Also present at the September 1929 recording session was Baby Jay on cornet. This instrumentation gave an exultant background, similar to a Pentecostal service, or the type of music played by the Salvation Army at Christmastime.

Two of the Paramount releases were excellent sellers: "Guitar Boogie," the first Paramount featuring a boogie by a guitarist from Mississippi, and

This November 1929 session, featuring Texas pianist Will Ezell, was the first guitar boogie recorded, although many piano boogies had been recorded previously. Wardlow collection.

"Crazy about My Baby." The most memorable sacred sides were "Take Your Burdens to the Lord" and "I Shall Not Be Moved."

Graves and his brother continued to make their living playing street corners in south Mississippi towns, until 1936, when Speir found them "down there in McComb City" and persuaded them to be in Hattiesburg on July 16. After arriving at the Hattiesburg hotel room for the ARC session directed by W.R. Calaway, they recorded a total of 14 songs. Unfortunately, only two sacred selections were issued, "Woke Up This Morning (With My Mind on Jesus)" and "I'll Be Rested." Pioneer gospel collector and advocate Bernie Klatzko noted that these songs were the last recorded examples of the older-style sacred music that had begun sweeping the South in the 1900s, and in 1966 he advocated their inclusion in the Origin Jazz Library albums *In the Spirit* (OJL 12–13).

At that 1936 session, Graves was teamed with local pianist Cooney Vaughn, one of the more reputable and influential piano players in Mississippi. At that time Vaughn had been playing for more than 20 years and had helped to establish Hattiesburg as a blues piano center (according to the research of Hattiesburg TV reporter Charlie Herrington, who produced a documentary on Hattiesburg musicians). These recordings were issued as by the Mississippi Jook Band in late 1936, and have been described by *Rolling Stone* columnist Robert Palmer as possessing the rhythmic elements that were to influence the beginning of the 1950s rock 'n' roll era. However, the prominence of the piano and guitar on these Jook Band sides can also be heard on the Paramount performances with cornet seven years earlier.

(A few more words about Cooney Vaughn: He is remembered as a "pop performer" and not a blues entertainer in my hometown of Meridian, where he played on radio station WCOC just before World War II. Mrs. Withers Gavin, wife of the deceased owner, recalls him fondly and says he had fifteen minutes a week and played "all types of songs." Sam Lovelady, a shoestore owner in Meridian's black business section, says he was present at a picnic at which Cooney shot and killed a man in Livingston, Alabama, in the late 1930s or early 1940s. Vaughn was sent to the Alabama State Penitentiary. Others have reported that Vaughn was killed by a train that hit him while he was either sleeping or in a drunken stupor on a railroad track in Hattiesburg. Vaughn seems to have played in Laurel, Hattiesburg, and Meridian at different times. No death certificate has been located to substantiate the death information.)

Blind Roosevelt Graves was only 19 when he went into his first major record company studio. Wardlow collection.

Chester House of Laurel, a close friend of Graves from their teenage years and beyond, saw him play many times on the streets of both Laurel

This document shows that Roosevelt Graves was only 53 when he died of a heart attack, brought on by diabetes. No photos of Roosevelt and Aaron have ever been found. Wardlow collection.

and Hattiesburg before Graves moved to Gulfport in the late 1950s. The two had met as early as 1926 at Rose Hill, near Hickory on Highway 80.

House recalled that Graves was as proficient with blues as he was with sacred songs, and with either a six- or a twelve-string guitar. He remembered traveling with him to the Delta, where they both performed blues with brother Aaron Graves at a country picnic. Later, Ishmon Bracey saw the two brothers singing gospel and blues in Jackson. Bracey went on to adapt, as his own, the song "Woke Up This Morning (With My Mind on Jesus)" after he was ordained as a Baptist minister, refusing to perform blues thereafter.

Around 1959, Aaron died suddenly near Summerland; no death certificate has been located by the Mississippi Department of Vital Records confirming this death. Then, a blind black woman named Elizabeth (nicknamed "Sis") from Gulfport found Graves hungry and dirty on Hattiesburg streets, and she took him to Gulfport to "keep him clean and cook for him," according to House. There, Graves joined the Baptist church, where he sang in an all-men's quartet. Graves never told members of the church that he had made records for Paramount and ARC in Hattiesburg, perhaps thinking he would not be believed. Nevertheless, Sis (his wife) listed his occupation as "musician" on the death certificate filed on January 18, 1963, instead of "laborer" or "disabled."

In late 1962 Graves suffered health problems from acute diabetes. He was treated by a Hattiesburg doctor from December 15, 1962, until his death on December 30. The doctor ruled the official cause of death as heart failure resulting from his diabetic condition. Graves was only 53. He was buried January 6, 1963, in an unmarked grave in the Mississippi City graveyard within the Gulfport city limits. Sis lived a few more years before her death in the late 1960s.

Graves was one of the youngest black musicians to make commercial blues recordings, along with Henry Townsend of St. Louis and Jesse Thomas of Shreveport. All three were only 19 when they went into major record company studios. Roosevelt Graves was also an example of the state's wealth of sacred and gospel recorded talent that included Blind Willie Davis, McIntorsh and Edwards, and Leontyne Price of Laurel, the heralded opera singer who has recorded much black religious music in her career.

"I ain't never see'd the light of day one time in my life," Graves told Chester House before he died. "Lord knows I tried to keep his teachings and live right, but I ain't never even seen the sun rise one time."

Stop, Look, and Listen
At the Cross Road

The continuing saga of Robert Johnson selling his soul to become the masterful blues legend that he was has not itself been factually investigated. After carefully reviewing the lyrics and the literature leading up to the 1988 movie Crossroads *that enhanced the myth for a worldwide audience, I have written this, my only commentary and opinion of Johnson's alleged pact with Satan. Interestingly, although Johnson and Elvis Presley died 39 years apart (in 1938 and 1977), these two cultural icons died on the same day of the year, August 16. (For details on Johnson's death, see "Searching for the Robert Johnson Death Certificate," page 86, and "Robert Johnson: New Details on the Death of a Bluesman," page 91.) —GDW*

The "crossroads" legend: is it sensationalism for profit, or factual? If indeed true, where is the fabled crossroads where Robert Johnson reputedly sold his soul to "the devil," to become the masterful bluesman whose 29 songs have earned more royalties than a Delta planter could have ever made?

The concept that a person may "sell his soul to the devil" is apparently rooted in both black and white American folklore. In 1824 Washington Irving published "The Devil and Tom Walker." Its storyline revolved around the character Tom Walker, who had made a pact with the devil (described as a "man of color") sitting on a stump in a swamp. Walker bested the "devil" and thus saved his own soul. Critics of American literature say the work was based upon actual folktales prevalent during the early 1700s in New Hampshire and Massachusetts, areas having little or no black cultural influence.

More than 100 years after Irving, Stephen Vincent Benet published his renowned short story, "The Devil and Daniel Webster" (1936), ironically the same year as Johnson's first session in San Antonio at which he recorded his "Cross Road Blues." The setting is

Record companies of the '20s utilized the "devil theme" to depict the dangers associated with playing the blues. Talking Machine World, *by Tim Grayck.*

also Massachusetts, and the devil also loses a soul that he had earlier claimed, this time to a person represented by famous lawyer and politician Daniel Webster.

In the 1960s when this writer began inquiring about Mississippi blues artists, both Ledell Johnson and Ishmon Bracey recounted stories of Tommy Johnson (Ledell's brother, but no relation to Robert) "selling his soul to the devil at a crossroad." Later, Ledell changed the setting to a graveyard at midnight on the darkest night of the month. Bracey relayed to me Tommy Johnson's boast that he had "sold his soul to the devil" to play the blues. But Bracey downplayed the claim, saying he had played the blues "as good as Tommy" and he never sold his soul for his musical talent.

Rev. Booker Miller (1910–1968), a Greenwood-based bluesman and Charlie Patton associate in the late 1920s who later became a Baptist minister, said: "Them old folks did believe the devil would get you for playin' the blues and livin' like that," meaning the sins of adultery, fornication, gambling, lying, and drinking. He confirmed that the idea of "selling your soul to the devil" came from "those old slavery times."

Additionally, Steve LaVere (1990) confirmed the graveyard aspect of the legend by reporting that guitarist Ike Zinnerman of Hazelhurst, who influenced Johnson's playing, claimed to have "learned to play a guitar in a graveyard at midnight while sitting atop tombstones."

Perhaps the greatest of Robert Johnson's recordings, this song was the impetus for rumors that Johnson "sold his soul" at a Delta crossroads. Wardlow collection.

Robert Johnson recorded two songs that many listeners felt strongly identified with Satan: "Hell Hound on My Trail," and "Me and the Devil Blues." Like Peetie Wheatstraw, who billed himself as the "Devil's Son-in-Law," Johnson apparently believed that this Satanic association would heighten his reputation among record buyers and juke house frolickers. Today we would call such devilment "hype," but it added to the image of Johnson, whose life's ambition was to "make records one day in New York," as he confided to his Robinsonville plantation friend Elizabeth Glynn Moore. In the late 1920s she had listened to the teenaged Johnson as he tried to learn the guitar accompaniment to the only song her husband "Hard Rock" Glynn knew; previously Johnson had only played the harmonica, which she told him "to go back to," because of his constant mistakes.

Western swing singer Dave Edwards recorded this song about the devil's influence on his actions, indicating that the "devil theme" also influenced white musicians. Wardlow collection.

Is "Hell Hound on My Trail" subject to some skepticism? Yes. In 1976, English blues enthusiast Dave

Moore responded to a three-part article on Robert Johnson by blues editor Bob Groom that had been printed in the English publication *Blues Unlimited* (Groom 1976). In his letter (*BU* no. 122 [1976]: 15), Moore pointed out that Oklahoma/Texas bluesman J.T. "Funny Paper" Smith had sung in his 1931 record "Howling Wolf Blues No. 3":

I take time when I'm prowlin'
an' wipe my tracks out with my tail.
I take time when I'm prowlin'
an' wipe my tracks out with my tail.
Get home an' get blue an' start howlin'
an' the hellhound get on my trail.

Oddly, in his "Hell Hound on My Trail," Robert Johnson uses the title words in one chorus only; had the lyrics been more developed, there would have been more mentions of the hellhound. Also, it is doubtful "Hell Hound on My Trail" occupied a central place in his repertoire, as it was recorded on the second day of his 1937 San Antonio session. Listening to a reissue of "Hell Hound" in the late 1960s, Elizabeth Moore said, "That's a surprise. I had never heard him sing that song before." She had heard him sing "live" on several occasions, including her Friar's Point juke house in 1937.

Skip James recorded a "devil theme" song as early as 1931. Johnson used James' melody for "Hell Hound on My Trail" in 1937. Wardlow collection.

It was common for a pre–World War II record company to record an artist at least once a year for 10 to 16 songs for release during the coming 12 months. This allowed the company to release a double-sided 78 rpm disc by that artist every two months or so. To meet this requirement, the artist would have to play material that would be considered "studio songs." Many of these songs were never performed live. But the more songs Johnson recorded, the more money from flat fees per side he received. Having that much material from him, the label could select and release only those sides that would sell. Of the 29 songs Johnson recorded in 1936 and 1937, 24 were released in the 78 rpm format.

Returning to Smith's song, "hellhound" can mean the police, and this meaning of the word can lead to a new explanation of Johnson's "Hell Hound on My Trail," in which the singer is on the run from the law, not from the devil. For Johnson, the threat of violence from the police

One of two songs Johnson recorded using the devil motif. Blues Archive.

was much more imminent than any supposed claims on his soul. In fact, he took several aliases (such as Robert Saunders, Robert Dusty, and Robert Saxton) to protect himself while traveling. Even so, he had to explain why he was cautious sometimes.

"[Johnson] told the people to quit callin' him that ('Robert Dusty') for the time bein'," remembered Elizabeth Moore. "I asked him why. He say, 'See, I be out on the road so much, girl, I might tell the folks I'm named Robert Dusty, and there might be a man goin' on down the road there done *done* somethin' [wrong], and I'm just wearin' that name.' A person [Johnson] could be wearin' the name of somebody else done killed a thousand people" (Wardlow and Calt 1989, 42).

No matter where he was and under which name, Johnson must have had access to Victrolas in Memphis or the Delta, on which he could listen closely to his contemporaries on records; Edward Komara's list (1996) of records whose melodies Johnson apparently borrowed appears at this article's end. But a careful inspection of the lyrics to "Cross Road Blues" and the other 28 songs Johnson recorded does not reveal any verse that remotely says, "I went to the crossroads and I sold my soul to the devil." It is not there.

Moreover, Johnson did not record "Cross Road Blues" (as it was spelled on the record's first release in 1937) until his third day of recording in an San Antonio hotel. It was his twelfth song recorded overall. H.C. Speir—who recommended Johnson to the American Recording Co. (ARC)—said a bluesman had to have at least four original songs for a company to record him.

"They always record their best song first, and they do the four songs they know best, you know, the ones they sing all the time."

Tommy Johnson had only one complete original song when he first met Speir in 1927 at a fish camp on the Pearl River. To prepare the musician for a possible recording session, Speir told him to write three more original songs to meet the industry's requirements. Conversely, Speir "turned down" Jimmie Rodgers because of his lack of four original songs. Rodgers did not audition with his "Blue Yodel," but instead performed two other songs.

Robert Johnson's first recorded song was "Kind Hearted Woman," the song Johnson auditioned for Speir at his store. The second was "Dust My Broom," followed by "Sweet Home Chicago" and "Rambling on My Mind"; four additional songs were cut that day. His next recording day produced only one song, "32-20 Blues." That Friday he recorded "Cross Road Blues" as the twelfth song of his sessions and the third song on that day, indicating it was one of his "studio sides."

In the postscript following this article, Edward Komara discusses the first apparent reference to Johnson's "selling his soul" interpretation in Pete

One of the "devil-theme" songs Robert Johnson recorded that linked him to the devil and the crossroads theme. Blues Archive.

Welding's 1966 *Down Beat Music* (no. 76: 103) article on Johnson. Later, in the 1975 book *Mystery Train,* Greil Marcus "symbolically" implied Johnson mastered the guitar because of his alleged pact with the devil.

Seven years later, in 1982, Peter Guralnick added the Ledell Johnson story of Tommy "selling his soul" at midnight at a Delta crossroad. In that region, a crossroad is simply a place where two dirt roads intersect. There is no such place as "The Cross Road." Additionally, in the 1988 Hollywood movie, a cross road became "The Crossroads," as it is now known. Many tourists believe that the intersection of Highways 49 and 61 at Clarksdale is "The Crossroads" where Johnson is believed to have made his deal with the devil (O'Neal 1990). Even Memphis uses the "crossroads" theme. Its promoters claim that Beale Street in Memphis is the actual location.

The *Crossroads* movie certainly gave the "crossroads" myth additional credibility. The movie's Willie Brown was a harmonica player who saved his own soul by leading a young guitarist to the Delta for Robert Johnson's missing thirtieth song; there, the youth "saved Willie's soul" by besting Satan in a guitar contest. The real-life Willie Brown died in 1952 and did not play the harmonica. Instead, he was a superb Delta guitarist who actually spent time with the teenaged Johnson, according to the eyewitness account of Elizabeth Moore. The myth of the missing Johnson song sprang from the 1959 Samuel Charters book *The Country Blues.* Charters reported (without giving a source) that other Johnson masters besides "32-20 Blues" were recorded but destroyed in a billiard parlor fight where the recording session took place. However, both the Chuck Wagon Gang and a Mexican group recorded before and after Johnson's lone recording that day, according to both the session research by LaVere (1990, 46) and independent verification by Texas blues authority Mack McCormick.

Therefore, the legend of Johnson's pact with the "devil" has been widely accepted as factual since the release of the *Crossroads* movie. In the same manner, the 1956 ballad "Davy Crockett" (composed by T. Blackbum and G. Bruns, and recorded by Fess Parker) heralded the story that Crockett killed a bear "when he was only three." From such examples, legends grow.

At the 1991 dedication of the Johnson memorial at Mt. Zion Baptist Church near Morgan City, Mississippi, the Reverend James Ratliff Jr. made favorable remarks about Johnson's life and said it was "up to God" to judge Robert Johnson's life and eternal destination. Perhaps that minister had heard the first verse of "Cross Road Blues," which has been totally overlooked in the many analyses of his lyrics. Stop, look and listen! The first verse begins:

I went to the cross road, fell down on my knees
I went to the cross road, fell down on my knees
Asked the Lord above "Have mercy,
Save poor Bob, if you please."

Nowhere does Johnson say that he had earlier been to the cross road (in Johnson's time "cross road" was two words, singular; today it is one word, plural) and sold his soul to the devil. Nor does he give an answer to the plea "for mercy," such as "But you know boys, the Lord didn't answer me."

In the apostle Paul's letters to the members of the early Christian churches he wrote: "Whosoever shall call upon the name of the Lord, shall be saved" (Romans 10:13). Traditional theologians would agree that Johnson did just that, and at the moment that he called, he was "saved" and had an eternal home in heaven, the same as that thief crucified with Jesus who asked Jesus to remember him in Paradise.

However, this interpretation spoils the romance around Johnson's life and its commercial possibilities. (For details about Johnson's death, see "Searching for the Robert Johnson Death Certificate, page 86" and "Robert Johnson: New Details on the Death of a Bluesman," page 91.)

Regardless of the contradictory information that seems to surface occasionally—such as claims that Johnson is *not* buried at Mt. Zion Church near Morgan City—Johnson's music continues to intrigue and hypnotize countless blues guitarists, as it did a young Eric Clapton and Keith Richards in the early 1960s.

So, here's hoping the Lord heard Johnson's plea and that he welcomed the bluesman to an eternity of peace, far removed from the hype and controversy that have surrounded his posthumous introduction to a worldwide audience. May the devil be chained in hell. The Lord and Robert won this one at the cross road.

◄◦►◄◦►◄◦► On Robert Johnson's Signature ◄◦►◄◦►◄◦►

Robert Johnson's ability to read and write was highly unusual for a black plantation child. In the late 1920s and '30s, few black children were able to advance beyond the elementary grades because of poorly equipped facilities—or none at all—for blacks. Schools were usually funded by plantation owners in the 1920s, and from the beginning of the cotton-picking season in September, all children were expected to work in the fields. As late as the 1950s, some Mississippi schools began in early summer, then letting out in the early fall, so children could work in the autumn harvest.

To be officially married in Mississippi and other southern states, the couple had to obtain a marriage license from the county clerk's office and pay a

The Robert Johnson signature is a registered trademark of the Johnson estate.

small fee. Robert Johnson was legally married twice, according to licenses on file at the courthouses in Tunica (Tunica County) and Hazelhurst (Copiah County). At both locations, Johnson, as well as the bride-to-be, were required to sign the document. For a black man born in 1911, Johnson's signature is fluent and readable. These documents are public records and cannot be copyrighted. For the 1991 documentary "Searching for Robert Johnson" these certificates were filmed, but only now has there been an opportunity to publish them. We have selected the 1931 license for his marriage to Callie Craft at Hazelhurst for this first publication of Robert Johnson's actual signature.

GDW and EK: One prewar musician who actually sang about selling his soul to the devil was not a bluesman, but a white Western swing singer, Dave Edwards. Not to be confused with Robert Johnson's acquaintance David "Honey Boy" Edwards, Dave Edwards and "his Alabamians" recorded "Done Sold My Soul to the Devil" in late 1937 for Decca Records. It was released in early 1938. Evidently during this time the devil lyric concept was treated by whites as well as blacks. Some of Edwards lyrics, especially "He tails me like a bloodhound" are similar to those in Robert Johnson's "Hell Hound on My Trail," and others as they appear on the printed page exceed the "pure, icy cold paranoia" that Robert Palmer (1981, 127) attributes to the Johnson blues. The proof, however, is in the performance (included on the accompanying CD), and Edwards' singing renders an ironic, even comic tinge to the words.

Verse: *I'm like a ship on the stormy seas*
    since my baby quit me flat.
    Along came the devil as high as you can see
    and he treats me like an old house cat.
    He says "I can make you happy
    and give you back your gal and all your lady friends."
    I was so blue that I took him up,
    and now look what a hole I'm in.

Chorus 1:   *I've done sold my soul, I've sold it to the devil*
    and my heart's done turned to stone.
    I've got lots of gold, I got it from the devil
    but he won't let me alone.
    He tails me like a bloodhound,
    he's crooked like a snake
    He's always right behind me
    every crooked turn I take.

Chorus 2:   *I've done sold my soul, I've sold it to the devil*
          and my heart's done turned to stone.
          I've got lots of gold, I got it from the devil
          but he won't let me alone.
          I'm stubborn and I'm hateful
          and I'll die before I'll run,
          I'll drink carbolic acid
          and I'll tote a Gatlin gun.

GDW: This song was previously recorded in 1924 by Clara Smith, a woman blues singer

◄o►◄o►◄o► Postscript ◄o►◄o►◄o►

EK: The present-day myth that Robert Johnson sold his soul to the devil at a cross road in exchange for phenomenal guitar skills has no single source. This tall tale was developed in full view by blues writers, not in private by unnamed folk.

As Wardlow notes above, nowhere in Johnson's "Cross Road Blues" and his other 28 recorded songs does he sing about going to the cross road to sell his soul to the devil. The early writings about Johnson, from the mention of him in the July 1937 *Melody Maker* through the various reviews of the Columbia *King of the Delta Blues Singers* LP in 1962, say nothing of such a trade.

Pete Welding's article "Hellhound on his Trail" (1966) provided the initial building block to the myth. Son House, as quoted by Welding (p. 76), "suggested in all seriousness that Johnson, in his months away from home, had 'sold his soul to the devil in exchange for learning to play like that.'" It is likely House was envious of Johnson's musical skills, rather than awed or horrified at the prospect of any supernatural means of attaining them.

At any rate, Welding did not think much of consequence about House's comment, since, instead of asking for more details, he discusses House's influence on Johnson (beginning with "Johnson's style, House pointed out, was basically patterned on the instrumental approaches that House and Brown employed at the time"). Welding died on November 17, 1995, so unless an interview tape survives, there is no means of checking the nature of House's quote to him.

On this matter I spoke with Dick Waterman, a co-rediscoverer of House who managed his rediscovery career. He remembered discussing Robert Johnson with the aged bluesman a few times while traveling between concerts. House told Waterman of seeing Johnson returning to Robinsonville after an absence of "a couple of years." Whenever the legend of Johnson and the devil was mentioned, House would dismiss it with a shrug of his shoulders or a wave of his hand. Waterman believes what House said to Welding is strongly dependent on the line of questioning.

In 1971, David Evans published his book *Tommy Johnson,* which contains no mention of Robert Johnson, since Tommy and Robert were not related.

On page 22, Evans gives, in an extended quote (beginning with "He knew his songs then . . ."), Ledell Johnson's story about his brother Tommy claiming to have gone to a cross road with a guitar and acquired superior guitar skills by having an unidentified "big black man" tune the guitar.

The next step in the Robert Johnson myth-building comes with Greil Marcus' *Mystery Train* in 1975. With the words "let us say" (p. 32) Marcus hypothesizes that Johnson did sell his soul, on the apparent basis of House's stray quote to Welding (here worded as "He [Johnson] must have sold his soul to the devil to get to play like that"), then elaborates on the symbolic consequences. Although Robert Palmer, in his 1981 book *Deep Blues*, admits that "some of Johnson's satanic references were simply macho posturing" (p. 127), he cannot avoid a little romantic touch (p. 126): "Robert Johnson, alone in similar circumstances, might have imagined he was hearing the approach of Papa Legba, the black Man." Since their first appearances, these books by Marcus and Palmer have influenced others' writings on Johnson.

The elements of Robert Johnson's life, the devil pact, the improvement in guitar technique, and the crossroads come together in Peter Guralnick's 1982 *Living Blues* article "Searching for Robert Johnson" (no. 53: 27–41), later reprinted as a book in 1989. Guralnick quotes Ledell Johnson's story, then follows it with the comment "Son House was convinced that Robert Johnson had done the same thing" without naming a source, although House's quote to Welding and its use by Marcus would have come to mind to anyone well-read in the blues books and magazines. Guralnick does not go so far as to say directly that Robert Johnson had gone to a cross road and made a deal with the devil to become a better guitarist; yet the juxtaposition of the Ledell Johnson quote and the Son House reference seems to have led many readers to integrate the two statements.

The "cross road" myth reached its present form with the film *Crossroads*, which blended the Robert Johnson premise, the devil pact lore, and Mississippi dirt crossroads. The sights and sounds of them were recorded and photographed, combined on a strip of celluloid, then projected on a large screen. The impact on moviegoers was and remains considerable. Today, tourists come to Mississippi to find the crossroad(s), obviously believing the legend enacted on film to be factual.

Recordings before November 1936 of melodic precedents of Robert Johnson's recorded songs.

Prepared by Edward Komara. (An early version of this chart appeared in Living Blues *no. 129 [1996].)*

Robert Johnson repertory
"Kindhearted Woman Blues"

Melodic precedents
"Cruel Hearted Woman Blues" (Bumble Bee Slim, 1934) / "Mean Mistreater Mama" (Leroy Carr, 1934)

"I Believe I'll Dust My Broom"	"I Believe I'll Make a Change" (Leroy Carr, 1934) / "I Believe I'll Make a Change" (Josh White, 1934) / "Believe I'll Go Back Home" (Jack Kelly, 1933) / "I Believe I'll Make a Change" (Sparks Brothers, 1932)
"Sweet Home Chicago"	"Original Old Kokomo Blues" (Kokomo Arnold, 1934) / "Kokomo Blues" (Scrapper Blackwell, 1928) / "Kokola Blues" (Madlyn Davis, 1927) / "One Time Blues" (Blind Blake, 1927)
"Rambling on My Mind"	"My Woman's Gone Wrong" (Leroy Carr, 1934) / "M. & O. Blues" (Walter Davis, 1930)
"When You Got a Good Friend"	Same as that for "Rambling on My Mind"
"Come On in My Kitchen"	"Six Feet in the Ground" (Jimmy Oden, 1934) / "Sitting on Top of the World" (Mississippi Sheiks, 1930) / "How Long How Long Blues" (Leroy Carr, 1928) / "How Long Daddy How Long" (Ida Cox with Papa Charlie Jackson, 1925)
"Terraplane Blues"	"Police Station Blues" (Peetie Wheatstraw, 1932) / "So Long Blues" (Peetie Wheatstraw, 1930)
"Phonograph Blues," take 1	Same as that for "Kindhearted Woman Blues"
"Phonograph Blues," take 2	Same as that for "Rambling on My Mind"
"32-20 Blues"	"22-20 Blues" (Skip James, 1931) / "32-20 Blues" (Roosevelt Sykes, 1930)
"They're Red Hot"	"Keep Your Hands off Her" (Big Bill Broonzy, 1935) / "Keep It to Yourself" (Memphis Minnie, 1934) / "What Is It That Tastes Like Gravy?" (Tampa Red, 1929)
"Dead Shrimp Blues"	Same as that for "Kindhearted Woman Blues"
"Cross Road Blues"	"Straight Alky Blues" [Vocalion matrix no. C-3144] (Leroy Carr, 1929)

"Walking Blues"	"My Black Mama" (Son House, 1930)
"Last Fair Deal Gone Down"	"You're Gonna Need Somebody When You Gone to Die" (Charlie Patton, 1929/1930)
"Preaching Blues"	"Preachin' the Blues" (Son House, 1930)
"If I Had Possession Over Judgment Day"	"Roll and Tumble Blues" (Hambone Willie Newbern, 1929)
"Stones in My Passway"	Same as that for "Terraplane Blues"
"I'm a Steady Rollin' Man"	"Johnnie Blues" (Peetie Wheatstraw, 1935)
"From Four Until Late"	"Georgia Bound" (Blind Blake, 1929)
"Hell Hound on My Trail"	"Evil Devil Blues" (Johnny Temple, 1935)/ "Evil Devil Woman Blues" (Joe McCoy, 1934)/ "Devil Got My Woman" (Skip James, 1931)/ "Yola My Blues Away" (Skip James, 1931)
"Little Queen of Spades"	"King of Spades" (Peetie Wheatstraw, 1935)/ "Ain't It a Pity and a Shame" (Peetie Wheatstraw, 1930)
"Malted Milk"	"Life Saver Blues" (Lonnie Johnson, 1927)/ "Ball and Chain Blues" (Lonnie Johnson, 1926)
"Drunken Hearted Man"	Same as that for "Malted Milk"
"Me and the Devil"	"Prison Bound Blues" (Leroy Carr, 1928)
"Stop Breakin' Down"	"Caught Me Wrong Agin" (Memphis Minnie, 1936)/ "Stop Hanging Around" (Buddy Moss, 1935)/ "You Got to Move" (Memphis Minnie and Joe McCoy, 1934)
"Traveling Riverside Blues"	"Banty Rooster Blues" (Charlie Patton, 1929)
"Honeymoon Blues"	Same as that for "Kindhearted Woman Blues"
"Love in Vain"	"When the Sun Goes Down" (Leroy Carr, 1935)
"Milkcow's Calf Blues"	Same as that for "Terraplane Blues"

Epilogue

One Last Walk up King Solomon Hill

After the Ishmon Bracey, Blind Joe Reynolds, and Willie Brown features for Blues Unlimited, *I felt compelled to explain the use of the name of King Solomon Hill, and thus reaffirm my 1967 statement (see "King Solomon Hill," this book's prologue, page 2) that Joe Holmes was the man who made records as King Solomon Hill, the name of a community containing the King Solomon Hill Baptist Church. That article had been termed a "fiasco" by David Evans in a* Blues World *review (1968b) of the first issue of 78* Quarterly. *The concrete evidence that the King Solomon Hill community was where Joe Holmes lived was documented by a published letter from a retired Minden postman, E.B. Wall, who ran the mail route through the Sibley and King Solomon Hill communities during and after Holmes' lifetime. This "last walk" was the leading feature in the last issue of* Blues Unlimited. *—GDW*

[Originally published in *Blues Unlimited* no. 148 (Winter 1987): 8–12.]

As blues historians began to assemble biographical data on the legendary blues singers of the '20s and '30s, among the mysteries most often debated was this: who was the tantalizing, eerie King Solomon Hill, who sang in falsetto—to a bottleneck guitar accompaniment—about his woman "making whoopee with the devil in hell tomorrow night"? What of his mysterious "Gone Dead Train"?

This record sparked a controversy over Joe Holmes' pronunciation of "Minden" as "Winden." Regardless, it led this writer to Minden, Louisiana (and on to Sibley), where Holmes lived and played music. Wardlow collection.

Some researchers speculated that he was a Texan because of his guitar riffs. Others, myself included, believed that his work showed similarities to that of Salty Dog Sam Collins and to some of the patterns used by Willard "Ramblin'" Thomas. In the '60s, no information had yet been published on Thomas and very little on Salty Dog Sam, except a brief note of mine to the Origin *Mississippi Blues* album, saying that Collins was from the McComb area. This information came from Ishmon Bracey, who said he saw Salty Dog Sam (he never knew his last name) in McComb. Bracey often traveled to New Orleans to visit his baby sister and would work his way back to Jackson by the Illinois Central main line, which ran through McComb.

As early as 1959, Sam Charters' book *The Country Blues* (which inspired many researchers, including me) identified King Solomon Hill as the crafty braggart Big Joe Williams, who worked out of Crawford, Mississippi. Charters said Big Joe claimed the Hill recordings as his, but Big Joe later told researchers like me that "words were put in my mouth." (Charters was unavailable to comment for this article.) Nevertheless, that statement, as well as the issue, in the early '60s, of the Sam Collins' Origin Jazz Library album (OJL-10)—which contained Hill's Paramounts (Pete Whelan of Origin obviously thought there was some connection between the two men)— sparked even more interest in his identity. It was speculated that the artist

This cartoon by Tony Mostrom, who has been published in a number of specialty magazines, pokes fun at the King Solomon Hill controversy. Unfortunately, this one was never published as intended. Tony Mostrom collection.

was named King Solomon after the Biblical figure, his last name genuinely being Hill—a plausible enough possibility.

In the article I published in the first issue of *78 Quarterly* in the fall of 1967, I identified "King Solomon Hill" as Joe Holmes. Within the year David Evans, who had been in contact with many of my discoveries—Ishmon Bracey, Johnny Temple, Mager Johnson (Tommy's brother), Dick Bankston, and especially H.C. Speir—wrote in *Blues World* 21 that my identification of King Solomon Hill was untrustworthy ("a fiasco").

In a letter published in *BU* 70 (February–March 1970), Stephen Calt challenged Evans to meet me in northern Louisiana to question my sources—something that Evans never attempted, with or without me, although the two primary informants were alive until the mid-'70s.

That the Evans article created a controversy is unquestionable. In the second edition of Godrich and Dixon (1969), the authors said in the "Late Additions" section that it appeared "doubtful" that Hill's name was actually Joe Holmes. Then in *BU* 147, Henry Thomas, reviewing an album of *Giants of Country Blues* (Wold WSE116), wrote: "The sense of urgency which marks [Rube] Lacy's performance is also crucial to the artistry of King Solomon Hill, whose identity has been the subject of much debate."

After 18 years of "waiting at the crossroads" for Evans to produce his King Solomon Hill or tell us who he really was—if *not* Joe Holmes—it is time to resolve this issue. [Evans has been asked by the *BU* editorial committee to state his present position on the matter, and his reply is given at the end of this article.] [EK: Such a reply was not appended to the published article, nor published elsewhere.] Joe Holmes deserves his rightful place in blues history for his accomplishments—not because his identity was discovered by Wardlow or rejected by Evans, but for his artistic ability to adapt a south Mississippi guitar style (most of it probably learned from Salty Dog Sam) with influences from northern Louisiana and east Texas (Ramblin' Thomas and Blind Lemon) into a complex, eerie bottleneck approach. Few people would disagree that Hill's "Gone Dead Train," "Whoopee Blues," and "Down on My Bended Knee" are masterpieces. Their reissue on the Wolf LP bears out the extent of Hill's reputation: he belongs in the same category as Son House, Willie Brown, and Rube Lacy.

The sources for this article were Roberta Allums (the primary informant for the *78 Quarterly* story "King Solomon Hill"), John Willis (found on a second research trip in 1968), Wesley Hall, and retired postal carrier

This is the church (rebuilt after World War II) that "sat on King Solomon's Hill," according to John Willis, a friend of Joe Holmes. Wardlow collection.

E.B. Wall of Minden. All sources except Wall were taped between 1967 and 1969, while listening to the Hill reissues. (Informants do not make as many errors in recalling a person's background or songs if they are able to hear his recordings.) The Willis interview, in which he talks of Joe Holmes singing about "his buddy Blind Lemon," was played for Simon Napier and the late Mike Leadbitter on an early-'70s trip to the South. Both agreed with the information they heard and said they had no doubt that Hill was indeed Joe Holmes, though neither ever published his opinion.

Late summer, 1968, in the community of Yellow Pine, Louisiana, with the temperature hovering in the low 90s. A short bespectacled man in his early sixties answers the door.

"Yeah, I'm John Willis. Did I know Joe Holmes? Yes, sir, I use to play guitar with 'im right here where we's at."

After several more minutes of chatting, Willis listened to the four King Solomon Hill recordings on the Origin (OJL-10) reissue.

"Did Joe Holmes ever use the name King Solomon Hill?" I asked him.

"No, sir," replied Willis. "But see that church over there?" He pointed about 100 yards up the asphalt pavement of the country road. "That's the King Solomon Hill Baptist Church, and right here where you's standing is the King Solomon Hill community."

Willis' statement hit like a bombshell. He did not realize he had solved a mystery that had seemed impenetrable. Such an easy answer to what seemed so difficult a puzzle.

Not only was his statement confirmed by other residents of the Yellow Pine community, but the former rural mail carrier from the Sibley post office, E.B. Wall, investigated the name in 1986 to verify the report. (The community is now called Salt Works by newer residents.)

Willis said Holmes never used the name King Solomon Hill, nor was he called by it. So why did "King Solomon Hill" appear on the labels of the 1932 Paramounts? Part of the answer might be: why not? The company issued alternative takes of Charlie Patton as by Elder J.J. Hadley and even gave composer credits to Hadley. Record companies often conferred names on artists, and scouts such as Birmingham's Harry Charles used false names to keep other companies from "jumping talent," as he termed the practice. "King Solomon Hill" certainly sounds better than a simple "Joe Holmes." It seems likely that Holmes gave Paramount officials his address as King Solomon Hill, Louisiana, and the idea started there.

◄◦►◄◦►◄◦► Paramount in Decline ◄◦►◄◦►◄◦►

By 1932 Paramount was in desperate financial straits. According to John Steiner of Milwaukee, who talked to company officials in the late '40s when he purchased Paramount's name and remaining assets, the company was unable to contemplate riding out the Depression like the larger labels. It would either have to buy new and more expensive equipment simply to stay in competition, or liquidate its assets. As early as April 1930, the company's name and assets were offered to talent scout H.C. Speir when he visited the Grafton, Wisconsin, offices to record the Delta Big Four.

Record sales were dismal throughout the industry in 1932. A ledger for the Superior label shows that new summer releases were shipped from the factory in quantities of 20- or 30-odd, or even fewer. August 1932 may have been the lowest point of the Depression for the recording industry. Paramount was pressing more than 30 copies a week during the early months of 1932; according to Alfred Schultz (pressing-room foreman in Grafton), the company was pressing two or three days a week before it ceased operations in the summer.

In late 1931, Paramount had fired its sales manager and recording director, Art Laibley. A native of Louisiana, Laibley then moved to Chicago to endure the Depression years and worked for Wassau Insurance. He died in the early '70s in a nursing home, after living for many years in Park Ridge, a northern suburb of Chicago.

Laibley's replacement was Henry Stephany, who had no background in recording but did have sales ability. Contacted by telephone in the early '70s, Stephany, then living in Milwaukee, refused to discuss his tenure with Paramount, saying that it was a "difficult time" and he had only "bad memories" of his association with the company. However, Mrs. Stephany, who was more willing to talk when her husband was not present, confirmed that the two of them had made at least two trips to Birmingham, continuing on to Dallas before returning to Chicago.

◄◦►◄◦►◄◦► The Birmingham Connection ◄◦►◄◦►◄◦►

Birmingham was the major southern outlet for Paramounts, and the Forbes Piano Company, which began distributing the label in 1923—at one time bringing Paramounts to nine states—was one of the company's leading wholesalers. Direct ties exist between Birmingham and the musician King Solomon Hill. Recorded at the same Grafton, Wisconsin, session as Hill were Ben Curry, the Famous Blue Jay Singers, and Marshall Owens. Curry, according to Roberta Allums, had played with Joe Holmes in Monroe and other northern Louisiana towns. (Some reports say that he moved from Arcadia, Louisiana, his hometown, to Birmingham at some time in the mid-'20s.)

Mrs. Allums said that Joe Holmes was discovered by Paramount in Minden, the county seat of Webster Parish, some 40 miles from Shreveport on Highway 80.

"He was in Minden. He was playin'—he had his guitar with 'im and he run up on this man and they talked," she recalled. "And this man come on home with him. I think the man was from Chicago. He come down here and went out in Texas. They [Joe and an unidentified musician, possibly George Young, a rub-board player] played one or two songs for the man.

He come back here after two or three weeks and took him [Joe] to Birmingham." From there, they went on to Grafton to record.

She placed the event in the spring of 1932, which is more probable than a winter date, since street musicians didn't play outside in cold weather. (Most blues musicians were either street singers—who performed for handouts or to advertise a party—or, less often, dance players, such as Charlie Patton or William Harris.)

Conceivably it was Curry who, having been found in Birmingham, suggested that Stephany locate Joe Holmes in Minden on his way to Texas. H.C. Speir has said it was not unusual for him and other talent scouts to travel long distances to seek out musicians held in high esteem by their contemporaries. That was what led him to Lake Providence, Louisiana, to search for and find bottleneck stylist Blind Joe Reynolds. Lake Providence was also the home of Freddie Spruell, according to his widow; he never lived in Mississippi. And earlier, Speir has said, he found the preacher and street vendor Moses Mason in that same river town.

On another occasion, Speir and Polk Brockman, the OKeh recording director in Atlanta, travelled to Vicksburg before a session to search for a piano player Speir had been told about, only to find that he had left for Ruston, Louisiana. When the two arrived in Ruston, the bluesman had already left, and they gave up looking for him. "They [talent] moved around all the time," said Speir. "They didn't stay in no one place."

◄◦►◄◦►◄◦► The White Blues Records ◄◦►◄◦►◄◦►

Joe told Roberta Allums that after the Paramount session in Grafton he had gone back to Birmingham for a couple of weeks. He showed up in Sibley carrying some records with "white labels" bearing handwriting.

"He brought three records," she remembered. "Two of 'em got burned up in a house fire and one of 'em was left at Roytown [a small sawmill community a mile below Castor]. He carried that record down there to play [for a Mrs. King, who died in 1967] and left it there." Roberta never saw a labelled Paramount issue, nor did anyone else interviewed.

Holmes also bragged to John Willis about making records. Willis didn't consider the items Joe brought from Grafton to be "real records" because they had no printed labels. Willis recalls the conversation.

"Joe say, he said, 'Well, I had some records made, John.' I said, 'You did?' He say, 'You'll hear them some day. They'll be out—I don't know when they'll be out.' I say, 'Oh, you know you's lyin'. You ain't made no records.' He say, 'They'll come out some day. You might hear it.'"

Willis tells a different story from Allums about the fate of the tests: "He gave one of 'em records to an old man." He didn't know about the other two.

When Willis heard "Gone Dead Train" and the other Paramount sides on the Origin reissue, he finally believed Holmes' story. He had always assumed that Holmes had the tests recorded for himself so that he could say he had made a recording.

Roberta Allums was only surprised that it took until 1932 for Joe Holmes to record. She said he had known personally, and played with, both Blind Lemon Jefferson and Ramblin' Thomas. "They [Lemon and Holmes] had spoken 'bout they was gonna make some records, but I don't know whether they make 'em or not."

"Lemon was Joe's idol," she remembered. "The two first met in uptown Minden about 1928. He met 'im [Lemon] in Minden. He come up there ridin' in a car. Joe was standin' on the street and somebody drove a car up there [with Lemon]. Looks like they couldn't get away from each other. They went to Shreveport and played one night and went down here to Ringgold [a town about 20 miles below Sibley] and played one night."

Lemon's reputation was legendary among blacks. "When Lemon comes, the folks wouldn't go to bed at night. They'd [Joe and Lemon] get together often. One time they went out in Texas. Now where was it they went? They went to Nacogdoches. Joe come back alone."

She also recalled a trip Lemon, Holmes, and George Young, Holmes' closest musical associate in the area, made to Wichita Falls, Texas. She said Joe told her the three played together for about two months in Texas, before Joe "showed back up" in Sibley.

It may be that Holmes auditioned unsuccessfully for the Dallas-based Paramount scout R.T. Ashford. If so, he probably failed the audition because he lacked original material. According to Laibley, Ashford was the primary scout for Paramount in the Southwest. Interestingly, Speir never heard of Ashford, while Harry Charles knew of neither Ashford nor Speir. Seemingly, Paramount kept its scouts unknown to each other.

Ramblin' Thomas was originally from Logansport, Louisiana, according to his brother Jesse. Ramblin' played a circuit of northeastern Louisiana from Monroe to Shreveport, including the Minden area.

"He [Joe] met Ramblin' Thomas here in Sibley," Allums recalled. "They went down there to Monroe."

The two met many times in Shreveport to play together. But Holmes' guitar approach was more emotional and dynamic than that of Thomas, who played in a slow bottleneck style—more typical of a street musician— on his Paramount recordings. Apparently Holmes' background led him to develop a faster, dance-oriented approach. Tracing this background takes us to Mississippi.

◄◦►◄◦►◄◦► The Mississippi Connection ◄◦►◄◦►◄◦►

Although no hard information has been discovered concerning the birthplace of Sam Collins, a number of people interviewed in the Summit-McComb area of southern Mississippi knew him, but only as "Salty Dog Sam." Several sources said he played in both those towns. (Summit is about five miles above McComb.) Ishmon Bracey saw Sam at least twice on McComb streets, and Gress Barnett of Quitman, Mississippi, identified

Collins' voice and playing as those of the man from whom he learned "Out West Blues" on a McComb street in the late '20s. (Speir could not remember ever hearing Collins play.)

Incidentally, it is possible that Collins was discovered in New Orleans, during Mardi Gras. Musicians would go there just for the festival. Bill Russell, the New Orleans jazz and ragtime authority, once heard a string band on the streets during Mardi Gras, but in order to record them for his American Music label he had to trace them to their hometown in southern Alabama, just below Montgomery. Also, Gennett had a major retailer in New Orleans, and their talent scout Frank Wiggens may possibly have been based there too. New Orleans was the major city closest to McComb, and during Mardi Gras, as at cotton-picking time in the Delta, the place would be full of tourists who would tip street singers.

John Willis moved to the McComb area to find a better job than he could get in northern Louisiana. "I was down in McComb, Mississippi, in '24," he recalled. "Salty Dog, he's all outta town. He drinked a lot. Say about four o'clock [Saturday afternoon] we hit 'em barrelhouses blues. Oh, man! I'd just say about four-thirty, five, the next morning, you could hear that guitar 'bout three miles."

Willis saw Holmes and Sam together on numerous occasions. "Him and Salty Dog sang that song ["Jailhouse Blues"] together. Oh, man, he [Sam] had a bunch of songs he could make up, some of the prettiest songs you ever listen to."

Willis also identified "Riverside Blues," "Loving Lady Blues," and "Devil and Lions' Den" [*sic*] as songs often sung by Salty Dog Sam. Joe told him that Collins "was 'bout the best he ever met."

Roberta Allums agreed. "He played a heap with Salty Dog Sam. Some nights they'd stay two or three nights before they'd come back . . . They'd go down in Beartown." Beartown was a black community south of Summit, in northern McComb, where, according to local residents, the Harlem Nightingale club was a weekend playing place for Collins in the '30s.

Allums emphasized the similarities in the two men's playing. "Both of 'em played just alike. If you didn't see, you wouldn't hardly know 'em apart."

Strangely, Allums said Joe met Salty Dog Sam not in the Summit area but "up near Crystal Springs, and he come on home with Joe." One source in McComb said he thought Collins' home was originally near Terry, but no substantial evidence has been uncovered to confirm that.

According to Allums, Joe Holmes was a native Mississippian. He was born around 1897 near McComb, and moved to northern Louisiana around 1915, following his older brother Charlie, who later ran a juke in the Yellow Pine community. By 1920 Joe had taken Allums to McComb, but their relationship deteriorated and she later went back alone to northern Louisiana. Holmes returned there in the mid-'20s and made it the base for his wanderings.

◄◦►◄◦►◄◦► The Songs of Joe Holmes ◄◦►◄◦►◄◦►

What songs was Joe Holmes playing in the early '20s?

"He was singing that song 'bout 'down on my bended knees,'" remembered Roberta Allums. "He also sung, 'He done lied to his wife and three little children'—that's what he said—'and his wife's sick in bed.'"

Holmes also sang "Gone Dead Train" when he was in McComb and Summit, and Collins' "Jailhouse Blues," which he later changed to "Going to Shreveport, Tell the Chief Police" or "Going to Helena, Tell the Chief Police."

John Willis also remembers "Gone Dead Train" from his McComb years, when he was working at a rock quarry as a gravel hauler. He said Holmes told him it was about "a train that killed people." The verse beginning "So many people have gone down today" meant that a lot of people "had died today."

Willis also recalled the words "going to the Western Union," which referred to Holmes' attempt to get money from home so that he could ride the train.

As for the opening words of the song, Willis interpreted them differently on two occasions. At first he thought that Holmes was singing "Lord, I'm goin' Winden," meaning Minden, but on a second listening he believed Holmes was saying "way down." "Joe sung it so many ways," he said. And he also spoke of a song about "the Minden train," probably a version of "Gone Dead Train."

The difficulty of understanding Holmes can be attributed to his speech impediment. "He couldn't talk plain," Willis recalled, though he said Holmes didn't stutter the way Tommy Johnson did.

Willis also explained another verse of "Gone Dead Train." "He sang, 'I once was a hobo, I crossed many a pome [palm]; but I decided I go down Fryeburg light [without any money] and take it as it comes [get what money he can beg for his playing].'" He said that Holmes often played for dances and parties in Fryeburg.

After playing with Jefferson and Thomas, Holmes' repertoire took in additional songs. "He got down perfect a lotta Lemon's records," said Willis. Thomas' as well: Willis remembered Holmes singing "Juke Head Blues," "Hard Dallas Blues," "Lock and Key Blues," and "Sawmill Blues." Also, "he sung that song 'bout 'poor boy long ways from home'"—a standard piece sung widely across the South.

But what of the undiscovered Paramount titles, "My Buddy Blind Papa Lemon" and "Times Has Done Got Out of Hand"? Where did they originate?

The former was remembered without prodding by both Willis and Allums, but the Depression-type song was apparently sung only in the Paramount studies; neither recalls Joe singing it.

"He sung that song a whole lot 'bout Blind Lemon," said Willis. "Said he loved his buddy 'some way better than anyone I know.'" Allums concurred with this wording.

Did Holmes, like Skip James and Charlie Patton, ever sing religious songs? If he did, neither Willis nor Allums ever heard him.

But Joe Holmes did use his bottleneck technique with a majestic touch. "He said he learned to play like that [with a bottle] in Mississippi," said Willis. "I tried to learn from him, but I never could get it down. He'd take a beer bottle, break it, and put it on his third finger."

Holmes also sang in a low register, as he did on one take of "Whoopee Blues." "He didn't raise his voice that high . . . late in the night he sang like that." Unfortunately, we do not know if Paramount recorded its talent at night; other companies sometimes did.

◄◦►◄◦►◄◦► "He Don't Stay No One Place" ◄◦►◄◦►◄◦►

Holmes was a nomadic personality, quick to leave if trouble began. He would be in Sibley one day and gone the next, Willis said, not to return for two or three months at a time.

"He went everywhere, I reckon," said Allums. And Willis recalled: "When he'd leave King Solomon Hill he'd be here today and tomorrow he liable to be in Memphis, Tennessee, or anywhere. He don't stay no one place."

Usually Willis didn't travel with Holmes—Willis said his mother claimed Holmes was an unstable influence upon him—but they did go together once to Jackson and then on to Memphis, where they parted, Willis returning to Louisiana and Holmes going on to some northern city. "It was three months 'fore I saw 'em again.

"There used to be a big juke here in Yellow Pine. It's another guy with 'im, he played rub-board [George Young], and I seconds behind him and we all three played . . . And we picked up another man and he had two handsaws and together we made the best music you wanna hear," Willis bragged.

But Holmes also played in nearby communities. "Roytown, Fryeburg, that's his hangouts here," Willis remembered. "I first met 'im in Yellow Pine [before moving to McComb]. I started to second him and I played near 'bout anything he could play."

A chain-smoker, Joe Holmes was also an entertainer—swinging the guitar over his head while playing, to impress his public. "People come over and give him a handout. Get in his palm right smart of money here, and he'd just take off."

Holmes' neighbor Wesley Hall, who heard Holmes play at his brother's juke in nearby Heflin, remembered that another number Holmes sang was a travelling song about Tennessee.

"'Tennessee, Tennessee, that's the place for me; I've traveled Georgia and part of Tennessee. Take your time, friend of mine . . .' That's all I know of it right now, but I can't sing it like he did," says Hall. "Yes, sir, he could sing it. Old Joe just had so many old songs."

◄◊►◄◊►◄◊► "Joe Just Kept Right On Goin'" ◄◊►◄◊►◄◊►

Because of strained relations with Allums, Willis said, Holmes didn't stay with her when he was in the area. "He'd stay around here three or four months when he's got a place to play, Ringgold or Roytown. He'd stay with anybody [rather than Allums]. He stayed some with me. His niece, he stayed with her practically all the time he's in here. He used to stay with a woman right across over here [in the King Solomon Hill community], Bessie Yazaday. He stayed with her a long time. He got in bad health when he's staying with her."

Allums admitted that after the recording session she and Holmes didn't stay together long. He moved to Monroe, remaining there for nearly three years. "He'd play at the juke houses there. A woman ran a cafe in west Monroe near the [Ouachita] river." Later he lived in Shreveport, and then came back to Sibley.

By the spring of 1949, Holmes, who was living about five miles from Sibley, near Heflin, with his brother's wife and daughter, was in bad health from his heavy drinking. Roberta Allums described his death in "King Solomon Hill," page 2.

The state of Louisiana has been unable to find any death certificate for Joe Holmes filed between 1945 and 1953, following information supplied by Allums and Willis. Since he did not see a doctor before his death, his body was probably just carried to a funeral home, which would not be required to report a death.

Afterword

In the early 1960s when I read jazz books from the early 1940s, I wondered where the authors were located then. I have included the names and locations of the persons I had associations with during the blues revival of the 1960s to 1980s.

Mary Katherine Aldin—
Los Angeles, CA

Bill Barth—Denmark

Bruce Bastin—England

Roy Book Binder—St Petersburg,
FL/Rounder Rcords

Stephen Calt—Astoria, NY

Samuel Charters—Massachusetts

Lawrence Cohn—California/Sony
Records

David Evans—Memphis, TN

John Fahey—Grant's Pass, OR

Paul Garon—Beasley Books,
Chicago, IL

Bob Groom—unknown

Stefan Grossman—Sparta, NJ

Peter Guralnick—Boston, MA

John Hammond—New Jersey

Bob Hite—deceased

Richard Hite—Ashland, MS

Tom Hoskins—Mill Spring, NC

Don Kent- Brooklyn

Bernie Klatzko—Queens, NY

Bob Koester—Chicago

Steve LaVere—Los Angeles, CA

Mike Leadbitter—deceased

Peter Lowry, New York, NY

Mack McCormick—Houston, TX

George Mitchell—Atlanta, GA

Simon Napier—deceased

Paul Oliver—England

Jim O'Neal—Kansas City, Missouri

Robert Palmer—deceased

Nick Perls—deceased

Mike Rowe—London, England

H.C. Speir—deceased

Dick Spottswood—Library of Congress, Washington, DC

Mike (Firk) Stewart—Mill Spring,
NC

Chris Strachwitz—Arhoolie Records,
El Cerrito, California

Maxey Tarpley—Edisto Island, SC

Henry Vestine—deceased

Gayle Dean Wardlow—Long Beach,
MS

Dick Waterman—Oxford, MS

Pete Welding—deceased

Pete Whelan—Key West, FL

References

Albertson, Chris. 1972. *Bessie*. New York: Stein and Day.

Anonymous. 1964. Looking for the blues. *Newsweek* 64, 2 (July 13): 82–83.

———. 1997. Access: New information found on the death of Robert Johnson. *Blues Access* 28 (Winter): 108.

Bastin, Bruce, and Pete Lowry. 1970. Blues from the south-east. Part 7: "It hurts me too." *Blues Unlimited* 73 (June): 4–5.

Benet, Stephen Vincent. 1936. "The Devil and Daniel Webster." *The Saturday Evening Post* 209, 17 (October): 8–9, 68–74.

Broonzy, William. 1955. *Big Bill Blues: William Broonzy's Story as Told to Yannick Bruynoghe*. London: Cassell.

Calt, Stephen. 1970. King Solomon Hill revisited. *Blues Unlimited* 70 (February/March): 4–6.

———. 1971. Robert Johnson recapitulated. *Blues Unlimited* 86 (November): 12–14.

———. 1994. *I'd Rather Be the Devil: Skip James and the Blues*. New York: Da Capo Press.

Cohen, Anne, and Norm Cohen. 1977. Folk and hillbilly music: further thoughts on their relation. *John Edwards Memorial Foundation Quarterly* 13: 50–57.

Charters, Samuel. 1959. *The Country Blues*. New York: Rinehart.

Crumb, Robert. 1975. That's life. *Arcade* 3 (Fall).

Dixon, Robert M.W., John Godrich, and Howard Rye. 1997. *Blues and Gospel Records 1890–1943*. Fourth edition. Oxford: Oxford University Press.

Driggs, Frank. 1962. Liner notes to Robert Johnson, *King of the Delta Blues Singers*. New York: Columbia CL 1654. LP record.

Eagle, Bob. 1975. Luther Huff. *Living Blues* 22 (July–August): 33–35.

Erlewine, Michael, Vladimir Bogdanov, Chris Woodstra, and Cub Koda. 1996. *All Music Guide to the Blues*. San Francisco: Miller Freeman Books.

Evans, David. 1968a. The Fiddlin' Joe Martin story. *Blues World* 20 (July): 3–5.

———. 1968b. The King Solomon Hill fiasco. *Blues World* 21 (October): 17–20.

———. 1971. *Tommy Johnson*. London: Studio Vista.

———. 1972. An interview with H.C. Speir. *John Edwards Memorial Foundation Quarterly* 8, part 3: 117–121.

———. 1981. Bitchin boogie: Response to Calt and Wardlow's open letter to blues fans. *Blues Unlimited* 141 (Autumn/Winter): 12–13.

———. 1982. *Big Road Blues: Tradition and Creativity in the Folk Blues*. Berkeley: University of California Press.

Godrich, John. 1964. The Victor race series. *Blues Unlimited* 10 (March): 8; 11 (April): 8; 13 (July): 12–13; 14 (August): 14–15; 16 (October): 13; 17 (November/December): 12.

Greenberg, Alan. 1983. *Love in Vain: The Life and Legend of Robert Johnson*. Garden City, NY: Dolphin/Doubleday.

Groom, Bob. 1965. A tribute to Sonny Boy. *Blues World* 3 (July): 3.

———. 1976. Standing at the crossroads: Robert Johnson's recordings. *Blues Unlimited* 118 (March/April): 17–20; 119 (May/June): 11–14; 120 (July/August): 15–17; 121 (September/October): 20–21.

Guralnick, Peter. 1989. *Searching for Robert Johnson*. Reprint in book form, New York: Dutton. Original article, *Living Blues* 53 (Summer/Autumn 1982): 27–41.

Hammond, John. 1938. Jim Crow blues. *The New Masses* (13 December): 27–28.

Handy, William Christopher. 1941. *Father of the Blues: An Autobiography*. New York: Macmillan.

Harris, Sheldon. 1994. *Blues Who's Who*. Reprint, New Rochelle: Arlington House. Original edition, 1979.

House, Son, as told to Julius Lester. 1965. "I can make my own songs." *Sing Out!* 15, 3 (July): 38–45.

Howse, Patrick. 1991. Blues researcher Gayle Dean Wardlow talks about Delta blues and the Robert Johnson mystery. *Monitor* (Peavey) 10, no. 3: 30–39.

Howse, Patrick, and Jimmy Phillips. 1994. Godfather of the blues: H.C. Speir. *Monitor* (Peavey) 13, 2: 34–44.

Hurley, F. Jack, and David Evans. 1981. Bukka White. In *Tom Ashley, Sam McGee, Bukka White: Tennessee Traditional Singers*, edited by Thomas G. Burton. Knoxville: University of Tennessee Press.

Irving, Washington. 1824. *Tales of a Traveler*. Philadelphia: Carey and Lea. Includes "The Devil and Tom Walker."

Keepnews, Orrin, and Bill Grauer. 1955. *A Pictorial History of Jazz*. New York: Crown.

Klatzko, Bernard. 1964a. The immortal Charlie Patton. Liner notes for *The Immortal Charlie Patton 1887–1934, No. 2*. Origin Jazz Library OJL-7. Originally credited to Klatzko alone. Contains a profile of Wardlow and a description, with direct quotes from Wardlow, of his fact-finding trip with Klatzko through the Mississippi Delta in August 1963.

———. 1964b. Finding Son House. *Blues Unlimited* 15 (September): 8–9.

———. 1966. Booklet notes accompanying *In the Spirit* vols. 1 and 2, Origin Jazz Library OJL-12/13. Two LP records.

Komara, Edward. 1996. From the archive (Robert Johnson melodic precedent chart). *Living Blues* 129 (September/October): 12.

LaVere, Stephen C. 1989. Charlie Booker. *Living Blues* 89 (November/December): 38–39.

———. 1990. Booklet notes to *Robert Johnson: The Complete Recordings*. Sony/Columbia C2K 46222. New York. Two compact discs.

Leadbitter, Mike. 1966. Post-war discographical comment. *Blues Unlimited* 30 (February): 13.

———. 1973. Bring it on home. *Blues Unlimited* 98 (January): 4–13.

Leadbitter, Mike, and Simon Napier. 1964. Note on Gayle Wardlow's rediscovery of Ishmon Bracey. *Blues Unlimited* 13 (July): 3.

Leadbitter, Mike, and Neil Slaven. 1968. *Blues Records 1943–1966*. London: Hanover.

Lomax, Alan. 1993. *The Land Where the Blues Began*. New York: Pantheon.

McCormick, Mack. 1974. Booklet notes to *Henry Thomas*. Herwin 209. Glen Cove, New York. Two-LP set.

McMurry, Lillian. Lillian McMurry/Trumpet Records Collection, Blues Archive, J.D. Williams Library, University of Mississippi.

Marcus, Greil. 1975. *Mystery Train*. New York: E.P. Dutton.

Misiewicz, Roger. 1991. Booklet notes to *Rev. D.C. Rice 1928–1930*. Document DOCD-5071. Vienna, Austria. Compact disc.

Moore, Dave. 1976. Letter to the editor. *Blues Unlimited* 122 (November/December): 15.

Oliver, Paul. 1961. *Bessie Smith*. New York : A.S. Barnes. Original edition, London: Cassell, 1959.

———. 1960. *Blues Fell This Morning*. London: Cassell.

———. 1969. *Story of the Blues*. London: Barrie and Jenkins.

O'Neal, Jim. 1981. Garfield Akers . . . to Beale Street and the juke joints. *Living Blues* 50 (Spring): 27–28.

———. 1986. *Living Blues* interview: Lillian McMurry. *Living Blues* 67 (February): 15–28.

———. 1990. A traveler's guide to the crossroads. *Living Blues* 94 (November/December): 21–24.

Palmer, Robert. 1981. *Deep Blues*. New York: Viking.

Pearlman, Bernard. 1965. John Lee. *Blues Unlimited* 19 (February): 11.

Perls, Nick, and Stephen Calt. 1967. Son House interview—part one. *78 Quarterly*, no. 1: 59–61.

Pratt, Jim. 1994. Tommy Lee's d.j. jamboree. *Living Blues* 102 (March/April): 32–33.

Roche, Jacques [Stephen Calt]. 1967. The words. *78 Quarterly* 1: 51–55.

Rowe, Mike. 1966. Liner notes to *Memphis . . . On Down*. PWB Records 2. LP record.

Rust, Brian. 1962. *Jazz Records A–Z, 1897–1931*. Second edition. Hatch End, Middlesex: self-published.

———. 1969a. *Jazz Records A–Z, 1897–1942*. Revised edition. London: Storyville.

———. 1969b. *Victor Master Book Vol. 2 (1925–1936)*. Hatch End, Middlesex: self-published.

Ryan, Marc. 1992. *Trumpet Records: An Illustrated History with Discography*. Milford, New Hampshire: Big Nickel.

Scott, Frank. 1974. Alabama boogie: John Lee. *Living Blues* 18 (Autumn): 12–13.

Scott, Frank, and Gary Paulsen. 1970. Joe and Jules Bihari. *Blues Unlimited* 74 (July): 11–13.

Slotnikoff, Joel. 1996. Gayle Dean Wardlow: The BLUES WORLD interview. *Blues World* World Wide Web page: http://www.bluesworld.com /GDW.html

Smith, Chris. 1990. Booklet notes to Sam Collins, *The Jail House Blues*. Yazoo 1079. New York. Compact disc.

Stephens, Cal. 1991. Booker White on Bullet Williams. *78 Quarterly* 6: 83–85.

Thomas, Henry. 1986. Review of Wolf WSE116, *Giants of the Country Blues, vol. 1. Blues Unlimited* 147 (Spring): 45.

Townsend, Charles R. 1976. *San Antonio Rose: The Life and Music of Bob Wills*. Urbana, Illinois: University of Illinois Press.

Vreede, Max. 1971. *Paramount 12000/13000 Series*. London: Storyville.

Wardlow, Gayle Dean. 1965. *OJL Supplement no.1: Biographical Notes for OJLs 2, 5, and 8*. New York: Origin Jazz Library. Capsule biographies of blues musicians whose sides were reissued in *Really! The Country Blues, 1927–1933* (Origin Jazz Library OJL-2), *Mississippi Blues, 1927–1940, vol. 1* (OJL-5), and *Country Blues Encores, 1927–1935* (OJL-8).

———. 1966a. Mysteries in Mississippi. *Blues Unlimited* 30 (February): 10.

————. 1966b. Legends of the lost. *Blues Unlimited* 31 (March): 3–4; 34 (July): 3; 35 (August): 3; 36 (September): 7. Reprinted with corrections in Simon Napier, comp., *Back Woods Blues*, pp. 25–28, 1968, Bexhill-on-Sea, Essex: Blues Unlimited.

————. 1966c. Biographical notes, appended to notes by Bernard Klatzko, for *In the Spirit No. 1 and No. 2.* Origin Jazz Library OJL-12 and -13. New York. Two records.

————. 1966d. Locations, note to John Godrich, in Blues and gospel amendments. *Blues Unlimited* 34 (July): 17.

————. 1967a. Son House (Collector Classics 14) comments and additions. *Blues Unlimited* 42 (March–April): 7–8.

————. 1967b. King Solomon Hill. *78 Quarterly* 1: 5–9.

————. 1967c. Ledell Johnson remembers his brother, Tommy. *78 Quarterly* 1: 63–65.

————. 1968. The Black Birds of Paradise. *78 Quarterly* 2: 7–12.

————. 1969a. Rev. D.C. Rice—gospel singer. *Storyville* 23 (June–July): 164–167.

————. 1969b. Highway 80 blues. *Blues Unlimited* 66 (October): 12–13.

————. 1969c. Gayle Wardlow's Memphis City Directory blues. *Blues Unlimited* 68 (December): 16–17.

————. 1970. Note to the editor on Charlie Booker and Houston Boines. *Blues Unlimited* 73. (June): 3.

————. 1973. "Greenville smokin'!" *Blues Unlimited* 99 (February–March): 2.

————. 1975a. Down at the depot: the story of John Lee. *Blues Unlimited* 113 (May–June): 12–13.

————. 1975b. Liner notes for John Lee, *Down at the Depot.* Rounder Records 2010.

————. 1981a. Garfield Akers and Mississippi Joe Callicott: From the Hernando cottonfields . . . *Living Blues* 50 (Spring): 26–27.

————. 1981b. A quick ramble with Ramblin' Thomas, Jesse Thomas, Will Ezell, Bessie Tucker, Elzadie Robinson and Texas Talent Scouts, R.T. Ashford and the Kendall Brothers. *Blues Unlimited* 141: 14–15.

————. 1982. Got four, five puppies, one little shaggy hound. *Blues Unlimited* 142: 4–11.

————. 1986. Can't tell my future: the mystery of Willie Brown. *Blues Unlimited* 147: 6–9.

————. 1987. One last walk up King Solomon Hill. *Blues Unlimited* 148 (Winter): 8–12.

————. 1988. Big Foot William Harris. *78 Quarterly* 3: 45–48.

————. 1990. Six who made recorded history. *78 Quarterly* 5: 93–96.

———. 1992. Searching for the Robert Johnson death certificate. *Blues Revue Quarterly* 6 (Fall): 26–27.

———. 1993a. Robert Johnson. In *The Roots of Robert Johnson* by Stefan Grossman and Woody Mann, 4–6. Pacific, Missouri: Mel Bay Publications.

———. 1993b. Letter to the editor, *Blues Revue Quarterly* 10 (1993): 7.

———. 1994. H.C. Speir (1895–1972). *78 Quarterly* 8: 11–33.

———. 1995. Ten most played blues 78s. *Victrola and 78 Journal* 6 (Summer): 50–51.

———. 1996a. Henry "Son" Sims: "Farrell Blues Mama, Sho' Don't Worry Me." *78 Quarterly* 9: 11–19.

———. 1996b. Knocking on doors for 78s: buying race records in the South. *Victrola and 78 Journal* 9 (Summer): 9–14.

———. 1996c. Robert Johnson: new details on the death of a bluesman. *Guitar Player* 30, 11 (November): 29–32.

———. 1996d. Sonny Boy Williamson. *Blues World* World Wide Web page: http://www.bluesworld.com/GDWSonny.htm

———. 1997. From Aberdeen to Parchman. Written for this volume.

———. 1997. Blind Roosevelt Graves. Written for this volume.

———. 1997. Stop, look, and listen at the cross road. Written for this volume.

Wardlow, Gayle Dean, and Jacques Roche [Stephen Calt]. 1967. Patton's murder—whitewash? Or hogwash? *78 Quarterly* 1: 10–17.

———. 1981. Bitchin boogie: an open letter to blues fans. *Blues Unlimited* 140 (Spring): 39. Also printed as An open letter to blues fans, *Living Blues* 50 (Spring 1981): 5.

———. 1984. He's a devil of a Joe. *Blues Unlimited* 146 (Fall–Winter): 16–20.

———. 1988. *King of the Delta Blues Singers: The Life and Music of Charlie Patton.* Newton, New Jersey: Rock Chapel Press.

———. 1989. Robert Johnson. *78 Quarterly* 4: 40–50.

———. 1990. The buying and selling of Paramounts. *78 Quarterly* 5: 7–24.

———. 1991. Paramount part 4: the advent of Arthur Laibley. *78 Quarterly* 6: 8–26.

———. 1992. Paramount's decline and fall. *78 Quarterly* 7: 7–29.

Wardlow, Gayle Dean and Mike Leadbitter. 1972. Canton, Mis'sippi breakdown. *Blues Unlimited* 91 (May): 5–10. Reprinted in *Blues Unlimited* 144 (Spring 1983): 4–8.

Welding, Pete. 1965. Homesick James Williamson. *Blues Unlimited Collector's Classic* 7 (May): 7–8.

———. 1966. Hell hound on his trail: Robert Johnson. *Down Beat Music '66*: 73–76, 103.

———. 1968. David "Honey Boy" Edwards. *Blues Unlimited* 54 (June): 3–13.

Whelan, Pete. 1965. Booklet notes to *Sam Collins*, Origin Jazz Library OJL-10. New York. LP record.

White, Bukka. 1963. Remembrance of Charlie Patton (talking). *Mississippi Blues vol. 1: Bukka White*. Takoma B1001. Berkeley. LP record.

Wilson, Alan. 1966. Son House. *Blues Unlimited Collectors Classics* 14 (October). First published in installments of *Broadside*, 1965, Boston.

Wolfe, Charles, and Kip Lornell. 1992. *The Life and Legend of Leadbelly*. New York: HarperCollins.

For published accounts of and interviews with Wardlow, see Calt 1970, 1971, and 1994; Howse 1991; Howse and Phillips 1994; Klatzko 1964a; and Slotnikoff 1996.

List of 78 rpm Record Issues Cited

In his articles, Wardlow refers to original issues of pre–World War II blues by title or record issue number. Here are longer citations of those records, arranged by label and issue number, with artist, titles, year or years of recording session(s), and references to the discographies listed below for those desiring matrix numbers and other data. For reissues, see the section that follows this one.

Key to References

DG: Dixon, Robert M.W., John Godrich, and Howard Rye. 1997. *Blues and Gospel Records 1890–1943*. Fourth edition. Oxford: Oxford University Press.

F: Franz, Steve. 1994. *Elmore James: The Ultimate Guide to the Master of the Slide*. St. Louis: Primal Art.

LS: Leadbitter, Mike, and Neil Slaven, with Les Fancourt and Paul Pelletier. 1994. *Blues Records 1943–1970*. London: Record Information Services.

P: Porterfield, Nolan. 1979. *Jimmie Rodgers: The Life and Times of America's Blue Yodeler*. Urbana, Illinois: University of Illinois Press.

Rust: Rust, Brian. 1969, 1970. *Jazz Records, 1897–1942*. London: Storyville.

Ryan: Ryan, Marc. 1992. *Trumpet Records: An Illustrated History with Discography*. Milford, New Hampshire: Big Nickel.

Ace 508: see Trumpet 146.

ARC 6-11-74: Blind Roosevelt Graves, "Woke Up This Morning with My Mind on Jesus"/ "I'll Be Rested When the Roll Is Called," 1936. [DG: 323]

ARC 7-01-70: Buddy Moss, "Stop Hanging Around"/ "My Baby Won't Pay Me No Mind," 1935. [DG: 669]

Atlantic 1016: Big Joe Turner, "TV Mama"/ "Oke-She-Moke-She Pop," 1953. [F: 14]

Black Patti 8025: see Gennett 6167.

Black Patti 8053: Black Birds of Paradise, "Razor Edge"/ "Stompin' Fool," 1927. [Rust: 153–154]

Bluebird B5861: Bo Chatman [Carter], "Let Me Roll Your Lemon"/ "Old

Shoe Blues," 1935. [DG: 152]

Bluebird B5877: Leroy Carr, "When the Sun Goes Down"/ "Ain't It a Shame," 1935. [DG: 144]

Bluebird B6188: Big Bill [Broonzy], "Keep Your Hands off Her"/ "The Sun Gonna Shine in My Door Someday," 1935. [DG: 62]

Bluebird B8159: Bo Chatman [Carter], "Your Biscuits Are Big Enough for Me"/ "Trouble in Blues," 1936, 1938. [DG: 152–153]

Blues & Rhythm 7003: Charlie Booker, "Rabbit Blues"/ "No Ridin' Blues," 1952. [LS: 130]

Broadway 5085: see Paramount 12651.

Brunswick 7042: Hattie Burleson, "Superstitious Blues"/ "Sadie's Servant Room Blues," 1928. [DG: 123]

Brunswick 7049: Rosie Mae Moore [Mary Butler], "Mad Dog Blues"/ "Electrocuted Blues," 1928. [DG:128]

Brunswick 7074: Southern Sanctified Singers, "Soon We'll Gather at the River"/ "Where He Leads Me I Will Follow," 1929. [DG: 845]

Brunswick 7114: Kid Bailey, "Mississippi Bottom Blues"/ "Rowdy Blues," 1929. [DG: 31]

Brunswick 7158: Robert Wilkins, "Get Away Blues"/ "I'll Go with Her Blues," 1930. [DG: 1028]

Brunswick 7166: Joe Callicott, "Fare Thee Well Blues"/ "Traveling Mama Blues," 1930. [DG: 133]

Champion 16058: Bessie Sanders [Alberta Jones], "River Bottom"/ "I Lost My Man," 1930. [DG: 484]

Champion 16718: James Cole String Band, "Undertaker Blues"/ "Mistreated the Only Friend You Had," 1932. [DG: 167]

Checker 777: Elmore James, "She Just Won't Do Right"/ "Country Boogie," 1953. [F:10]

Columbia A3844: Bessie Smith, "Down Hearted Blues"/ "Gulf Coast Blues," 1923. [DG: 803]

Columbia 14042: Bessie Smith, "Weeping Willow Blues"/ "Bye Bye Blues," 1924. [DG: 805]

Decca 7017: St. Louis Jimmy Oden, "Six Feet in the Ground"/ "Pipe Layin' Blues," 1934. [DG: 689]

Decca 7021: Bumble Bee Slim, "Cruel Hearted Woman Blues" Parts I and II, 1934. [DG: 233]

Decca 7026: Kokomo Arnold, "Original Old Kokomo Blues"/ "Milk Cow Blues," 1934. [DG: 25]

Decca 7037: Memphis Minnie, "Keep It to Yourself"/ "Moaning the Blues," 1934. [DG: 619]

Decca 7038: Memphis Minnie, "You Got to Move" Parts I and II, 1934. [DG: 513]

Decca 7822: Joe McCoy, "Evil Devil Woman Blues"/ "Please Baby," 1934, 1935. [DG: 563, 564]

Decca 7828: Joe McCoy (as Georgia Pine Boy), "Look Who's Coming Down the Road"/ "The World Is a Hard Place to Live In," 1935. [DG: 564]

Delta 403: Tommy Lee, "Highway 80 Blues"/ "Packing Up My Blues," 1952. [LS: 37]

Federal 12054: John Lee, "Down at the Depot"/ "Alabama Boogie," 1951. [LS: 33]

Federal 12089: John Lee, "Blind's Blues"/ "Baby Blues," 1951. [LS: 33]

Flair 1022: Elmore James, "Please Find My Baby"/ "Strange Kinda Feeling," 1952, 1953. [F: 8, 13]

Flair 1039: Elmore James, "1839 Blues"/ "Sho' Nuff I Do," 1954. [F: 15]

Flair 1057: Elmore James, "Standing at the Crossroads"/ "Sunny Land," 1954. [F: 16]

Flair 1074: Elmore James, "Dust My Blues"/ "I Was a Fool," 1955. [F: 16]

Gennett 6106: Sunny Boy and His Pals [Papa Harvey Hull], "Hey Lawdy Mama—The France Blues"/ "Don't You Leave Me Here," 1927. [DG: 410–411]

Gennett 6122: Daddy Moon Mayer [Papa Harvey Hull], "Two Little Tommie Blues"/ "Gang of Brown Skin Women," 1927. [DG: 410–411]

Gennett 6146: Sam Collins, "Loving Lady Blues"/ "Yellow Dog Blues," 1927. [DG: 172]

Gennett 6167: Sam Collins, "The Jail House Blues"/ "Riverside Blues," 1927. [DG: 172]

Gennett 6181: Sam Collins, "Devil in the Lion's Den"/Jelly Roll Anderson, "Good Time Blues," 1927. [DG: 44, 172]

Gennett 6210: Black Birds of Paradise, "Bugahoma Blues"/ "Tishomingo Blues," 1927. [Rust: 153]

Gennett 6211: Black Birds of Paradise, "Muddy Water"/ "Sugar," 1927. [Rust: 153]

Gennett 6307: Sam Collins, "Midnight Special Blues"/ "Do That Thing," 1927. [DG: 172]

Gennett 6379: Sam Collins, "Hesitation Blues"/ "It Won't Be Long," 1927. [DG: 172]

Herwin 92001: Alberta Jones, "Lucky Number Blues"/ "I'm Gonna Put You Right in Jail," 1926. [DG: 483]

Melotone M12812: Jack Kelly and His South Memphis Jug Band, "Believe I'll Go Back Home"/ "Ko-Ko-Mo Blues," 1933. [DG: 505]

Melotone M13196: Josh White [pseud. Pinewood Tom], "I Believe I'll Make a Change"/ "Friendless City Blues," 1934. [DG: 1020]

Meteor 5000: Elmore James, "I Believe"/ "I Held My Baby Last Night," 1952. [F: 9]

Modern 878: Charlie Booker, "Moonrise Blues"/ "Charlie's Boogie Woogie," 1952. [LS: 130]

OKeh 8422: Mr. Freddie Spruell, "Milk Cow Blues"/ "Muddy Water Blues," 1926. [DG: 857]

OKeh 8435: Lonnie Johnson, "Ball and Chain Blues"/ "Sweet Woman, See for Yourself," 1926. [DG: 459]

OKeh 8437: Bertha "Chippie" Hill, "Mess, Katie, Mess"/ "Street Walker Blues," 1926. [DG: 394-395]

OKeh 8557: Lonnie Johnson, "Life Saver Blues"/ "Blue Ghost Blues," 1927. [DG: 460]

OKeh 8560: Mississippi John Hurt, "Frankie"/ "Nobody's Dirty Business," 1928. [DG: 418]

OKeh 8679: Hambone Willie Newbern, "Roll and Tumble Blues"/ "Nobody Knows," 1929. [DG: 678]

OKeh 8784: Mississippi Sheiks, "Sitting on Top of the World"/ "Lonely One in This Town," 1930. [DG: 642]

OKeh 8871: Slim Duckett and Pig Norwood, "Sister Mary Wore Three Lengths of Chain"/ "You Gotta Stand Judgment for Yourself," 1930. [DG: 227]

OKeh 8899: Slim Duckett and Pig Norwood, "When the Saints Go Marching In"/ "I Want to Go Where Jesus Is," 1930. [DG: 227]

Paramount 12325: Ida Cox, "How Long Daddy How Long?"/ "One Time Woman Blues," 1925. [DG: 183]

Paramount 12407: Blind Lemon Jefferson, "That Black Snake Moan"/ "Stocking Feet Blues," 1926. [DG: 442]

Paramount 12608: Blind Lemon Jefferson, "'Lectric Chair Blues"/ "See That My Grave Is Kept Clean," 1928. [DG: 444]

Paramount 12615: Madlyn Davis, "Kokola Blues"/ "Winter Blues," 1927. [DG: 204]

Paramount 12629: Rube Lacy, "Mississippi Jail House Groan"/ "Ham Hound Crave," 1928. [DG: 515]

Paramount 12651: George "Bullet" Williams, "The Escaped Convict"/ "Frisco Leaving Birmingham," 1928. [DG: 1037–1038]

Paramount 12680: George "Bullet" Williams, "Touch Me Light, Mama"/ "Middlin' Blues," 1928. [DG: 1037–1038]

Paramount 12792: Charlie Patton, "Pony Blues"/ "Banty Rooster Blues," 1929. [DG: 707]

Paramount 12803: Freezone, "Indian Squaw Blues"/Raymond Barrow, "Walking Blues," 1929. [DG: 42, 275]

Paramount 12805: Charlie Patton, "Mississippi Bo Weavil Blues"/ "Screamin' and Hollerin' the Blues," 1929. [DG: 707]

Paramount 12820: Blind Roosevelt Graves, "Guitar Boogie"/ "New York Blues," 1929. [DG: 323]

Paramount 12824: Blind Blake, "Georgia Bound"/ "Too Tight No. 2," 1929. [DG: 80]

Paramount 12854: Charlie Patton, "It Won't Be Long"/ "Down the Dirt Road Blues," 1929. [DG: 707]

Paramount 12859: Blind Roosevelt Graves, "Crazy about My Baby"/ "Bustin' the Jug," 1929. [DG: 323]

Paramount 12873: Tenderfoot Edwards [Edward Thompson], "Florida Bound"/ "Seven Sister Blues," 1929. [DG: 921]

Paramount 12874: Blind Roosevelt Graves, "Take Your Burdens to the Lord"/ "Telephone to Glory," 1929. [DG: 323]

Paramount 12877: Charlie Patton, "Tom Rushen Blues"/ "Pea Vine Blues," 1929. [DG: 707]

Paramount 12909: Charlie Patton, "High Water Everywhere" Parts I and II, 1929. [DG: 708]

Paramount 12924: Charlie Patton, "Rattlesnake Blues"/ "Runnin' Wild," 1929. [DG: 708]

Paramount 12925: Rev. Emmett Dickinson, "Sermon on Tight Like That"/ "Is There Harm in Singing the Blues?" 1929. [DG: 213]

Paramount 12927: Blind Joe Reynolds, "Outside Woman Blues"/ "Nehi Blues," 1929. [DG: 750]

Paramount 12941: Ishmon Bracey, "Jake Liquor Blues"/ "Family Stirving [*sic* = Striving]," 1930. [DG: 97]

Paramount 12949: Charlie Taylor (with Ishmon Bracey), "Too Damp to Be Wet"/ "Where My Shoes At," 1930. [DG: 893]

Paramount 12950: Tommy Johnson, "Ridin' Horse"/ "Alcohol and Jake Blues," 1930. [DG: 481]

Paramount 12966: Rev. T.T. Rose, "Roll the Old Chariot Along"/ "See the Sign of Judgment," 1930. [DG: 772]

Paramount 12967: Charley Taylor, "Heavy Suitcase Blues"/ "Louisiana Bound," 1930. [DG: 893]

Paramount 12970: Ishmon Bracey, "Woman Woman Blues"/ "Suitcase Full of Blues," 1930. [DG: 97]

Paramount 12972: Charlie Patton, "Green River Blues"/ "Elder Greene Blues," 1929. [DG: 708]

Paramount 12974: Blind Roosevelt Graves, "I Shall Not Be Moved"/ "When I Lay My Burdens Down," 1929. [DG: 323]

Paramount 12975: Tommy Johnson, "Slidin' Delta"/ "I Wonder to Myself," 1930. [DG: 480]

Paramount 12980: New Orleans Nehi Boys, "Mobile Stomp"/ "Farrish St. Rag," 1930. [DG: 677]

Paramount 12983: Blind Joe Reynolds, "Cold Woman Blues"/ "Ninety Nine Blues," 1929 (unrecovered). [DG: 750]

Paramount 12990: Son House, "Dry Spell Blues" Parts I and II, 1930. [DG: 404]

Paramount 13000: Tommy Johnson, "Lonesome Home Blues"/ "Black Mare Blues," 1930. [DG: 480]

Paramount 13006: Little Brother Montgomery, "No Special Rider Blues"/ "Vicksburg Blues," 1930. [DG: 651]

Paramount 13013: Son House, "Preaching the Blues" Parts I and II, 1930. [DG: 404]

Paramount 13014: Charlie Patton, "Moon Going Down"/ "Going to Move to Alabama," 1929, 1930. [DG: 708]

Paramount 13031: Charlie Patton, "You're Gonna Need Somebody When You Gone to Die"/ "Some Happy Day," 1929. [DG: 708]

Paramount 13038: Ishmon Bracey, "Pay Me No Mind"/ "Bust Up Blues," 1930. [DG: 97]

Paramount 13042: Son House, "My Black Mama" Parts I and II, 1930. [DG: 404]

Paramount 13066: Skip James, "22-20 Blues"/ "If You Haven't Any Hay Get On down the Road," 1931. [DG: 437]

Paramount 13074: Geeshie Wiley, "Eagles on a Half"/ "Pick Poor Robin Clean," 1931. [DG: 1028]

Paramount 13088: Skip James, "Devil Got My Woman"/ "Cypress Grove Blues," 1931 [DG: 437]

Paramount 13090: Willie Brown, "Future Blues"/ "M & O Blues," 1930. [DG: 117]

Paramount 13096: Son House, "Mississippi County Farm Blues"/ "Clarksdale Moan" (unrecovered), 1930. [DG: 404]

Paramount 13110: Charlie Patton, "Frankie and Albert"/ "Some These Days I'll Be Gone," 1929. [DG: 708]

Paramount 13116: King Solomon Hill, "Whoopee Blues"/ "Down on My Bended Knee," 1932. [DG: 396]

Paramount 13117: Marshall Owens, "Texas Blues"/ "Try Me One More Time," 1932. [DG: 695]

Paramount 13121: Charlie Taylor (with the New Orleans Nehi Boys), "P.C. Railroad Blues"/ Irene Scruggs, "You've Got What I Want," 1930. [DG: 783, 894]

Paramount 13125: King Solomon Hill, "My Buddy Blind Papa Lemon"/ "Times Has Done Got out of Hand" (unrecovered), 1932. [DG: 396]

Paramount 13129: King Solomon Hill, "The Gone Dead Train"/ "Tell Me Baby," 1932. [DG: 396]

Sittin' In With 621: Lightnin' Hopkins, "New York Boogie"/ "Give Me Central 209," 1951. [LS: 602]

Sun 187, Little Junior Parker, "Feelin' Good"/ "Fussin' and Fightin' Blues," 1953. [LS: 342]

Trumpet 129: Sonny Boy Williamson, "Eyesight to the Blind"/ "Crazy 'Bout You, Baby," 1951. [Ryan: 82]

Trumpet 132: Luther Huff, "Dirty Disposition"/ "1951 Blues," 1951. [Ryan: 82]

Trumpet 141: Luther Huff, "Bull Dog Blues"/ "Rosalee," 1951. [Ryan: 83]

Trumpet 146: Elmore James, "Dust My Broom"/ Elmo James [Bobo "Slim" Thomas], "Catfish Blues," 1951. [F: 7; Ryan: 84]

Victor 20864: Jimmie Rodgers, "Sleep, Baby, Sleep"/ "The Soldier's Sweetheart," 1927. [P: 390]

Victor 21142: Jimmie Rodgers, "Blue Yodel"/ "Away Out on the Mountain," 1928. [P: 391]

Victor 21279: Tommy Johnson, "Cool Drink of Water Blues"/ "Big Road Blues," 1928. [DG: 480]

Victor 21349: Ishmon Bracey, "Saturday Blues"/ "Left Alone Blues," 1928. [DG: 97]

Victor 21409: Tommy Johnson, "Maggie Campbell Blues"/ "Bye Bye Blues," 1928. [DG: 480]

Victor 21691: Ishmon Bracey, "Brown Mamma Blues"/ "Trouble Hearted Blues," 1928. [DG: 97]

Victor 23258: Blind Willie Reynolds [Joe Reynolds], "Married Man Blues"/ "Third St. Woman Blues," 1930. [DG: 750]

Victor 23359: Sparks Brothers, "I Believe I'll Make a Change"/ "Louisiana Bound," 1932. [DG: 849]

Victor 23381: Jesse Thomas, "Down in Texas Blues"/ "My Heart's a Rolling Stone," 1929. [DG: 919]

Victor 38535: Tommy Johnson, "Canned Heat Blues"/ "Big Fat Mama Blues," 1928. [DG: 480]

Victor 38542: Bessie Tucker, "Katy Blues"/ "Better Boot That Thing," 1929. [DG: 931]

Victor 38555: Jesse Thomas, "Blue Goose Blues"/ "No Good Woman Blues," 1929. [DG: 919]

Victor 38560: Ishmon Bracey, "Leavin' Town Blues"/ "Four Day Blues," 1928. [DG: 97]

Victor 38619: Willie Kelly [Roosevelt Sykes], "32-20 Blues"/ "Give Me Your Change," 1930. [DG: 872]

Vocalion 1144: Jim Jackson, "Jim Jackson's Kansas City Blues" Parts I and II, 1927. [DG: 428]

Vocalion 1178: Rev. D.C. Rice, "The Angels Rolled the Stone Away"/ "A Sure Foundation," 1928. [DG: 753]

Vocalion 1191: Leroy Carr, "How Long—How Long Blues" / "My Own Lonesome Blues," 1928. [DG: 139]

Vocalion 1192: Scrapper Blackwell, "Kokomo Blues"/ "Penal Farm Blues," 1928. [DG: 76]

Vocalion 1201: Rev. D.C. Rice, "The Wise and Foolish Virgins"/ "Shall Not a Dog Move His Tongue," 1928. [DG: 753]

Vocalion 1241: Leroy Carr, "Prison Bound Blues"/ "How Long How Long Part 2," 1928. [DG: 139]

Vocalion 1289: Rev. D.C. Rice, "I'm Pressing On"/ "No Night There," 1929. [DG: 753]

Vocalion 1290: Leroy Carr, "Straight Alky Blues" Parts I and II, 1929. [DG: 140]

Vocalion 1426: Tampa Red, "What Is It That Tastes Like Gravy?"/ "You Better Tighten Up on It," 1929. [DG: 883]

Vocalion 1442: Garfield Akers, "Cottonfield Blues" Parts I and II, 1929. [DG: 2]

Vocalion 1476: Memphis Minnie and Kansas Joe McCoy, "Bumble Bee"/ "I'm Talking About You," 1930. [DG: 616]

Vocalion 1480: Mattie Delaney, "Tallahatchie River Blues"/ "Down the Big Road Blues," 1930. [DG: 212]

Vocalion 1481: Garfield Akers, "Dough Roller Blues"/ "Jumpin' and Shoutin' Blues," 1930. [DG: 2]

Vocalion 1620: Peetie Wheatstraw, "So Long Blues"/ "Mama's Advice," 1930. [DG: 1007]

Vocalion 1649: Peetie Wheatstraw, "Ain't It a Pity and a Shame?"/ "Don't Hang My Clothes on a Barb Wire Line," 1930. [DG: 1007]

Vocalion 1722: Peetie Wheatstraw, "Police Station Blues"/ "All Alone Blues," 1932. [DG: 1008]

Vocalion 02650: Bertha Lee, "Yellow Bee"/ "Mind Reader Blues, " 1934. [DG: 533]

Vocalion 02651: Charlie Patton, "34 Blues"/ "Poor Me," 1934. [DG: 709]

Vocalion 02657: Leroy Carr, "Mean Mistreater Mama"/ "Blues Before Sunrise," 1934. [DG: 142]

Vocalion 02680: Charlie Patton, "High Sheriff Blues"/ "Stone Pony Blues," 1934. [DG: 709]

Vocalion 02820: Leroy Carr, "I Believe I'll Make a Change"/ "Barrel House Woman No. 2," 1934. [DG: 143]

Vocalion 02950: Leroy Carr, "My Woman's Gone Wrong"/ "I Ain't Got No Money Now," 1934. [DG: 143]

Vocalion 02987: Johnnie Temple, "The Evil Devil Blues"/ "Jacksonville Blues," 1935. [DG: 906]

Vocalion 03066: Peetie Wheatstraw, "King of Spades"/ "Rising Sun Blues," 1935. [DG: 1008–1009]

Vocalion 03155: Peetie Wheatstraw, "Johnnie Blues"/ "Midnight Blues," 1934, 1935. [DG: 1008–1009]

Vocalion 03416: Robert Johnson, "Terraplane Blues"/ "Kind Hearted Woman Blues," 1936. [DG: 476]

Vocalion 03445: Robert Johnson, "32–20 Blues"/ "Last Fair Deal Gone Down," 1936. [DG: 477]

Vocalion 03475: Robert Johnson, "I Believe I'll Dust My Broom"/ "Dead Shrimp Blues," 1936. [DG: 476–477]

Vocalion 03519: Robert Johnson, "Cross Road Blues"/ "Ramblin' on My Mind," 1936. [DG: 476–477]

Vocalion 03563: Robert Johnson, "Come On in My Kitchen"/ "They're Red Hot," 1936. [DG: 476–477]

Vocalion 03601: Robert Johnson, "Sweet Home Chicago"/ "Walking Blues," 1936. [DG: 476–477]

Vocalion 03623: Robert Johnson, "Hell Hound on My Trail"/ "From Four Until Late," 1937. [DG: 477]

Vocalion 03665: Robert Johnson, "Malted Milk"/ "Milkcow's Calf Blues," 1937. [DG: 477–478]

Vocalion 03711: Bukka White, "Shake 'Em On Down"/ "Pinebluff, Arkansas," 1937. [DG: 1024]

Vocalion 03723: Robert Johnson, "Stones in My Passway"/ "I'm a Steady Rolling Man," 1937. [DG: 477]

Vocalion 04002: Robert Johnson, "Stop Breakin' Down"/ "Honeymoon Blues," 1937. [DG: 478]

Vocalion 04108: Robert Johnson, "Me and the Devil"/ "Little Queen of Spades," 1937. [DG: 477–478]

Vocalion 04630: Robert Johnson, "Preaching Blues"/ "Love in Vain," 1936, 1937. [DG: 477–478]

Index to 78s

Akers, Garfield: Vocalion 1442, 1481. Anderson, Jelly Roll: Gennett 6181. Arnold, Kokomo: Decca 7026.

Bailey, Kid: Brunswick 7114. Barrow, Raymond: Paramount 12803. Black Birds of Paradise: Black Patti 8053, Gennett 6210, 6211. Blackwell, Scrapper: Vocalion 1192. Blake, Blind: Paramount 12824. Booker, Charlie: Blues & Rhythm 7003, Modern 878. Bracey, Ishmon: Paramount 12941, 12970, 13038, Victor 21349, 21691, 38560. Broonzy, Big Bill: Bluebird B6188. Brown, Willie: Paramount 13090. Bumble Bee Slim—see Easton, Amos. Bunch, William—see Wheatstraw, Peetie. Burleson, Hattie: Brunswick 7042. Butler, Mary—see Moore, Rosie Mae.

Callicott, Joe: Brunswick 7166. Carr, Leroy: Bluebird B5877, Vocalion 1191, 1241, 1290, 02657, 02820, 02950. Carter, Bo—see Chatman, Bo. Chatman, Bo: Bluebird B5861, B8159. Cole, James: Champion 16718. Collins, Sam: Gennett 6146, 6167, 6181, 6307, 6379. Cox, Ida: Paramount 12325.

Davis, Madlyn: Paramount 12615. Delaney, Mattie: Vocalion 1480. Dickinson, Rev. Emmett: Paramount 12925. Douglas, Lizzie—see Memphis Minnie. Duckett, Slim, and Pig (One Leg) Norwood: OKeh 8871, 8899.

Easton, Amos: Decca 7021.

Freezone: Paramount 12803.

Graves, Blind Roosevelt: ARC 6-11-74, Paramount 12820, 12859, 12874, 12974.

Hill, Bertha "Chippie": OKeh 8437. Hill, King Solomon: Paramount 13116, 13125, 13129. Holmes, Joe—see Hill, King Solomon. Hopkins, Sam "Lightnin'": Sittin In With 621. House, Eddie "Son," Jr.: Paramount 12990, 13013, 13042, 13096. Huff, Luther: Trumpet 132, 141. Hull, Papa Harvey: Gennett 6106, 6122. Hurt, "Mississippi" John, OKeh 8560.

Jackson, Jim: Vocalion 1144. James, Elmore: Checker 777, Flair 1022, 1039, 1057, 1074, Meteor 5000, Trumpet 146. James, Nehemiah "Skip": Paramount 13066, 13088. Jefferson, Blind Lemon: Paramount 12407, 12608. Johnson, Lonnie: OKeh 8435, 8557. Johnson, Robert: Vocalion 03416, 03445, 03475, 03519, 03563, 03601, 03623, 03665, 03723, 04002, 04108, 04630. Johnson, Tommy: Paramount 12950, 12975, 13000, Victor 21279, 21409, 38535. Jones, Alberta: Champion 16038, Herwin 92001.

Kelly, Jack: Melotone M12812.

Lacy, Rube: Paramount 12629. Lee, Bertha: Vocalion 02650. Lee, John: Federal 12054, 12089. Lee, Tommy: Delta 403.

McCoy, Joe: Decca 7822, 7828, Vocalion 1476. Memphis Minnie: Decca 7037, 7038. Mississippi Sheiks: OKeh 8784. Montgomery, Eurreal "Little Brother": Paramount 13006. Moore, Rosie Mae: Brunswick 7049. Moss, Buddy: ARC 7-10-70.

New Orleans Nehi Boys: Paramount 12980. Newbern, Hambone Willie: OKeh 8679. Norwood, Sam "Pig" or "One Leg"—see Duckett, Slim.

Oden, "St. Louis" Jimmy: Decca 7017. Owens, Marshall: Paramount 13117.

Parker, "Little" Junior: Sun 187. Patton, Charlie: Paramount 12792, 12805, 12854, 12877, 12909, 12924, 12972, 13014, 13110, Vocalion 02651, 02680.

Reynolds, Blind Joe (see also Reynolds, Blind Willie): Paramount 12927, 12883. Reynolds, Blind Willie: Victor 23258. Rice, Rev. D.C.: Vocalion 1178, 1201, 1289. Rodgers, Jimmie: Victor 20864, 21142. Rose, Rev. T.T.: Paramount 12966.

Scruggs, Irene: Paramount 13121. Sheppard, Joe—see Reynolds, Blind Joe (and) Willie. Smith, Bessie: Columbia A3844, 14042. Southern Sanctified Singers: Brunswick 7074. Sparks Brothers: Victor 23359. Spruell, Freddie: OKeh 8422. Sykes, Roosevelt: Victor 38619.

Tampa Red: Vocalion 1426. Taylor, Charlie: Paramount 12949, 12967, 13121. Temple, Johnnie: Vocalion 02987. Tenderfoot Edwards—see Thompson, Edward. Thomas, Bobo "Slim": Trumpet 146. Thomas, Jesse: Victor 23381, 38555. Thompson, Edward: Paramount 12873. Tucker, Bessie, Victor 38542. Turner, Big Joe: Atlantic 1016.

Wheatstraw, Peetie: Vocalion 1620, 1649, 1722, 03066, 03155. White, Bukka: Vocalion 03711. White, Josh: Melotone M13196. Wiley, Geeshie: Paramount 13074. Wilkins, Robert: Brunswick 7158. Williams, George "Bullet": Paramount 12651, 12680. Williamson, Sonny Boy, II [Aleck Miller]: Trumpet 129.

Chasing Down Ishmon Bracey's Records:
Paramount L Masters Recorded at Grafton, Wisconsin

This list is reconstructed using Dixon and Godrich (1997). Possibly, Johnson's and Bracey's master number could be interchanged, but any transfer still leaves Bracey with eighteen sides, Johnson six, and Taylor five. Although Bracey said his first song recorded at Grafton was "Doodleville Blues," Dixon and Godrich shows his first master as Pm 12941, "Jake Liquor Blues."

Bracey 12941 — "Jake Liquor Blues" [Matrix L-225-3]
Bracey 12941 — "Family Stirving" [L-226-1]
Bracey (missing) [L-227]
Johnson 12975 — "I Wonder to Myself" [L-228-1]
Johnson 12975 — "Slidin' Delta" [L-229-2]
Johnson 13000 — "Lonesome Home Blues" [L-230-2]
Bracey (missing) [L-231]
Bracey (missing) [L-232]
Nehi Boys 12980 — "Mobile Stomp" [L-233-1]
Nehi Boys 12980 — "Farish St. Rag" [L-234-1]
Bracey (missing) — [L-235]
Bracey (missing) — [L-236]
Bracey (missing) — [L-237]
Bracey (missing) — [L-238]
Bracey 12970 — "Woman Woman Blues" [L-239-2]
Bracey 12970 — "Suitcase Full of Blues" [L-240-1]
Bracey 13038 — "Bust Up Blues" [L-241-2]
Bracey 13038 — "Pay Me No Mind" [L-242-2]
Bracey (probably) [L-243]
Bracey (probably) [L-244]
Johnson 13000 — "Black Mare Blues" [L-245-2]
Bracey (missing) [L-246]
Bracey (missing) [L-247]
Bracey (missing) [L-248]
Johnson 12950 — "Ridin' Horse" [L-249-1]
Johnson 12950 — "Alcohol and Jake Blues" [L-250-2]
Taylor 12967 — "Heavy Suitcase Blues" [L-251-1]
Taylor 12967 — "Louisiana Bound" [L-252-2]
Taylor 12949 — "Too Damp to Be Wet" [L-253-1]
Taylor 12949 — "Where My Shoes At?" [L-254-1]
Taylor 13121 (probably) [L-255?]

Some of the missing Braceys may be among the following open Paramount items:

12962
13011
13012
13027
13029
13073
13079

◄o►◄o►◄o►

List of Interviews Cited

A. Tape interviews conducted by Gayle Wardlow

Ordinal numbers refer to tape designation in the Wardlow Tape Collection, Blues Archive, J.D. Williams Library, University of Mississippi. Bracketed [#] numbers refer to the tape designation at the Center for Popular Music, Middle Tennessee State University.

4–5. Hayes McMullan, Willie and Elizabeth Moore, Tutwiler, MS, August 12, 1967. [0182 D and E]

6. Hayes McMullan, Willie and Elizabeth Moore, Willie Young, Tutwiler, MS, August 12, 1967. [0182 F]

7. Hayes McMullan, Tutwiler, MS, August 12, 1967. [0182 G]

8. Hayes McMullan, July 29, 1967. [0182 H]

9. Hayes McMullan, July 29, 1967; H.C. Speir, Jackson, MS, February 8, 1970; Alfred Schultz, Grafton, WI, August 2, 1970. [0182 I]

10. P.C. Brockman, March 20, 1970; Harry Charles, 1968. [0182 J]

11. Harry Charles, 1968. [0182 K]

13. Tommy Lee (no date); Robert Gildart, juke owner (no date). [0182 N]

15–19. Willie and Elizabeth Moore, December 13, 1969. [0182 P, Q, R, S, and T]

20. Henry Austin and Hayes McMullan (no date); Willie Moore (no date). [0182 U]

21. Willie and Elizabeth Moore. [0182 V]

22. H.C. Speir, Jackson, MS, May 18, 1968. [0182 W]

23. Hayes McMullan (no date). [0182 X]

24. Hayes McMullan (no date); Willie Moore (no date). [0182 Y]

25. Lila Mae Braxton (no date); Rev. Frank Howard, December 1967. [0182 Z]

26. Roberta Holmes Allums, May 26, 1968; Wesley Hall. [0182 AA]

27. Sammy Watkins and Fred Gordon, 1967; Leroy Willis; Grant Maxell; Reed Jones; Ishmon Bracey. [0182 BB]

28. Ishmon Bracey (no date); Joe Callicott (December 13, 1967). [0182 CC]

29. Ishmon Bracey, (no date). [0182 DD]

30. Booker Miller, 1968. [0182 EE]

31. Booker Miller, (no date). Dick Bankston, August 13, 1967. [0182 FF]

32. Dick Bankston, August 13, 1967; Jack Cooper, August 15, 1967. [0182 GG]

33. H.C. Speir, Jackson, MS, 1969. [0182 HH]

34. Chester House, (no date). Percy Huff, April 12, 1968. [0182 II]

35. John Willis, September 12, 1968. [0182 JJ]

36. King Abram, (no date). John Willis, 1968. [0182 KK]

37–38. Booker Miller, 1968. [0182 LL and MM]

39. Ledell Johnson, 1967. [0182 NN]

41–42. Blind Joe Sheppard (Reynolds) acquaintances. [0182 PP and QQ]

43. Blind Joe Sheppard acquaintances; King Solomon Hill acquaintances. [0182 RR]

44–45. Gress Barnett. [0182 SS and TT]

47. King Solomon Hill acquaintances. [0182 VV]

Index to Tapes (with references to articles)

Allums, Roberta Holmes, 26 (One Last Walk)

Bankston, Dick, 31–32 (Can't Tell My Future)

Barnett, Gress, 44–45 (Six Who Made Recorded History; Four, Five Puppies)

Bracey, Ishmon, 27–29 (OJL; A Quick Ramble; Six Who Made Recorded History; Got Four, Five Puppies; Garfield Akers and Joe Callicott; Devil of a Joe; One Last Walk; Stop, Look, and Listen)

Brown, Jack: See Sheppard, Joe, acquaintances of.

Callicott, Joe, 28 (From Aberdeen to Parchman; Garfield Akers and Joe Callicott; Devil of a Joe)

Charles, Henry, 10–11 (A Quick Ramble; One Last Walk)

B. Wardlow's written notes from untaped interviews

The following are held in the Wardlow Collection, Blues Archive, University of Mississippi, and may be available for examination with Wardlow's permission. References to use in this book are in parentheses.

Davis, Skeeter, acquaintances of, Drew, MS, 1967. (Can't Tell My Future)

Johnson, Ledell, 8, 17, July 21, 1967; August 13, 1967. (Ledell Johnson Re members; Stop, Look, and Listen)

Lee, John, 1967. (Down at the Depot)

Miller, Booker, July 29, 1967; August 3 and 4, 1967. (Six Who Made Recorded History)

Rice, Rev. D.C., January 27, 1967. (Rev. D.C. Rice)

Speir, H.C., no date (A Quick Ramble; Godfather; Patton's Murder; Devil of a Joe; One Last Walk; Blind Roosevelt Graves; Stop, Look, and Listen)

Temple, Johnny, March 20, 1965 (OJL; Six Who Made Recorded History)

C. Additional interviews and documents cited by Wardlow but not held in the Blues Archive, University of Mississippi

Bell, James, and Tom Ivery, by Wardlow, Birmingham, Alabama, March 1967. (Black Birds)

Booker, Charlie, telephone conversation with Wardlow, 1971. (Greenville Smokin')

Bracey, Anne, taped interview with Wardlow. (Got Four, Five Puppies)

Bracey, Ishmon, interview notes by Wardlow, 1965. (Mysteries; OJL)

Edwards, David "Honey Boy," to Stephen Calt, Vienna, Virginia, 1971. (From Aberdeen to Parchman)

Franklin, Minnie, by Wardlow, July 1963. (Mysteries)

Gavin, Mrs. Withers, taped interview with Wardlow. (Got Four, Five Pup pies)

Gueston, John Junior, interview with Wardlow. (Canton, Mis'sippi Break down)

Halston, Robert, interview with Wardlow. (Canton, Mis'sippi Breakdown)

Jacobs, Walter (Vincson), interview notes by Wardlow. (Mysteries; Got Four, Five Puppies, One Little Shaggy Hound)

James, Elmore, acquaintances and sources of, including Eddie Burns,

Homesick James Williamson, Cilla Huggins, Darryl Stolper, Sonny Boy Williamson II [Aleck Miller]; interviews by Mike Leadbitter, 1963–1970. (Canton, Mis'sippi Breakdown)

James, Skip, interview with Stephen Calt, Philadelphia, PA. (Patton's Mur der; Devil of a Joe)

Laibley, Arthur, phone interviews and correspondence with Wardlow. (A Quick Ramble; Got Four, Five Puppies)

Lee, Bertha, interview with Bernard Klatzko, Chicago (Patton's Murder)

Lovelady, Sam, interview with Wardlow. (Got Four, Five Puppies, One Little Shaggy Hound)

Morris, Willie (musician), to Stephen Calt, Vienna, Virginia, 1971. (From Aberdeen to Parchman)

Olsson, Bengt, correspondence with Wardlow, 1976. (Got Four, Five Pup pies, One Little Shaggy Hound)

O'Neal, Jim, phone conversation with Wardlow, 1981. (A Quick Ramble)

Russell, Bill, correspondence with Wardlow. (One Last Walk)

Stephany, Henry, and wife, interview with Wardlow. (One Last Walk)

Temple, Johnny, taped interview with Wardlow, 1968. (Got Four, Five Pup pies, One Little Shaggy Hound; Garfield Akers and Joe Callicott)

Thomas, Jesse, taped interview conducted by Wardlow and Bill Woodward. (A Quick Ramble)

Williams, Mayo, interview conducted by Stephen Calt, Chicago. (Got Four, Five Puppies, One Little Shaggy Hound)

Reissues

Blues music research has long been hampered by the lack of reissues of the records cited in various articles. Until the mid-1990s, for those records not available on LP reissues, blues writers had to seek the original records through trade, door-to-door canvassing, or listening to copies held by other blues collectors. It was a time-consuming process—before the contemporary surge of compact disc reissues, the record research for a topic that now takes *days,* could take *years* to complete. However, once collectors finished piecing together an artist's work on 78s, they made their treasures available through LP and CD reissues.

The first great reissue series was Origin Jazz Library (OJL), which between 1960 and 1975 issued over two dozen LPs of prewar blues. Started by Pete Whelan and Bill Givens, OJL's first reissue was devoted to Charlie Patton, and its subsequent releases made available the legendary 78s of Son House and Skip James as they were found, one by one. A notable OJL issue was the two-LP set *In the Spirit* (OJL 12 and 13, 1966), collecting 32 rare examples of prewar sacred music performed by bluesmen and sanctified groups, with notes by Bernard Klatzko and Wardlow. In addition to laying a firm foundation for studies in sanctified music, the set also paid tribute to Harry Smith, Robert Waller, and especially James McKune—pioneering collectors of the 1940s and 1950s of prewar blues and religious records, who encouraged younger collectors like Klatzko and Whelan to seek and promote the same.

In 1967, Bill Givens took over the OJL label, and Whelan went on to begin *78 Quarterly.* Meanwhile, Yazoo Records (originally Belzona Records) was founded by Nick Perls, the son of New York City art dealers. Perls, along with Dick Waterman and Phil Spiro, had rediscovered Son House in 1964, yet he apparently decided to concentrate his energies on the records rather than on the musicians who made them. From 1966 through his death in 1986, Perls released over 75 Yazoo LPs and developed plans for several additional ones.

After his death, his 78 rpm record collection and Yazoo label were purchased by Shanachie Records. Under the supervision of Richard Nevins and Don Kent, Yazoo made a successful transition to the compact disc medium, issuing new releases, and re-releasing previous ones in improved remasterings.

Yet OJL and Yazoo were not the only blues reissue labels of the 1960s and 1970s. To name a few, there were also Klatzko's revival of the Herwin label, Chris Strachwitz's Blues Classics and Arhoolie, Don Kent's Mamlish, and Johnny and Evelyn Parth's Roots. Herwin brought forth the outstanding complete reissues of Gus Cannon and of Henry Thomas. Still, the general nature of the reissues of this era remained piecemeal, either presenting selections of an artist's work or a cross-section of a particular genre, or offering "the rest of" an artist's output left incomplete by another reissue label.

In all fairness, though, one must acknowledge that most of these reissue labels could afford to issue only one LP at a time, thus limiting the contents to 48 minutes of music, or 16 three-minute performances. The reissuers had to make some difficult choices.

Columbia Records was one of the few LP labels involved in prewar blues and jazz reissues that could afford to issue multidisc sets. Among Columbia's reissue achievements (brought about in large part by Frank Driggs) were the box sets of Duke Ellington, Billie Holiday, and Fletcher Henderson, and the five double-LP albums collecting Bessie Smith's complete recordings. Yet its most celebrated reissue of prewar music was the 1962 single LP *Robert Johnson: King of the Delta Blues Singers*, which caught the attention of not only historical collectors, but also budding rock musicians such as Keith Richard and Eric Clapton. The treatment of Johnson's songs by rock musicians and critics exposed the dead bluesman to a wider audience, thus keeping the Columbia LP in print, enabling a second Johnson LP on Columbia, and paving the way for the widespread success of the Johnson CD set in 1990.

The 1990 compact disc reissue of Robert Johnson's complete recordings was a milestone in the record industry, and not just for blues records. Developed in the early 1980s, the compact disc could hold up to 72 minutes of music, or 24 three-minute sides. Thus, a bulky three-LP set could be re-released as a two-CD set. It was, and still is, remarkable that the CD technology could result in a musician's complete output fitting in the palm of one's hand. Fortunately, Johnson's recordings fit onto two CDs; a single CD issue would have seemed unremarkable, while three or more CDs would have been too expensive. The mainstream success of the Robert Johnson box—at a retail price of $20 apiece—showed what could be done with issues of prewar music, and that there was a large audience willing to invest in blues CDs.

Over the next six years, in the wake of the Robert Johnson success, Columbia's Roots and Blues subsidary brought forth additional reissues from its vaults, including Bessie Smith, John Hurt, Blind Willie McTell, and Booker "Bukka" White.

Yet the most extensive use of CD technology for blues reissues has been the Document series undertaken by Johnny Parth. Perhaps upon realizing that at least 24 78 rpm sides could be crammed onto a single CD, Parth discontinued the Document LP series in the late 1980s and planned the CD series. As stated in Parth's latest Document CD catalog, Parth's reissue program aims to bring back into print "the complete recordings of all early blues and gospel singers in chronological order" (with the exception of those artists reissued by Columbia, Rounder, and other active labels). In spite of the various reservations that have been published in reviews regarding its reissue procedure and variable sound quality, the Document series has enabled more critical evaluations of blues music research and more informed analyses of individual blues performances than previously possible.

Reissues of the performances mentioned in this book are listed and described below in order of the performer(s). CD reissues are cited whenever possible, since they are in print at the time of publication (1998) and easily available. Articles in which the performers are mentioned in this book are also cited. Document CDs are cited only by their issue number, as most of them are organized by performer. Many LPs, especially those on OJL, have been out of print for many years and are now almost as hard to find as the 78s they reissued; however, a few of them are cited if a CD reissue is not yet available.

Several labels, such as Columbia's Legacy/Roots series, Rhino, and Flair/Virgin, may be mail-ordered if not found at most record stores. For Yazoo and Document, it is best to order by mail; both labels have excellent catalogs worth writing for:

Yazoo Mailorder, P.O. Box 1004, Cooper Station, New York, NY 10276.

Document Records, Johnny Parth, Eipeldauerstrasse 23/43/5, A-1220, Vienna, Austria. (American readers may wish to write to Document's American distributor, Arhoolie Records, 10341 San Pablo Ave., El Cerrito, CA 94530.)

The reissues in order of performer:

Acuff, Roy (1903–1992) (Knocking; Godfather): Leading Grand Ole Opry star from the late 1930s on. His early recordings, including those from his first session in 1936, are on Roy Acuff, *Columbia Historic Edition* (Columbia 39998).

Akers, Garfield (circa 1902–circa 1962) (Country Blues and Gospel Pioneers; Garfield Akers and Joe Callicott): His four surviving sides are on Document DOCD 5002.

Anderson, Jelly Roll (rec. 1927): His records, made for the Gennett label in 1927, are on Document DOCD 5181.

Armstrong, Louis (1901–1971) (Got Four, Five Puppies; Legends): The first three volumes of the Columbia/Legacy series (*The Hot Fives, vol. 1* [Columbia/Legacy CK-44049] and *The Hot Fives and Hot Sevens, vols. 2 and 3* [Columbia/Legacy CK-44253 and -44422]) collect Armstrong's band work from 1925 into 1928, the same period in which Speir saw him perform on a riverboat, and when Bracey claimed (perhaps falsely) that he met Armstrong.

Arnold, James "Kokomo" (1901–1968) (Legends): His collected prewar records are on Document DOCD 5037–5039.

Bailey, Kid (rec. 1929) (Immortal Charlie Patton; Country Blues and Gospel Pioneers; Got Four, Five Puppies; Garfield Akers and Joe Callicott; Can't Tell My Future): *Masters of the Delta Blues* (Yazoo 2002) has his two surviving recordings, with better sound than on the Document DOCD 5002 release.

Barefoot Bill (rec. 1930) (Depot): His sides are issued with those of Ed Bell on Document DOCD 5090.

Barrow, Raymond (rec. 1928) (Knocking): His one side, a piano instrumental for Paramount, is on Document DOCD 5103.

Beck, Elder Charles (rec. 1930–1939) (Country Blues and Gospel Pioneers; Legends): His performances at Speir's 1930 Jackson sessions for OKeh may be heard on Document BDCD 6035 (with sides by Elder Curry) and Document DOCD 5524.

Bell, Ed (1905–c. 1966) (Down at the Depot): The collected sides of this Alabama bluesman are on Document DOCD 5090.

Big Chief Henry (rec. 1929) (Godfather): Discovered by Speir at a Philadelphia Choctaw Festival, and recorded for Victor in Dallas in 1929. One of his performances, "Indian Tom Tom," is available on the cassette *Push Them Clouds Away* from the Musical Traditions label.

Bingham, Zeke (rec. 1936) (Legends): Recorded at Speir's 1936 ARC session in Hattiesburg; none of the sides were released.

Black Birds of Paradise (Black Birds): Their various sides were reissued on the LP *By Ways of Jazz* (Origin Jazz Library OJL-9) around 1964.

Blackwell, Francis "Scrapper" (1903–1962) (Stop, Look, and Listen): His prewar solo recordings are on Document BDCD 6029 and 6030; see also Leroy Carr.

Blake, Blind Arthur (rec. 1926–1932) (Godfather): Document reissued the complete recordings of this Florida guitar-picker on seven CDs (DOCD 5024 through 5027, 5062, 5150, 5216). Those who wish for a representative sample should get Yazoo's Blind Blake anthology *Ragtime Guitar's Foremost Fingerpicker* (Yazoo 1068).

Boines, Houston (rec. 1952–1953) (Greenville Smokin'): See the entry for Charlie Booker (below).

Booker, Charlie (1925–1989) (Greenville Smokin'): Houston Boines and Charlie Booker's original 78s are hard to find, and locating reissues of them is not much easier. In the late 1960s, Kent Records reissued their Modern and Blues & Rhythm sides on the LP *Anthology of the Blues: Mississippi Blues* (Kent LP 9009). Some of their respective Sun sides were first issued on the *Sun Records: The Blues Years* on Sun Box (Charly) 105, although a few remain unissued.

Bracey, Mississippi Coleman (or Caldwell) (rec. 1930) (Legends): Recorded at Speir's 1930 Jackson session for OKeh; those sides are on Document DOCD 5157.

Bracey, Ishmon (1901–1970) (Country Blues and Gospel Pioneers; Got Four, Five Puppies): Collected recordings are on Document DOCD 5059. A few selected recordings are featured, with two photos of Bracey, on *Masters of the Delta Blues* (Yazoo 2002).

Broonzy, Bill (1893–1958) (Country Blues and Gospel Pioneers; Stop, Look, and Listen): His 1927–42 recordings are collected on Document DOCD 5050–5052, 5126–5133.

Brown, Willie (1900–1952) (Immortal Charlie Patton; Country Blues and Gospel Pioneers; Legends; Can't Tell My Future): The two 1929 sides backing Kid Bailey and the two 1930 sides by Brown himself are on Yazoo 2002, *Masters of the Delta Blues*, and in lesser sound on Document DOCD 5002. The sides of him accompanying Charlie Patton on second guitar may be found on many anthologies, not least the Patton discs in the Yazoo and Document series (see Patton, below). The 1941 Library of Congress recordings with Son House are on House, *Delta Blues* (Biograph BCD 118), although Brown's solo performance of "Make Me a Pallet on the Floor" is on the Flyright LP 541 (*Walking Blues*).

Bumble Bee Slim: See Easton, Amos.

Burleson, Hattie (rec. 1929–1930) (Knocking): Her sides are on Document DOCD 5471.

Butler, Sam. See listing under his pseudonym, Bo Weavil Jackson.

Bryant, Elder Richard (rec. 1928) (Country Blues and Gospel Pioneers): His supreme sanctified performances are on Document 5300.

Butler, Sam. See Jackson, Bo Weavil (recording pseudonym).

Byrd, John (rec. 1929–1930) (Country Blues and Gospel Pioneers; Six Who Made Recorded History; Got Four, Five Puppies): Collected recordings on the CD label Story of Blues da CD 3517-2.

Callicott, Joe (1901–1969) (Garfield Akers and Joe Callicott): His prewar recordings alone and with Garfield Akers are on Document DOCD 5002.

Campbell College Quartet (rec. 1930) (Legends): Recorded at Speir's 1930 Jackson session for OKeh; two sides were released on OKeh 8900. No LP or CD reissues as yet.

Carr, Leroy (1905–1935) (Knocking; Stop, Look, and Listen): His records with guitarist Scrapper Blackwell were hugely popular in their day, exerting an indelible influence on St. Louis and Mississippi musicians. They are collected on Document DOCD 5134–5139, with additional sides on DOCD 5411, 5465, and BDCD 6045.

Chatman, Bo [Carter] (1893–1964) (Godfather): Document DOCD 5078–5082, with 5150 and 5216, collects the various Bo Carter solos sides. See also Mississippi Sheiks.

Coleman, Jaybird (1896–1950) (Country Blues and Gospel Pioneers): His harmonica performances are on Document DOCD 5140.

Collins, Sam (1887–1949) (King Solomon Hill; Knocking; Country Blues and Gospel Pioneers; Got Four, Five Puppies; One Last Walk): Collected sides are on Document DOCD 5034, although most of them can be heard in better sound on Yazoo 1079 (Sam Collins, *Jailhouse Blues*).

Cox, Ida (1896-1967) (Stop, Look, and Listen): Collected prewar records are on Document DOCD 5322–5325.

Crudup, Arthur "Big Boy" (1905–1974) (Got Four, Five Puppies): His 1941–1954 sides are on Document DOCD 5201 through 5204, including his 1946 "That's All Right," which Elvis Presley would cover on his first commercial record.

Curry, Ben (c.1900–1935?) (King Solomon Hill): His handful of recordings may be found on Document DOCD-5166.

Curry, Elder (rec. 1930–1938) (Country Blues and Gospel Pioneers; Legends): Recorded for Speir's 1930 Jackson session for OKeh. Collected recordings on Document BDCD 6035.

Davis, Madlyn (rec. 1927–1928) (Stop, Look, and Listen): Her "Kokola Blues" (a precursor to "Kokomo Blues" and "Sweet Home Chicago") and other records may be heard on Document DOCD 5073 and 5509.

Davis, Blind Willie (rec. 1928–1929) (Blind Roosevelt Graves): First reissued on the OJL *In the Spirit* LPs. His collected performances are on Document DOCD 5190.

Delaney, Mattie (rec. 1930) (Knocking): Her two sides are on Document DOCD 5157.

Delta Big Four (rec. 1930) (Legends): Lula, Mississippi-based sacred quartet. Discovered and driven to their Paramount session by Speir in late April 1930. Sides reissued on Document DOCD 5538.

Dickinson, Rev. Emmett (rec. 1929–1930) (Rev. D.C. Rice): Surviving sides on Document DOCD 5441 and 5490.

Dorsey, Thomas A. (1899–1993) (Knocking): The blues records from his "Georgia Tom" years are on Document BDCD 6021–6022. See also Tampa Red.

Duckett, Luceen "Slim," and Sam "Pig" or "One Leg" Norwood (rec. 1930) (Country Blues and Gospel Pioneers; Got Four, Five Puppies): Blues duo that recorded sacred sides at Speir's 1930 Jackson session for OKeh. Those sides are on Document DOCD 5165.

Easton, Amos (1905–1968) (Stop, Look, and Listen): Better known as Bumble Bee Slim, his collected 1931–1952 records are on Document DOCD 5262–5268.

Edwards, Tenderfoot: See Edward Thompson.

Ezell, Will (rec. 1927–1931) (A Quick Ramble): Ezell's sides are reissued complete on Document BDCD-6033.

Famous Blue Jay Singers of Birmingham (rec. 1932) (King Solomon Hill): Recorded at Paramount on the same day as Joe Holmes; resulting sides reissued on Document DOCD 5538.

Fancy, Sister Cally (rec. 1929–1931) (Country Blues and Gospel Pioneers): Her religious sides are on Document DOCD 5313.

Forehand, Blind Mamie (rec. 1927) (Country Blues and Gospel Pioneers): Her records with husband A.C. Forehand are on Document DOCD 5054.

Freeny Barn Dance Orchestra (rec. 1930s) (Godfather): Hillbilly band from Freeny, Mississippi, that recorded at Speir's 1930 Jackson session for OKeh; their sides are coveted by fiddling aficionados. Several sides were reissued on County LP 529 *Mississippi Fiddle Bands vol. 2.*

Freezone (rec. 1929) (Knocking): His lone title, "Indian Squaw Blues," is on Document DOCD 5103.

Garnett, Blind Leroy (rec. 1929) (Legends): Recordings reissued on Document DOCD 5103.

Graves, Blind Roosevelt (1909–1963) (Country Blues and Gospel Pioneers; Blind Roosevelt Graves; Got Four, Five Puppies; Legends): Collected sides under his name and as part of the Mississippi Jook Band may be found on Document BDCD 6033 and DOCD 5105.

Green, Lee (c. 1900?–1945?) (Legends): The St. Louis piano player's collected sides are on Document BDCD 6045 and DOCD 5187–5188.

Harris, James (Legends): Recording pseudonym for James Wiggins.

Harris, William (rec. 1927–1928) (Country Blues and Gospel Pioneers; Legends): Among Speir's first discoveries. Collected recordings are on Document DOCD 5035 and 5276.

Hill, Bertha "Chippie" (rec. 1925–1929) (Knocking): Her records are sought after for the trumpet fills of young Louis Armstrong. They appear on Document DOCD 5053 and 5330, as well as on a number of jazz reissues.

Hill, King Solomon: Recording pseudonym for Joe Holmes. See also Famous Blue Jay Singers of Birmingham.

Holmes, Joe (c.1897–c. 1949) (King Solomon Hill; One Last Walk): Collected sides are on Document DOCD 5036.

Holy Ghost Sanctified Singers (rec. 1930) (Country Blues and Gospel Pioneers): On Document DOCD 5300.

Hopkins, Sam "Lightnin'" (1912–1982) (Depot): His "New York Boogie," later to serve as the model for John Lee's "Alabama Boogie," is on *Sittin' in with Lightnin' Hopkins* on the British label Mainstream.

House, Eddie "Son," Jr. (1902–1988) (Immortal Charlie Patton; Country Blues and Gospel Pioneers; Legends; Godfather; Can't Tell My Future): The seven surviving performances from 1930 are on Yazoo's *Masters of the Delta Blues* (Yazoo 2002), and in lesser sound on Document DOCD 5002. His 1941 and 1942 Library of Congress recordings are gathered for the most part on Biograph CD 118 (House, *Delta Blues*). His best-known recordings after his 1964 rediscovery remain those made for Columbia in 1965 and reissued as *Father of the Delta Blues* (Columbia/Legacy C2K-48867).

Huff, Luther (1910–1973) (Huff Brothers): The four Trumpet sides with his brother Percy (b. 1912) are on Big Joe Williams/Willie Love/Luther Huff, *Delta Blues–1951* (Alligator ALCD 2702)."

Hull, Papa Harvey (rec. 1927) (Country Blues and Gospel Pioneers): His performances, evoking what Wardlow calls "pre-blues," are on Document DOCD 5045.

Hurt, "Mississippi" John (1893–1966) (Country Blues and Gospel Pioneers; Godfather): His 1928 performances for OKeh are best remastered on Yazoo 1065 (Hurt, *1928 Sessions*), although they may also be found in the Document series (Document DOCD 5003).

Jackson, Bo Weavil (recording pseudonym of Sam Butler) (rec. 1926) (Legends): An early discovery of Birmingham-based Paramount scout Harry Charles, his collected sides are on Document DOCD 5036.

Jackson, Jim (1890–1937) (Garfield Akers and Joe Callicott; Legends): Best known for his hit "Jim Jackson's Kansas City Blues." That and his other surviving performances are on Doument DOCD 5114–5115, 5216, and 5276.

James, Elmore (1918–1963) (Highway 80 Blues; Canton, Mis'sippi Breakdown): The first recording of "Dust My Broom," his lone featured side before jumping Trumpet in 1951, is available on a number of compact discs, especially on Sonny Boy Williamson, *King Biscuit Time* (Arhoolie CD 310). His sessions for the Bihari brothers labels are presented on *Elmore James: The Classic Early Recordings* (Virgin/America 7243-8-39631-2-6). His later sides, especially for Bobby Robinson, have fallen in and out of print. *King of the Slide Guitar* (Capricorn CD42006-2) was a notable two-CD selection in the United States; the Charlie four-CD set—a British box, also titled *King of the Slide Guitar* (CDRED Box 4)—had the complete Robinson sessions and the Chess recordings to boot. Rhino offers an overview, *The Sky Is Crying: The History of Elmore James* (Rhino R2-71190), that includes Big Joe Turner's "T.V. Mama" with James. Yet, collecting Elmore James reissues has become as difficult as gathering the original releases. A discography that thoroughly matches the mass of James reissues to each session is Steve Franz's *Elmore James: The Ultimate Guide to the Master of the Slide* (St. Louis: Primal Art, 1994); serious Elmore addicts who want to know more about this guide should write to Franz at 8816 Manchester Rd., No. 408, St. Louis, MO, 63144-2602.

James, Nehemiah "Skip" (1902–1969) (Country Blues and Gospel Pioneers; Legends; Godfather; Got Four, Five Puppies; Stop, Look, and Listen): Although mentioned only in passing in the articles reprinted here, Skip James and his 1931 recordings merit close listening. *The Complete Early Recordings* on Yazoo 2009 is the best mastering yet of these rare (and scratchy) 78s. Those holding the Document series will find the same session on DOCD-5005.

Jefferson, Blind Lemon (1893–1929) (Knocking; Godfather; One Last Walk; Got Four, Five Puppies): Texas bluesman whose commercial success on Paramount Records in 1926 led to more country blues artists getting recorded. His complete recordings are on Document DOCD 5017–5020, 5150, and 5321; a selection is available on Yazoo 1069, *Blind Lemon Jefferson: King of the Country Blues.*

Johnson, Bessie (rec. 1927–1929) (Country Blues and Gospel Pioneers): This outstanding sanctified singer's various sides are on Document DOCD 5072.

Johnson, Buster (rec. 1932) (Country Blues and Gospel Pioneers): His record with James Cole is on Document DOCD 5189.

Johnson, Louise (rec. 1930) (Knocking; Legends): This Delta barrelhouse piano player recorded her Paramount label sides in 1930 in the presence of Charlie Patton, Son House, and Willie Brown. The various sides appear on Document DOCD- 5157 and 5321.

Johnson, Lonnie (1894–1970) (Stop, Look, and Listen): This great prewar guitarist recorded solo or with early jazz greats; his 1925–32 discs, including those that influenced Robert Johnson in Mississippi, are on Document DOCD 5063–5068.

Johnson, Robert (1911–1938) (Knocking; From Aberdeen to Parchman; Godfather; Canton; Stop, Look, and Listen): The reissues of this ill-fated Mississippi bluesman are now the best-selling of any prewar blues artist.

The 1990 two-CD set *Robert Johnson: The Complete Recordings* (Columbia/Legacy C2K-46222) enjoyed phenomenal sales beyond anyone's expectation. In 1996, the set was remastered with cleaner matrix sources and better digital technology, and issued under the same title but a different label number (Columbia/Legacy C2K 64916).

Johnson, Tommy (c.1896–1956) (Country Blues and Gospel Pioneers; Ledell Johnson Remembers; Highway 80; Got Four, Five Puppies; Legends; Godfather): The recordings of this legendary early Mississippi bluesman continue to be highly regarded. Document DOCD 5001 has the famous Victor sessions and the recently recovered Paramount sides.

Johnson, Blind Willie (c.1902–c.1947) (Country Blues and Gospel Pioneers): The records of this unparalleled Texas sacred performer are collected on *The Complete Blind Willie Johnson,* Columbia CK 52835.

Jones, Alberta (rec. 1923–1930) (Knocking): Reissues, if any, are untraced.

Jordan, Charlie (1890–1954) (Country Blues and Gospel Pioneers): Collected sides on Document DOCD 5097–5099.

Karnes, Alfred (rec. 1927–1928) (Country Blues and Gospel Pioneers): Two of his performances are on *The Music of Kentucky Vol. 1* on Yazoo 2013.

Kelly, Jack (rec. 1933–1939) (Canton; Stop, Look, and Listen): Complete recordings are on Document BDCD 6005.

Kid Stormy Weather (rec. 1935) (Legends): Pianist who recorded at Speir's 1935 Jackson session for ARC. The two sides that were issued in 1935 can be found on Document DOCD 5233.

Lacy, Rube (1901–c.1972) (Got Four, Five Puppies; Legends): Among the first Mississippi bluesmen on records, his two surviving sides may be found on Document DOCD 5002.

Laurel Firemen's Quartet (rec. 1930) (Legends): Group that recorded at Speir's 1930 Jackson sessions for OKeh; sides may have been unissued, or unreissued.

Lawlers, Ernest "Little Son Joe" (1900–1961) (Legends): Recorded at Speir's 1935 Jackson sessions for ARC, but the sides were not issued. Later he made commercial releases by himself (reissued on Document BDCD 6011–6012 and Wolf WBCD-010) and with Memphis Minnie.

Leake County Revelers (rec. 1930s) (Godfather): A hillbilly band from Carthage, Mississippi, they recorded for Columbia. No comprehensive CD reissues yet; several Revelers sides were reissued on the 1968 Columbia LP *Ballads and Breakdowns of the Golden Era.*

Lee, Bertha (1902–1975) (Patton's Murder; Godfather): The sides she performed with Charlie Patton in 1934 are on volume 3 of Patton's collected recordings in the Document series (Document DOCD 5001).

Lee, John (1915–) (Down at the Depot): The 1951 Federal session is on Document DOCD 5223. After Wardlow's *Blues Unlimited* article, Lee recorded a rediscovery LP for Rounder, *Down at the Depot* (Rounder 2010).

Lee, Tommy (1915–) (Highway 80): No LP or CD reissues of his Delta label 78 rpm release have yet emerged.

McCollum, Mother (rec. 1930) (Country Blues and Gospel Pioneers): Her sides are on Document DOCD 5101.

McCoy, Charlie (1909–1959) (Got Four, Five Puppies; Legends): Collected solo recordings are on Document BDCD 6018–6020.

McCoy, Joe (1905–1950) (Garfield Akers and Joe Callicott): His records with Memphis Minnie are on Document 5028–5031, 5150, and 5216, and his records with his brother Charlie McCoy are on Document BDCD 6019–6020. Later he joined the Harlem Hamfats, whose performances are on Document DOCD 5271–5274.

McIntorsh, Lonnie, and Edwards (rec. 1928) (Country Blues and Gospel Pioneers): Creators of some of the finest early sanctified records, which are brought together on Document DOCD 5072.

Macon, "Uncle" Dave (1870–1952) (Country Blues and Gospel Pioneers; Legends): Selected performances of this pioneering Grand Ole Opry star have been reissued on CD by County, under the title *Go Long Mule* (County CD 3505).

Mason, Moses (rec. 1928) (Godfather; Legends): His sides are gathered on Document DOCD 5165 and 5216.

Memphis Jug Band: See Shade, Will.

Memphis Minnie (Lizzie Douglas) (1897–1973): Her years with Kansas Joe McCoy (1929–1934) are presented on Document DOCD 5028–5031, and her 1935–41 solo career is on Document BDCD 6008–6012.

Mississippi Jook Band; see Graves, Blind Roosevelt.

Mississippi Sheiks (1930–1935) (Got Four, Five Puppies; Legends; Stop, Look, and Listen): Collected recordings of this popular group are on Document 5083–5086.

Montgomery, Eurreal "Little Brother" (1906–1985) (Knocking; Got Four, Five Puppies): His prewar performances are on Document DOCD 5109, and BDCD 6034 and 6045.

Moore, Rosie Mae (rec. 1928) (Got Four, Five Puppies): This Jackson singer is on Document DOCD 5049 and BDCD 6018.

Moore, William (rec. 1928) (Country Blues and Gospel Pioneers): Not to be confused with Wardlow's source Will Moore. This guitarist's sides are on Document DOCD 5062.

Moss, Buddy (1914–1984) (Stop, Look, and Listen): Collected sides are on Document DOCD 5123–5125.

Moten, Bennie (1894–1935) (Godfather): A leading Kansas City jazz bandleader until his untimely death, his best sessions, including his legendary 1932 "Toby" date, are on Moten, *1930–1932* (Classics 578).

Morton, Ferdinand "Jelly Roll" (c.1895–1941) (Godfather): Pioneering jazz composer and pianist. BMG/RCA released as a five-CD set *Jelly Roll Morton Centennial: His Complete Victor Recordings* (Bluebird 2361-2-RB); his most famous sides, though, may be found on the two-CD *Jelly Roll Morton and His Red Hot Peppers (1926–1938)* (Bluebird 6588-2-RB).

Nelson, Charlie "Dad" (rec. 1926) (Legends): His surviving records are on Document DOCD 5277.

Nelson, Tom (rec. 1928) (Got Four, Five Puppies): His recordings with T.C. Johnson are on Document DOCD 5169.

Nettles, Isaiah (rec. 1935) (Six Who Made Recorded History; Godfather): Recorded for Speir's 1935 Jackson session for Vocalion, which issued his sides under the name "The Mississippi Moaner." Reissued on Document DOCD 5157.

New Orleans Nehi Boys (rec. 1929–1930) (Got Four, Five Puppies): Document has reissued their backings for Tommy Johnson (DOCD 5001) and Ishmon Bracey (DOCD 5049).

Newbern, Hambone Willie (rec. 1929) (Stop, Look, and Listen): His "Roll and Tumble Blues" and other records are on Document DOCD 5003.

Newton County Hillbillies (rec. 1930) (Godfather): This hillbilly band recorded at Speir's 1930 Jackson sessions for OKeh. No LP or CD reissues yet.

Oden, St. Louis Jimmy (1903–1977) (Stop, Look, and Listen): Collected prewar sides are on Document DOCD 5234–5235.

Owens, Marshall (1880–1974) (King Solomon Hill): Texas/Alabama guitarist was at the Paramount studio at the same time as Joe Holmes. His recordings are on Document DOCD 5165.

Parker, "Little" Junior (1932–1971) (Highway 80): Best known for recording "Mystery Train," a blues later covered by Elvis Presley. His Sun recordings may be found on the set *Sun Records: The Blues Years* (Charlie/Sun Box 105).

Patton, Charlie (1891–1934) (Immortal Charlie Patton; Mysteries; Legends; Godfather; Patton's Death): An archetypal Mississippi bluesman, Patton's posthumous reissues are rivaled only by those of Robert Johnson with respect to packaging and liner/booklet notes. Pete Whelan did the first reissues on his OJL (Origin Jazz Library) label, namely *Charlie Patton* (OJL-

1) and *Charlie Patton vol. 2* (OJL-7). In the early 1970s, Nick Perls issued the two-LP set *Charlie Patton: Founder of the Delta Blues* (Yazoo L-1020) with notes and lyric transcriptions. Among CD reissues, Yazoo has done very well with its two Patton CDs, *Founder of the Delta Blues* (Yazoo 2010, which has a different selection than the earlier Yazoo LP of the same title) and *King of the Delta Blues* (Yazoo 2001). For Patton's complete recordings, the Document series (Document DOCD 5009–5011) will have to be consulted, although the sound remastering is not as well done as Yazoo's.

Phillips, Washington (rec. 1927–1929) (Country Blues and Gospel Pioneers): Accompanying himself with a rare dulceola instrument, Phillips' sacred performances have a delicate, even ethereal quality. They are collected on Phillips, *I Am Born to Preach the Gospel* on Yazoo 2003, and on Document DOCD 5054.

Rainey, Gertrude "Ma" (1886–1939) (Godfather): Her 1928 recordings are on Document DOCD -5156. Black Swan reissued her records of 1923–25 with the outtakes (Black Swan HCD-12001–12002), while King Jazz has issued her 1923–28 commercial releases without outtakes (King Jazz KJ-181–184).

Reynolds, Blind Joe [Joe Sheppard] (1900–1968) (Got Four, Five Puppies; Legends; Godfather; Devil of a Joe): His four surviving recordings are on Document DOCD 5002.

Rice, Rev. D.C. (c.1888–1973) (Country Blues and Gospel Pioneers; Rev. D.C. Rice): His collected sides are on Document DOCD 5071. See also Southern Sanctified Singers.

Robinson, Elzadie (rec. 1926–1929) (A Quick Ramble): Her recordings are gathered on Document DOCD 5248 and 5249.

Rodgers, Jimmie (1897–1933) (Godfather): RCA Victor issued all its "Singing Brakeman" sides on LP during the early 1960s. Recently, Rounder has completed a chronological Rodgers reissue on eight CDs (Rounder ROUN-1056 through -1063).

Rose, Rev. T.T. (rec. 1927–1930) (Rev. D.C. Rice): His sacred sides have not yet been reissued.

Scott, Sonny (rec. 1933) (Six Who Made Recorded History): His sides have been reissued on Document DOCD 5144 and 5450.

Shade, Will (1898–1966) (Legends): The records he made with the Memphis Jug Band are collected on Document DOCD 5021–5023, 5150, 5276, and BDCD 6002 and 6028; additional sides are on Wolf WBCD-004. Yazoo released a well-mastered selection on CD as *The Memphis Jug Band* (Yazoo 1067).

Sheppard, Joe: See Reynolds, Blind Joe.

Sims, Henry "Son" (1890–1958) (Country Blues and Gospel Pioneers; God-father): The records he made with Charlie Patton can be found on the Document volumes for Patton (particularly Document DOCD 5010 and 5011). His later performances with Muddy Waters at Stovall's plantation are on Muddy Waters, *The Complete Plantation Recordings/The Historic 1941–1942 Library of Congress Field Recordings* (MCA/Chess CHD 9344).

Smith, Bessie (1894–1937) (Knocking; Godfather): Her complete record-ings are on five deluxe-packaged sets on Columbia/Legacy C2K-47091, -47471, -47474, -52838, and -57546.

Southern Sanctified Singers (Rev. D.C. Rice): The two lone sides issued under this name have been reissued on Document DOCD 5186.

Sparks Brothers (rec. 1932-1935) (Stop, Look, and Listen): Their "I Be-lieve I'll Make a Change" of 1932, later reworked by later bluesmen as "Dust My Broom," may be heard on Document DOCD 5315.

Spruell, Freddie (d. 1956) (Knocking; Six Who Made Recorded History): His various sides are on Document DOCD 5158.

Sykes, Roosevelt (1906–1984) (Stop, Look, and Listen): Popular singer and pianist who brought much prewar St. Louis talent to the recording studios. His own prewar sides are on Document DOCD 5116–5122.

Tampa Red (Hudson Whittaker) (1904–1981) (Knocking): His 1928–1934 performances, including those with Thomas A. Dorsey, are on Document 5073–5077.

Taylor, Charlie (rec. 1930) (Got Four, Five Puppies): The recordings he made in the company of Ishmon Bracey are on Document DOCD 5049. See also Bracey, Ishmon, and the New Orleans Nehi Boys.

Taylor, Melinda (Country Blues and Gospel Pioneers): See Johnson, Bessie, and McIntorsh and Edwards.

Taylor, Walter (rec. 1930) (Legends): The recordings he made with John Byrd are on Story of Blues da CD 3517-2.

Temple, Johnny (1906–1968) (Stop, Look, and Listen): A Jackson, Missis-sippi, bluesman, he made a successful transition to Chicago clubs in the mid-1930s. Collected sides are on Document DOCD 5238–5240.

Thomas, Bobo "Slim" (rec. 1950) (Highway 80 Blues): His only recording, "Catfish Blues," has been reissued on Sonny Boy Williamson, *Goin' in Your Direction* (Alligator ALCD 2803).

Thomas, Elvie (rec. 1930) (Legends; Six Who Made Recorded History): Her sides by herself and with Geechie Wiley are reissued on Document DOCD 5157.

Thomas, Henry (1874–perhaps 1949?) (Country Blues and Gospel Pioneers): The performances of this itinerant Texas songster indicate the deepest roots of the blues on record. Complete recordings are on Henry Thomas, *Texas Worried Blues,* Yazoo 1080/1081.

Thomas, Jesse (1911–1995) (A Quick Ramble): His prewar recordings are on Document DOCD 5107 and 5276, and BDCD 6044.

Thomas, Willard "Ramblin'" (c.1902–c.1930s) (King Solomon Hill; A Quick Ramble): His collected sides are on Document DOCD 5107 and 5216.

Thompson, Edward (rec. 1929) (Depot): Also known as Tenderfoot Edwards. On Document DOCD 5165.

Tucker, Bessie (rec. 1928–1929) (A Quick Ramble): Her recordings are on Document DOCD 5070 and 5150.

Turner, "Big" Joe (1911–1985) (Canton, Mis'sippi Breakdown): His recording of "T.V. Mama" with Elmore James may be found on the CD *The Sky Is Crying: The History of Elmore James* (Rhino R2-71190).

Vaughan, Cooney (rec. 1936) (Legends; Blind Roosevelt Graves): Recorded solo and with Blind Roosevelt Graves during the 1936 Speir sessions in Hattiesburg for ARC. Unfortunately, the solo sides were not issued; however, the "Mississippi Jook Band" sides with Graves may be found on Document DOCD 5105.

Wallace, Minnie (rec. 1929–1935) (Legends): Recorded at Speir's 1935 Jackson session for Vocalion. Her collected sides are on Document DOCD 5022 and BDCD-6028, and Wolf WBCD-004.

Waters, Muddy [McKinley Morganfield] (1915–1983) (Godfather): His 1941–1942 Library of Congress recordings may be heard in full on *Muddy Waters: The Complete Plantation Recordings* (MCA/Chess CHD-9344). An overview of his star years is *Muddy Waters: The Chess Box* (MCA/Chess CHD3-80002).

Wheatstraw, Peetie [William Bunch] (1902–1941) (Stop, Look, and Listen): Pianist and vocalist whose "ooh, well well" was copied by a generation of blues musicians. Collected sides are on Document DOCD 5241–5247.

White, Booker T. Washington "Bukka" (1909–1977) (Country Blues and Gospel Pioneers; From Aberdeen to Parchman; Godfather): Two of his 1930 Victor recordings are on *Master of the Delta Blues* (Yazoo 2002). *The Complete Bukka White* (Columbia/Legacy CK-52782) has his 1937 and 1940 sessions, including the hit "Shake 'Em On Down"; this disc belongs next to the Robert Johnson complete recordings set on every acoustic blues-lover's shelf. Those seeking White's two Library of Congress sides recorded during his 1937–40 Parchman imprisonment will find them on Document DOCD 5320.

White, Josh (1914–1969) (Canton; Stop, Look, and Listen): His 1929–40 recordings are gathered together on Document DOCD 5194–5196.

Wiggins, James (aka James Harris) (d. 1929/1930?) (Legends): His surviving performances have been reissued on Document DOCD 5103.

Wiley, Geeshie (rec. 1930–1931) (Got Four, Five Puppies; Legends): Moviegoers may remember Wiley's "Last Kind Words Blues" during a Robert Crumb montage in Zwigoff's documentary *Crumb*. That side and her remaining others (including the superb "Eagles on a Half") are on Document DOCD 5157.

Wilkins, Robert (1886–1987) (Country Blues and Gospel Pioneers; Garfield Akers and Joe Callicott): His collected recordings are on Document DOCD 5014, yet Yazoo offers a better-mastered version on Robert Wilkins, *The Original Rolling Stone* (Yazoo 1077).

Wills, Bob (1905–1975) (Knocking; Godfather): The father of Texas swing; many of his most famous sides are on *The Essential Bob Wills* (Columbia/Legacy 48958).

Williams, George "Bullet" (rec. 1928) (Immortal Charlie Patton; Country Blues and Gospel Pioneers): His sides are on Document DOCD 5100 and 5150.

Williams, Jabo (rec. 1932) (Down at the Depot): This Birmingham pianist's sides rank among the finest in prewar piano blues. However, he recorded for Paramount when the company was ceasing operation; therefore the original issues were pressed in low runs and poorly distributed. Fortunately, today his surviving sides are available on CD on Document DOCD-5102.

Williamson, Sonny Boy [Aleck Miller] (1910–1965) (Canton, Mis'sippi Breakdown): His Trumpet sides can be found on *King Biscuit Time* (Arhoolie CD-310), *Goin' in Your Direction* (Alligator ALCD 2803), and *Clownin' with the World* (Alligator ALCD-2700). *The Essential Sonny Boy Williamson* (MCA/Chess CHD 9343) offers an overview of his later Chess years. *Keep It to Ourselves* (Alligator ALCD 4787) is a wonderful memento of his European appearances.

Index of Names

CD Liner Notes

Produced by Gayle Dean Wardlow, Mastered by MasterDigital Corporation, Parker Dinkins. All selections from the Wardlow collection except: Tommy Johnson, "Alcohol and Jake Blues," Pete Whelan collection; and Son House, "Jinx Blues," Herwin collection/Library of Congress. All interviews from Wardlow collection.

The *Chasin that Devil Music* CD includes more than 20 great blues performances by premier Delta bluesmen who recorded various "Delta styles" in the late 1920s. Many of the songs are done by bottleneck players such as Charlie Patton, Son House, King Solomon Hill, Blind Joe Reynolds, and others who either lived or played in the Delta. As an added point of interest, this CD is culled from records in my own collection, including three postwar recordings by Delta musicians, to demonstrate how bluesmen of the Delta sounded, as compared to the Chicago sound of Muddy Waters, Howlin' Wolf and others in the early 1950s. Most of the bluesmen who are common subjects of book articles are represented on this CD. This recording also has gospel recordings by Rev. D.C. Rice and Blind Roosevelt Graves and his brother Aaron. Also featured here are short memories by personalities such as Jackson talent scout H.C. Speir, Ishmon Bracey, Joe Callicott and Rev. Booker Miller. I did not include any of Robert Johnson's or Elmore James's recordings, as they are widely available in so many formats. Briefly, the CD highlights these bluesmen:

1. Charley Patton, "Green River Blues," 1929 (3:06). This song is one of his foremost. He hits the side of the guitar and stomps his feet for dance rhythm. Paramount 12972, by Charlie Patton.
2. "Booker Miller on Patton, part 1," 1968 (0:58). Booker Miller talking of memories about Patton. Wardlow interview.
3. Willie Brown, "Future Blues," 1930 (2:53). His greatest blues done for "shimmy" dancing, using Spanish G tuning, but capoed to the A-flat position. Paramount 13090, by Willie Brown.
4. "H.C. Speir on Patton and Brown," 1968 (0:54). Speir talking of memories about Patton and Brown. Wardlow interview.
5. Hayes McMullan, "Looka Here Woman," 1968 (1:59). A 1968 recording of his 1920s playing. Hayes was never a professional musician; he sharecropped for his living. Wardlow studio session, Jackson, MS. Previously unissued, by Hayes McMullan.
6. "Joe Callicott on Garfield Akers," 1967 (0:29). Joe Callicott remembers

about the record he and Garfield Akers made in 1929. Wardlow interview.

7. Garfield Akers with Joe Callicott, "Cottonfield Blues, pt.1," 1929 (2:52). One of the greatest two-guitar blues ever recorded. Vocalion 1442, by Garfield Akers. Courtesy MCA Records, Inc.; under license from Universal Music Special Markets, Inc.

8. William Harris, "Bull Frog Blues," 1928 (3:05). One of the more primitive Delta guitar styles for dancing, played in the key of D, in standard tunings. Gennett 6661, by William Harris.

9. Rube Lacy, "Ham Hound and Gravy," 1928 (2:55). A 1928 recording [Ham Hound Crave] showing his Delta influences through the stomping of his feet to keep rhythm for dancers. Paramount 12629, by Rube Lacy.

10. Rev. D.C. Rice, "I'm Pressing On," 1929 (2:45). This song is one of the most dynamic sanctified recordings with group singing. Vocalion 1289, by Rev. D.C. Rice. Courtesy MCA Records, Inc.; under license from Universal Music Special Markets, Inc.

11. "Ishmon Bracey on performing," 1969 (0:36). Ishmon Bracey talking about playing with Tommy Johnson and his drinking problems. Wardlow interview.

12. Ishmon Bracey, "Woman Woman Blues," 1930 (3:25). This song is perhaps Bracey's finest blues, in what he refered to as his "G-minor" tuning. Paramount 12970, by Ishmon Bracey.

13. Blind Joe Reynolds, "Outside Woman Blues," 1929 (2:53). This song was performed with a bottleneck, in Open D tuning that he learned in the Louisiana Delta, across the river from Vicksburg. The British rock band Cream did this song in the late 1960s. Paramount 12927, by Joe Reynolds.

14. Son House, "Jinx Blues," 1942 (3:21). This song is Son's version of a Willie Brown song. Library of Congress matrix 6608-A-3, by Son House.

15. Junior Brooks, "Lone Town Blues," 1951 (2:46). This song is a 1951 recording by Brooks, from Little Rock, Arkansas. His singing style is highly similar to that of Son House in his 1930 recordings. RPM 343, by Junior Brooks.

16. King Solomon Hill, "The Gone Dead Train," 1932 (3:15). This song was the inspiration for the article of the same name in this book. Joe Holmes used a bottleneck in a style similar to that of Salty Dog Sam, whom he played with in south Mississippi. Paramount 13129, by Joe Holmes.

17. "Booker Miller on Charlie Patton," 1968 (0:57). Booker Miller talking about Patton's "trick" of staying sober by eating fat meat at parties. Wardlow interview.

18. Charley Patton, "A Spoonful Blues," 1929 (3:08). The same-titled song that Howlin' Wolf later recorded for Chess. Charley's version is different, with great bottleneck playing. Paramount 12869, by Charley Patton.

19. Charley Booker, "No Ridin' Blues," 1952 (2:52). This song is Booker's rendition of Patton licks from "Green River Blues," which he learned

from a relative who played with Patton. Blues and Rhythm 7003, by Charley Booker.

20. The Confiners, "Harmonica Boogie," 1961 (2:32). This song is a 1961 recording by a blues band of Parchman inmates, one of whom reportedly was from Hattiesburg, where the record label Central was located that released the obscure recordings. Electro 261, by The Confiners.

21. Skip James, "Illinois Blues," 1931 (3:01). This is one of Skippy's more obscure blues recordings in E minor tuning. The song is about a lumber camp where James once worked. Paramount 13072, by Skip James.

22. Tommy Johnson, "Alcohol and Jake Blues," 1930 (3:18). This song is a remake of "Canned Heat Blues," with Bracey talking to Tommy as he sings. Paramount 12950, by Tommy Johnson.

23. "Ishmon Bracey on Tommy Johnson's Death," 1969 (0:55). Ishmon Bracey talking about Tommy Johnson's 1956 death from alcoholism. Wardlow interview.

24. Blind Roosevelt Graves, "Take Your Burdens to the Lord," 3:09 (1929). This type of song was sung at church revivals to win "sinners" to God. Paramount 12874, by Rev. Charles A. Tindley.

25. Dave Edwards, "Done Sold My Soul to the Devil," 1937 (3:02). This song expresses the fact that both rural blacks and rural whites faced the same teachings about blues being the "Devil's Music." Decca 5493, by Harold Gray. Courtesy MCA Records, Inc.; under license from Universal Music Special Markets, Inc.

About the Author and Editor

Gayle Dean Wardlow

Gayle Dean Wardlow co-authored *King of the Delta Blues: The Life of Charlie Patton* (1989) and has written for publications such as *Blues Unlimited, Living Blues, 78 Quarterly,* and *Guitar Player* since 1965. His life and work are described in the "Editor's Introduction" on page vii of this book.

Edward Komara

Edward Komara has been the Music Librarian and Director of the Blues Archive at the University of Mississippi since 1993. He received his degrees at the State University of New York at Buffalo (M.A. in music history, 1992; M.L.S. in library science, 1991) and St. John's College, Annapolis (B.A. in liberal arts, 1988). In addition to his contribution to *Chasin That Devil Music,* he is the author of *The Dial Recordings of Charlie Parker* (Greenwood Press, 1998). His articles have been published in *Guitar One, Black Music Research Journal, Tri-State Blues,* and *Living Blues.*

When it Comes to Music We Wrote the Book

All Music Guide to the Blues
The Experts' Guide to the Best Blues Recordings
Third Edition

Edited by Michael Erlewine, Vladimir Bogdanov, Chris Woodstra, and Cub Koda "...easily the best blues guide to hit the market, both as an encyclopedia and as a tool to help readers pick discs for purchase...a real winner."
—Real Blues

Fully updated and expanded to cover hundreds more artists and recordings, the All Music Guide to The Blues reviews and rates over 3,500 classic blues recordings in all major styles and profiles the lives of 700-plus musicians. This second edition adds a section on gospel—the spiritual sister of the blues.
Softcover, 700pp, ISBN 0-87930-736-6, $24.95.

Roadhouse Blues
Stevie Ray Vaughan and Texas R&B

By Hugh Gregory
Roadhouse Blues profiles the context and traditions of Texas R&B that made Stevie Ray Vaughan one of the best guitarists of the rock era. It examines the roots that the Vaughan brothers drew upon, illuminates the key events from their musical careers, and concludes by evaluating the legacy of Stevie Ray Vaughan following his tragic early death in 1990.
Softcover, 192 pages, ISBN 0-87930-747-1, $19.95

Elwood's Blues
Interviews with the Blues Legends & Stars

By Dan Aykroyd and Ben Manilla
The House of Blues Radio Hour is hosted by Dan Aykroyd in the character of Elwood Blues of The Blues Brothers, and since 1993 he has interviewed over 900 blues and rock greats. This book compiles the best of those, including B.B. King, John Lee Hooker, Ray Charles, Junior Wells, Bobby "Blue" Bland, Bo Diddley and Buddy Guy.
Softcover, 256 pages, ISBN 0-87930-809-5, $17.95

Incurable Blues
The Troubles and Triumph of Blues Legend Hubert Sumlin

By Will Romano
Heard on most of Howlin' Wolf's classic Chess recordings, Hubert Sumlin's guitar style has influenced Eric Clapton, Jimi Hendrix, Keith Richards, and Stevie Ray Vaughn. This authorized biography recounts Sumlin's life, from his birth in the Deep South to the '50s and '60s Chicago blues scene and on to the 21st century.
Softcover, 272 pages, ISBN 0-87930-833-8, $17.95

Slide Guitar
Know the Players, Play the Music

By Pete Madsen
Another entry in the Fretmaster series, this book teaches the history and technique of slide guitar and provides lessons on the playing styles of masters like Robert Johnson, Bonnie Raitt and Brian Jones. The accompanying CD offers specially recorded backing tracks in blues, folk, country and rock, allowing guitarists to explore new sounds.
Spiral with CD, 160 pages, ISBN 0-87930-852-4, $24.95

Guitar Licks of the Brit-Rock Heroes
Clapton, Beck & Page

By Jesse Gress
This guide details the lead guitar styles of three legendary musicians—Eric Clapton, Jeff Beck, and Jimmy Page. Written by guitar expert Jesse Gress, this volume contains 100 easily understood licks that have been constructed after careful study of dozens of the artists' greatest live performances. Every lick features its own mini-lesson and is performed by the author on the accompanying CD.
Softcover w/CD, 112 pages, ISBN 0-87930-796-X, $19.95

AVAILABLE AT FINE BOOK AND MUSIC STORES. OR CONTACT:

Backbeat Books
San Francisco

6600 Silacci Way • Gilroy, California 95020 USA
phone 866 222-5232 fax 408 848-5784
e-mail: backbeat@rushorder.com   www.backbeatbooks.com

Here's what kids have to say to
Mary Pope Osborne, author of
the Magic Tree House series:

*If you didn't make the Magic Tree House Books
I would go nuts!!!!*—Anthony

*Jack gave me the idea of getting a notebook
myself.*—Reid K.

*I hope that you make more Magic Tree House
books. They bring magic to my life.*
—Michell R.

You gave me the courage to read. Thanks!
—Lydia K.

*I like your books because they are very exciting.
It's like I'm traveling around the world with
Jack and Annie.*—Elizabeth C.

Our imaginations are soaring thanks to you!
—Julie M.

Your books inspired me to read, read, read!
—Eliza C.

*Reading your books gave me the idea to write
a book myself.*—Tyler

*I think your books are great. I can't sleep
without reading one.*—Leah Y.

Teachers and librarians love Magic Tree House books, too!

Your stories have been a very special part of every day in our class for the last two years. I read aloud to the class each day and we choose someone who gets to be "Jack/Annie," complete with backpack, glasses and journal. We have props from every book. . . . The children act out what is going on.—L. Horist

Introducing my students to your books is the best thing I've done. . . . Jack and Annie have incredibly helped my students' growth in reading. —D. Boyd

Thank you for these great books. They truly "light the fire within" that helps motivate students to read. I enjoy them myself!—D. Chatwin

It is refreshing as a classroom teacher to be able to use such interesting, informational adventure books to motivate and encourage good reading habits.—R. Trump

You have created a terrific tool for motivating children to learn about historical moments and places.—L. George

As a teacher I love how easily your books tie in with curriculum studies. Science and Social Studies units can easily be supplemented using your series. . . . Your books let my students experience other places and times beyond their front door.—T. Gaussoin

Due to your wide variety of settings, my students are learning an invaluable amount of information about history and the world around them, sometimes without even realizing it.
—L. Arnts

It amazes me how these books easily lured my students into wanting to read.—T. Lovelady

Dear Readers,

Last year, while my husband Will and I were doing research for our Magic Tree House Research Guide on rain forests, we visited the Bronx Zoo in New York. As we passed by the gorilla area, we saw a large gorilla sitting under a tree. She was staring very intently at us. We said hi to her—and she stuck out her tongue at us! I'm convinced she was just trying to make us laugh. And we did! In fact, we still laugh whenever we think about that moment.

We found out later that the gorilla's name is Pattycake. I keep a photograph of Pattycake on my desk, and I feel as if she's a giant, friendly spirit who overlooks all my work.

I love gorillas more than I can say. And I hope that by the time you finish reading Good Morning, Gorillas, you'll love them as much as I do.

All my best,

Mary Pope Osborne

MAGIC TREE HOUSE® #26

Good Morning, Gorillas

by Mary Pope Osborne

illustrated by Sal Murdocca

SCHOLASTIC INC.

New York Toronto London Auckland Sydney
Mexico City New Delhi Hong Kong Buenos Aires

For Dr. Michael Pope

ISBN 0-439-54012-7

36 35 34 33 32   13 14 15 16/0

Printed in the U.S.A.   40

First Scholastic printing, September 2003

Contents

Prologue

One summer day in Frog Creek, Pennsylvania, a mysterious tree house appeared in the woods.

Eight-year-old Jack and his seven-year-old sister, Annie, climbed into the tree house. They found that it was filled with books.

Jack and Annie soon discovered that the tree house was magic. It could take them to the places in the books. All they had to do was point to a picture and wish to go there. While they are gone, no time at all passes in Frog Creek.

Along the way, Jack and Annie discovered that the tree house belongs to Morgan le Fay. Morgan is a magical librarian of Camelot, the long-ago kingdom of King Arthur. She travels through time and space, gathering books.

In Magic Tree House Books #5–8, Jack and Annie help free Morgan from a spell. In Books #9–12, they solve four ancient riddles and become Master Librarians.

In Magic Tree House Books #13–16, Jack and Annie have to save four ancient stories from being lost forever. In Magic Tree House Books #17–20, Jack and Annie free a mysterious little dog from a magic spell. In Magic Tree House Books #21–24, Jack and Annie help save Camelot. In Magic Tree House Books #25–28, Jack and Annie learn about different kinds of magic.

1

Dark and Rainy

Tap-tap-tap.

Jack sat up in bed. Rain tapped against his window. His clock said 5 A.M. It was still dark outside.

Annie peeked into his room.

"Are you awake?" she whispered.

"Yep," said Jack.

"Ready to find some special magic?" she asked.

"Maybe we should wait," said Jack. "It's so dark and rainy."

3

"*No* waiting," said Annie. "I'll get an umbrella. You bring a flashlight. Meet you downstairs."

"Okay, okay," said Jack.

He jumped out of bed. He pulled on his clothes and put on a jacket. Then he grabbed his backpack and flashlight.

Jack slipped downstairs and out the front door. Annie stood on the porch in jeans and a T-shirt. The air was chilly and breezy.

"Don't you need a sweater or something?" said Jack.

"I'm okay," she said. "Let's go."

Annie raised the umbrella. Jack turned on the flashlight. They followed a circle of rainy light down their street into the woods.

They headed through the Frog Creek woods. The flashlight lit up the trees—the wet leaves and dark branches. Then it shined on a dangling rope ladder.

Jack raised the flashlight beam.

"There it is," he said.

A circle of light lit the magic tree house.

"Morgan's not there," said Annie. "I can tell."

"Maybe she left us a message," said Jack.

Jack grabbed the rope ladder and started up. Annie put the umbrella down and followed. When they climbed inside, Jack shined the flashlight around the tree house.

Morgan le Fay wasn't there. But the scrolls from their trip to old England were.

"Here's proof we found a special magic yesterday," she said.

"Yeah," said Jack, smiling. "*Theater* magic." He had great memories of acting in a play by their friend William Shakespeare.

"Did Morgan leave us a new secret rhyme?" asked Jack.

He shined the flashlight on a book lying under the window. A piece of paper was sticking out of the book.

"Yes!" said Annie. She picked up the book and pulled out the paper.

Jack shined his light on the paper while Annie read aloud:

Dear Annie and Jack,

Good luck on your second journey to find a special magic. This secret rhyme will guide you:

*To find a special kind of magic
in worlds so far apart,
speak a special language,
talk with your hands and heart.*

*Thank you,
Morgan*

"What kind of language does she mean?" Jack asked.

"I guess we'll find out," said Annie. "Where are we going?"

Jack shined the flashlight on the cover of the book. It showed huge trees partly hidden by mist. The title was:

AN AFRICAN RAIN FOREST

"*Rain* forest?" said Jack. "Good thing we brought our umbrella and flashlight. Remember the rain in the *Amazon* rain forest? Remember how dark it was under the treetops?"

"Yeah," said Annie. "Remember the spiders and scary ants?"

"Well . . . ," Jack said, "not all rain forests have the same bugs."

"Remember the river snakes?" said Annie. "And the crocodiles?"

7

"Well . . . ," said Jack, "not all rain forests have big rivers. There are different kinds of rain forests, you know."

"Right," said Annie. She pointed to the cover of the book. "I wish we could go there."

The wind started to blow.

"Oh, remember the jaguar?" said Annie. "And the vampire bats?"

"Wait!" said Jack.

But it was too late. The wind was blowing harder. The tree house started to spin.

It spun faster and faster.

Then everything was still.

Absolutely still.

2

Cloud Forest

Jack opened his eyes.

"I can't tell *what* kind of rain forest this is," said Annie. She stared out the window.

Jack looked out, too. It seemed to be daytime, but he couldn't see much of anything. The quiet forest was covered with fog.

Jack opened their research book and read:

> The misty rain forest in the mountains of central Africa is called a "cloud forest."

"Oh, I get it," said Annie. "We're up so high, it's like we're in a cloud."

"Cool," said Jack. He pulled out his notebook and wrote:

cloud forest—rain forest high

up in mountains

10

Then he read more:

**The African cloud forest is home to
many animals, including elephants,
water buffaloes, black leopards ...**

Jack looked up.
"Black leopards?" he said.

11

"Don't worry," said Annie.

Jack cleared his throat and kept reading:

. . . antelopes, wild hogs, and gorillas.

"*Gorillas?*" said Annie.

"Don't worry," said Jack.

"I'm not worried. I *love* gorillas," said Annie. "They're totally great!"

"I don't know about that," said Jack. He pictured huge apes pounding their chests. "I'd like to study them, though. Write down their habits and behavior, just like a real scientist."

"Whatever," said Annie. "Let's just go. This'll be a fun adventure!" She took off down the ladder.

Jack threw his notebook, the research book, and the flashlight into his pack. He hooked the umbrella over his arm. Then he followed Annie.

When they stepped onto the ground, Jack could see better. The fog had turned into a fine mist.

Jack and Annie started through the cloud forest. They walked around huge trees draped with moss. They pushed past tall shrubs and leafy plants.

"Wow, look at *that* tree," said Annie.

She pointed to a fat tree. It had wide lower limbs padded with thick cushions of moss.

"It looks like a piece of furniture," said Annie, "like an armchair."

"Yeah," said Jack. "I better draw it."

He put the umbrella on the ground. He pulled the flashlight out of his pack and put it next to the umbrella. Then he took out his notebook and pencil.

As Annie walked ahead, Jack started to draw a simple picture of the fat tree.

"Hey, Jack," Annie called in a whispery voice. "Come here. Quick!"

Jack grabbed his pack. He moved around the tree and caught up with Annie.

"Listen," she said.

Jack heard branches snap.

Crack!

A leopard? he wondered.

Crack! Crack!

Jack nervously looked around the forest.

"Maybe we should go back up to the tree house," he said. "We could read a little more and learn a little more."

Annie didn't answer. Jack turned to her.

She was grinning from ear to ear as she stared into the bushes. Jack followed her gaze.

A dark, shaggy little head was peeking out from a cluster of leaves.

"Bu, bu?" a small gorilla asked.

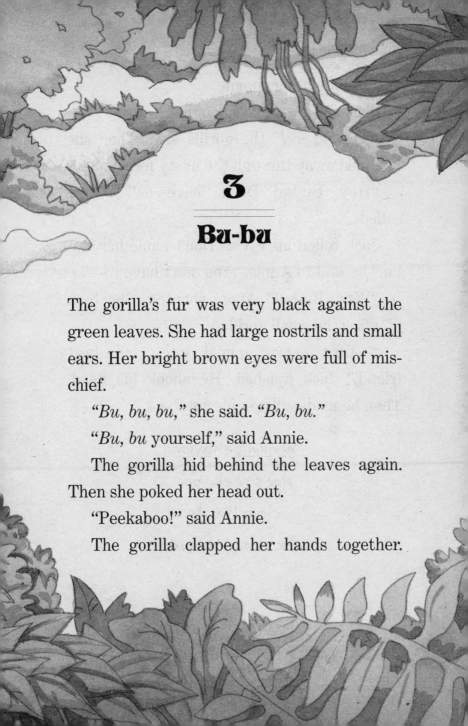

3

Bu-bu

The gorilla's fur was very black against the green leaves. She had large nostrils and small ears. Her bright brown eyes were full of mischief.

"*Bu, bu, bu,*" she said. "*Bu, bu.*"

"*Bu, bu* yourself," said Annie.

The gorilla hid behind the leaves again. Then she poked her head out.

"Peekaboo!" said Annie.

The gorilla clapped her hands together.

She stuck out her tongue.

Jack and Annie both laughed.

"Bu, bu, bu!" the gorilla said. Then she bounded away through the misty forest.

"Hey, Bu-bu! Don't leave us!" Annie called.

Jack rolled his eyes. "Don't name her Bu-bu," he said to Annie. "You don't have to—"

"Wait, Bu-bu!" Annie shouted. She took off after the small gorilla.

"—turn every animal into your best friend," Jack finished. He shook his head. Then he made a list in his notebook.

<u>gorilla behavior</u>

plays peekaboo

claps hands

sticks out tongue

As he wrote, Jack heard Annie laughing. But then he heard high shrieks.

He caught his breath. *A leopard?* he wondered.

Carrying his notebook, Jack hurried in the direction of the noise. He found Annie and the small gorilla perched in two trees.

"What's wrong?" said Jack, standing beneath the trees.

"Nothing!" called Annie. "We're just playing."

The small gorilla screeched again. Then she scratched her head and hiccuped.

Annie screeched, too. She scratched *her* head and hiccuped.

While they played, Jack studied the gorilla a bit more.

He noticed she was about the size of a

three-year-old kid. Her fingers looked like human fingers. They even had fingernails! He made a new list:

<u>young gorilla</u>
size of 3-year-old
fingers like humans'
fingernails

Jack heard the tree leaves shaking. He looked up. Annie and the gorilla had both climbed higher.

"Hey, come down, Annie!" Jack called. "You might fall. Plus, it's getting dark."

Jack looked around. Light was fading quickly from the forest. *Is night falling?* he wondered. *Or is a storm coming?*

The small gorilla screeched again and climbed even higher.

"Hey, Bu-bu! Where you going?" said Annie. She climbed even higher, too.

"That's enough, Annie. Come down *now*!" said Jack. "I'm serious."

To his relief, the gorilla settled on a branch. Annie did the same.

The gorilla broke off a piece of tree bark. She nibbled it like a candy bar.

Annie broke off a piece of bark. She nibbled it like a candy bar, too.

The gorilla threw down her bark. She grabbed a tree branch and swung to another tree.

"Don't try it, Annie!" shouted Jack.

But his warning came too late.

Annie threw down her bark. She grabbed a tree branch and *tried* to swing to another tree.

Annie didn't swing like a gorilla. She fell

from the tree—and crashed down to the ground near Jack.

"Annie!" he cried.

4

Nightmare

Jack knelt beside Annie. She was gasping for breath.

The gorilla bounded down the tree and over to Annie. She bit her lower lip as if she were worried.

"Are you okay?" Jack asked Annie.

"Yes—" Annie panted, "just—got the breath—knocked out of me—"

"Wiggle your arms and your legs," said Jack.

23

Annie wiggled her arms and her legs.

"Good, nothing's broken," said Jack.

Just then, he felt a drop of water hit his arm. The mist had turned to rain.

"Uh-oh," said Jack. He threw his notebook into his pack.

"I better get our umbrella and flashlight," he said. "I left them near that tree that looked like a chair."

"I'll come, too," said Annie. She started to sit up.

"No, no, catch your breath," said Jack. "It's not far. I'll be right back."

He took off his jacket and draped it over her. "This'll help you stay dry," he said. He pulled on his pack and stood up.

The gorilla screeched.

"Stay with Annie!" said Jack.

Then he dashed back through the cloud forest. He looked for the fat tree with the wide limbs padded with moss.

As he peered through the growing darkness, Jack saw *many* fat trees. He saw *many* limbs padded with moss.

Soon he could hardly see trees at all. He realized that both a storm *and* night had come to the forest.

Forget the umbrella and flashlight, he thought. It was more important to get back to Annie before it was too dark. They could wait together for daylight.

As Jack started back to Annie, he could hardly see. He didn't know which way to go.

"Annie! Bu-bu!" he shouted. He felt silly shouting, "Bu-bu." But he didn't know what else to call the small gorilla.

Jack put out his hands. He moved slowly through the dark, rainy forest. He kept calling for Annie and Bu-bu. He listened for them. But he couldn't hear anything above the loud patter of the rain.

"Ahh!" he shouted. He had run into something that felt like a ball of spiderwebs!

As he jumped back, he slipped and fell in the mud. He crawled over to a tree and huddled between two of its giant roots.

I'll just wait here until morning, he thought. *Then I'll find Annie. Or she'll find me.*

As rain dripped all around him, Jack wondered if leopards came out at night. He quickly pushed the thought away. He tried to think about morning and finding Annie and going home.

He was *really* ready to go home.

Why did Morgan even send us to the cloud forest? he wondered. He tried to remember the secret rhyme.

"To find a special magic . . . ," he whispered. He couldn't remember the rest. He felt tired and miserable. He took his backpack off and rested his head on it. He closed his eyes.

"To find a special magic . . . ," he mumbled.

But he couldn't find the magic. He couldn't even find the words that finished the rhyme. Worst of all, he couldn't find Annie.

Their fun adventure in the cloud forest had turned into a nightmare.

5

Silverback

Jack felt something tugging on his sleeve. He opened his eyes.

Bu-bu. The small gorilla was staring at him in the dawn light.

Jack stood up. His arms and legs felt stiff and achy. His wet clothes stuck to his skin.

He looked around the cloud forest. Misty sunlight shined through the tree branches.

"Where's Annie?" he asked the small gorilla.

Bu-bu waved her arms. Then she bounded off between the trees. Jack pulled on his pack and followed.

As the small gorilla led him through the cloud forest, her head bobbed above the leafy plants. Finally, she stopped before a row of shrubs.

Jack took a few steps forward and peered over the shrubs.

"Oh, man," he whispered.

Large dark figures were sleeping in an open, grassy area—*gorillas!* There were at least ten of them. Some slept on their backs. Some slept on their bellies.

The gorillas were all sizes. The smallest was a baby sleeping in its mother's arms. The biggest was a giant with black and silver fur.

Jack pulled the book out of his pack. He

found a chapter on gorillas and read:

Mountain gorillas live together in families. The leader of the family is a large male called a "silverback" because he has silver fur on his back and shoulders. Gorillas do not hunt other animals. They mainly eat the plant growth of the forest. They are known to be shy and gentle giants.

"Shy and gentle giants," Jack repeated. That sounded good.

He peered over the shrubs again. Bu-bu waved at him. She was standing at the far edge of the clearing. She pointed to something in the tall grass.

Annie was fast asleep in the grass!

Jack didn't know what to do. If he called her name, the gorillas would wake up. He had

30

only one choice. He had to sneak over to her.

Jack put his book in his pack. He pushed past the shrubs and stepped into the clearing. His heart was pounding. He thought of the words from the book—*shy and gentle giants*.

As he started toward Annie, he heard a grunt. The giant gorilla with silver fur opened his eyes. When the gorilla saw Jack, he sat up.

Jack stopped in his tracks.

The gorilla just glared. *This* giant did not seem shy or gentle at all.

Jack saw a stick lying on the ground. He picked it up—just in case.

Jack's stick made the gorilla growl. He stood up. He was *very* tall and *very* wide.

Jack dropped his stick.

Bu-bu ran and hid behind a tree.

The silverback growled again. His long, shaggy arms touched the ground. His fingers curled under. Walking on his knuckles, he stepped toward Jack.

Jack stepped back.

The gorilla stepped forward.

Jack stepped back again.

The gorilla kept stepping forward. Jack kept stepping back until he had stepped out of the clearing.

But the silverback kept coming. Jack stumbled back through the brush until he came to a thick wall of plants.

The gorilla kept coming. Jack couldn't move back anymore.

"Uh . . . hi," he said nervously. He held up his hand. "I come in—"

Before Jack could say "peace," the giant gorilla went crazy. He hooted and leaped to his feet.

Jack crouched down in a panic.

The gorilla kept hooting. He grabbed a tree limb. He shook it wildly. He ripped leaves from branches.

He gnashed his teeth. He cupped his hands. He beat his chest.

WRAAGH! he roared. *WRAAGH!*

The gorilla dropped on all fours. He charged back and forth past Jack. Then he threw himself on his belly. He began bashing the ground with his palms. He bashed and bashed and bashed.

Jack scrambled on his hands and knees over to a tree. He hid behind the trunk, hugging his head.

He waited for the maniac gorilla to find him and tear him to pieces.

6

Good Morning, Gorillas

The pounding ended. There was silence . . . a long silence.

Jack opened his eyes. He peeked around the tree. The silverback was sitting on the ground. His lips were curved in a smile. He looked pleased with himself.

Was his whole act a fake? Jack wondered.

Jack didn't know whether to be scared or to laugh. The only thing he *did* know was he still had to get to Annie!

Jack pulled out the research book. He found the gorilla chapter again. He read:

> To safely get close to gorillas in the wild, it's wise to act like a gorilla yourself. Crouch down and rest on your knuckles like a gorilla. Keep your head down and act friendly!

Jack packed up his research book. He put his pack on his back. Then he went down on his knees.

Jack took a deep breath. He smiled a friendly smile. Pressing down on his knuckles, he moved out from behind the tree. His fingers hurt as he walked on them.

The silverback grunted.

Jack didn't look up. He kept smiling a friendly smile as he crawled through the brush toward the clearing.

When he got to the edge of the clearing, he glanced back. The giant gorilla was following him. He was frowning, but he didn't seem about to attack.

Jack kept going. He moved into the clearing. Then he stopped.

More gorillas were waking up. A large gorilla hugged Bu-bu as if to comfort her.

When Bu-bu saw Jack, she screeched joyfully.

All the other gorillas turned to look at him. They made nervous sounds.

Jack's heart pounded. But he just smiled his friendly smile and kept crawling. He crawled around the gorillas and over to Annie.

"Wake up!" he said, shaking her.

Annie yawned, then opened her eyes.

"Oh, hi!" she said.

38

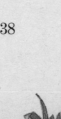

"Are you okay?" asked Jack.

"Sure," she said. She sat up and looked around. She gasped.

The gorillas were staring at Jack and Annie with bright, darting eyes. The silverback stared the hardest.

"Oh, wow!" said Annie. A joyful smile crossed her face. "Good morning, gorillas!"

7

Eating Out

Annie kept smiling at the gorillas. "Wow!" she said. "Wow, wow, wow."

"Didn't you know you were sleeping next to them?" Jack asked.

"No!" she said. "When you didn't come back, Bu-bu led me here. But I couldn't see anything. It was too dark."

Just then, Bu-bu left her mother's arms and bounded over to Annie. She climbed into Annie's lap and hugged her.

Another small gorilla left his mother and ran over to Annie, too. He was about the size of a two-year-old kid.

"*Ho, ho!*" he said. He gave Annie a playful poke.

"Ho, ho yourself!" said Annie. "Is Ho-ho your name?"

She tickled Ho-ho. She tickled Bu-bu, too. The two small gorillas made laughing sounds and fell onto their backs.

The two mother gorillas laughed, too. *Huh-huh-huh*, they said.

Jack felt a little jealous. He wanted the gorillas to like him as well. But he didn't know how to join in the fun. So he just sighed and pulled out his notebook. He added to his "gorilla behavior" list:

gorillas like to tickle and laugh

41

Suddenly, he heard a low growl.

He looked up. The silverback had moved closer to him. He was glaring.

"That big guy doesn't understand what you're doing!" Annie called to Jack. "He's never seen anyone take notes before."

Jack quickly put his notebook away.

The giant gorilla huffed. Then he turned to his family and gave a short bark.

The gorillas began lining up behind the silverback. The baby traveled in his mother's arms. Ho-ho traveled on his mother's back. Bu-bu and Annie held hands. They all followed the silverback out of the clearing.

"Come on!" Annie called to Jack. "Let's go with Big Guy and the gang!"

Jack shook his head.

"I don't think they want *me* to come along," he said.

Bu-bu screeched at Jack. She held out her free hand to him.

"*Bu-bu* wants you!" said Annie.

Jack smiled shyly. He took Bu-bu's small, warm hand. Then he walked with Annie and the gorillas out of the clearing.

On their ramble through the cloud forest, the gorillas found food everywhere. They munched flowers and ferns and leaves. They swallowed and burped.

They munched twigs and branches and pieces of bark and bamboo. They swallowed and burped.

As the gorillas ate breakfast, it started to rain again. But they didn't seem to mind.

Annie didn't seem to mind, either. She and Bu-bu played tag in the drizzly woods. They ran around the trees, laughing and screeching.

43

Jack tried to follow them, but he gave up. He was tired and cold. Shivering, he stood under a mossy tree to keep dry.

While he was alone, Jack sneaked his notebook out of his pack. He made a new list:

gorilla foods

flowers

ferns

leaves

twigs

bark

branches

bamboo

As he wrote, he heard a low growl. He looked up.

Big Guy had spotted him. The silverback

was standing close by. He was frowning at Jack, his lips tucked in a tight line.

"Sorry, sorry!" said Jack. He quickly put away his notebook.

Big Guy kept frowning.

Jack quickly tried to act like a gorilla. He went down on all fours. He tore off the leaf of a plant. He took a bite. It tasted bitter, like vinegar. Jack pretended to munch and swallow and burp.

Big Guy huffed, then moved on. As soon as he was gone, Jack spat out the leaf.

"Yuck, yuck, yuck!" he said, wiping his tongue.

Jack felt a tap on his back. He jumped. But it was just Ho-ho. The small gorilla offered him a twig to eat.

"Oh, no thanks, Ho-ho," said Jack.

Ho-ho kept holding out the twig.

"Oh, okay," said Jack, politely taking it. "I'll eat it later." He put the twig into his backpack.

Ho-ho's mom came over to Jack. She held some berries to his lips.

"Uh, no thanks," Jack said.

The gorilla stared at him with a sad look.

"Oh, okay," said Jack. He opened his mouth. And Ho-ho's mom fed him the berries.

Jack munched the berries. To his surprise, they tasted good. He swallowed, then burped just like a gorilla. This time, he wasn't pretending.

Bu-bu's mom then came over to Jack. She offered him some rainwater from a cupped plant. Jack was very thirsty. He sipped the water. It tasted fresh and cold.

46

Bu-bu's mom took Jack's hand in her wide hand. She led him through the forest to Annie and Bu-bu.

Bu-bu screeched happily when she saw Jack. She threw her furry arms around him.

"Hi! We missed you!" Annie said to Jack. "Are you having fun?"

Jack smiled and nodded.

Actually, he *was* having fun now. He didn't mind the rain so much anymore. He didn't feel so left out. Some of the gorillas really seemed to like him, he thought. They seemed to like him a lot.

8

A Special Language

The rain ended. Slowly the feeding came to a stop.

Big Guy led his family into a clearing. The tall grass sparkled with misty sunlight.

The silverback lay down and tucked his arms under his head.

The other gorillas gathered around him. Some beat the grasses until they were flat.

Ho-ho's mom made a bed of weed stalks for Ho-ho. Bu-bu's mom made a bed of leaves for Bu-bu. Then she made two extra beds for Jack and Annie.

They lay down with all the gorillas to take their naps. Jack used his backpack for a pillow.

Lying on his leafy bed, Jack watched the mother of the baby gorilla groom her small baby. The mother parted his hair and searched through it, picking at his skin now and then.

The baby soon wiggled free and crawled around in the grass. His mother's gaze then rested on Annie. She moved over to Annie and gently grabbed one of her pigtails. She studied it carefully.

"What are you doing?" Annie asked.

"She's looking for bugs, I think," said Jack.

"Oh, yuck!" said Annie, sitting up.

Jack laughed. Just then, the baby's mother reached for him.

"Oops! No thanks! No bugs on me!" he said, and he sat up, too.

The mother gorilla lay back in the grass and closed her eyes. Her baby crawled over to Annie.

"Hi, Little Guy," Annie said tenderly. She picked up the baby and stroked his head. The baby smiled at her and closed his eyes.

While all the gorillas napped, Jack sneaked the book out of his pack. He found the gorilla chapter. He read softly to Annie:

> Gorillas are very smart. A captive gorilla named Koko has even learned sign language. Sign language is a special language used by people who cannot hear. Koko can say—

51

"*What?*" Annie said loudly. "*Sign* language? A *special language?*"

Her voice woke Bu-bu and Ho-ho. They sat up and rubbed their eyes.

"So?" said Jack.

"Morgan's secret *rhyme!*" said Annie. "Don't you remember?" She repeated the rhyme:

*To find a special kind of magic
in worlds so far apart,
speak a special language,
talk with your hands and heart.*

"Oh . . . yeah!" said Jack.

"I even know a little sign language," said Annie. "In school, we learned how to sign *I love you.*"

Annie held up a closed hand. Slowly she lifted her thumb, index finger, and little finger. She showed the sign to Bu-bu and Ho-ho.

"I—love—you," she said slowly.

The small gorillas looked curious.

Jack made the sign, too.

"I—love—you," he said to Bu-bu and Ho-ho.

The two little gorillas stared at Annie and Jack. Then both of them held up their hands. They tried to make the same sign.

"They love us, too!" said Annie.

"Wow," said Jack. He glanced over at Big Guy.

The silverback's eyes were open! He was watching them. Jack quickly closed the book. To his relief, the giant gorilla turned over.

"Well," Annie said with a sigh, "I guess that does it."

"We spoke a special language," said Jack. "We talked with our—" Before he could finish his sentence, Bu-bu pushed him.

"Whoa!" said Jack.

Ho-ho held his little arms above his head. He reared back and charged at Jack. With a flying tackle, he knocked Jack over.

"What's going on?" said Jack.

"They want to play with you!" said Annie.

Bu-bu jumped on Jack and put him in a headlock. Jack broke free from the two small

54

gorillas. He jumped up and dashed into the forest.

Bu-bu and Ho-ho charged after him.

Annie carried Little Guy and followed. She laughed as the small gorillas looked for Jack.

Jack hid behind a tree. He pushed his glasses into place. He waited for Bu-bu.

In a moment, she walked by.

"BOO!" Jack shouted, jumping out.

Bu-bu screeched and leaped straight up in the air. Jack cracked up laughing.

Bu-bu didn't laugh, though. She bit her lip. She hid her face behind her hands.

"Ohhh, Bu-bu," said Annie. "Don't be scared."

She gently put the baby on the ground. She reached out to comfort Bu-bu.

Bu-bu wrapped her arms around Annie's

neck. She buried her furry head in Annie's shoulder.

"Jack was just playing," said Annie.

Bu-bu raised her head. She looked at Jack over Annie's shoulder.

"Friends?" he asked softly.

Bu-bu stuck her tongue out at him.

Jack laughed. Bu-bu showed her teeth in a big smile.

"Friends!" said Jack.

Just then, Ho-ho started screeching. Jack and Annie looked around. Ho-ho was pointing into the bushes.

"Where's Little Guy?" said Annie. She and Jack dashed around the shrubs.

The baby had crawled to a tree. He was looking up at a branch.

A huge, sleek cat with black fur was sitting on the branch. His pale green eyes stared down at the baby gorilla. He looked hungry.

"*A black leopard,*" breathed Jack.

The leopard leaped lightly down from his perch. He faced Little Guy. The baby looked scared.

"No!" cried Annie.

She ran over to the baby gorilla and scooped him into her arms.

The leopard let out a snarl. He lowered his head and started slowly toward Annie and the baby.

Jack panicked. He didn't know what to do at first. Then he remembered Big Guy's act. Jack took a deep breath. When he let it out, he made a loud hooting sound.

He tore out from the brush. Hooting like a silverback, he ran between Annie and the leopard.

Jack grabbed a tree limb and shook it. He ripped leaves from branches.

He cupped his hands. He beat his chest.

"WRAAGH!" he roared. *"WRAAGH!"*

Then Jack leaned over and charged back and forth past the leopard.

Finally, he threw himself on his belly. He began bashing the ground with his palms. He bashed and bashed and bashed.

"Jack!" Annie called. "Jack!"

Jack looked up.

"He's gone," Annie said in a quiet voice. "The leopard's gone. He left a while ago."

"Oh," said Jack.

He sat up.

He pushed his glasses into place. He looked around. Then he smiled.

9

Good-bye, Gorillas

Jack couldn't stop smiling. He had scared off a leopard!

Bu-bu and Ho-ho stared at Jack with awe. Annie looked at him with awe, too.

"When did you learn to do *that*?" she asked.

Before Jack could answer, he heard a rustling in the brush. Then Big Guy stepped out from the shrubs.

The giant gorilla walked silently over to Annie. He took Little Guy from her and put the baby on his back. Then he touched Annie's cheek gently.

Annie grinned at him.

Bu-bu and Ho-ho ran to Big Guy and clung to his legs.

The giant gorilla barked at the small ones, directing them to come with him.

As he walked past Jack, Big Guy stopped.

Huh-huh-huh, he said in a low voice. He reached out toward Jack.

Jack ducked.

But the silverback patted him on the head. Then he and the small gorillas moved out of sight.

Jack felt as if the top of his head were glowing.

"Wow," he whispered. "Did you see what he just did?"

"Yeah," said Annie. "He must have

watched the show you put on. He was proud of you."

"Well, he was proud of you, too," Jack said modestly.

Annie nodded, smiling. "I guess it's time to leave now," she said.

"Leave?" said Jack.

"We have to say good-bye now," said Annie.

"Good-bye?" said Jack. He didn't want to say good-bye to the gorillas. He loved them. They were totally great.

"Yeah," Annie said softly. "Come on."

She led the way back through the shrubs, around the trees, to the clearing.

They found all the gorillas awake. Some were stretching and yawning. Others were munching on grass or leaves.

The baby was back in his mother's arms. Bu-bu and Ho-ho were chattering away to their moms.

They're probably telling them what I did, Jack thought.

He and Annie walked over to Big Guy and stood in front of him. The other gorillas gathered around.

"We have to go now," Annie said to all of them.

"We have to say good-bye," said Jack.

"Thanks for letting us be a part of your family," said Annie.

She and Jack held up their hands and waved. The gorillas looked sad. They murmured soft sounds.

Big Guy lifted his hand in the air as if he were about to wave. But instead, the

63

silverback raised his thumb, his index finger, and his little finger.

I love you, the giant gorilla signed.

Jack couldn't believe his eyes.

Annie signed back, *I love you.*

Jack signed, too.

The silverback stared at them for a long moment with a gentle, shy look. Then he turned away and gave a short bark to his family.

All the gorillas lined up behind him. The baby's mother held her baby close. Ho-ho rode piggyback on his mom. Bu-bu held her mom's hand.

The silverback started away from the clearing. The others followed.

Bu-bu was the only one who looked back. She screeched and waved at Jack and Annie. Then she walked away, out of sight.

Jack couldn't talk. His heart was too full. He took a few steps in the direction of the gorillas.

"Hey—" Annie said softly. "You're going the wrong way."

Jack looked back at her.

"The tree house is over there," she said. She pointed in the opposite direction—at the tree house peeking out from the fog.

Jack sighed. Then he turned and started to follow her out of the clearing.

"Oh, don't forget this," said Annie.

She leaned over and picked up Jack's backpack from the grass. She handed it to him.

"Thanks," he said.

They kept walking.

"And don't forget *this*," said Annie. She picked up Jack's jacket from under a tree. She handed it to him.

"Thanks," said Jack. He tied his jacket around his waist. They kept walking.

"And don't forget *these*," said Annie. She pointed to the flashlight and umbrella. They lay on the grass under the wide, mossy limbs of a fat tree.

Annie picked them up and carried them herself.

It started to drizzle again just as she and Jack got to the rope ladder. They climbed up into the tree house.

When they got inside, they looked out the window. Jack hoped to catch one last glimpse of the gorilla family.

But there was nothing to see. A white mist covered the cloud forest.

Annie picked up the Pennsylvania book. She pointed to a picture of Frog Creek woods.

"I wish we could go home," she said.

Suddenly, a joyous screech rang out. The

happy, wild sound shot through the white mist, through the cool rain, straight into Jack's heart.

He opened his mouth to answer the call of the gorillas. But it was too late. The wind began to blow.

The tree house started to spin.

It spun faster and faster.

Then everything was still.

Absolutely still.

10

A Special Magic

Tap-tap-tap.

Jack opened his eyes.

The Frog Creek woods were still dark and rainy.

"We're home," Annie said.

Jack sighed.

"I miss them already," he said.

"Me too," said Annie. "Did you take a lot of notes on their habits and behavior?"

Jack shrugged.

"I listed a few things about them," he said. "But sometimes lists don't tell you much. You have to love gorillas to *really* know them."

"Yeah. That's right," said Annie.

Jack opened his backpack. He pulled out their research book and put it in the corner.

Then he pulled out the twig that Ho-ho had given him. He smiled as he showed it to Annie.

"I promised Ho-ho I'd eat this later," he said. "But I think we should save it for Morgan instead."

"Good idea," said Annie. "It'll prove to her that we found a special magic."

"Yeah, *gorilla* magic," said Jack.

"The magic of *all* animals," said Annie.

"Yeah," said Jack.

He placed the twig next to the scrolls they'd brought back from old England.

"Let's go," said Annie. She started down.

Jack pulled on his backpack. He put the flashlight in his pack. Then he grabbed the umbrella and followed Annie.

They started through the Frog Creek woods. It was still cool and dark and rainy.

Jack didn't mind, though. He didn't put on his jacket. He didn't take out the flashlight. He didn't put up the umbrella.

Jack felt as if he weren't completely human yet. There was still a bit of gorilla left in him.

"*Ho, ho, ho,*" he said in a low voice.

"*Bu, bu,*" Annie said back.

"*Huh, huh, huh,*" they said together.

71

MORE FACTS FOR
JACK AND ANNIE AND *YOU*!

Gorillas are the biggest members of the group of animals we call *primates*. Other primates include chimpanzees, orangutans, gibbons, baboons, monkeys, and humans.

All gorillas live in Africa. There are three groups of gorillas—western lowland gorillas, eastern lowland gorillas, and mountain gorillas. Mountain gorillas are the largest gorillas. They have longer hair and longer jaws and teeth than lowland gorillas.

Mountain gorillas live in the volcanic mountains of Virunga in east-central Africa. The word *virunga* means "a lonely mountain that reaches to the clouds."

Gorillas are mainly *herbivores*, or plant-eaters. They keep on the move, so they will not deplete a feeding area. A silverback gorilla can eat up to 50 pounds of forest vegetation in only one day.

ENDANGERED SPECIES

All gorillas are on the endangered species list. But the ones most threatened are the mountain gorillas. Fewer than 650 still live in the wild. None live in captivity. A woman named Dian Fossey lived for almost 20 years with the mountain gorillas. During her life, she fought very hard for their protection.

GORILLAS AND
AMERICAN SIGN LANGUAGE

Since 1971, a lowland gorilla named Koko has been part of a gorilla language project in California. Gorillas will never be able to talk like people because their vocal cords cannot make the necessary range of sounds. But a woman named Penny Patterson taught Koko the gorilla how to use *American Sign Language.* American Sign Language is a special language using hand gestures. It is primarily used by people who are unable to hear. Koko has learned to make more than 1,000 signs. And she understands about 2,000 English words. She proves that gorillas have extraordinary intelligence, as well as many thoughts and feelings similar to those of humans.

Discover the facts behind the fiction!

Do you love the *real* things you find out in the Magic Tree House books? Join Jack and Annie as they share all the great research they've done about the cool places they've been in the

MAGIC TREE HOUSE® RESEARCH GUIDES

The must-have companions for your favorite Magic Tree House adventures!

Don't miss the next Magic Tree House book,
when Jack and Annie meet the Pilgrims and
nearly burn dinner in . . .

MAGIC TREE HOUSE® #27

THANKSGIVING ON THURSDAY

September 2003

*ALSO AVAILABLE ON AUDIO FROM LISTENING LIBRARY, READ BY MARY POPE OSBORNE!

Where have *you* traveled in the

MAGIC TREE HOUSE®?

#1–4: The Mystery of the Tree House*

❏ **#1 DINOSAURS BEFORE DARK** Jack and Annie find the tree house and travel to the time of dinosaurs.

❏ **#2 THE KNIGHT AT DAWN** Jack and Annie go to the time of knights and explore a castle.

❏ **#3 MUMMIES IN THE MORNING** Jack and Annie go to ancient Egypt and get lost in a pyramid while helping a ghost queen.

❏ **#4 PIRATES PAST NOON** Jack and Annie travel back in time and meet pirates with a treasure map.

#5–8: The Mystery of the Magic Spell*

☐ **#5 NIGHT OF THE NINJAS** Jack and Annie go to old Japan and learn the secrets of the ninjas.

☐ **#6 AFTERNOON ON THE AMAZON** Jack and Annie go to the Amazon rain forest and are greeted by army ants, crocodiles, and flesh-eating piranhas.

☐ **#7 SUNSET OF THE SABERTOOTH** Jack and Annie go back to the Ice Age—the world of woolly mammoths, sabertooth tigers, and a mysterious sorcerer.

☐ **#8 MIDNIGHT ON THE MOON** Jack and Annie go *forward* in time and explore the moon.

#9–12: The Mystery of the Ancient Riddles*

☐ **#9 DOLPHINS AT DAYBREAK** Jack and Annie take a mini-submarine into the world of sharks and dolphins.

❏ **#10 GHOST TOWN AT SUNDOWN** Jack and Annie travel to the Wild West, where they battle horse thieves, meet a kindly cowboy, and get help from a ghost.

❏ **#11 LIONS AT LUNCHTIME** Jack and Annie go to the plains of Africa, where they help wild animals cross a rushing river and have a picnic with a Masai warrior.

❏ **#12 POLAR BEARS PAST BEDTIME** Jack and Annie go to the Arctic, where they meet a seal hunter, play with polar bear cubs, and get trapped on thin ice.

#13–16: The Mystery of the Lost Stories*

❏ **#13 VACATION UNDER THE VOLCANO** Jack and Annie land in Pompeii during Roman times, on the very day Mount Vesuvius erupts!

❏ **#14 DAY OF THE DRAGON KING** Jack and Annie travel back to ancient China, where they must face an emperor who burns books.

❑ **#15 VIKING SHIPS AT SUNRISE** Jack and Annie visit a monastery in medieval Ireland on the day the Vikings attack!

❑ **#16 HOUR OF THE OLYMPICS** Jack and Annie go back to ancient Greece and the first Olympic games.

#17–20: The Mystery of the Enchanted Dog*

❑ **#17 TONIGHT ON THE TITANIC** Jack and Annie travel back to the decks of the *Titanic* and help two children escape from the sinking ship.

❑ **#18 BUFFALO BEFORE BREAKFAST** Jack and Annie go back in time to the Great Plains, where they meet a Lakota boy and stop a buffalo stampede!

❑ **#19 TIGERS AT TWILIGHT** Jack and Annie are whisked to a forest in India, where they are stalked by a hungry tiger!

❑ **#20 DINGOES AT DINNERTIME** Jack and Annie go to Australia and help a baby kangaroo and a koala bear escape from a wildfire.

#21–24: The Mystery of Morgan's Library

❏ **#21 CIVIL WAR ON SUNDAY** Jack and Annie go back in time to the War Between the States and help a famous nurse named Clara Barton.

❏ **#22 REVOLUTIONARY WAR ON WEDNESDAY** Jack and Annie go to the shores of the Delaware River the night George Washington and his troops prepare for their famous crossing!

❏ **#23 TWISTER ON TUESDAY** Jack and Annie help save students in a frontier schoolhouse when a tornado hits.

❏ **#24 EARTHQUAKE IN THE EARLY MORNING** Jack and Annie go to San Francisco in 1906—just as the famous earthquake is shaking things up!

#25–28: The Mystery of Morgan's Rhymes

❑ **#25 STAGE FRIGHT ON A SUMMER NIGHT** Jack and Annie travel to Elizabethan England and help William Shakespeare put on a play.

Paul Coughlin

About the Author

Mary Pope Osborne is the award-winning author of over fifty books for young people, including *American Tall Tales*, *Favorite Greek Myths*, the *Spider Kane* mystery books, and *One World, Many Religions*, an Orbis Pictus Honor Book. She recently completed two terms as president of the Authors Guild, the leading writers' organization in the United States. She lives in New York City and Connecticut with her husband, Will, and their Norfolk terrier, Bailey.